PERSONALITIES AND CULTURES

Robert Hunt
is professor of anthropology at Brandeis University, having previously taught at the University of Illinois at Chicago Circle and Northwestern University. Born in Binghamton, New York, he graduated from Hamilton College, received his M.A. from the University of Chicago, and was awarded his Ph.D. by Northwestern University.

With his wife, Eva Hunt, he spent eighteen months between 1963 and 1966 among the Cuicatecs, in southern Mexico. He is the author of various technical articles in anthropology and of a history of anthropological studies of national character.

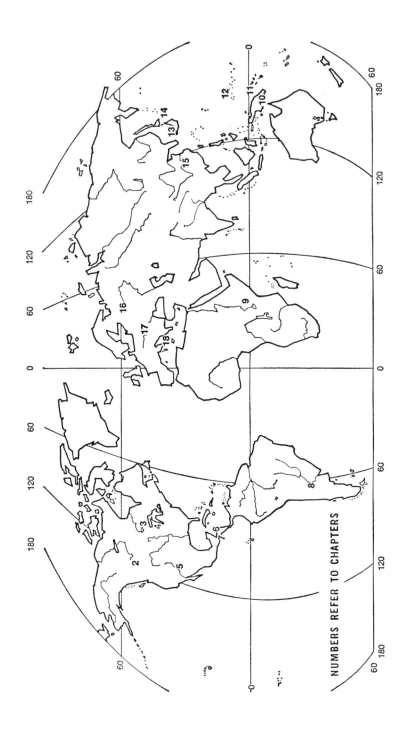

Texas Press Sourcebooks in Anthropology
were originally published by the Natural History Press, a division of Doubleday and Company, Inc. Responsibility for the series now resides with the University of Texas Press, Box 7819, Austin, Texas 78712. Whereas the series has been a joint effort between the American Museum of Natural History and the Natural History Press, future volumes in the series will be selected through the auspices of the editorial offices of the University of Texas Press.

The purpose of the series will remain unchanged in its effort to make available inexpensive, up-to-date, and authoritative volumes for the student and the general reader in the field of anthropology.

Personalities and Cultures

Readings in Psychological Anthropology

Edited by Robert Hunt

University of Texas Press
Austin and London

Library of Congress Cataloging in Publication Data

Hunt, Robert Cushman, ed.
    Personalities and cultures

    (Texas Press sourcebooks in anthropology; 3)
    Reprint of the ed. published for the American Museum of Natural History by the Natural History Press, Garden City, N.Y., issued in series: American Museum sourcebooks in anthropology.
    Bibliography: p.
    Includes index.
    CONTENTS: Personality: Hall, C. S., and Lindzey, G. Freud's psychoanalytic theory of personality.—New World: Honigmann, J. World view and self-view of the Kaska Indians. [etc.]
    1. Personality and culture—Addresses, essays, lectures.　2. Ethnopsychology—Addresses, essays, lectures.　I. Title.　II. Series.　III. Series: American Museum sourcebooks in anthropology.
[GN504.H86 1976]　　155.8　　75-44402

ISBN 0-292-76429-4

Copyright © 1967 by Robert Hunt
All rights reserved
Printed in the United States of America

Second Printing, 1979

Published by arrangement with Doubleday & Company, Inc.
Previously published by the Natural History Press in cooperation with Doubleday & Company, Inc.

CONTENTS

Introduction ix

PART I PERSONALITY

1. CALVIN S. HALL AND GARDNER LINDZEY Freud's Psychoanalytic Theory of Personality   3

PART II NEW WORLD

2. JOHN HONIGMANN World View and Self-View of the Kaska Indians   33
3. A. IRVING HALLOWELL Intelligence of Northeastern Indians   49
4. LOUISE AND GEORGE SPINDLER Male and Female Adaptations in Culture Change: Menomini   56
5. DAVID FRIEND ABERLE The Psychosocial Analysis of a Hopi Life-History   79
6. JOHN GILLIN The Balance of Threat and Security in Mesoamerica: San Carlos   139
7. BENJAMIN D. PAUL Mental Disorder and Self-Regulating Processes in Culture: A Guatemalan Illustration   150
8. JULES HENRY Some Cultural Determinants of Hostility in Pilaga Indian Children   166

PART III AFRICA AND OCEANIA

9. ROBERT A. LEVINE The Internalization of Political Values in Stateless Societies   185
10. GREGORY BATESON Sex Ethos and the Iatmul *Naven* Ceremony   204
11. MARGARET MEAD An Investigation of the Thought of Primitive Children, with Special Reference to Animism   213

12. MELFORD E. SPIRO Ifaluk Ghosts: An Anthropological Inquiry into Learning and Perception   238
13. ALEXANDER LEIGHTON AND MORRIS OPLER Psychological Warfare and the Japanese Emperor   251
14. GEORGE DE VOS The Relation of Guilt Toward Parents to Achievement and Arranged Marriage Among the Japanese   261

PART IV EURASIA

15. FRANCIS L. K. HSU Family System and the Economy: China   291
16. ALEX INKELES, EUGENIA HANFMANN, AND HELEN BEIER Modal Personality and Adjustment to the Soviet Socio-Political System   312
17. RUTH BENEDICT Child Rearing in Eastern European Countries   340
18. ANNE PARSONS Is the Oedipus Complex Universal? A South Italian "Nuclear Complex"   352

Bibliography   400

Index   421

INTRODUCTION

Psychological anthropology—also known as Culture and Personality—is often thought to be a recent addition to the roster of anthropological sub-disciplines. Insofar as it has been concerned with personality as the primary psychological variable, it is generally agreed that the field dates from the mid-1920s with the work of Seligman, Malinowski, Boas, Mead, Sapir, and Benedict (cf. Gladwin 1961, Honigmann 1961, Singer 1961). This view, however, ignores the Torres Straits Expedition (1898), some of the members of which had a very strong interest in pursuing psychological researches in the East Indies.

Psychological anthropology can conveniently (although admittedly somewhat summarily) be divided into two aspects: the cross-cultural testing of hypotheses derived from psychology (a cross-cultural empirical psychology), and the generation of more meaningful and efficient theories about human behavior with the attempted integration or interdigitation of social and psychological theory (cf. Spiro 1961a). The anthropologist is therefore offered several different research strategies: he can test psychological hypotheses in his cross-cultural laboratory; he can attempt to make more sense out of his data by adding psychological theory to the social theory which he already has; and he can attempt to build a more effective theory of human behavior. (These strategies are not mutually exclusive.)

Much of the field work to date has been cross-cultural psychology, and most of the theorizing has been directed to the job of devising more effective theory of human behavior. Some anthropologists have been trying explicitly to utilize psychological and socio-cultural insights in the analysis of empirical data, and one of the results is a better understanding of religious, political, economic, and family systems (cf. Bateson, LeVine, Hsu, and Parsons in this volume). I think that we may confidently look forward to more of this work in the future. The anthropologist can also, of course, take what is already accepted as known in the two dimensions and apply them to a practical problem. Much of the anthropological work on national character has been this sort of social engineering, for it has been done in the context of governmental management of practical problems such as World War II and the cold war (Hunt 1965). The Leighton and Opler, Benedict, and Inkeles, Hanfmann, and Beier selections in the volume reflect this orientation; the first is concerned with World War II, and the others with cold war issues.

PSYCHOLOGICAL AND SOCIO-CULTURAL VARIABLES

The psychological anthropologist by definition works with what can be called *psychological variables,* and *socio-cultural*[1] *variables.* He is interested in the relationships between them, and one of the most important questions he can ask in this context is what are the effects these two kinds of variables have upon each other. Does one determine the other, and if so, which? Or, if they are not dependently related, what is the nature of their relationship? Knowledge of the answers that behavioral scientists in general and anthropologists in particular have found to these questions is a prerequisite to understanding of this field. There are many psychological variables to choose from, including intelligence, perception, hostility, security, etc. Anthropologists, however, have been primarily interested in personality, for it is more central to the science of human behavior than they are seeking than the others, or at least this would seem to be the thinking of many in the field. Al-

[1] For the purposes of this discussion, we are lumping social and cultural together and calling them "socio-cultural." Cf. Geertz 1957, for a recent discussion of the relationship of social and cultural variables.

Introduction xi

most all of the selections in this volume, therefore, focus upon *personality,* and this reflects the field as a whole.

As already mentioned, the relationship between the psychic variables on the one hand and the socio-cultural variables on the other has been the main concern of psychological anthropology. It has been hypothesized (1) that the psychic variables may be irrelevant to the socio-cultural ones, (2) that the psychic variables are dependent upon the socio-cultural ones, (3) that the socio-cultural variables are dependent upon the psychic, and (4) that they may be distinct but interdependent.

Durkheim is often—and not always accurately—cited as an exponent of the first view. Durkheim said that social factors could best be explained by other social factors (1897).

The second position—that psychic variables are dependent upon socio-cultural variables—has been the dominant position in psychological anthropology. Freud's discovery that many parts of the adult personality are shaped by early experiences, the most crucial of which occur in the nuclear family, stimulated cross-cultural investigation of how the particular kind of a family in a particular culture affects the psychic development of the child. Since the impact of the family upon the child was shaped by tradition or custom (in other words, the society and the culture), personality (a psychological variable) depended upon (was caused by) socio-cultural variables. Most cross-cultural work on personality has been interested in the degree of correlation between the culture and the personalities found in that culture, and most workers in this field have found at least some degree of correlation. By now it is considered axiomatic that most psychic variables, and especially much of the personality, are largely determined by cultural conditioning. This position is represented in almost all of the articles reprinted here.

Another approach represented in the work of some psychological anthropologists is that which places the psychological variables in an intermediate position between different socio-cultural variables. One example of this view is to be found in Fromm's *Escape from Freedom,* where the economy influences the form and function of the family, and of the practices of child rearing, which then affect the personality. The personality in turn affects social process[2] (1941:296–97). Kardiner's work may also be seen in this light. In his view the primary socio-cultural institutions establish the basic personality, which then in turn affect the secondary socio-cultural institutions (1939, 1945).

The third possibility, less discussed among behavioral scientists in this day and age, is to view socio-cultural variables as dependent upon psychological ones. Here the form of society, or some of its institutions, or social behavior, are caused by primary psychological needs, or something of the sort. Malinowski (1925) seems to have viewed the complex of religious rituals as in part a response to man's anxiety about the life cycle. Emphasis on the importance of the behavior learned in social contexts has helped to make this kind of analysis very rare—as Malinowski himself would probably have conceded.

Finally, it is possible to view psychic and socio-cultural variables as interdependent, mutually influencing, and incapable of being brought together in unidirectional linear strings of dependence-independence. Bateson presents this view when he defines *ethos* (culturally standardized emotional tone) and *eidos* (culturally standardized mode of cognition) as aspects of patterned human behavior, fully equivalent to other aspects, such as social structure, or the economic system (1936). Spiro has recently utilized the same kind of argument using society, culture, and personality as the three kinds of interdependent variables (1961a, 1961b).

PSYCHOLOGICAL VARIABLES

There are many psychological variables, and most of them have been used in studies of non-western cultures. Price-Williams, for example, has studied various aspects of intellectual functioning among the Tiv (1961a, 1961b, 1962a, 1962b); Segal, Campbell and Herskovits wrote on perception (1963). A number of psychiatrists have been interested in cross-cultural

[2] "... ideologies and culture in general are rooted in the social character; the social character itself is molded by the mode of existence of a given society; and in their turn the dominant character traits become productive forces shaping the social process" (Fromm 1941:296–97).

aspects of mental illness (cf. Tooth 1950; Carstairs 1957; Field 1960), and in social psychiatry (cf. Hollingshead and Redlich 1958; Leighton, A. 1963; Hughes et. al. 1960; Srole et. al. 1962).

Among anthropologists, as we have pointed out, the most popular variable has been personality. Unfortunately, personality is a nebulous concept—in the sense that it cannot be readily defined. Hall and Lindzey, in their book, *Theories of Personality,* state that:

> . . . it is our conviction that no substantitive definition of personality can be applied with any generality. By this we mean simply that the way in which a given individual will define personality will depend completely upon his theoretical preference (1957:9).

(The same conditions hold for the concept of culture, as witness the huge number of definitions amassed by Kroeber and Kluckhohn [1952].)

However, some of the characteristic dimensions of the notion of personality are clear. First of all, it refers to the individual organism. Second, it usually refers to the long-term, relatively permanent organization of energies, capacities, and processes in that organism. Third, a personality is almost totally acquired from other individuals, and in two manners, biologically (including genetically) and by learning. Fourth, each individual is unique—no other human personality is the same in every detail. Every human being is a unique combination of genetically inherited traits and goes through a unique (in however small degree) sequence of social experiences. His personality is the end result of this non-recurring complex set of events. Kluckhohn and Murray put it succinctly: "Every man is in certain respects

"a. like all other men,
b. like some other men,
c. like no other man" (1953:53)

The major interest of psychological anthropologists has been in *b.* above. Kluckhohn and Murray point out that a man in Culture A will in some respects be like some men in Culture B, and in some respects like other men in Culture A (op. cit.). The former refers to psychological types, and there has been virtually no progress made in isolating and explaining such types, even though anthropologists in the field usually find some individuals who remind them very strongly of people back home.

The other notion—of group personality or shared personality traits—is a very old one, and the idea is perhaps close to a cultural universal. Herodotus, for example, remarked upon psychological characteristics of nations foreign to the Greeks. The idea persists in popular stereotypes. It also persists in the social sciences and the humanities; there is a huge literature on national character (cf. Duijker and Frijda 1960). In psychological anthropology, the idea that a culture, or a significant number of its representatives, share personality characteristics has been a fundamental assumption, and, on occasion, hypothesis.

In 1939 Kardiner explicitly gave the idea a psychoanalytic underpinning. Since personality is formed as a response to early environment, and since in a culture the early environment is similar for all individuals, significant parts of the personalities will be similar. Since early environments vary from culture to culture, personalities vary from culture to culture (1939).

It was not until the 1950s, however, that rigorous testing of this assumption began. (DuBois' study of Alor was claimed by Kardiner to be a test of the proposition, but there was no random sampling of the Alorese population, and, therefore, on that ground alone the results were inconclusive [DuBois 1944]). Wallace took a large random sample of Tuscarora Indians, administered the Rorschach to this sample, and then inspected his data to see how similar the Tuscarora were to each other (1952). Using a statistical definition of similarity, he found that fewer than 40 per cent of his subjects (and by inference, of the population) were like one another. Furthermore, he found no personality subgrouping by age, sex, social position, etc. Very few other studies even kept open, let alone tested for, the possibility that there would be only a very low degree of similarity between individuals. One of them is presented in this volume (Inkeles et. al.). In general, psychological anthropologists have assumed that similarities between individuals in a given culture existed and that these were important similarities. Wallace has pointed out, however, that it is not logically necessary to use this model, which he calls the replication of uniformity. Instead, he argues that complex human culture could not exist or operate unless individual organizations differ in fundamental ways, and

Introduction

he calls this the organization of diversity model (1961). Here he supports the idea that the division of labor in a culture demands, in effect, a psychic division of labor (op. cit.).

Research on these points, and even thinking about them, suffers from the ambiguities inherent in the term "personality." Wallace in 1952 defined personality in terms of scoring Rorschach protocols, whereas Kardiner typically deduced the basic personality from information about institutions on the basis of psychoanalytic theory. Overlap between these two definitions of the concept of personality is difficult to ascertain and is possibly quite small. It is therefore not very meaningful to compare the Kardiner theory with the Wallace results; the same word, "personality," obscures the fact that quite different things are being talked about. This difficulty has continually plagued research and delayed progress in psychological anthropology.

Many have considered projective techniques an ideal answer to this problem, since they provide the "same" stimulus, and can be scored in a relatively objective way. Unfortunately, however, their validity and reliability are often in doubt (Lindzey 1961), and the part of the personality that the test probes varies from individual to individual (cf. Wm. Henry 1947).

Instead, therefore, of wrestling with relatively difficult methodological problems, many scholars have recently chosen more modest problems. Attention has been focused on one or a few personality processes, or on the way that one personality variable such as aggression is related to religion or the political organization (cf. LeVine, in this volume), rather than on the whole personality, or on the degree to which large numbers of variables are similar for many members of a culture.

Most psychological anthropologists, being interested in personality, have chosen the individual as the locus of the psychological trait. A few scholars have, however, suggested that we may also study the psychological organization of socio-cultural features such as rituals, family structure, etc. This is what Mead (1928, 1930b, 1935), Benedict (1930, 1934), and Bateson (1936) were doing when they utilized the concept of ethos, which for them meant the emotional organization of an agegrade (Samoan adolescence), the two sexes (Mead 1935, Bateson op. cit.), or the whole culture (Benedict 1934, Hsu 1953).

This theory has also been used (usually covertly) by other anthropologists. Most social anthropologists are interested in the institutional location of these variables. Many students of kinship, for example, concern themselves in part with such topics as the typical attitudes of sons toward fathers (cf. F. Eggan 1950:31–42). More extensive treatment of this phenomenon may be found in Spiro (1961a).

There has been little study of the relationship between the idea of ethos and personality. It is perfectly obvious that there must be considerable overlap, and that where there is contradiction between what the social and cultural organization require, and what the individual wants to do, or is capable of doing, there will be difficulties of one sort or another (cf. Paul in this volume). The Aberle selection in this volume explores the relationship between an individual personality and the psychological demands of the society and culture in which the individual lives.

Anthropologists utilize psychological variables because it is thought possible to explain more about a culture with them than without them. Bateson, as we see in the section reprinted here, was able to make more sense out of the Iatmul *naven* ceremony with the variable of ethos than without it. It has been argued that the maintenance of social and cultural systems can not be explained without the use of personality theory (cf. Spiro 1916b). Moreover anthropologists have taken the opportunity of cross-cultural research to test the validity of many propositions concerning human nature and human psychological processes (Spiro 1961a). Mead, for example, went to Samoa to test the notion that adolescence was a time of strain and stress (Mead 1959), and concluded that the Western response to adolescence was culture-determined and culture-bound (1928). Malinowski, after working in the matrilineal Trobriand Islands, claimed that the Oedipus complex as described by Freud was not a human universal but a feature of some particular societies (cf. Parsons in this volume).

Other variables, however, have not as yet been invalidated. Projection, repression, sublimination, and perception as processes seem to be similarly structured in all normal human beings, although the content of these processes of course varies from culture to culture. Also, such entities as love, hate, aggression,

Introduction xvii

anxiety, and the like are assumed to be universally present in all normal human beings, although again the strength and the expression they take varies from culture to culture as well as from one individual to another.

THE SCOPE OF PSYCHOLOGICAL ANTHROPOLOGY

In addition to the research directions illustrated in this source book, there are other concerns that could be (and in some cases have been) fruitfully attacked by the psychological anthropologist. Two can be singled out for brief attention here.

Human evolution has long been the special bailiwick of the anthropologist. We have a crude notion of how man's soma and his society and culture have evolved.

However, little of scientific importance has been learned about the evolution of man's psyche. Lévy-Bruhl's idea that primitive thought was "pre-logical" is shown by the Mead selection in this volume to be indefensible—a point Lévy-Bruhl conceded toward the end of his life. More recently, Hallowell, Kroeber, and a few others have addressed themselves to this problem. Kroeber has pointed out that the great apes do not have the patience necessary for inventing on a human scale. He has also argued that civilizations require more reality testing and more deferral of impulse gratification than primitive cultures (1948). Hallowell has written extensively on the evolution of the self (cf. 1950, 1960). Hockett and Ascher have reopened the question of the origins of human language, and in the course of so doing have considered evolutional psychological problems such as symbolization and communication (1964). Work on infra-human primates (DeVore 1965; Schrier 1965) may provide additional information on the evolution of the human psyche.

Another very important topic is the validity of the psychological assumptions which lurk in social theory. Economists today know that "economic man" is a straw man—a model—but what of Radcliffe-Brown's use of "sentiments" in the analysis of kinship? There are doubtless many more. Since most social theory contains psychological assumptions of some sort or other, in part based upon research on Western man and in part on mere assumption, it should be very illuminating to hold them up to the light to see if they are justifiable. Here the psychological anthropologist can bring to the arena not only psychology but also his invaluable empirical evidence from non-Western cultures.

SELECTION OF ARTICLES

The American Museum Sourcebooks in Anthropology are designed to present a large body of factual data, and the theory which explains these facts. We have, because of the emphasis on ethnography, left out the important cross-cultural studies generated by John W. M. Whiting (cf. Whiting 1961, for an excellent example of this work), and some stimulating theoretical articles and books, such as the pioneer works of Sapir, Linton, and Wallace.

In addition, many publications in psychological anthropology are heavily technical in language. Most psychoanalytically oriented studies are virtually unintelligible to the uninitiated. The same is true of the analysis of projective tests. One can, however, consult Lindzey's superb survey of the cross-cultural application of projective techniques (1961).

All of the articles in this volume save one are loaded with ethnography. The first one, a summary of Freudian psychoanalytic conceptions of the personality, of course, is not. This has been included because the majority of the articles presented in this book utilize a terminology which is somewhat technical and esoteric and is the more difficult to use and understand because many of the words occur in ordinary parlance (such as aggressive, anxious, etc.). Since the ambiguities of usage are subtle and complex, all readers should be made aware of their existence before moving on into the data. Few anthropologists are dogmatically or even overtly psychoanalytic (Gorer is a notable exception), but most owe a tremendous intellectual debt to psychoanalysis. Therefore most of these selections to one degree or another operate with psychoanalytic concepts. The introductory article is designed to provide a sketch map of the territory, with a few place names.

In the process of selecting the articles for this volume, it be-

Introduction

came more and more evident that there is little or no correlation between, on the one hand, the analysis of societies organized according to level of socio-economic integration, level of political complexity, or any other such criterion that is common in anthropology, and on the other hand, the results of studies in psychological anthropology. In fact, this sort of hypothesis has not been congenial to anthropologists. Aside from a few statements concerning the demands put upon man in an industrialized society such as the need for deferment of gratification, the increase in general anxiety and alienation, the demands for punctuality and orderliness, and the like, there is no empirical study known to me in which the psychological demands of other forms of socio-cultural integration have been explored, much less classified.

It is true, moreover, that there has been no successful attempt to rank psychic processes or personality organizations into an order progressing from most primitive, archaic, or early primate, to the most human, or even from most primitive to most civilized.

As a consequence, there is (since I am not grinding theoretical axes in the organization of this book) no more rational way of organizing this book than by area. Accordingly I have started with northern North America, proceeded southward through the southwest and Mesoamerica to the Argentine Chaco, and thence across the Atlantic to the Nuer and Gusii of East Africa, and then to New Guinea and Oceania. From there we proceed to Japan and the land mass of Eurasia, from China to Russia and Central Europe, ending in Italy. The difference in number of articles per area—the large number for North America and Oceania, for example—is in part a direct reflection of the fact that psychological anthropologists discuss some regions of the world more than others.

The reader will note that while there are but very few sections devoted explicitly to the United States (the native culture of all but a very few of the authors represented here), many of these articles have a great deal to say about American culture and personality. In many ways the underlying psychic organization of Americans is more exotic to the layman than are the details of the economy, the polity, the religions, etc., which are after all covered, however mythically, in the primary and secondary schools. But the American unconscious is not examined in the schools. Many of the authors presented here contrast statements about aggression or anxiety in the culture they studied with comparative statements about American culture. Since our space is limited we have therefore felt justified in not presenting any of the studies which are explicitly and exclusively concerned with America (e.g. Mead 1942; Riesman 1950). A good introduction to the specialized literature on America is the reader edited by Smelser and Smelser (1963). We have also left out studies of mental hospitals (cf. Caudill 1958, and Stanton and Schwartz 1954) due to limitations of space.

ADDITIONAL READING

There are several sources that are indispensable to the student for their evaluations of the field or of studies in the field, for their bibliographies, or for the articles reprinted there. There are now two textbooks in the field, by Honigmann (1954) and Barnouw (1963). Collections of original articles are to be found in Hsu (1954, 1961), Kaplan (1961), and Sargent and Smith (1949). There are several readers: the pioneering *Personality in Nature, Society and Culture* (Kluckhohn, Murray, and Schneider 1953), a book by Haring (1956) which contains a good bibliography, Cohen's case book emphasizing the relationship of personality and social structure rather than culture (1961) and Marvin Opler's collection on mental illness (1959). Duijker and Frijda (1960) and Hunt (1965) have surveyed the national character literature, and Lindzey has covered the field of cross-cultural application of projective techniques with admirable skill and sensitivity (1961). Wallace's volume on Culture and Personality (1961) is a stimulating theoretical treatise. The papers of Hallowell, Mead, and Benedict have been published in single volumes (Hallowell 1955, Mead 1964, and Mead 1959). Treatments of child rearing and socialization are to be found in Whiting and Child's volume on cross-cultural research (1953) and in the first two volumes of Whiting's Child Rearing in Six Cultures project (Whiting 1963, Mintern and Lambert 1964). In addition, valuable information about theory and method is to be found in the *Handbook of Social Psychology* (Lindzey 1954), especially

Introduction

chapters by Kluckhohn, Whiting, Inkeles and Levinson, Murphy, Child, Riecken and Homans, and Hebb and Thompson. The chapters on psychological anthropology in the *Biennial Review of Anthropology* edited by Siegel (1959, 1961, 1963, 1965) cover the recent literature extensively if not always deeply.

NOTE ON THE TEXT. The articles reprinted in this volume are in all important respects the same as in the original publication, except that I have shortened some of them. The only changes involved the correcting of obvious typographical errors in the original, and the references and footnotes have been made to conform with the *American Anthropologist*.

I am indebted to Paul Bohannan, Francis Hsu, and Eva Hunt for critical comments.

Stephanie Alnot helped me with the references cited at the end of the book.

Robert Hunt

Chicago, Illinois
1966

Part I PERSONALITY

1 FREUD'S PSYCHOANALYTIC THEORY OF PERSONALITY

Calvin S. Hall and Gardner Lindzey

THE STRUCTURE OF PERSONALITY

The personality is made up of three major systems, the *id,* the *ego,* and the *superego.* Although each of these provinces of the total personality has its own functions, properties, components, operating principles, dynamisms, and mechanisms, they interact so closely with one another that it is difficult if not impossible to disentangle their effects and weigh their relative contribution to man's behavior. Behavior is nearly always the product of an interaction among these three systems; rarely does one system operate to the exclusion of the other two.

THE ID. The id is the original system of the personality; it is the matrix within which the ego and the superego become differentiated. The id consists of everything psychological that is inherited and that is present at birth, including the instincts. It is the reservoir of psychic energy and furnishes all the power for the operation of the other two systems. It is in close touch with the bodily processes from which it derives its energy. Freud called the id the "true psychic reality" because it represents the inner world of subjective experience and has no knowledge of objective reality.

The id cannot tolerate increases of energy which are experienced as uncomfortable states of tension. Consequently, when the tension level of the organism is raised, either as a result of

FROM Calvin S. Hall and Gardner Lindzey, *Theories of Personality,* 1957:32–55, by permission of the authors and the publisher, John Wiley and Sons.

external stimulation or of internally produced excitations, the id functions in such a manner as to discharge the tension immediately and return the organism to a comfortably constant and low energy level. This principle of tension reduction by which the id operates is called the *pleasure principle*.

In order to accomplish its aim of avoiding pain and obtaining pleasure, the id has at its command two processes. These are *reflex action* and the *primary process*. Reflex actions are inborn and automatic reactions like sneezing and blinking; they usually reduce tension immediately. The organism is equipped with a number of such reflexes for dealing with relatively simple forms of excitation. The primary process involves a somewhat more complicated psychological reaction. It attempts to discharge tension by forming an image of an object that will remove the tension. For example, the primary process provides the hungry person with a mental picture of food. This hallucinatory experience in which the desired object is present in the form of a memory image is called *wish-fulfillment*. The best example of the primary process in normal people is the nocturnal dream which Freud believed always represents the fulfillment or attempted fulfillment of a wish. The hallucinations and visions of psychotic patients are also examples of the primary process. Autistic or wishful thinking is highly colored by the action of the primary process. These wish-fulfilling mental images are the only reality that the id knows.

Obviously the primary process by itself is not capable of reducing tension. The hungry person cannot eat mental images of food. Consequently, a new or secondary psychological process develops, and when this occurs the structure of the second system of the personality, the ego, begins to take form.

THE EGO. The ego comes into existence because the needs of the organism require appropriate transactions with the objective world of reality. The hungry person has to seek, find, and eat food before the tension of hunger can be eliminated. This means that he has to learn to differentiate between a memory image of food and an actual perception of food as it exists in the outer world. Having made this crucial differentiation it is then necessary for him to convert the image into a perception which is accomplished by locating food in the environment. In other words, the person matches his memory image of food with the sight or smell of food as they come to him through his senses. The basic distinction between the id and the ego is that the former knows only the subjective reality of the mind whereas the latter distinguishes between things in the mind and things in the external world.

The ego is said to obey the *reality principle* and to operate by means of the *secondary process*. The aim of the reality principle is to prevent the discharge of tension until an object which is appropriate for the satisfaction of the need has been discovered. The reality principle suspends the pleasure principle temporarily because the pleasure principle is eventually served when the needed object is found and the tension is thereby reduced. The reality principle asks in effect whether an experience is true or false, that is, whether it has external existence or not, while the pleasure principle is only interested in whether the experience is painful or pleasurable.

The secondary process is realistic thinking. By means of the secondary process the ego formulates a plan for the satisfaction of the need and then tests this plan, usually by some kind of action, in order to see whether or not it will work. The hungry person thinks where he may find food and then proceeds to look in that place. This is called *reality testing*. In order to perform its role efficiently the ego has control over all of the cognitive and intellectual functions; these higher mental processes are placed at the service of the secondary process.

The ego is said to be the executive of the personality because it controls the gateways to action, selects the features of the environment to which it will respond, and decides what instincts will be satisfied and in what manner. In performing these highly important executive functions, the ego has to try to integrate the often conflicting demands of the id, the superego, and the external world. This is not an easy task and often places a great strain upon the ego.

It should be kept in mind, however, that the ego is the organized portion of the id, that it comes into existence in order to forward the aims of the id and not to frustrate them, and that all of its power is derived from the id. It has no existence apart from the id, and it never becomes completely independent of the id.

Its principal role is to mediate between the instinctual requirements of the organism and the conditions of the surrounding environment; its superordinate objectives are to maintain the life of the individual and to see that the species is reproduced.

THE SUPEREGO. The third and last system of personality to be developed is the superego. It is the internal representative of the traditional values and ideals of society as interpreted to the child by his parents, and enforced by means of a system of rewards and punishments imposed upon the child. The superego is the moral arm of personality; it represents the ideal rather than the real and it strives for perfection rather than pleasure. Its main concern is to decide whether something is right or wrong so that it can act in accordance with the moral standards authorized by the agents of society.

The superego as the internalized moral arbiter of conduct develops in response to the rewards and punishments meted out by the parents. To obtain the rewards and avoid the punishments, the child learns to guide his behavior along the lines laid down by the parents. Whatever they say is improper and punish him for doing tends to become incorporated into his *conscience* which is one of the two subsystems of the superego. Whatever they approve of and reward him for doing tends to become incorporated into his *ego-ideal* which is the other subsystem of the superego. The mechanism by which this incorporation takes place is called *introjection*. The conscience punishes the person by making him feel guilty, the ego-ideal rewards the person by making him feel proud of himself. With the formation of the superego, self-control is substituted for parental control.

The main functions of the superego are (1) to inhibit the impulses of the id, particularly those of a sexual or aggressive nature, since these are the impulses whose expression is most highly condemned by society, (2) to persuade the ego to substitute moralistic goals for realistic ones, and (3) to strive for perfection. That is, the superego is inclined to oppose both the id and the ego, and to make the world over into its own image. However, it is like the id in being non-rational and like the ego in attempting to exercise control over the instincts. Unlike the ego, the superego does not merely postpone instinctual gratification; it tries to block it permanently.

In concluding this brief description of the three systems of the personality, it should be pointed out that the id, ego, and superego are not to be thought of as manikins which operate the personality. They are merely names for various psychological processes which obey different system principles. Under ordinary circumstances these different principles do not collide with one another nor do they work at cross purposes. On the contrary, they work together as a team under the administrative leadership of the ego. The personality normally functions as a whole rather than as three separate segments. In a very general way, the id may be thought of as the biological component of personality, the ego as the psychological component, and the superego as the social component.

THE DYNAMICS OF PERSONALITY

Freud was brought up under the influence of the strongly deterministic and positivistic philosophy of nineteenth century science and regarded the human organism as a complex energy system, which derives its energy from the food it consumes and expends it for such various purposes as circulation, respiration, muscular exercise, perceiving, thinking, and remembering. Freud saw no reason to assume that the energy which furnishes the power for breathing or digesting is any different, save in form, from the energy which furnishes the power for thinking and remembering. After all, as nineteenth century physicists were firmly insisting, energy has to be defined in terms of the work it performs. If the work consists of a psychological activity such as thinking, then it is perfectly legitimate, Freud believed, to call this form of energy *psychic energy*. According to the doctrine of the conservation of energy, energy may be transformed from one state into another state but can never be lost from the total cosmic system; it follows from this that psychic energy may be transformed into physiological energy and vice versa. The point of contact or bridge between the energy of the body and that of the personality is the id and its instincts.

INSTINCT. An instinct is defined as an inborn psychological representation of an inner somatic source of excitation. The psychological representation is called a *wish,* and the bodily excitation from which it stems is called a *need.* Thus, the state of hunger may be described in physiological terms as a condition of nutritional deficit in the tissues of the body whereas psychologically it is represented as a wish for food. The wish acts as a motive for behavior. The hungry person seeks food. Instincts are considered therefore to be the propelling factors of personality. Not only do they drive behavior but they also determine the direction that the behavior will take. In other words, an instinct exercises selective control over conduct by increasing one's sensitivity for particular kinds of stimulation. The hungry person is more sensitive to food stimuli, the sexually aroused person is more likely to respond to erotic stimuli.

Parenthetically, may be observed that the organism can also be activated by stimuli from the external world. Freud felt, however, that these environmental sources of excitation play a less important role in the dynamics of personality than do the inborn instincts. In general, external stimuli make fewer demands upon the individual and require less complicated forms of adjustment than do the needs. One can always flee from an external stimulus but it is impossible to run away from a need. Although Freud relegated environmental stimuli to a secondary place, he did not deny their importance under certain conditions. For example, excessive stimulation during the early years of life when the immature ego lacks the capacity for binding large amounts of free energy (tension) may have drastic effects upon the personality, as we shall see when we consider Freud's theory of anxiety.

An instinct is a quantum of psychic energy or as Freud put it "a measure of the demand made upon the mind for work" (1905a:168). All of the instincts taken together constitute the sum total of psychic energy available to the personality. As was previously pointed out, the id is the reservoir of this energy and it is also the seat of the instincts. The id may be considered to be a dynamo which furnishes psychological power for running the manifold operations of personality. This power is derived, of course, from the metabolic processes of the body.

An instinct has four characteristic features: a *source,* an *aim,* an *object,* and an *impetus.* The source has already been defined as a bodily condition or a need. The aim is the removal of the bodily excitation. The aim of the hunger instinct, for example, is to abolish the nutritional deficiency, which is accomplished, of course, by eating food. All of the activity which intervenes between the appearance of the wish and its fulfillment is subsumed under the heading of *object*. That is, object refers not only to the particular thing or condition which will satisfy the need but it also includes all of the behavior which takes place in securing the necessary thing or condition. For instance, when a person is hungry he usually has to perform a number of actions before he can reach the final consummatory goal of eating.

The impetus of an instinct is its force or strength which is determined by the intensity of the underlying need. As the nutritional deficiency becomes greater, up to the point where physical weakness sets in, the force of the instinct becomes correspondingly greater.

Let us briefly consider some of the implications that inhere in this way of conceptualizing an instinct. In the first place, the model which Freud provides is a tension-reduction one. The behavior of a person is activated by internal irritants and subsides as soon as an appropriate action removes or diminishes the irritation. This means that the aim of an instinct is essentially *regressive* in character since it returns the person to a prior state to which the personality returns is one of relative quiescence. An instinct is also said to be *conservative* because its aim is to conserve the equilibrium of the organism by abolishing disturbing excitations. Thus, we can picture an instinct as a process which repeats as often as it appears a cycle of events starting with excitement and terminating with repose. Freud called this aspect of an instinct *repetition compulsion*. The personality is compelled to repeat over and over again the inevitable cycle from excitation to quiescence. (The term repetition compulsion is also employed to describe perseverative behavior which occurs when the means adopted for satisfying the need are not completely appropriate. A child may perseverate in sucking its thumb when it is hungry.)

According to Freud's theory of instincts, the source and aim of an instinct remain constant throughout life, unless the source is changed or eliminated by physical maturation. New instincts may appear as new bodily needs develop. In contrast to this constancy of source and aim, the object or means by which the person attempts to satisfy the need can and does vary considerably during the lifetime of the person. This variation in object choice is possible because psychic energy is *displaceable;* it can be expended in various ways. Consequently, if one object is not available either by virtue of its absence or by virtue of barriers within the personality, energy can be invested in another object. If that object proves also to be inaccessible another displacement can occur, and so forth, until an available object is found. In other words, objects can be substituted for one another, which is definitely not the case with either the source or the aim of an instinct.

When the energy of an instinct is more or less permanently invested in a substitute object, that is, one which is not the original and innately determined object, the resulting behavior is said to be an *instinct derivative.* Thus, if the first sexual object choice of the baby is the manipulation of his own sex organs and he is forced to give up this pleasure in favor of more innocuous forms of bodily stimulation such as sucking his thumb or playing with his toes, the substitute activities are derivatives of the sexual instinct. The aim of the sexual instinct does not change one whit when a substitution takes place; the goal sought is still that of sexual gratification.

The displacement of energy from one object to another is the most important feature of personality dynamics. It accounts for the apparent plasticity of human nature and the remarkable versatility of man's behavior. Practically all of the adult person's interests, preferences, tastes, habits, and attitudes represent the displacements of energy from original instinctual object-choices. They are almost all instinct derivatives. Freud's theory of motivation was based solidly on the assumption that the instincts are *the* sole energy sources for man's behavior. We shall have a great deal more to say about displacement in subsequent sections of this chapter.

Number and kinds of instincts. Freud did not attempt to draw up a list of instincts because he felt that not enough was known about the bodily states upon which the instincts depend. The identification of these organic needs is a job for the physiologist,

Freud's Psychoanalytic Theory of Personality

not the psychologist. Although Freud did not pretend to know how many instincts there are, he did assume that they could all be classified under two general headings, the *life* instincts and the *death* instincts.

The life instincts serve the purpose of individual survival and racial propagation. Hunger, thirst, and sex fall in this category. The form of energy by which the life instincts perform their work is called *libido*.

The life instinct to which Freud paid the greatest attention is that of sex, and in the early years of psychoanalysis almost everything the person did was attributed to this ubiquitous drive. (Freud 1905a). Actually, the sex instinct is not one instinct but many. That is, there are a number of separate bodily needs which give rise to erotic wishes. Each of these wishes has its source in a different bodily region which are referred to collectively as *erogenous zones*. An erogenous zone is a part of the skin or mucous membrane which is extremely sensitive to irritation and which when manipulated in a certain way removes the irritation and produces pleasurable feelings. The lips and oral cavity constitute one such erogenous zone, the anal region another, and the sex organs a third. Sucking produces oral pleasure, elimination anal pleasure, and massaging or rubbing genital pleasure. In childhood, the sexual instincts are relatively independent of one another but when the person reaches puberty they tend to fuse together and to serve jointly the aim of reproduction.

The death instincts, or, as Freud sometimes called them, the destructive instincts, perform their work much less conspicuously than the life instincts, and for this reason little is known about them, other than that they inevitably accomplish their mission. Every person does eventually die, a fact which caused Freud to formulate the famous dictum, "the goal of all life is death" 1920a:38). Freud assumed specifically that the person has a wish, usually of course unconscious, to die. He did not attempt to identify the somatic sources of the death instincts although one may wish to speculate that they reside in the catabolic or breaking-down processes of the body. Nor did he assign a name to the energy by which the death instincts carry on their work.

Freud's assumption of a death wish is based upon the constancy principle as formulated by Fechner. This principle asserts that all living processes tend to return to the stability of the inorganic world. In *Beyond the Pleasure Principle* (1920a), Freud made the following argument in favor of the concept of the death wish. Living matter evolved by the action of cosmic forces upon inorganic matter. These changes were highly unstable at first and quickly reverted to their prior inorganic state. Gradually, however, the length of life increased because of evolutionary changes in the world but these unstable animate forms always eventually regressed to the stability of inanimate matter. With the development of reproductive mechanisms, living things were able to reproduce their own kind, and did not have to depend upon being created out of the inorganic world. Yet even with this advance the individual member of a species inevitably obeyed the constancy principle, since this was the principle that governed its existence when it was endowed with life. Life, Freud said, is but a roundabout way to death. Disturbed out of its stable existence, organic matter strives to return to a quiescent state. The death wish in the human being is the psychological representation of the constancy principle.

An important derivative of the death instincts is the *aggressive drive*. Aggressiveness is self-destruction turned outward against substitute objects. A person fights with other people and is destructive because his death wish is blocked by the forces of the life instincts and by other obstacles in his personality which counteract the death instincts. It took the Great War of 1914–1918 to convince Freud that aggression was as sovereign a motive as sex.

The life and death instincts and their derivates may fuse together, neutralize each other, or replace one another. Eating, for example, represents a fusion of hunger and destructiveness which is satisfied by biting, chewing, and swallowing food. Love, a derivative of the sex instinct, can neutralize hate, a derivation of the death instinct. Or love can replace hate, and hate love.

Since the instincts contain all of the energy by which the three systems of the personality perform their work, let us turn now to consider the ways in which the id, ego, and superego gain control over and utilize psychic energy.

THE DISTRIBUTION AND UTILIZATION OF PSYCHIC ENERGY. The dynamics of personality consists of the way in which psychic energy is distributed and used by the id, ego, and superego. Since the amount of energy is a limited quantity there is competition among the three systems for the energy that is available. One system gains control over the available energy at the expense of the other two systems. As one system becomes stronger the other two necessarily become weaker, unless new energy is added to the total system.

Originally the id possesses all of the energy and uses it for reflex action and wish-fulfillment by means of the primary process. Both of these activities are in the direct service of the pleasure principle by which the id operates. The investment of energy in an action or image which will gratify an instinct is called an instinctual *object-choice* or *object-cathexis*.

The energy of the id is in a very fluid state which means that it can easily be shunted from one action or image to another action or image. The displaceable quality of this instinctual energy is due to the id's inability to form fine discriminations between objects. Objects that are different are treated as though they were the same. The hungry baby, for instance, will take up almost anything that it can hold and put it to its lips.

Since the ego has no source of power of its own it has to borrow it from the id. The diversion of energy from the id into the processes that make up the ego is accomplished by a mechanism known as *identification*. This is one of the most important concepts in Freudian psychology, and one of the most difficult to comprehend. It will be recalled from a previous discussion that the id does not distinguish between subjective imagery and objective reality. When it cathects an image of an object it is the same as cathecting the object itself. However, since a mental image cannot satisfy a need, the person is forced to differentiate between the world of the mind and the outer world. He has to learn the difference between a memory or idea of an object which is not present and a sensory impression or perception of an object which is present. Then, in order to satisfy a need, he must learn to match what is in his mind with its counterpart in the external world by means of the secondary process. This matching of a mental representation with physical reality, of something that is in the mind with something that is in the outer world, is what is meant by identification.

Since the id makes no distinction between any of the contents of the mind, whether they be perceptions, memory images, ideas, or hallucinations, a cathexis may be formed for a realistic perception as readily as for a wish-fulfilling memory image. In this way, energy is diverted from the purely autistic psychological processes of the id into the realistic, logical, ideational processes of the ego. In both cases, energy is used for strictly psychological purposes, but in the case of the id no distinction is made between the mental symbol and the physical referent whereas in the case of the ego this distinction is made. The ego attempts to make the symbol accurately represent the referent. In other words, identification enables the secondary process to supersede the primary process. Since the secondary process is so much more successful in reducing tensions, more and more ego cathexes are formed. Gradually the more efficient ego obtains a virtual monopoly over the store of psychic energy. This monopoly is only relative, however, because if the ego fails to satisfy the instincts, the id reasserts its power.

Once the ego has trapped enough energy it can use it for other purposes than that of gratifying the instincts by means of the secondary process. Some of the energy is used to bring the various psychological processes such as perceiving, remembering, judging, discriminating, abstracting, generalizing, and reasoning to a higher level of development. Some of the energy has to be used by the ego to restrain the id from acting impulsively and irrationally. These restraining forces are known as *anticathexes* in contradistinction to the driving forces or cathexes. If the id becomes too threatening, the ego erects defenses against the id. These defense mechanisms, which will be discussed in a later section, may also be used to cope with the pressures of the superego upon the ego. Energy, of course, is required for the maintenance of these defenses.

Ego energy may also be displaced to form new object-cathexes, so that a whole network of derived interests, attitudes, and preferences is formed within the ego. These ego-cathexes may not directly satisfy the basic needs of the organism but they are connected by associative links with objects that do. The energy of the hunger drive, for example, may fan out to include such cathexes as an interest in collecting recipes, visiting unusual

Freud's Psychoanalytic Theory of Personality

restaurants, and selling chinaware. This spreading of cathexes into channels that are only remotely connected with the original object of an instinct is made possible by the greater efficiency of the ego in performing its fundamental job of gratifying the instincts. The ego has a surplus of energy to use for other purposes.

Finally, the ego as the executive of the personality organization uses energy to effect an integration among the three systems. The purpose of this integrative function of the ego is to produce an inner harmony within the personality so that the ego's transactions with the environment may be made smoothly and effectively.

The mechanism of identification also accounts for the energizing of the superego system. This, too, is a complex matter and takes place in the following way. Among the first object-cathexes of the baby are those of the parents. These cathexes develop early and become very firmly entrenched because the baby is completely dependent upon his parents or parent-substitutes for the satisfaction of his needs. The parents also play the role of disciplinary agents; they teach the child the moral code and the traditional values and ideals of the society in which the child is raised. They do this by rewarding the child when he does the right thing and punishing him when he does the wrong thing. A reward is anything that reduces tensions or promises to do so. A piece of candy, a smile, or a kind word may be an effective reward. A punishment is anything that increases tension. It may be a spanking, a disapproving look, or a denial of some pleasure. Thus, the child learns to identify, that is, to match his behavior with the sanctions and prohibitions laid down by the parents. He introjects the moral imperatives of his parents by virtue of the original cathexes he has for them as need-satisfying agents. He cathects their ideals and these become his ego-ideal; he cathects their prohibitions and these become his conscience. Thus, the superego gains access to the reservoir of energy in the id by means of the child's identification with his parents.

The work performed by the superego is often, although not always, in direct opposition to the impulses of the id. This is the case because the moral code represents society's attempt to control and even to inhibit the expression of the primitive drives, especially those of sex and aggression. Being good usually means being obedient and not saying or doing "dirty" things. Being bad means being disobedient, rebellious, and lustful. The virtuous person inhibits his impulses, the sinful person indulges them. However, the superego can sometimes be corrupted by the id. This happens, for example, when a person in a fit of moralistic fervor takes aggressive measures against those whom he considers to be wicked and sinful. The expression of aggression in such instances is cloaked by the mantle of righteous indignation.

Once the energy furnished by the instincts has been channeled into the ego and the superego by the mechanism of identification, a complicated interplay of driving and restraining forces becomes possible. The id, it will be recalled, possesses only driving forces or cathexes whereas the energy of the ego and the superego is used both to forward and to frustrate the aims of the instincts. The ego has to check both the id and the superego if it is to govern the personality wisely, yet it must have enough energy left over to engage in necessary intercourse with the external world. If the id retains control over a large share of the energy, the behavior of the person will tend to be impulsive and primitive in character. On the other hand, if the superego gains control of an undue amount of energy, the functioning of the personality will be dominated by moralistic considerations rather than by realistic ones. The anticathexes of the conscience may tie up the ego in moral knots and prevent action of any sort, while the cathexes of the ego-ideal may set such high standards for the ego that the person is being continually frustrated and may eventually develop a depressing sense of failure.

Moreover, sudden and unpredictable shifts of energy from one system to another and from cathexes to anticathexes are common, especially during the first two decades of life before the distribution of energy has become more or less stabilized. These shifts of energy keep the personality in a state of dynamic flux. Freud was pessimistic about the chances of psychology ever becoming a very exact science because, as he pointed out, even a very small change in the distribution of energy might tip the scale in favor of one form of behavior rather than its opposite (Freud 1920b). Who can say whether the man poised on the window ledge is going to jump or not, or whether the batter is going to strike out or hit a winning home run?

In the final analysis, the dynamics of personality consist of the interplay of the driving forces, cathexes, and the restraining forces, anticathexes. All of the conflicts within the personality may be reduced to the opposition of these two sets of forces. All prolonged tension is due to the counteraction of a driving force by a restraining force. Whether it be an anticathexis of the ego opposed to a cathexis of the id or an anticathexis of the superego opposed to a cathexis of the ego, the result in terms of tension is the same. As Freud was fond of saying, psychoanalysis is "a dynamic conception which reduces mental life to the interplay of reciprocally urging and checking forces" (1910b:107).

ANXIETY. The dynamics of personality is to a large extent governed by the necessity for gratifying one's needs by means of transactions with objects in the external world. The surrounding environment provides the hungry organism with food, the thirsty one with water. In addition to its role as the source of supplies, the external world plays another part in shaping the destiny of personality. The environment contains regions of danger and insecurity; it can threaten as well as satisfy. The environment has the power to produce pain and increase tension as well as to bring pleasure and reduce tension. It disturbs as well as comforts.

The individual's customary reaction to external threats of pain and destruction with which it is not prepared to cope is to become afraid. The threatened person is ordinarily a fearful person. Overwhelmed by excessive stimulation which the ego is unable to bring under control, the ego becomes flooded with anxiety.

Freud recognized three types of anxiety: *reality* anxiety, *neurotic* anxiety, and *moral* anxiety or feelings of guilt (1926b). The basic type is reality anxiety or fear of real dangers in the external world; from it are derived the other two types. Neurotic anxiety is the fear that the instincts will get out of control and cause the person to do something for which he will be punished. Neurotic anxiety is not so much a fear of the instincts themselves as it is a fear of the punishment that is likely to ensue from instinctual gratification. Neurotic anxiety has a basis in reality, because the world as represented by the parents and other authorities does punish the child for impulsive actions. Moral anxiety is fear of the conscience. The person with a well-developed superego tends to feel guilty when he does something or even thinks of doing something that is contrary to the moral code by which he has been raised. He is said to feel conscience-stricken. Moral anxiety also has a realistic basis; the person has been punished in the past for violating the moral code and may be punished again.

The function of anxiety is to warn the person of impending danger; it is a signal to the ego that unless appropriate measures are taken the danger may increase until the ego is overthrown. Anxiety is a state of tension; it is a drive like hunger or sex but instead of arising from internal tissue conditions it is produced originally by external causes. When anxiety is aroused it motivates the person to do something. He may flee from the threatening region, inhibit the dangerous impulse, or obey the voice of conscience.

Anxiety which cannot be dealt with by effective measures is said to be traumatic. It reduces the person to a state of infantile helplessness. In fact, the prototype of all later anxiety is the *birth trauma*. The neonate is bombarded with stimuli from the world for which he is not prepared and to which he cannot adapt. The baby needs a sheltered environment until his ego has had a chance to develop to the point where it can master strong stimuli from the environment. When the ego cannot cope with anxiety by rational methods it has to fall back upon unrealistic ones. These are the so-called *defense mechanisms* of the ego which will be discussed in the following section.

THE DEVELOPMENT OF PERSONALITY

Freud was probably the first psychological theorist to emphasize the developmental aspects of personality and in particular to stress the decisive role of the early years of infancy and childhood in laying down the basic character structure of the person. Indeed, Freud felt that personality was pretty well formed by the end of the fifth year, and that subsequent growth consisted for the most part of elaborating this basic structure. He

Freud's Psychoanalytic Theory of Personality

arrived at this conclusion on the basis of his experiences with patients undergoing psychoanalysis. Inevitably, their mental explorations led them back to early childhood experiences which appeared to be decisive for the development of a neurosis later in life. Freud believed that the child is father of the man. It is interesting in view of this strong preference for genetic explanations of adult behavior that Freud rarely studied young children directly. He preferred to reconstruct the past life of a person from evidence furnished by his adult recollections.

Personality develops in response to four major sources of tension: (1) physiological growth processes, (2) frustrations, (3) conflicts, and (4) threats. As a direct consequence of increases in tension emanating from these sources, the person is forced to learn new methods of reducing tension. This learning is what is meant by personality development.

Identification and *displacement* are two methods by which the individual learns to resolve his frustrations, conflicts, and anxieties.

IDENTIFICATION. This concept was introduced in an earlier section to help account for the formation of the ego and superego. In the present context, identification may be defined as the method by which a person takes over the features of another person and makes them a corporate part of his own personality. He learns to reduce tension by modeling his behavior after that of someone else. Freud preferred the term *identification* to the more familiar one *imitation* because he felt that imitation denotes a kind of superficial and transient copying behavior whereas he wanted a word that would convey the idea of a more or less permanent acquisition to personality.

We chose as models those who seem to be more successful in gratifying their needs than we are. The child identifies with his parents because they appear to him to be omnipotent, at least during the years of early childhood. As the child grows older, he finds other people to identify with whose accomplishments are more in line with his current wishes. Each period tends to have its own characteristic identification figures. Needless to say, most of this identification takes place unconsciously and not, as it may sound, with conscious intention.

It is not necessary for a person to identify with someone else in every respect. He usually selects and incorporates just those features which he believes will help him achieve a desired goal. There is a good deal of trial and error in the identification process because one is usually not quite sure what it is about another person that accounts for his success. The ultimate test is whether the identification helps to reduce tension; if it does the quality is taken over, if it does not it is discarded. One may identify with animals, imaginary characters, institutions, abstract ideas, and inanimate objects as well as with other human beings.

Identification is also a method by which one may regain an object that has been lost. By identifying with a loved person who has died or from whom one has been separated, the lost person becomes reincarnated as an incorporated feature of one's personality. Children who have been rejected by their parents tend to form strong identifications with them in the hope of regaining their love. One may also identify with a person out of fear. The child identifies with the prohibitions of the parents in order to avoid punishment. This kind of identification is the basis for the formation of the superego.

The final personality structure represents an accumulation of numerous identifications made at various periods of the person's life, although the mother and father are probably the most important identification figures in anyone's life.

DISPLACEMENT. When an original object-choice of an instinct is rendered inaccessible by external or internal barriers (anticathexes), a new cathexis is formed unless a strong repression occurs. If this new cathexis is also blocked, another displacement takes place, and so on, until an object is found which yields some relief for the pent-up tension. This object is then cathected until it loses its power to reduce tension, at which time another search for an appropriate goal object is instituted. Throughout the series of displacements that constitute, in such large measure, the development of personality, the source and aim of the instinct remains constant; it is only the object that varies.

A substitute object is rarely if ever as satisfying or tension-reducing as the original object, and the less tension is reduced the more remote the displacement is from the original object. As a consequence of numerous displacements a pool of undischarged tension accumulates which acts as a permanent motivating force for behavior. The person is constantly seeking new

Freud's Psychoanalytic Theory of Personality 21

and better ways of reducing tension. This accounts for the variability and diversity of behavior, as well as for man's restlessness. On the other hand, the personality does become more or less stabilized with age owing to the compromises that are made between the urging forces of the instincts and the resistances of the ego and superego.

As we have written in another place (Hall 1954):

> Interests, attachments, and all the other forms of acquired motives endure because they are to some degree frustrating as well as satisfying. They persist because they fail to yield complete satisfaction. . . . Every compromise is at the same time a renunciation. A person gives up something that he really wants but cannot have, and accepts something second or third best that he can have (p. 104).

Freud pointed out that the development of civilization was made possible by the inhibition of primitive object-choices and the diversion of instinctual energy into socially acceptable and culturally creative channels (1930). A displacement which produces a higher cultural achievement is called a *sublimation*. Freud observed in this connection that Leonardo da Vinci's interest in painting Madonnas was a sublimated expression of a longing for intimacy with his mother from whom he had been separated at a tender age (1910a). Since sublimation does not result in complete satisfaction, any more than any displacement does, there is always some residual tension. This tension may discharge itself in the form of nervousness or restlessness, conditions which Freud pointed out were the price that man paid for his civilized status (1908).

The direction taken by a displacement is determined by two factors. These are (1) the resemblance of the substitute object to the original one, and (2) the sanctions and prohibitions imposed by society. The factor of resemblance is actually the degree to which the two objects are identified in the mind of the person. Da Vinci painted Madonnas rather than peasant women or aristocrats because he conceived of his mother as resembling the Madonna more than any other type of woman. Society acting through the parents and other authority figures authorizes certain displacements and outlaws others. The child learns that it is permissible to suck a lollipop but not to suck his thumb.

The ability to form substitute object-cathexes is the most powerful mechanism for the development of personality. The complex network of interests, preferences, values, attitudes, and attachments that characterize the personality of the adult human being is made possible by displacement. If psychic energy were not displaceable and distributive there would be no development of personality. The person would be merely a mechanical robot driven to perform fixed patterns of behavior by his instincts.

THE DEFENSE MECHANISMS OF THE EGO. Under the pressure of excessive anxiety, the ego is sometimes forced to take extreme measures to relieve the pressure. These measures are called defense mechanisms. The principal defenses are repression, projection, reaction formation, fixation, and regression (Anna Freud 1946). All defense mechanisms have two characteristics in common: (1) they deny, falsify, or distort reality, and (2) they operate unconsciously so that the person is not aware of what is taking place.

Repression. This is one of the earliest concepts of psychoanalysis. Before Freud arrived at his final formulation of personality theory in terms of the id, ego, and superego, he divided the mind into three regions, consciousness, preconsciousness, and unconsciousness. The preconscious consisted of psychological material that could become concious when the need arose. Material in the unconscious, however, was regarded by Freud as being relatively inaccessible to conscious awareness; it was said to be in a state of repression.

When Freud revised his theory of personality, the concept of repression was retained as one of the defense mechanisms of the ego. Repression is said to occur when an object-choice that arouses undue alarm is forced out of consciousness by an anticathexis. For example, a disturbing memory may be prevented from becoming conscious or a person may not see something that is in plain sight because the perception of it is repressed. Repression can even interfere with the normal functioning of the body. Someone may become sexually impotent because he is afraid of the sex impulse, or he may develop arthritis as a consequence of repressing feelings of hostility.

Repressions may force their way through the opposing anticathexes or they may find expression in the form of a displacement. If the displacement is to be successful in preventing the reawakening of anxiety it must be disguised in some suitable symbolic form. A son who has repressed his hostile feelings towards his father may express these hostile feelings against other symbols of authority.

Repressions once formed are difficult to abolish. The person must reassure himself that the danger no longer exists, but he cannot get such reassurance until the repression is lifted so that he can test reality. It is a vicious circle. That is why the adult carries around with him a lot of childish fears; he never gets a chance to discover that they have no basis in reality.

Projection. Reality anxiety is usually easier for the ego to deal with than is either neurotic or moral anxiety. Consequently, if the source of the anxiety can be attributed to the external world rather than to the individual's own primitive impulses or to the threats of his conscience, he is likely to achieve greater relief for his anxious condition. This mechanism by which neurotic or moral anxiety is converted into an objective fear is called projection. This conversion is easily made because the original source of both neurotic and moral anxiety is fear of punishment from an external agent. In projection, one simply says "He hates me" instead of "I hate him," or "He is persecuting me" instead of "My conscience is bothering me." Projection often serves a dual purpose. It reduces anxiety by substituting a lesser danger for a greater one, and it enables the projecting person to express his impulses under the guise of defending himself against his enemies.

Reaction formation. This defensive measure involves the replacement in consciousness of an anxiety-producing impulse or feeling by its opposite. For example, hate is replaced by love. The original impulse still exists but it is glossed over or masked by one that does not cause anxiety.

The question often arises as to how a reaction formation may be distinguished from a genuine expression of an impulse or feeling. For instance, how can reactive love be differentiated from true love? Usually, a reaction formation is marked by extravagant showiness—the person protests too much—and by compulsiveness. Extreme forms of behavior of any kind usually denote a reaction formation. Sometimes the reaction formation succeeds in satisfying the original impulse which is being defended against, as when a mother smothers her child with affection and attention.

Fixation and regression. In the course of normal development, as we shall see in the next section, the personality passes through a series of rather well-defined stages until it reaches maturity. Each new step that is taken, however, entails a certain amount of frustration and anxiety and if these become too great, normal growth may be temporarily or permanently halted. In other words, the person may become fixated on one of the early stages of development because taking the next step is fraught with anxiety. The overly dependent child exemplifies defense by fixation; anxiety prevents him from learning how to become independent.

A closely related type of defense is that of regression. In this case, a person who encounters traumatic experiences retreats to an earlier stage of development. For example, a child who is frightened by his first day at school may indulge in infantile behavior, such as weeping, sucking his thumb, hanging on to the teacher, or hiding in a corner. A young married woman who has difficulties with her husband may return to the security of her parents' home, or a man who has lost his job may seek comfort in drink. The path of regression is usually determined by the earlier fixations of the person. That is, a person tends to regress to a stage upon which he has been previously fixated. If he was overly dependent as a child, he will be likely to become overly dependent again when his anxiety increases to an unbearable level.

Fixation and regression are ordinarily relative conditions; a person rarely fixates or regresses completely. Rather his personality tends to include infantilisms, that is, immature forms of behavior, and predispositions to display childish conduct when thwarted. Fixations and regressions are responsible for the unevenness in personality development.

STAGES OF DEVELOPMENT. Freud believed that the child passes through a series of dynamically differentiated stages during the first five years of life, following which for a period of five or six years—the period of latency—the dynamics become more or less stabilized. With the advent of adolescence, the dynamics erupt again and then gradually settle down as the adolescent moves into adulthood. For Freud, *the first few years of life are decisive for the formation of personality.*

Each stage of development during the first five years is defined in terms of the modes of reaction of a particular zone of the body. During the first stage, which lasts for about a year, the mouth is the principal region of dynamic activity. The *oral* stage is followed by the development of cathexes and anticathexes around the eliminative functions, and is called the *anal* stage. This lasts during the second year and is succeeded by the *phallic* stage in which the sex organs become the leading erogenous zones. These three stages, the oral, anal, and phallic, are called the pregenital stages. The child then goes into a prolonged latency period, the so-called quiet years dynamically speaking. During this period the impulses tend to be held in a state of repression. The dynamic resurgence of adolescence reactivates the pregenital impulses; if these are successfully displaced and sublimated by the ego, the person passes into the final stage of maturity, the *genital* stage.

The oral stage. The principal source of pleasure derived from the mouth is that of eating. Eating involves tactual stimulation of the lips and oral cavity, and swallowing or, if the food is unpleasant, spitting out. Later when the teeth erupt the mouth is used for biting and chewing. These two modes of oral activity, incorporation of food and biting, are the prototypes for many later character traits that develop. Pleasure derived from oral incorporation may be displaced to other modes of incorporation such as the pleasure gained from acquiring knowledge or possessions. A gullible person, for example, is one who is fixated on the oral incorporative level of personality; he will swallow almost anything he is told. Biting or oral aggression may be displaced in the form of sarcasm and argumentativeness. By displacements and sublimations of various kinds, as well as by defenses against the primitive oral impulses, these prototypic modes of oral functioning provide the basis for the development of a vast network of interests, attitudes, and character traits.

Furthermore, since the oral stage occurs at a time when the baby is almost completely dependent upon his mother for sustenance, when he is cradled and nursed by her and protected from discomfort, feelings of dependency arise during this period.

These feelings of dependency tend to persist throughout life, in spite of later ego developments, and are apt to come to the fore whenever the person feels anxious and insecure. Freud believed that the most extreme symptom of dependency is the desire to return to the womb.

The anal stage. After the food has been digested, the residue accumulates in the lower end of the intestinal tract and is reflexly discharged when the pressure upon the anal sphincters reaches a certain level. The expulsion of the feces removes the source of discomfort and produces a feeling of relief. When toilet training is initiated, usually during the second year of life, the child has his first decisive experience with the external regulation of an instinctual impulse. He has to learn to postpone the pleasure that comes from relieving his anal tensions. Depending upon the particular method of toilet training used by the mother and her feelings concerning defecation, the consequences of this training may have far-reaching effects upon the formation of specific traits and values. If the mother is very strict and repressive in her methods, the child may hold back his feces and become constipated. If this mode of reaction generalizes to other ways of behaving, the child will develop a retentive character. He will become obstinate and stingy. Or under the duress of repressive measures the child may vent his rage by expelling his feces at the most inappropriate times. This is the prototype for all kinds of expulsive traits—cruelty, wanton destructiveness, temper tantrums, and messy disorderliness, to mention only a few. On the other hand, if the mother is the type of person who pleads with her child to have a bowel movement and who praises him extravagantly when he does, the child will acquire the notion that the whole activity of producing feces is extremely important. This idea may be the basis for creativity and productivity. Innumerable other traits of character are said to have their roots laid down in the anal stage.

The phallic stage. During this stage of personality development sexual and aggressive feelings associated with the functioning of the genital organs come into focus. The pleasures of masturbation and the fantasy life of the child which accompanies autoerotic activity set the stage for the appearance of the *Oedipus complex.* Freud considered the identification of the

Oedipus complex to be one of his greatest discoveries. The Oedipus complex is named for the king of Thebes who killed his father and married his mother.

Briefly defined, the Oedipus complex consists of a sexual cathexis for the parent of the opposite sex and a hostile cathexis for the parent of the same sex. The boy wants to possess his mother and remove his father, the girl wants to possess her father and displace her mother. These feelings express themselves in the child's fantasies during masturbation and in the alternation of loving and rebellious actions toward his parents. The behavior of the three- to five-year-old child is marked to a large extent by the operation of the Oedipus complex, and although it is modified and suffers repression after the age of five it remains a vital force in the personality throughout life. Attitudes toward the opposite sex and toward people in authority, for instance, are largely conditioned by the Oedipus complex.

The history and fate of the Oedipus complex differ for males and females. To begin with, both sexes love the mother because she satisfies their needs and resent the father because he is regarded as a rival for the mother's affections. These feelings persist in the boy but change in the girl. Let us consider first the sequence of events which characterize the development of the male Oedipus complex.

The boy's incestuous craving for the mother and his growing resentment toward the father bring him into conflict with his parents, especially the father. He imagines that his dominant rival is going to harm him, and his fears may actually be confirmed by threats from a resentful and punitive father. His fears concerning what the father may do to him center around harm to his genital organs because they are the source of his lustful feelings. He is afraid that his jealous father will remove the offending organs. Fear of castration or, as Freud called it, *castration anxiety* induces a repression of the sexual desire for the mother and hostility toward the father. It also helps to bring about an identification of the boy with his father. By identifying with the father, the boy also gains some vicarious satisfaction for his sexual impulses toward the mother. At the same time, his dangerous erotic feeling for the mother is converted into harmless tender affection for her. Lastly, the repression of the Oedipus complex causes the superego to undergo its final development. In Freud's words, the superego is the heir of the male Oedipus complex. It is the bulwark against incest and aggression.

The sequence of events in the development and dissolution of the female Oedipus complex is more involved. In the first place, she exchanges her original love object, the mother, for a new object, the father. Why this takes place depends upon the girl's reaction of disappointment when she discovers that a boy possesses a protruding sex organ, the penis, while she has only a cavity. Several important consequences follow from this traumatic discovery. In the first place, she holds her mother responsible for her castrated condition which weakens the cathexis for the mother. In the second place, she transfers her love to the father because he has the valued organ which she aspires to share with him. However, her love for the father and for other men as well is mixed with a feeling of envy because they possess something she lacks. Penis envy is the female counterpart of castration anxiety in the boy, and collectively they are called the *castration complex*. She imagines that she has lost something valuable, while the boy is afraid he is going to lose it. To some extent, the lack of a penis is compensated for when a woman has a baby, especially if it is a boy baby.

In the girl the castration complex initiates the Oedipus complex by weakening her cathexis for the mother and instituting a cathexis for the father. Unlike the boy's Oedipus complex which is repressed or otherwise changed by castration anxiety, the girl's Oedipus complex tends to persist although it undergoes some modification due to the realistic barriers that prevent her from gratifying her sexual desire for the father. But it does not fall under the strong repression that the boy's does. These differences in the nature of the Oedipus and castration complexes are the basis for many psychological differences between the sexes.

Freud assumed that every person is inherently bisexual; each sex is attracted to members of the same sex as well as to members of the opposite sex. This is the constitutional basis for homosexuality, although in most people the homosexual impulses remain latent. This condition of bisexuality complicates the

Oedipus complex by inducing sexual cathexes for the same sex parent. Consequently, the boy's feelings for his father and the girl's feelings for her mother are said to be ambivalent rather than univalent in character. The assumption of bisexuality has been supported by investigations on the endocrine glands which show rather conclusively that both male and female sex hormones are present in each sex.

The emergence and development of the Oedipus and castration complexes are the chief events of the phallic period, and leave a host of deposits in the personality.

The genital stage. The cathexes of the pregenital periods are narcissistic in character. This means that the individual obtains gratification from the stimulation and manipulation of his own body and other people are cathected only because they help to provide additional forms of body pleasure to the child. During adolescence, some of this self-love or narcissism becomes channeled into genuine object choices. The adolescent begins to love others for altruistic motives and not simply for selfish or narcissistic reasons. Sexual attraction, socialization, group activities, vocational planning, and preparations for marrying and raising a family begin to manifest themselves. By the end of adolescence, these socialized, altruistic cathexes have become fairly well stabilized in the form of habitual displacements, sublimations, and identifications. The person becomes transformed from a pleasure-seeking, narcissistic infant into a reality-oriented, socialized adult. However, it should not be thought that the pregenital impulses are displaced by genital ones. Rather, the cathexes of the oral, anal, and phallic stages become fused and synthesized with the genital impulses. The principal biological function of the genital stage is that of reproduction; the psychological aspects help to achieve this end by providing a certain measure of stability and security.

In spite of the fact that Freud differentiated four stages of personality growth, he did not assume that there were any sharp breaks or abrupt transitions in passing out of one stage into another. The final organization of personality represents contributions from all four stages.

Part II NEW WORLD

2 WORLD VIEW AND SELF-VIEW OF THE KASKA INDIANS

John Honigmann

WORLD VIEW AND SELF-VIEW

The Kaska view of the world wavers between an idea that experience is manageable and an awareness that life is threatening and difficult. These opposite attitudes lead to two principal means of responding to adaptive and adjustive problems. For many of the hazards of existence, there are tested problem solutions with the aid of which one can efficiently overcome a harsh and rigorous environment. In these situations it is possible to be resourceful, capable, and masterful. Unfortunately, the context of life offering security is extremely limited. To stay within the area of safety requires constant watchfulness and caution. As soon as experiential boundaries widen, catastrophe may be expected. The uncertainties of life must be avoided lest by testing resourcefulness too sharply they promote failure. Society, like the physical environment, also holds dangers. Here safety lies in avoiding interpersonal relations which promise to stir up intense emotions or invite excessive effort against which there are no effective safeguards and which tax the resources of the ego.

Two divergent attitudes toward the self, self-reliance and helplessness, complement the double view of the world in Kaska personality. The most acceptable is the notion of self-confidence that seems to say: "I can do this, but I must do it alone." The

FROM John Honigmann, "Culture and Ethos of Kaska Society," 1949, *Yale University Publications in Anthropology* ⚹40, Yale University Press, pp. 305–15, by permission of the author and the publisher.

independence and self-containment involved in this formula partly rest on feelings of being socially detached, lonely, and afraid. To deny these anxious notes, a person must prove his effectiveness lest by failure he admit his need for social support.

Completely inacceptable is the idea of personal helplessness, the doubt that promises failure and which urges the person to relax from striving. In life's critical situations—and these are frequent and inevitable for an uncertain personality—the responsible feelings of the individual, to his great dismay, quickly give ground. There ensues a blind reaching out for all the things that are equivalent to failure—relaxation from striving, affection, and protection. The person is touched with guilt for his helplessness and threatened by anxiety which he dares not release for fear of further imperiling his safety. So long as the Kaska can contain their physical and social environmental participation within narrow limits, they feel resourceful, capable, and safe; trouble is avoided; life is simple, and the individual is supreme. As soon as the protective boundaries are upset, however, there follows a wave of worry and anxiety that signifies the penalty of failure.

Development of the Ethos

Our study of Kaska ethos now concerns itself with the development of the dominant motivations in which this system has its roots. In pursuing this aim we find it more significant to concentrate on how learning takes place than on the cultural content which is transmitted by direct learning, although explicit instruction which reinforces dominant motivations will not be neglected. In the words of Bateson and Mead, our assumption is that, "An individual's character structure, his attitudes toward himself and his interpretation of experience are conditioned not only by what he learns, but also by the method of learning" (Bateson and Mead 1942:84). For this analysis, the most significant aspects of socialization may be grouped under five headings: infant care, emotional rejection, parental attitudes and authority, identifications, and activities of later childhood.

Infant care. A newborn infant occupies an extremely favorable

World View and Self-View of the Kaska Indians 35

position in Kaska society. The baby is carefully kept warm and comfortable and fed whenever it cries. Crying also brings a quick response in the way of other comforts and attention. The early relationship between mother and child is a warm one and during the first two years of life the child is usually in close proximity to its mother, although the manner of blanketing the infant permits little direct contact between the mother's arms and the baby's naked body. Weaning is gradual and tolerant, the satisfactions of suckling being prolonged by continuing to allow nursing from a bottle once weaning is terminated. Punishment is as rare in the baby's life as attention is plentiful.

What are the effects of these patterns of infant care in the personality of the developing child and adult? Good maternal care in infancy, by gratifying the child's craving for physical comfort and alimentary needs, may be considered the initial stimulus for the development of feelings of mastery and control and to instill confidence for later investigating and dealing with the external world. It is therefore the basis for the development of egocentricity and self-sufficiency, the self-assertive motives of Kaska personality, which determine the emotional significance of many adaptive situations. The prompt satisfactions produced by crying also condition the child to expectations of being able to control his environment resourcefully, capably, and empirically. In other words, good care in childhood is a strong stimulus for developing the executive functions of the ego. The cherished position of the Kaska baby is responsible for creating active coping techniques in the personality, which later become expressed in attitudes toward the world and self characterized by self-confidence, independence, and ego strength.

On the other hand, as Kardiner has pointed out, a readiness for passive forms of adaptation and adjustment is one of the "bad effects" of good maternal care (Kardiner 1945:345, 347–48). Such passivity results primarily from the infant's unconscious idealization of the mother as a powerful and resourceful figure. The satisfactions of Kaska infancy, kinaesthetic and oral, are well nigh complete and extremely gratifying. Their very fullness sets the stage for an unconscious attraction to this period of easy gratification. In later life passive reactions occur when, under situations of stress and crisis, the person unconsciously attempts to restore the omnipotence which maternal gratification encouraged in the very early years of life. The appearance of passive adaptive and passive receptive techniques, in which the person surrenders active striving, are therefore indices of an unconscious process called regression.

Thus we see that in the state of infancy Kaska society begins to shape both the relatively assertive and the passive coping techniques of the personality. It endows the personality with a capacity for mastery and accomplishment by inducing confidence in the self to command the resources of the environment. On the other hand, indulgent care creates a readiness to relinquish such techniques when, under conditions of stress, the ego no longer feels capable of achieving its goals. At what level of aspiration that stress will induce passivity seems to depend largely upon the development of personality beyond infancy.

Emotional rejection. Although the Kaska child receives a good start in life, this favorable situation is soon interrupted when the emotionally isolating tendencies of early childhood are instituted by the hitherto indulgent mother. At about two or three years of age the child begins to be denied the emotional warmth and generous attention to which he has been accustomed. He still receives sufficient nourishment, so long as good food is available in camp, but affectionally he is rejected; attention is withdrawn, fondling and playing with the child discontinued, the mother withdraws into impersonal aloofness. Following upon the initial period of extreme gratification these new attitudes are exceedingly traumatic for development. The self-confident expectations which the child was encouraged to experience toward the world are suddenly disappointed; his capacities for securing comfort and attention fail. There follow feelings of abandonment, of being reduced to struggling for satisfactions and creating comforts. The consequences of emotional isolation include the blocked development of active forms of mastery, affect hunger, institution of the first regressive trends, development of emotional aloofness, and the creation of various projective systems organized to deal with the persistent traumatic effects of this situation. We will now discuss these effects in greater detail.

We have emphasized the importance of good infant care in Kaska society for developing security and encouraging capacities

World View and Self-View of the Kaska Indians

for self-assertion and mastery. Such results are not only derived from social responsiveness to the child's bodily needs but are also built up in the process of inducing affection. The combined effect of these gratifications is to stimulate a congenial view of the world and faith in the self. When affectional stimulation is interrupted by the mother's emotional rejection, the development of the self-assertive aims receives a setback. Although the initial impetus to activity permits a conscious compensatory development of ego striving to continue (this will be discussed below), the removal of the heartening stimuli to such growth leaves ego strength in a precarious position, which in later life leads to narrowing the field of effective participation and strong readiness to succumb to crises with passivity and regression.

Emotional rejection institutes the first regressive trends because it intensifies the memory of infantile omnipotence. The highlighting of a past and more favorable period of adjustment, together with a simultaneous blow to ego development, help institute a chronic dependence that continues to underlie all forms of active mastery. Affect hunger is one feature of this phenomenon. Emotional rejection leaves the Kaska individual unable to form close emotional attachments for two main reasons. In the first place it must be remembered that the expression of love requires inducement; that is, it must be stimulated by the experience of being loved. When such indirect learning is early discontinued, as it is when the three year old is emotionally rejected, the individual is left without sufficient capacity to cathect love objects. He has not been sufficiently prepared for love. Second, emotional responsiveness may be inhibited by serious affectional disappointments encountered in the course of development. The Kaska child meets such disappointment when expected affectional gratification is abruptly withdrawn by the primary source of this reward—the mother. The seriousness of this withdrawal is reflected in the prolonged trauma that characterizes Kaska personality. As a result of that shock, the child becomes afraid ever again to lose his identity in strong love relationships which might once more be destroyed at the individual's expense. Both these factors help to institute emotional aloofness, leading the person to regard with fear all strong love relationships while at the same time he longs for a return to the period when affectional gratification was abundantly available. Realistically, regression is impossible; so the person comes to perceive one avenue of safety in the maintenance of personal inviolability and self-sufficiency. What happens is that emotional rejection secondarily reinforces the earlier patterned egocentric aim of mastery—independence comes to be valued as an active defense. The fact that such an assertive defense system can be patterned testifies to the importance of good infantile care for developing sufficient ego strength to institute such defenses. But emotional rejection also sets the stage for passive receptive techniques, which represent attempted or symbolic regression to the gratifications that were effortlessly available in infancy. Stealing and food leeching in childhood, the earliest ethological expression of this regressive process, originate from the child's awareness that his demands will not be adequately fulfilled. Stealing is largely confined to trinkets and food, objects symbolic of love. Food leeching is a means of securing oral indulgence, the mouth having been the organ most intensely associated with infantile gratification and unconsciously remaining a channel for trying to approximate those early rewards. Since children are punished for stealing, the behavior does not often continue into adulthood but its underlying aims continue to operate in the demandingness of the adult and in the high evaluation of generosity. The fact that demandingness is most directly expressed toward the government and whites, suggests that these sources are unconsciously regarded as parental substitutes who have in abundance what the individual needs and so suggest themselves as suitable sources for restoring the balance of frustrated parent-child relations. The statement of Nitla referring to the traders as "Just the same your daddy" is significant in this respect. The conception of authority, or bosses, as sources of protection also equates these concepts with the early parental ideal.

These facts show how closely emotional isolation is related to dependence. In dependence, the search for love is partially affirmed but in emotional aloofness (which, in turn, is related to the motives of egocentricity and utilitarianism) the need for love is denied. "I don't need anybody," the individual seems to say. While intrinsically this is not true, the expression of aloofness is important because of its effects in keeping down passivity and in encouraging the self-assertive motives. The extremes to which emotional aloofness is carried in Kaska society are striking. It leads to the isolation of the individual from all intense social contacts and constantly seeks to guard him against internal and external exciting stimuli which might activate the trauma of emotional rejection. The personality characterized by these trends bears many resemblances to Balinese character structure and certain etiological factors in the two situations are also broadly similar (Bateson and Mead op. cit.; Mead 1939).

The development of a psychoanalytic approach to culture and personality by workers like Roheim, Mead, and Kardiner has stimulated interest in the elucidation of projective systems. Such systems are "the records of traumatic experiences . . . excrescences developed from nuclear traumatic experiences within the growth pattern of the individual" (Kardiner 1945:39). Following such a definition we would expect to find the emotional rejection of the Kaska child reflected in projective systems and this is indeed the case. In order to distinguish between "records of traumatic experiences" and the ethological expressions of all early experiences in the ethos, we are using the term projective systems for the symbolic representation of a patterned traumatic experience (or persons related to such an experience) in the socially patterned behavior and ideas of a society.[1] Such representations may be regarded as the symbolic reenactment of the individual's roles in an early traumatic experience and involves the assumptions that the trauma still persists vividly in the individual's unconscious memory and that he is anxious to assume control over it (Fenichel 1945:120).

The principal projections of emotional isolation are found in the representations of women in Kaska folktales. We have already alluded to the story, "The Girl Who Turned Into An Owl."[2] Now we turn to another function of this tale, seeing it as the projection of emotional rejection and a representation of the mother pictured as a deceiver. The story also indicates a certain equivalence between the husband-wife and parent-child relationships. The girl's mother, taking the wife's place, symbolizes the equivalence of the maternal and wifely roles. Unconsciously,

---

[1] This definition seems implicit in the work of Mead (cf. 1939:24).
[2] Not reprinted here.

husbands are children fed by their mothers. They are dependent on wives as they were dependent on the maternal care in infancy, but in the tale the mother reveals her deceitfulness and must be punished. Similar unconscious ideas may also be at the root of the aggression which men direct against women during intoxication, and also in the rejection of the breasts as erotic stimuli in sexual situations. A similar story of a deceitful wife is found in "The Blind Old Man," in which the man again kills the mother equivalent. In "A Tribe of Women" we see represented a flight from parents and the discovery of new mothers. When the younger brother allows himself to be killed by these women he gives in to a regressive wish to be incorporated by the mother and attains his passive goal by being buried in the women's camp. That men should be indicated in these tales as experiencing somewhat greater frustration from emotional rejection than women can perhaps be partly explained in terms of the girl's greater opportunities to repair the wound of rejection. This will be discussed below in connection with identifications and childhood activities.

The grizzly bear fantasy may be regarded as another example of a projective system repeating the child's terror upon encountering emotional rejection. The mother is here represented (familiarly, as far as western clinical practice is concerned) in a large and dangerous animal against which the person feels powerless. It is not coincidental that another function of this fantasy is to express the anxiety which girls feel in the face of sexual situations, whose intensity threatens to break down the emotional isolation adopted as a defense against rejection.

Parental attitudes and authority. Parental authority plays a relatively slight and nontraumatic role in the Kaska child's life. Attitudes toward toilet training are not severe and sphincter regulation is not seriously expected before the child possesses the capacities for voluntary control. Punishment is rare and generally limited to situations of defaulting while overprotection has no soil in which to grow. There is an absence of authoritarian supervision such as would emphasize the child's humiliation and complete submission to his parents. Native education is also characterized by this lack of authoritarianism; little effort is made to specifically direct the child's assimilation of cultural routines and

World View and Self-View of the Kaska Indians 41

in a great deal of learning children are left to work out their own answers to problems. In general, the child grows up easily and independently and with a large amount of freedom from supervision and authority. What are the consequences of these patterns for Kaska personality?

In the first place, we note that sphincter training is not severe and therefore is not a situation in which parental disciplines can frustrate the child's capacities. Integrated as it is with other parental attitudes, toilet training is conducive to developing a sense of independence and personal responsibility. The absence of severe discipline or authoritarian attitudes therefore lends to the oedipal situation a flavor of permissiveness. The child's individuality is respected and no sense of blind obedience is ever imposed. Among the most important results of these patterns are the development of deference, egocentricity, and flexibility.

Deference is directly learned from the injunctions of parents warning children against aggression but is also indirectly assimilated in the absence of a frustrating and authoritarian oedipal situation. Following the child's emotional rejection, no new blocks or frustrations are set in the path of the developing ego, although it cannot be denied that the personality continues to carry the memory of this trauma whose anxieties continue to interfere with the richest development of ego functions. Kaska parents, therefore, do not demand submission and self-abnegation which in an authoritarian climate may undermine self-esteem and engender hostility (cf. Fromm 1939:514; Schilder 1942:49–50; Levy 1943:357–58). In the absence of such instigations to hostility, the positive lessons of parents against aggression can take a firm hold. This learning, it must be pointed out, further takes place in a personality whose emotional expressiveness, because of the emotionally isolating tendencies of the parents, is not being strongly stimulated. Positive injunctions to deference are therefore uncontested by alien forces or labile emotionality. The picture may be characterized as one of introversive isolation, and is in such a restrictive setting that the tendencies of egocentricity, emotional isolation, and deference become intensified. The nonauthoritarian parents influence the adoption of a religious view lacking a stern, authoritarian, nondeferent deity such as might be traced back to a harsh parental image.

The previously achieved degree of ego tonicity is maintained by the fact that shame and ridicule are not used as disciplinary measures. In the absence of a strongly inculcated sense of duty and obedience, the child, to a considerable extent, decides his own course of behavior against the introjected standards of his group. This does not imply failure to teach the child what is expected of him. The emphasis in such teaching, however, is to preserve the child's initiative, an effect that is further aided by the absence of constant adult watchfulness, supervision, or overprotection. The Kaska child finds this freedom to develop responsibility and independence congenial, perceiving the value of these attitudes as defenses against the traumatic effects of emotional rejection and regressive dependence. He gradually drops the overt forms of a compulsive search for love and is better off than he would be in a society that not only patterned a withdrawal of affection but also prevented the development of egocentric attitudes. The expressed fear lest a child be "pleased" too much (that is, lest the child be spoiled) may be understood as a desire to avoid inordinate permissiveness. Apparently it is not rare for permissiveness to be carried to extremes. On the other hand, it must be recognized that some parents exercise closer supervision and stricter discipline than is generally approved of.

The lack of strong parental direction and the fact that the child is left to learn many cultural routines for himself have consequences not only in further preventing the formation of a strong superego (based on the parental image) but in encouraging resourcefulness and self-sufficiency. They also make any idea of submission distasteful in later life. Such encouragement would be of little avail without the good infantile care which originally prepared the ego to exercise forms of active mastery. Early necessity for resourcefulness, in providing the emotional readiness to invent problem solutions, plays a large role in developing the practicality of the Kaska adult. From this we also learn more about how the empirical reality system gets its start in childhood. Among the Kaska, empiricism is related to good infant care, an oedipal pattern which stresses independent learning, discouragement from playing with impractical toys, encouragement of independence and self-sufficiency as defenses against emotional isolation, and the impossibility of overtly indulging passive dependent attitudes in parents.

The oedipal pattern we have described can certainly not lead to the projection of a strong authoritarian deity, and indeed the Kaska have refurbished the creation myth partially taken over from the Bible. Jesus (or God) is several times puzzled by his problems and there is no idea of God as omnipotent. The lasting idea of people as fallible and limited in their resources is another effect of the oedipal pattern and goes to reinforce the egocentric dictum: "I must do this by myself."

The influences of early parental attitudes, in association with moderate ego tonicity, on other aspects of flexibility are not hard to discern. With few rewards for the fulfillment of obligations, children are not required to learn the meaning of futurity. Compulsive qualities like duty and perfectionism are not demanded of the child nor are they available in his social environment for imitation. Similarly such compulsive ways of behaving are not acquired by the child while undergoing toilet training, where the stress on the child's preparedness and conformity are relatively mild. Few rules or formalized methods of procedure are given the child to follow. He sees no emphasis on planning and his moderate ego strength does not lead him to attempt to develop such notions. As a result, the adult is marked by a flexible approach to life which is largely used for passive purposes, to remove him from critical situations which threaten his ego resources.[3]

Identifications. Important stimulation is given to the dominant motivations by the identifications which the child creates in the oedipal situation. One expression of the effects of these identifications occurs in the conscious and unconscious attitudes characterizing adult interpersonal relations. There is no doubt that in the very early oedipal situation, before the institution of maternal

[3] Among the South African Lobvedu, the absence of stern parental authority also appears to be correlated with a lack of compulsiveness and tolerance for personal variation. In this society, too, we find that sphincter control is not expected before three years of age. Nevertheless there is evidence that Lobvedu spontaneity is something different from Kaska flexibility, being related to a feeling for moderation and a distaste for striving. Among the Kaska flexibility is essentially a passive reaction *from* striving. (See Krige and Krige 1943:290–92.)

emotional rejection, the mother is the most important figure in the child's life. Largely this importance is due to the mother's gratificatory role, but it also follows from the fact that the father's economic routines frequently separate him from his family. In later childhood the mother remains a powerful and significant figure but the father now becomes an equally important personage and one who suggests himself as a target for identification by children of both sexes. It must be pointed out, however, that identification with a father, or adequate father substitute, is often difficult when families are broken and children are raised by the mother or a mother surrogate like the mother's sister or the child's grandmother. Such broken families are quite common among the Kaska. The structure of the family too has an important bearing on what identifications can be cathected. The Kaska do not pattern the diffusion of parental roles among many parent extensions. The family tends to be centered in its own dwelling and parents, very much as in western society, originate most action to children. Other adults with whom the child comes into contact cannot be regarded as important for early identifications.

Following withdrawal of the mother's affectional stimulation we find in both the boy and girl a tendency to identify with the father. Undoubtedly this is due to the experience of the mother as a frustrating object, whose emotional rejection continues to live in the child's personality. In the boy identification with the father is indulged; in the girl, unless the family lacks an older son, identificatory aims are often difficult to realize. We will discuss the boy's identification first.

Following his emotional rejection, the boy sees the father as generally more assertive than the mother. The father, however, is not a warmly demonstrative person in whom the boy can realize his denied affective needs. A son may, however, associate with his father, offering the latter simple assistance. In so doing he strengthens his own egocentric and utilitarian motives as further defenses against isolation and passive tendencies. Idealization of fathers by sons is also possible because of the latters' socially important role as the chief providers of the family. As a result of the precarious emotional balance of the isolated boy, identification with the father assumes an ingratiatory quality,

World View and Self-View of the Kaska Indians

not because of the male parent's tyrannical family role but because the boy is afraid of losing what remains as a sole, if insufficient source of gratification. Ingratiation to the father is demonstrated in adult relationships between men, especially between Indians and white men—police, traders, the missionaries —and was also manifested toward the ethnographer. The relationship is, however, a deferent one; the father is rarely authoritarian and his behavior toward the boy expresses respect. These attitudes are also expressed between adult men and are partly responsible for the deferent individualism that is maintained in interpersonal relations. Yet the boy, for all the permissiveness extended to him, is not a tyrant in the family. He cannot deliberately offend or refuse to obey, although he can remain absent from camp for long periods. Tact, therefore, becomes essential in interpersonal relations lest hostility be aroused. This attitude also persists through life in the organization of deference.

Like her brother, the girl cannot successfully identify with the mother who emotionally isolates her. She too forms an early emotional attachment to the father and, particularly in the absence of an older son, often earns considerable satisfaction from this identification, accompanying her father on short hunting and trapping trips and, as she matures, striving to emulate the father's role as a food provider. Fathers may even offer daughters a certain amount of encouragement in this behavior. The girl's identification with the father encourages her ego development by developing the same goals, egocentricity and utilitarianism, which are patterned in the boy. We can now understand the masculine striving of women as a phenomenon partly following from identification with the father and generalization from maternal rejection to the feminine maternal role. Because of her cross-sexed identification, the girl probably becomes better able to manage intersexual relations than is the boy. Her warm attitudes toward men and her readiness to offer men emotional comforts are partially derived from this relationship.

One important class of identifications may be briefly stated, that occurring between like-sexed siblings. Between brothers this relationship often has an ambivalent quality, the functions of which are not clear, but between sisters the ties are very warm and probably give the girl a greater measure of emotional security than the boy has any opportunity of achieving. Yet sibling relationships are also influenced by the emotional isolation which never permits the child to relax completely affectional detachment.

Childhood activities. From six or seven years of age the Kaska girl is introduced to household duties, often in spite of her reluctance, while the boy's economically productive role does not begin for many more years. From this age, however, both sexes are usually thrown increasingly in the company of like-sexed parents or siblings from whom they begin to perceive the nature of their economic roles. Meanwhile play continues until with adolescence there begins the first stirring of the sexual impulse signalling adulthood.

The early domestic role of the girl has important effects in modifying, to some extent, the egocentric component of her personality and preparing her for the relatively passive female role. She is given an opportunity to develop capacities around the camp and unconsciously utilizes her serving role to remove some of the pain of isolation. The cooperation of the family's female relatives further provides some affectional gratification and is accompanied by a slight diminution of egocentricity. In general, however, the girl executes her role in autonomous terms and with a degree of individual responsibility which prevents any great development of passivity.

Egocentricity is less hindered in the boy. In the absence of early tasks, his career is freer and less subject to control and demands. On the other hand his development is more discontinuous than the girl's for, following childhood's period of freedom, he is confronted with the responsibilities of a man-sized role. The situation is one which invites confusion. The fact that the boy is not trained for active serving is an important factor in this confusion and one which, in a setting of moderate ego tonicity, is responsible for the conflicts over responsibility in the adult male. On the other hand the boy comes to appreciate the values of work and general self-assertion as defenses against emotional isolation, but the fact that with adolescence these gratifications entail more of a sense of duty and become less a matter of choice adds to confusion and increases readiness for dependence (cf. Fromm 1941:30).

World View and Self-View of the Kaska Indians 47

With puberty the personalities of both sexes are quite fully formed. Two behaviors appear in puberty which, perhaps, have not been clearly accounted for in the earlier development of the personality—homosexuality and promiscuity.

Three factors seem responsible for male homosexuality. The first of these is affectional neglect by the mother. This leads to the second factor, the boy's ambivalence to women, or his greater confidence in relations with youths who respect egocentric demands and do not immediately threaten emotional isolation. In other words, the passivity of homosexuality is not as threatening as dependence on women. Ambivalent feelings toward girls are also expressed in childhood, in the boy's teasing of girls, for example, a behavior which culminates in sexual teasing. The third factor in male homosexuality is identification with the father and the consequent development of positive attitudes toward all men; homosexuality, therefore, is unconsciously directed toward securing stronger emotional satisfactions from men than could originally be obtained from the father and than dare be sought from women who, unconsciously, are mother equivalents.

The development of homosexuality in girls is not so clear. Important factors seem to include the strong positive ties between sisters, the girl's greater ability, conditioned by early cooperation among female members of the family, and fear of the aggressive components of intersexual sexual interaction. As a result of her egocentricity, the girl is not attracted to being a masochistic sexual object. Among members of her own sex she has greater opportunity to receive affectional gratification without threat to egocentricity.

The developmental significance of promiscuity has already been mentioned as signalling a woman's rebellion against the serving role which was never wholly congenial to her egocentric orientations. In the boy varied sexual intercourse complements his economic self-assertive roles and is also a means of overcoming the potency anxieties which appear with his awakening genitality (Fromm 1943).

Conclusion. Our survey of the development of Kaska ethos in childhood has stressed the patterning of the dominant motivations, to a lesser extent illustrating their early expression. We have remained conscious of the need to avoid such simplification as would lead to correlating a dominant motive with any one specific childhood pattern. The situation is far more complex. At each moment in development, impacts on the child operate on what is already present and this cumulative process continues throughout childhood.

3 INTELLIGENCE OF NORTHEASTERN INDIANS

A. Irving Hallowell

INTELLIGENCE LEVEL

In view of the heated debate in modern times about the differential mental capacities of the various races of Man, the almost complete unanimity with which seventeenth-century observers equate the Indians with Europeans is striking. Apparently the idea never arose in the minds of those who had first-hand knowledge of them that the Indians were in any way mentally inferior to whites. Bressani, for example, who had been a missionary in Huronia from 1645 until 1649, and later wrote a general account of the New World natives, points out that they "are hardly Barbarians, save in name. There is no occasion to think of them as half beasts, shaggy, black and hideous." (*The Jesuit Relations,* XXXVIII, 257 ff., hereafter cited as J. R.) (Coues 1897, I:37 n.) He goes on to remark the acuteness of their senses and their tenacious memory. He is particularly impressed by their "marvellous faculty for remembering places, and for describing them to one another," for finding their way about and for recalling details that whites "could not rehearse without writing." Bressani even goes so far as to say that, "they have often persuaded us in affairs of importance, and made us change the resolution which, after mature deliberation, we had taken for the

FROM A. Irving Hallowell, "Some Psychological Characteristics of the Northeastern Indians," 1946, as reprinted in *Culture and Experience,* 1955: 125–50, by permission of the author and the University of Pennsylvania Press.

weal of the country. I doubt not that they are capable of the sciences. . . ."

Other Jesuits who, being intellectually trained men themselves, may be accepted as good common-sense judges of intellectual functioning, give similar reports. Du Peron (J. R., XV [1639], 157) writes of the Huron, and Ragueneau (J. R., XXIX, 281) corroborates him: "They nearly all show more intelligence in their business, speeches, courtesies, intercourse, tricks and subtleties, than do the shrewdest citizens and merchants in France." Jerome Lalemant writes, ". . . for I can say in truth that, as regards Intelligence, they are in no wise inferior to Europeans and to those who dwell in France. I would never have believed that, without instruction, nature could have supplied a most ready and vigorous eloquence, which I have admired in many Hurons; or more clear-sightedness in affairs, or a more discreet management in things to which they are accustomed" (J. R., XXVIII, 63).

The Micmac were said by Le Clercq not only to "have naturally a sound mind and a common sense beyond that which is supposed in France," (Le Clercq 1910:241) but "they conduct their affairs cleverly." The editor of Le Clercq remarks, "indeed they were able to outwit the French captains in trade, as Denys makes very plain," for which there is likewise evidence in Father Biard's account.

It is worth noting, too, that Father Le Jeune, that sage Jesuit, appears to have sensed the importance of training in relation to the full exercise of native capacities. For he observes that, "Those who cross over here from your France are almost all mistaken on one point,—they have a very low opinion of our Savages, thinking them dull and slow-witted; but as soon as they have associated with them they confess that only education, and not intelligence, is lacking in these peoples" (J. R., XIX [1640], 39). In another *Relation,* after remarking that the "mind of the Savages" is of good quality, he goes on to write, "Education and instruction alone are lacking. . . . I naturally compare our Savages with certain villagers, because both are usually without education; though our Peasants are superior in this regard; and yet I have not seen any one thus far, of those who have come to this country, who does not confess and frankly admit that the

Savages are more intelligent than our ordinary peasants." (J. R., VI, 231) Cadillac, referring to the Ottawa at Mackinac (1695), makes this general statement, "We may say without flattery, that all the Indians are naturally intelligent" (Kinietz 1940:232).

These are extremely interesting appraisals and, so far as we know, as honest as could be desired. While other citations, supporting the high level of intelligence attributed to the Indians in their native state, could be given,[1] those referred to must suffice as an index of the general impression created upon the early observers.

Is this impression supported by the more refined methods and observational techniques we now have at our disposal? It is impossible to answer this question specifically for the Northeastern Indians since no attempt has ever been made to rate their level of intelligence in terms of the results of a systematic application of standard intelligence tests. When such studies have been made the same questions arise that have plagued all the investigators who have used such tests on other American Indians or native peoples on other continents. For example, a study was made of children of the Six Nations Reserve (Iroquois). They all spoke English, but on the whole their command of the language was not that of white children, a fact that adversely affected their scores in the verbal tests. In non-verbal tests they approximated white norms.[2] While test results, when taken at their face value, may show the subjects to be "retarded" in terms of the average I.Q. (the majority of I.Q.'s obtained from studies of Indians at large fall between 70 and 90) (Klineberg op. cit.:153) sophisticated students are now aware that differences in language facility, schooling, speed in performance, motivation, and other factors related to the cultural background of the subject, all affect the results. Anne Anastasi writes,

> Thus it would seem that intelligence tests measure only the ability to succeed in our particular culture. Each culture, partly through the physical conditions of its environment and partly through

[1] Cf. Duncan Cameron (on the Saulteaux) in R. L. Masson 1890, II: 238.
[2] E. Jamieson and P. Sandiford (1929):536–51. See also T. R. Garth (1931); Blackwood (1927); Klineberg (1935), Chap. 8; Mann (1940): 366–95; Anastasi (1937), Chap. 7.

social tradition, "selects" certain activities as the most significant. These it encourages and stimulates; others it neglects or definitely suppresses. The relative standing of different cultural groups in "intelligence" is a function of the traits included under the concept of intelligence, or, to state the same point differently, it is a function of the particular culture in which the test was constructed (Anastasi op. cit.:511).

Consequently, until intra-cultural variables are properly weighed in inter-cultural comparisons, the results of intelligence tests may be highly misleading in the conclusions they suggest. Anastasi elaborates this point for primitive peoples:

> Tests of abstract abilities, for example, are considered more diagnostic of "intelligence" than those dealing with the manipulation of concrete objects or with the perception of spatial relationships. The aptitude for dealing with symbolic materials, especially of a verbal or numerical nature, is regarded as the acme of intellectual attainment. The "primitive" man's skill in responding to very slight sensory cues, his talents in the construction of objects, or the powers of sustained attention and muscular control which he may display in his hunting behavior, are regarded as interesting anthropological curios which have, however, little or no intellectual worth. As a result, such activities have not usually been incorporated in intelligence scales but have been relegated to a relatively minor position in mental testing (Ibid.:510–11).

The difference in the criteria used for evaluating superiority or inferiority of intelligence is strikingly brought out by the reports of the Indians' opinion of whites compared to themselves. They did not accept naïvely the white man's evaluation of himself as superior; actually, they considered themselves to be superior to whites. Europeans were sometimes perplexed by such an odd notion. Biard, for example, writes: "You will see these poor barbarians, notwithstanding their great lack of government, power, letters, art and riches, yet holding their heads so high that they greatly underrate us, regarding themselves as our superiors" (J. R., III, 73). Peter Grant, referring to the Saulteaux of a much later date, indicates quite clearly the nature of some of the criteria employed in judging the whites. After observing that, "Though they acknowledge the superiority of our arts and manufactures and their own incapacity to imitate us, yet, as a people, they think us far inferior to themselves," he adds, "They pity our want of skill in hunting and our incapacity for travel-

Intelligence of Northeastern Indians

ling through their immense forests without guides or food" (Masson, op. cit.; II:325). It is evident that the qualities of mind required for success in such pursuits are quite different from those exercised in abstract thinking or the manipulation of quantitative concepts.

The Standard Intelligence Tests, however, are not the only tool now at our disposal for gaining information about the intelligence level of nonliterate peoples. While designed as a technique for arriving at a more inclusive picture of personality structure and functioning, the Rorschach test permits judgments of general intelligence level that the expert, also familiar with intelligence tests, can translate into I.Q. points with a fair degree of accuracy. "Form level rating," as a means of arriving at a more precise appraisal of the intellectual functioning of the subject, has been recently discussed by Bruno Klopfer (Klopfer 1944). The advantage of this technique is that the subject's intellectual approach to things is evaluated as only one facet of the personality picture the Rorschach protocol reveals. This means that the *qualitative* aspects of intelligence can be judged in relation to the functioning of the personality as a whole and not as something abstracted from it. The range of the individual's intellectual aptitudes can be evaluated, for the test material itself is not weighted in any particular direction. Thus, it is possible to discern whether the subject shows capacities for intellectual functioning on an abstract or concrete level; how far either type of functioning predominates, and the quality of such functioning. When the group results from an adequate sample of a population are considered it is possible to see how far the intellectual functioning of an individual is typical of the general trend of the group. Furthermore, since verbal facility, speed, and other factors that have complicated the interpretation of the results of intelligence tests among primitive peoples play quite a different role in the Rorschach, it can be used with very little difficulty among native peoples, and the results obtained are comparable with those obtained on white subjects.

The results of an analysis of the Rorschach records of 102 adult Saulteaux and 49 children, so far as general level of intelligence is concerned, are interesting to compare with the evaluation of the intelligence of the Northeastern Indians given by early observers, and the somewhat equivocal results obtained when Indians have been given intelligence tests. Of course, the contemporary Saulteaux cannot be fully equated with the Indians of the Northeast in the seventeenth century, yet there are basic cultural and linguistic connections and the inland Saulteaux of the Berens River still maintain today a modicum of their aboriginal life. Like the Indians of an earlier day the chief problems they have to solve are the practical ones that face them daily in order to make a living. There are no large ventures to be planned by anyone, nor has the individual any responsibilities that extend beyond the members of his family group. (Even a chief has very little more.) There was nothing in the aboriginal culture to stimulate abstract thinking and the very elementary schooling some individuals have received is not directed toward this end. Furthermore, there is nothing in the culture to call forth any imaginative powers of a highly creative sort. Myths and tales are *recounted,* not invented, and the same situation holds true for most of their music. The only art that seems to call out any inventiveness is beadwork. It is not strange to find, then, that the results of the Rorschach technique indicate that the intelligence of the Saulteaux functions at a concrete, practical, common-sense level and that their characteristic intellectual approach to things is very cautious and precise. Many of them add to this a capacity for observing acutely fine details that might escape other observers, but they show little interest in organizing such details into wholes with a significant meaning. The details are of interest for their own sake rather than as part of some larger pattern. Related to this concrete approach to things is the passive fantasy, a kind of idling imaginative activity, without boldness or genuine creativeness, which is also shown in the Rorschach protocols.

From this brief resumé we can readily see that the Saulteaux, on the average, could hardly be expected to rate as high as educated whites on any intelligence test which stressed a qualitatively different type of intellectual functioning. They are not an intellectual people; abstract concepts of the order of those developed in Western culture are tools that are lacking for the development of their theoretical or artistic thinking. Saulteaux culture has encouraged intelligence to concentrate on such capacities as sharpness of perception and detailed memory. A few individuals do show tendencies toward more abstract and combinatorial thinking. One of these men is a conjurer whose personal history shows him to be ill-adapted to the practical exigencies that the life of a hunter and trapper demands. His Rorschach record shows him to have superior intelligence and a genuine capacity for abstract thought. His lack of social adjustment may be due to the fact that he has found no adequate scope for the exercise of his abilities in Saulteaux society.

Turning again to the statements of the early observers, we see that their estimates of the intelligence of the Indians were based on some of the same intellectual qualities that emerge from the picture which the Rorschach presents of Saulteaux intelligence. They were highly appreciative of the "practical intelligence" of the Indian as evinced in judgment about everyday affairs, a detailed knowledge of place and events, and so on. It was probably for this reason, too, that the Indians were compared to the peasantry of Europe rather than to the educated classes. The comparison was an apt one, since it is not unlikely that the qualitative aspects of the intelligence of both groups is rooted in comparable modes of meeting the problems of life.

4 MALE AND FEMALE ADAPTATIONS IN CULTURE CHANGE: MENOMINI

Louise and George Spindler

THE PROBLEM

This paper has a dual purpose: to compare the psychological adaptations of adult males and females to the exigencies of sociocultural change in an historically primitive but rapidly acculturating population—the Menomini Indians of Wisconsin—and to present the methodology that makes it possible to describe these differences accurately.[1] In so doing, we hope to help to fill a lacuna in anthropological literature on the differential adjustment of the two sexes in culture change situations, and to illustrate a method of analysis for such situations that may prove useful as a model for comparisons in other situations.

Although an awareness of the problem has long existed, few anthropologists have explicitly dealt with differences between the adaptations of males and females in their adjustment to a new environment created by the impact of an alien culture. Among those writing on American Indians, Mead (1932) was one of the first to recognize that acculturating females in one Plains Indian group undergo fewer abrupt changes in role playing than

FROM Louise and George Spindler, "Male and Female Adaptations in Culture Change," 1958, *American Anthropologist,* 60:217–33, by permission of the authors and publisher.

[1] Grateful acknowledgment is made to the Center for Advanced Study in the Behavioral Science for the time and support that enabled us to collaborate on this article and do the analysis upon which it is based. A shortened version of the paper was presented at the American Anthropological Association meetings in Chicago, December 1957.

do the males. Joffe (1940) was impressed with the conservatism displayed by Fox Indian women in acculturation, as were the Hanks (1950) in their study of the Blackfoot, Vogt (1951) in his study of the Navaho, Elkin (1940) with the Arapaho, and Caudill (1949) with the Ojibwa. In studies where psychological tests such as the Rorschach were used, male-female differences in adjustment were again noted by Hallowell (1942), who found that Saulteaux women were in general making a better adjustment to white culture than were the males. Caudill (1949) likewise found acculturating Ojibwa women less anxious than the men. While these studies are suggestive, they were not mainly concerned with male-female differences, and make little or no attempt to analyze these observed differences systematically.

In a general way, the Menomini data fit the model of male-female differences in culture change suggested by these studies. Menomini males appear to be more anxious and less controlled than do the women. And the women are psychologically more conservative. This suggests that for some reason the disruptions created in rapid culture change hit the men more directly, leaving the women less changed and less anxious. We will first demonstrate that these psychological differences are present, and in so doing apply some new techniques of analysis to Rorschach data that will permit accurate location of the sources of these differences on the Menomini acculturative continuum. Then we will turn to the sociocultural context, and particularly to differences in male and female roles, to seek explanation of the psychological observations.

Particular attention is given in this paper to methodology and its derivation. This is done in part because the Rorschach technique is used in this study and we wish to illustrate a method of analyzing Rorschach data that is not dependent upon acceptance of the usual interpretations of the meanings of scores developed by Western psychologists, since the validity of many of them has been questioned. Further, we wish to show how the technique used in this manner can provide essential information on modalities and distribution of psychological adaptations in culture change that would be difficult to gather or treat without a tool that provides quantitative data. And finally, we hope to show that when the subjects from whom protocols are taken are accurately located with respect to group identifications, acculturative and social status, and degree of social deviancy, meaningful relationships may be inferred between the psychological and the sociocultural processes in culture change.

The data and sample used in this study consist of 68 Rorschachs from males, and 61 from females, all over 21 years of age, one-half Menomini or more, and in the same acculturative categories (70 per cent of the females are married to Menomini males in the sample)[2]; a schedule of 23 sociocultural indices for each subject (house type, language, religious identification, etc.) which afforded data for placing subjects on an acculturative continuum and defining explicit values associated with the native or American culture; and short autobiographies expressly structured in terms of culture change process (15 from women, 8 from men) collected from individuals in each acculturative category and selected for their representation of both modal and deviant characteristics.[3] Interviews of each individual in the sample (and many others), participant observation over seven summers of field work, and ethnohistorical data, provide context for the sample data listed above.[4]

Initial Treatment of the Data

So that new procedures developed in this paper will be clear, it is necessary to summarize the methodological steps taken up to this point and described in detail elsewhere (G. Spindler 1955; L. Spindler 1956).

[2] The sample was selected sociometrically. Persons with whom necessary rapport had been established, and who represented known sociocultural characteristics, were asked to recommend others to be studied who were "like" and "unlike" themselves. The process was repeated with each new case.

[3] See L. Spindler (1956) for a full treatment of relevant data for Menomini women.

[4] All Rorschachs for both males and females, sixteen short autobiographies from women and eight for the men, and personal documents collected from Menomini Peyotists are included in *Primary Records in Culture and Personality*. Vol. II, edited by Bert Kaplan. Microcard Foundation, Madison, Wisconsin, 1957.

For purposes of study, the Menomini sample was divided into four acculturative categories, ranging from a native-oriented group, through transitional levels, to a fully acculturated category. Religious identification and participation were used as initial criteria for tentative placement of individuals (first men, later women). The categories thus constituted were then validated for both sexes separately by application of a measure of association (tetrachoric r) to each sociocultural index from the schedule of indices referred to previously, in relationship to the posited placement of individuals in the acculturative categories, and by statistical tests of differences between categories with respect to these same items (using chi square). The fully acculturated category was then subdivided into two socioeconomic status groups on the basis of group memberships, residence, income, and occupation.

The five categories thus distinguished for both males and females are:

1. *Native-oriented*—all members of the Medicine Lodge and/or Dream Dance group where the patterns of traditional culture survive to the greatest extent.

2. *Peyote Cult*—composed of participating members of the Cult and constitutes a unique variation of culture conflict resolution within the transitional position.

3. *Transitional*—consisting of persons in cultural transition who have participated in native-oriented religious activities and groups but have moved towards Catholicism and Western culture during their lifetimes, and are at present not clearly identified with either Western or native-oriented groups and values.

4. *Lower status acculturated*—persons who were born Catholic and maintained this identification, know little or nothing of native traditions, but who have acculturated to a laboring class standard.

5. *Elite acculturated*—composed of persons who participate regularly in Catholic services, are members of the prestigeful Catholic Mother's and Holy Name Societies, and, if male, occupy managerial or semiprofessional positions in the reservation lumber industry or agency.

The figure below expresses the relationship between these categories in graphic form.

FIG. 1. Sociocultural Categories in Menomini Acculturation

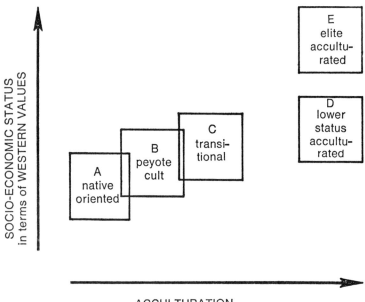

Standard statistical techniques (chi square and "exact probability") were applied first to the Rorschach data for the male sample to discover what statistically significant differences existed in the distributions of various Rorschach scores and combinations of scores among the acculturative categories. The differences revealed for the males were numerous, highly significant statistically, and "made sense" with respect to convergences between psychological and sociocultural process. There is no space here for discussion of the psychological content of these differences (G. Spindler 1955:107–66). In summary, this application of standard statistical techniques revealed that there was a homogeneous psychological structure characterizing the native-oriented males which was like that of Hallowell's least acculturated Ojibwa (1951) and which apparently represented psychological as well as cultural continuity with the past. This structure tended to persist among the ungrouped transitionals but exhibited clear signs of corrosion in anxiety and breakdown of emotional control. The Peyotists exhibited high homogeneity of psychological structure marked by the same signs of anxiety and loss of control that appeared among the ungrouped transitionals, but exhibited special and deviant (within the Menomini sample) forms of introspective fantasy and self-concern that seemed to be a direct function of identification with cult ideology and experience in cult ritual. The lower-status acculturated were not clearly differentiated from either the transitionals or elite acculturated. The latter exhibited a dramatic psychological reformulation, in the setting of the Menomini continuum, that is apparently appropriate to their comparatively full participation in the structure of behaviors and rewards associated with middle class American culture.

GROSS MALE-FEMALE DIFFERENCES

We anticipated that the same order of differences would be exhibited by the females. Consequently, the same statistical procedures were initially applied to the Rorschach data from females. The laborious process of applying exact probability and chi square tests (where size of sample permitted) to all possible comparisons of acculturative categories among the women, and between comparable categories of men versus women, revealed very little by way of either statistically significant or logically consistent differences. Apparently the females were a sample of a universe that was not responding to the same forces as the males. Or they were responding to the same forces, but differently.

In an attempt to discover statistically the differences in Rorschach responses between the two sexes that we hypothesized as existing on the basis of participant observation, autobiographies, and interviews, we applied chi square tests to the Rorschach data of all females compared to all males, in a massive test of difference without respect to acculturative categories. Significant differences were revealed by this technique.[5]

1. Women as a whole respond to the Rorschach ink blots with quicker reaction time than do the males (significant at .005).

2. Women exhibit less loss of emotional control (.05), in spite of the fact that they tend to express their emotions more openly (marginally significant at .06).

3. Women use more animal content than do men, to the greater exclusion of other types of content, indicating a less wide range of interests and experience (.001).

4. Protocols of the women contain more animal movement than do those of the men. There is thus the possibility that women are more involved with biologically oriented drives (eating, sex, reproduction) and exhibit less compulsion to produce abstract concepts (.05).

5. Women exhibit fewer tension and anxiety indicators than do the men: less anxiety of a free floating type (.05); less tension and conflict awareness (.005); and less attempt at introspection as a possible resolution of personal problems (.02).

6. Women as a whole show a higher degree of reality control than do the men (.05).

While we do not wish to make a case for these differences at this point, it is apparent that they are psychologically consistent within themselves. Women appear to be more controlled both intellectually and emotionally and yet retain enough open affect to be flexible. They appear to ruminate less about problems of conflict and are more involved with the problems of everyday life. There is apparently some significant tendency for females to adapt with less difficulty to the exigencies of culture change than do the males. All of the separate signs listed above, and they are all the signs isolated by this technique, are consistent in this respect.

But this information is not a very sizable advance over what

---

[5] The Rorschach signs and scores used in these tests of difference are not included in this paper because they are meaningless to readers not trained in their usage without explanation for which we do not have space. L. Spindler (1956) includes this information. A probability at .05 or less is considered significant.

Male and Female Adaptations in Culture Change

we already had hypothesized on the basis of other data, and does not go very significantly beyond what other studies have revealed. Furthermore, this technique affords no way of discovering the contribution of the various separate acculturative categories to the overall differences exhibited by the two sexes. Nor is it possible to isolate the contribution of what might be quite unlike personality types to the fractionated differences in specific indices that were revealed. In short, the differences in psychological adaptations for males and females thus revealed are too abstract and too gross, and do not permit the positing of relationships between psychological and sociocultural adaptations in discriminating terms.

THE APPLICATION OF A MODAL PERSONALITY TECHNIQUE

With the knowledge that these gross overall differences did exist between males and females in the adaptive processes, the problem became one of finding a technique that would make it possible to refine and exploit the meaning of these differences and explicate the contributions to them of personality type and acculturative position. After much exploration it was decided that the modal personality technique applied to Tuscarora Rorschachs by Wallace (1952:60–68) would serve best. In contrast to the application of the technique in Wallace's study, however, the modal personality is related to the acculturative groups delineated for the Menomini. The technique was first applied to the data from the Menomini women in a separate study by Louise Spindler (1956), then to the males and in terms of relationship to the females in the present study.

A brief description of the technique will be necessary in order to make its application intelligible. One of the most crucial values in the technique is that the personality structure (as revealed by the Rorschach) is not fractionated—it permits expression of a holistic configuration of interrelated psychological characteristics. This configuration is most directly expressed by the Rorschach psychogram, a bar graph of the thirteen most important determinants of perception (see Fig. 2) such as human movement (M), animal movement (FM), form in outline (F), form-controlled shading (Fc), form-controlled color (FC), color predominant (CF), and so on, in usages standardized in the Klopfer system of scoring responses (1956). A psychogram of this kind, summarizing the total number of responses given in each determinant category, can be constructed for any individual protocol or for a group of protocols in some expression of central tendency such as the mean.

The difficulty with using the mean of a group of protocols as a measure of central tendency is that the distribution of most scores in Rorschach usage are highly skewed (most people give 1 or 2 "M" for example, but some give a few, or many more), and the extreme scores bias the mean out of proportion to their significance. Other objections of this kind apply also to the raw mode and the median. In addition, what is wanted is an expression of range around the measures of central tendency that will include the Rorschach records of all those individuals who are enough alike to be psychologically indistinguishable, so that this "class" of individuals can be located wherever they may be in the acculturative continuum.

The following is the procedure of construction of modal personality types, in the form of modal Rorschach psychograms, with expressions of acceptable range. First, the crude mode was found for each score (of which there are 21) for all males and all females separately. Then a function of the standard error of measurement for Rorschach scores, based on an estimated reliability for the Rorschach test of 0.800 (Wallace 1952:65), was used to set limits on either side of these crude modes. This operation defined the "modal range" for each score. All scores falling in the modal range are considered indistinguishable from each other. Therefore, all individuals whose Rorschach protocol scores fall within the modal ranges for all 21 scores were regarded as belonging to a "modal class." One such modal class was found for the males, and one for the females. The scores of all the individual protocols in each modal class were then averaged, so that a modal psychogram could be drawn for the men and for the women. The results are expressed in Figure 2, and will be discussed later.

It will be noted that the use of twenty-one Rorschach indices (thirteen of which are expressed in the modal psychograms) provides rigorous selective criteria for what is modal or most representative. In most populations, even homogeneous ones, the selective criteria will eliminate more from the modal class than are included. But the fact that the number of indices used as criteria is large, and that the indices are organized in the form of a personality type, means that selection is dependent upon a configuration of indices rather than upon single criteria.

With a modal psychogram established for the Menomini women, and another for the men, it became possible to answer certain questions that could not be asked until now. What are the salient features of difference in these psychograms, as complex expressions of psychological adaptation, between males and females in the Menomini sample? Do these modal characteristics account for the differences between the sexes in psychological adaptation which were uncovered in the statistical test of fractionated factors? Or are the latter the result of fortuitous, nonrepresentative convergences? What is the distribution of the modal psychological type throughout the continuum of acculturation for the two sexes? What is the location of what we have chosen to call "the psychocultural center of gravity" for the men and women in the acculturative continuum, and how is it different for the two sexes? The remaining pages will be devoted to analysis of data relevant to these questions and to discussion of the corollary sociocultural processes.

MODAL MENOMINI: MALE AND FEMALE

The modal psychograms for Menomini males and females are presented in Figure 2 below.

We will try to avoid the technical language of standard Rorschach interpretation and confine the following discussion to application of "middle range" interpretive hypotheses that make extremes of nonoperational assumptions about the meaning of scores unnecessary. Later we will demonstrate a technique that makes even these modest assumptions unnecessary. Upon examination of the modal psychograms, it is apparent that the one for the males is quite different from that for the females. The "m," "k," "Fk," and "C'," determinants are represented in

FIG. 2. Modal Menomini Rorschach Profiles

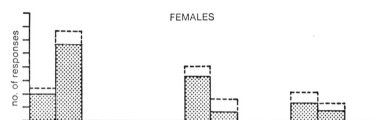

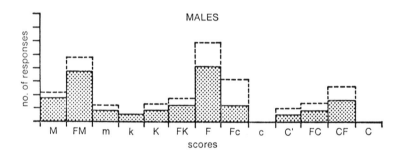

the former and absent in the latter, and the "FC"/"CF" ratios are reversed. These determinants express inanimate movement in tension or conflict (m), "squeezed down" two-dimensional percepts of what are ordinarily three-dimensional concepts (k), diffuse, vague percepts (K), vista (introspective) percepts (FK), and use of achromatic color (C'). The CF dominance over FC in the male psychogram indicates that there is less control by form perception (F) over color perception (C) than is the case with the modal women. These determinants together, as usually interpreted, combine to produce a picture of disturbance, tension, and diffuse anxiety, and decrease in emotional controls among the modal males that is not represented among the females. While the presence or absence of one or two of these indices would be insufficient evidence, and while specific interpretive hypotheses for any one of them may be only tentatively acceptable, the presence of a complex of factors pointing to an internally consistent picture in one case, and the total absence of this same complex in the other, is highly convincing.

It is interesting that all of the differences uncovered by the gross test of male-female difference described previously are represented by the differences between the two modal psychograms (with the exception of the difference in reaction time, which cannot be represented in a psychogram). These factors are all congruent in contributing to a complex of less anxiety and disturbance for females in adaptation. And apparently it is the modal type in the sample of each sex, and from all acculturative categories, that is contributing to this differential relationship, and not fortuitous convergence of fractionated psychological factors drawn from diverse psychological types.

THE PSYCHOCULTURAL CENTER OF GRAVITY

With the modal psychological structures established and compared, the next problem in the analysis of male-females adaptations in culture change is to locate them for males and females separately on the acculturative continuum. The points on the continuum where these structures are concentrated, as located by three convergent techniques to be described below, we have chosen to call "psychocultural centers of gravity." We are not strongly committed to the label but wish to use it as a matter of convenience. The ramifications of the concept will become clear as we locate the p.c.g.'s (as they will henceforth be called) for men and women, compare them, and compare the departures from them in the acculturative continuum. This application of the Rorschach, combined with data on acculturative position, requires minimal acceptance of conventional interpretive hypotheses about the meaning of scores. While the other usages developed in this paper have been as operational as possible, given the purposes of the analysis, this application depends primarily upon the concentration and dispersion of a complex of behavioral indices of psychological process and not upon the formal psychological meaning ascribed to Rorschach scores. The only assumption we must grant is that the Rorschach reliably samples psychological, perceptual process.[6] We do not have to grant the validity of the conventional meanings of the sampling in order for the results to have significance for the study of psychological adaptation in culture change.

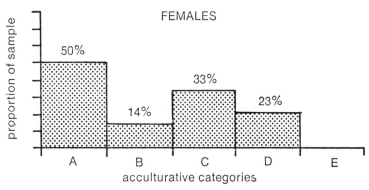

Fig. 3. Distribution of Modal Personality Type in Acculturative Categories

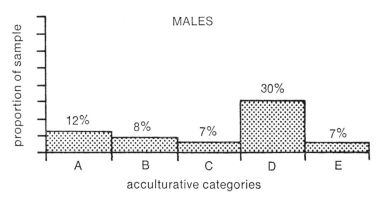

[6] For various reasons the usual test-retest and split-half tests of reliability are not strictly appropriate for the Rorschach. Despite the difficulties, coefficients of reliability are obtained ranging from .40 to above .90 for the various scores and ratios. See Ainsworth's review of Rorschach validity and reliability in Klopfer 1954.

Male and Female Adaptations in Culture Change

TABLE 1. DISTRIBUTION OF MODAL PERSONALITY TYPE IN ACCULTURATIVE CATEGORIES

Category	No. Protocols	No. Modal Cases	Modal as Per Cent of Category
Males			
A	17	2	12
B	13	1	8
C	15	1	7
D	10	3	30
E	13	1	7
Totals	68	8	
Females			
A	8	4	50
B	7	1	14
C	12	4	33.3
D	26	6	23
E	8	0	0
Totals	61	15	

The p.c.g. can be located through several convergent procedures. The first is to compare the modal psychogram for each sex to the typical psychograms of each acculturative category. The construction of typical psychograms for each category requires a separate operation not described in this paper, but presented elsewhere by G. Spindler (1955:169–70). When this is done for the male sample of Menomini it is clear that the modal male psychogram for the whole sample is most like that of the transitional acculturative category, and that for the females is most like that of the native-oriented group. This location of the p.c.g. by inspection is a simple but forthright procedure which suggests that Menomini females tend typically to be psychologically more conservative than do males. It also suggests that the males typically tend to be neither acculturated nor native-oriented, psychologically speaking, but suspended between the two more culturally coherent stages of acculturation.

The second procedure for locating the p.c.g. is to find the proportion of each acculturative category which is composed of members of the modal class for males and for females, on which the modal psychograms for each sex are based. Figure 3 presents this information in graphic form; Table 1 details the basis for the chart. The percentages of each acculturative category composed of modal class representatives are denoted. Of course, the percentages do not total 100 percent, since they are proportions of different total numbers. For example, the native-oriented female category "A" numbers 8 women, 4 of whom are in the modal class; "C" numbers 12 women, 4 of whom are in the modal class; and "D" totals 26 women, 6 of whom are in the modal class.

This procedure produces additional information concerning the p.c.g., and affords new data on the distribution of typical psychological adaptation for each sex. The p.c.g. for the women is still clearly the native-oriented group. The picture of psychological conservatism is strengthened. It is also important that all acculturative categories excepting that of the elite acculturated contributes significantly to the female modal class. The prototype is the native-oriented psychological structure and cultural position but apparently this prototype, in both of its dimensions (as indicated by data to be analyzed shortly), exhibits continuity throughout the acculturative continuum for the women until the elite acculturated position is reached. At this point there is a "cutoff." Elite Menomini women are clearly deviant in terms of central tendency in the Menomini acculturative continuum.

The distributional chart for males both confirms and modifies the interpretation of the results of location of the p.c.g. by inspection. The p.c.g. is even further along the acculturative continuum than the inspection procedure indicated—in the lower status acculturated category. The psychocultural position of the males is therefore practically the reverse of that for the females. The central tendency in psychological adaptation for Menomini males is far toward full acculturation. For females it is toward a least acculturated status. The distributional chart also conveys the information that each acculturative category contributes in some degree to the male modal class. Apparently there is continuity here also, but in lesser degree, and the continuity is in terms of transitional psychological characteristics and cultural position rather than native.

The third procedure for locating the p.c.g. is to turn to the actual people composing the modal class for each sex and ask what characteristics, in both psychological and sociocultural dimensions, they exhibit with respect to the norms of their groups. Such an analysis could quickly reach proportions that would be unfeasible for presentation in this paper, so only a summary of salient features will be included.

The native-oriented women in the female modal class are typical members of their group. They all exhibit a full complement of nativistic cultural retentions, and self-consciously try to raise their children as Indians. The one modal class woman in the Peyote Cult group was born a Peyotist, not driven to it by the experience of culture conflict as were most others, and retains social and cultural ties with the native-oriented group. She is thus deviant in the context of the cult. The nature of the Peyote group as a "systematic deviation" within the Menomini continuum must be taken into account here (G. Spindler 1955: 89–90). The transitional women in the modal class lack any clear-cut group identifications but express traditional Menomini values in their behaviors. They are not psychologically deviant within their group in the sense that 75 percent of the women in this acculturative category either fall within the modal class or exhibit all but one scoring criterion of this class—a fact that dramatically bespeaks the psychological conservatism of this group. With one exception, the modal class lower status acculturated women self-consciously chose to interact and identify with older relatives who had experience with the traditional Menomini culture, even though these modal women themselves have had no direct experience in groups or patterns representative of it. They are deviant in their group, since the majority of lower status acculturated women are second or third generation Catholics who, at the verbal level at least, exhibit values not unlike those of middle class white women. There are no modal class women in the elite acculturated group. This category is composed of women striving for acceptance on middle class white terms, but they represent a marked deviant minority in the acculturative continuum for women (see L. Spindler 1956), together with others from the lower status acculturated category, though these two status groups are separated by rather impermeable social barriers.

The analysis of individual cases in the modal class of Menomini males does not require so full a treatment. The males in this class all express in varying degrees, in both their Rorschach records and in other behaviors,[7] the psychological features of disorganization in emotional control, presence of anxiety and tension, and worrisome introspection that are aspects of what may be called a transitional syndrome in the Menomini acculturative continuum. There are three partial exceptions to this statement. They are men who exhibit highly constricted personality structures that presumably represent the result of social withdrawal and psychological defense against threat. This latter structure may be considered a permutation of the first.

These modal class males represent the central tendency of psychological adaptation in the male acculturative continuum. However, they are all deviant in some degree within their particular acculturative categories. This is necessarily the case because the male categories are so sharply differentiated from each other, as the statistical treatment of the male Rorschach data indicated. Each represents an ingroup homogeneity of psychological adaptation which differentiates it from each other category—with the exception of the transitionals. This group is psychologically more heterogeneous than the others. The process of adaptation for the males is apparently more disjunctive than for the females.

The picture of disjunctive psychological adaptation for the males and continuous adaptation for the females is strengthened by the fact that only 12 percent of the males in the whole sample are in the modal class, and 25 percent of the females. This means that there is a greater tendency for the latter to exhibit psychological homogeneity in adaptation; it also helps to account for the fact that no important differences were found between the various acculturative categories for women, and conversely, for the fact that acculturative categories for males were highly differentiated, in the initial statistical tests applied to the sample.

The information revealed by individual case analysis confirms and amplifies conclusions concerning the p.c.g. for each

[7] By "other behaviors" we mean drinking, fighting, wife-beating, political outbreaks, social withdrawal, and feelings expressed in interviews and autobiographies.

sex in the acculturative process existing at present among the Menomini. The p.c.g. for women is the native-oriented type, which is retained in surprising degree all the way through the acculturative continuum (disregarding the Peyote group as a special case) until the acculturated departure, which represents a small minority, takes place. Other forms of adaptation constitute deviations from the p.c.g. For males, the information again conveys a quite different picture. The male p.c.g. in terms of individual cases is transitional-disturbed. The acculturative process is sharply disjunctive for males, but permits the maintenance of psychological continuity for women in conservative terms.

CONTRIBUTING SOCIOCULTURAL FACTORS

Having observed covariance in psychological and sociocultural process, and having compared this covariance for Menomini males and females, we are obliged to attempt an explanation of the observed processes. Our attempt to explain rests at the level of plausibility, and with reference to role expectations and life experience in the social environment patterned by the influence of traditional Menomini culture, the impact of Western culture, and the conditions of contemporary reservation life. We can only draw selectively from this complex of factors and summarize briefly what appear to be factors of possible significance.[8]

Important social factors which serve to generate and support female psychological differences are found in the dynamics of the Menomini reservation social system. For example, it is pertinent that the mobility pattern for the males differs markedly from that for the females. Women may change groups readily and easily, by marriage and by adoption of the accessory behaviors, among the native-oriented, Peyote Cult, and Transitional categories. By definition, only those males and females who are born Catholic and have no religious identification with native groups comprise the acculturated categories. However, unlike the

---

[8] Extended treatment of the sociocultural context of psychological adaptations among the women is given by L. Spindler (1956).

situation found for the males, comparatively impermeable class barriers exist for the acculturating females between the lower status acculturated group and the elite. Lower status acculturated females are rarely accepted in the elite group, where status is almost hereditary. The males, on the other hand, through gaining occupational and economic success and the proper symbols of middle class culture, do move from lower status to elite status within the reservation community. Having achieved elite status, the males select wives who are less than one-half Indian or entirely white, since middle class values are associated with white skin color, in Menomini perception.

Many lower status acculturated women, realizing that the status and goals of white middle class culture are unavailable to them, either choose to identify with relatives raised in Menomini traditions, join the drinking crowd of women, or attempt to achieve the material symbols of middle class culture, disregarding the appropriate means for attainment. The female modal psychological structure was exhibited by all those women in the lower status acculturated category who chose to identify with Menomini relatives, and by no others. But none of these kinds of adjustments facilitate the radical psychological reorganization necessary for a change from a Menomini cultural position to that of a middle class white.

Another explanation lies in the relationship between traditional and contemporary role expectations, values, and their psychological corollaries. Historically speaking, Menomini culture was male oriented, with most public activities such as hunting, warfare, ceremony and ritual, centering on the male. The men, who took these important public "instrumental" roles, operated within rigidly defined role prescriptions.[9] On the other hand, women's roles, almost by default, were loosely defined and were interpreted in a flexible manner. Women had the choice of either assuming traditional female roles or they could gain respect without censure if they chose also to engage in male activities such as

[9] The concepts "instrumental," and "expressive" roles are taken from Parsons, Bales et al. (1955). Instrumental roles are those concerned with relations of the larger socioeconomic system to the family group. Expressive roles are those concerned with the maintenance of integrative relations between members of the family group.

fishing, hunting, dancing in a male fashion, or foot racing. They could even become practitioners of native medicine. During the acculturative process, women continue to adapt in this flexible fashion. Except in the most acculturated categories, Menomini women continue to play the affective, supportive, "expressive" roles (Parsons et al. 307–20) of wife, mother, and social participant in a more or less traditional Menomini fashion, unhampered by rigid role prescriptions stemming from either the traditional culture or from Western culture. It is hypothesized that because of this role continuity, they do not find the flux and conflict of rapid culture change as disturbing as do the males.

In contrast to the females, the acculturating Menomini males continue to take instrumental roles of public leadership and gaining of livelihood in the acculturation situation, as they did in the pattern of native culture, but roles in which the prescriptions for behavior have changed drastically. The male wage earner, for example, is forced into making immediate accommodations to role expectations patterned into the socioeconomic structure in which he must make his own and his family's living, and from which he must in part derive his self-concept. And these expectations are often discontinuous or in direct conflict with those of his traditional Menomini culture, even the attenuated part that is "built into" his personality under contemporary conditions. He must learn to be punctual in his arrivals and departures, and run his daily and weekly cycle by the clock and calendar. He has to learn that accumulation of property and money is the way "to get ahead." And he has to learn that getting ahead in this fashion is the most important thing a man can do. There are no precedents for these and many other expectations in the traditional pattern of instrumental roles for males in Menomini culture. Not only does the male have to learn new behavior patterns and accept new goals that are in conflict with the traditional ones, but in so doing he meets with prejudicial attitudes of whites toward Indians, even in the relatively favorable situation of the Menomini, that women encounter more infrequently in their habitual roles. So in his very striving toward acculturated values he experiences rejection, and this must in many instances engender anxieties and self-doubt. In short, the crucial respects in which contemporary American culture conflicts with native culture and maintains barriers against full acceptance, are encountered most directly and dramatically by the males in their exercise of instrumental roles. Furthermore, the wives of these men, in continuing to play their expressive roles in more or less traditional fashion, make it more difficult for their husbands to play the contemporary male instrumental roles appropriately, since the men are encountering problems of adjustment which their wives do not fully understand, at least at the emotional level. Therefore, the women cannot play the supportive aspect of their expressive roles adequately, and this probably helps to account for the insecurity of males in the instrumental roles.

A dimension of behavior lending support to this interpretation is furnished by the comparatively high degree of retention of traditional Menomini values exhibited by the women. These values apparently are not directly contested during the acculturative process and the only drastic changes that take place in value retention are at the elite acculturated level where women have had little or no contact with the old culture.

Table 2 presents a few explicit indices from which the differential rate of value change between males and females may be inferred.

The data are self-explanatory. These indices of specific value retentions begin to drop sharply in the Peyote Cult category for the males, while females retain them in much greater proportion through the lower status acculturated category.

Conclusion

Menomini women do not encounter the sharply disjunctive role expectations in acculturation that the men do, as long as they continue to play the feminine, expressive roles. Even when they move into the arena of instrumental roles in acculturation, as a minority of women do, the traditional flexibility of the feminine position probably helps make it possible for them to adapt to new expectations without much disturbance and without deep psychological reformulation. Furthermore, these movements into the instrumental roles are usually tentative or partial, and rarely

Male and Female Adaptations in Culture Change

dominate the woman's purposes or energies. But for the males, the new roles that they must necessarily appropriate in acculturation and that dominate their lives, are in sharp conflict with what they have had "built into" their personality systems by their usually less acculturated parents, and particularly by their mothers, who, being women, maintain in greatest degree the traditional cultural patterns and their psychological concomitants and must pass them on to their children. The struggle of psy-

TABLE 2. COMPARISON OF THE RETENTION OF NATIVE VALUES BETWEEN MALES AND FEMALES

Acculturative Category	Sex	No.	Know Some Native Lore	Use Indian Medicines	Full Knowledge of Menomini	Display of Native Objects
A	F	8	100%	100%	100%	100%
	M	17	100	100	88	88
B	F	7	100	100	86	100
	M	13	84	92	54	15
C	F	12	100	100	67	100
	M	15	67	86	40	6
D	F	26	73	61	50	12
	M	10	10	10	30	0
E	F	8	25	12	25	0
	M	13	30	7	30	0

chocultural forces—values, attitudes, and role expectations internalized during early socialization, versus their contemporary complements in the role expectations which men must adopt in getting a living and acting in the context of public affairs—is mirrored in the anxiety, tension, constriction, and breakdown of emotional controls characterizing the modal Menomini male in acculturation. This role conflict, the preconditions for which are laid down in socialization, is maintained and heightened by the acculturative lag between husbands and wives. The discontinuity of roles for males is concomitant with the psychological discontinuity they exhibit. And the impelling nature of the new instrumental roles they must adopt is projected in the location of their psychocultural center of gravity further along the continuum of acculturation than is the case with the women. The psychological differences between Menomini males and females may therefore be seen as the result of a complex of interlocking factors that appear to assume the form of a self-sustaining cycle, the key factor of which may be the psychocultural position of the women.

5 THE PSYCHOSOCIAL ANALYSIS OF A HOPI LIFE-HISTORY

David Friend Aberle

INTRODUCTION

This study analyzes a single life-history for the light it sheds on the society in which the subject lives. The life-history is that of Don C. Talayesva, a Hopi Indian, edited by Leo W. Simmons. It is the fullest and frankest life-history of a member of a nonliterate society[1] yet available to us (Simmons 1942); indeed, for purposes of social and psychological analysis it ranks above many autobiographies of individuals in Western societies. Some of the autobiographies may be as frank and some are longer, but few cover so many aspects of experience over so long a period of time.

In using the life-history for a new approach to the Hopi, the chief problem is that of relating two aspects of the society as it has been described by various authorities. Hopi society is often

Copyright by the Regents of the University of California. Reprinted from "The Psychosocial Analysis of a Hopi Life-History" 1951 (*Comparative Psychology Monographs*), Vol. XXI, No. 1, by permission of the Regents and the author.

[1] In conformity with current anthropological usage, *nonliterate society* will be used to refer to any society that lacked a system of writing prior to its contact with Western culture. The term *primitive society,* which is more common, has unfortunate connotations of "early," "backward," and often "prelogical." *Life-history* will be used to refer to an extensive record of a man's life as he reports it—whether in writing or in interviews. It will not be used to refer to a case study based on observations of the subject or on others' accounts of his life. The peculiarity of idiom involved in referring to the *autobiography* of an individual from a nonliterate society makes it necessary to avoid the more familiar term, even though Don wrote parts of his life-history himself.

described as peaceful, harmonious, and operating with a minimum of physical coercion. Yet child rearing is said to be repressive and adult life constrained, and the Hopi are often characterized as anxious, mistrustful, and full of suppressed hostility. It is the contention of this study that these features of Hopi society are closely related to one another—that the truth does not just lie "somewhere in between" but lies in understanding how these two aspects are bound together.[2]

Hopi Culture

For present purposes a selective presentation of Hopi culture is required. Points of particular significance for the life-history analysis which follows will be brought out; inevitably some areas of the culture will be stressed and others will be neglected. Thus, child rearing, initiation, kinship, and the ethic and system of belief of the Hopi will be emphasized, and ceremonialism and technology will be given little attention. Instead, implications of particular significance for the task at hand will be drawn, with particular reference to aggression, witchcraft, the prestige system, marriage, and child training. Since Don lives in Oraibi, and since information on Oraibi is most adequate, data from that community will predominate in the presentation.

HISTORY[3]

The Hopi are a group of Shoshonean-speaking American Indians living in the well-known pueblo type of "primitive apartment-house" towns placed on and at the foot of three mesas—extensions of the larger Black Mesa—in northeastern Arizona.

---

[2] For an account of so-called divergences of interpretation, see Bennett (1946). The Hopi studies he refers to are Titiev (1944, 1946), D. Eggan (1943), Goldfrank (1945), Kennard (1937), Thompson and Joseph (1944), and Dennis (1940). My analysis of the life-history and interpretation of Hopi society lead me to think that a majority of the "divergences" can be reconciled within the framework offered here. This problem, however, requires a long, separate analysis, the results of which, it is hoped, will appear at a later date.

[3] This section is based on Titiev (1944:69–95), except as noted.

The area has long been inhabited by the Hopi, Oraibi, for example, having been settled about 1200 A.D. The history of the group, though it includes little aggressive warfare, is full of conflict with the Spanish,[4] with non-Pueblo Indians, and with Americans. Farthest from Santa Fe of all the Pueblo groups, the Hopi were influenced by the Spanish less than any other Pueblo Indians were. Oraibi, the westernmost of the Hopi towns,[5] had even less contact with the Spanish than other Hopi towns. Nevertheless, from them its people acquired new crops, stock, and herding practices, and perhaps some religious behavior and witchcraft beliefs. A period of loosened control of the Southwest by the Spanish and Mexican governments was marked by greater and more frequent incursions of marauding non-Pueblo groups. Extensive contact with the American government began in the 1870's. Pro- and anti-American factional sentiments beginning in the 1880's recall similar developments during the period of Spanish contact. Oraibi was particularly hostile to the Americans, resisting schooling, census, and land surveying. Factionalism in this town reached so high a pitch that, in 1906, the anti-American faction, the Hostiles, were forced to leave Oraibi and found a new town, Hotevilla, which itself later gave rise to still a third town, Bakabi. The formerly pro-American, friendly Village chief of Oraibi changed his attitude and expelled Christian converts from the village. They founded New Oraibi. Migration from Oraibi to all these settlements and to Moenkopi reduced the population from 600 (in 1906) to 112 (in 1933). Furthermore, though Hotcvilla and Bakabi were able to set up full-scale ceremonial cycles after the split, Oraibi suffered a marked deterioration in its ritual cycle. Oraibi is perhaps more antagonistic to the Americans than are other Hopi towns, and possibly it is more tension-filled.

[4] Twenty years after the Pueblo revolt of 1680, the residents of Awatovi, on Antelope Mesa, permitted the Catholic priests to return. Apparently other Hopi attacked the town and killed a substantial number of Hopi. The town seems to have been uninhabited from that time on. See Montgomery, Smith, and Brew (1949:18–19).

[5] Except for Moenkopi, forty miles farther west, a farming "suburb," politically a part of Oraibi.

In considering the Oraibi split of 1906, two aspects of the event must be kept in mind: the structural features of Hopi social organization which make such splits a recurrent possibility, and the tensions which occasion the splits. Hopi social organization is characterized by a weak development of central political control and organized hierarchical office, little executive and legislative power, and the strong orientation of individuals to their clans and religious societies rather than to the village as such. This means that there are comparatively few institutional barriers to prevent fission and the resultant formation and growth of new towns. In addition, in 1906 there was a set of tensions that provided the motor force for the split: a struggle for land rights among groups in the town, and a division among the Hopi on the question whether they should adopt a friendly or a hostile attitude toward the Americans. Leaders of the Hostile faction, which was also the faction whose members considered themselves deprived of their rightful share of land, resorted to a reinterpretation of mythology as a basis for claiming that their actions were legitimate.

Authorities disagree as to whether splits are invariably the product of serious internal tension or are occasionally the result of an amicable decision to handle overcrowding and similar problems by division and resettlement (cf. Titiev 1944:96–99, 194: 431; Thompson and Joseph 1944:47–48).

ENVIRONMENT AND ECONOMY[6]

The Hopi country is exigent for a farming and herding people, and the life of a Hopi is arduous and filled with uncertainties. Scarce and uncertain rainfall, a short growing season with the possibility of killing frosts at the beginning or the end of the crop cycle, cold winters, and hot summers all make hard work necessary and its products unpredictable. Sources of water include rainfall, springs, intermittent washes, and seepage from springs which collects in dunes. Crops can be grown on these dunes. Planting is done principally in May and June, harvesting in September. The Hopi raise a variety of field and garden crops and cultivate fruit trees; corn and beans are the main

[6] This section is based on Hack (1942:5–38, 70–80), except as noted.

agricultural base.[7] Men do most of the field work, and women do the garden work. Most farming is with hoe and digging stick. Fields and gardens require constant attention, which extends sometimes to the building of individual shelters to protect plants from flying sand, and the digging of small individual ditches to bring water to each plant. Rain, when it comes, may be so violent as to wash out crops in wash-irrigated fields. In spite of the Hopi's use of drought-resistant breeds of corn, hard work, and constant vigilance, famine has always been a threat; even today it is customary to have a year's corn supply stored away as a safeguard. The story of the famine of 1860–1862 is still told (Titiev 1944:199).

Herding of sheep, goats, cattle, and other animals is men's work, with its own complications: the hazards of freezing weather in winter and hail in summer, and the decrease of forage as a result of soil erosion. Two recent events have contributed to Hopi attitudes of frustration, anxiety, and aggression in connection with the occupation of herding. The Hopi consider that the new boundaries between their reservation and that of the Navaho have reduced their grazing land (Page 1940). In addition, the American government has carried out a drastic stock-reduction program. Third Mesa, on which Oraibi is situated, was worst hit, its flocks being cut by 44 per cent (Thompson 1947:465). Herding is done by a group of men, each taking his turn. Cattle coöperatives exist and are strongest on First Mesa (Thompson and Joseph 1947:21).

Hunting and the gathering of wild plants have little economic significance today.[8] Trading in various goods is carried on among the Hopi towns, with other Pueblo Indians, and with and through the Navaho. Goods are also sold to white traders in the Hopi towns.

About 54 per cent of Hopi income (including goods produced for consumption only) derives from agriculture, about 10 per cent from livestock, a little more than 1 per cent from trade, and about 32 per cent from wages. Wages come principally

[7] For a detailed account, see Whiting (1939). Foodstuffs were introduced by the Spanish, American Mormons, and other whites (op. cit., 12–13).
[8] Data in this paragraph are from Beaglehole (1937:18–19, 49–52, 81–86).

from the government—for schoolteaching and upkeep of schools, hospital and road work, and other activities—a new source of income in recent years.[9] The balance in favor of agriculture is clear and is consistent with the strong feeling of the Hopi that they are predominantly an agricultural people (Titiev 1944: 194 n.). Hopi ritual is aimed principally at promoting the crops, though some attention is given to herds.[10]

Men do the heavy work of housebuilding, carry the firewood, often from long distances, and dig coal.[11] Women prepare foods for eating and for storage. This preparation includes the arduous and continuous task of grinding corn. They make pottery and baskets, assist in housebuilding, care for house and children, and work in the gardens and occasionally in the larger work parties in the fields.

SOCIOPOLITICAL ORGANIZATION[12]

Hopi society is characterized by a weak development of a central political authority, by the absence of a clear-cut hierarchy among offices and among groups within the society, by the lack of any true techniques of legislation to meet novel situations (reinterpretations of tradition are the bases for decisions), and by the lack of a well-implemented executive arm in the central political unit. The chief groupings of significance are the clan, the religious society, and the household; the "chief's talk," the only central grouping in the society, plays a definitely subordinate part.

The most significant unit of the kinship system is the matrilineal clan. These clans are substantially identical in every village.

---

[9] Hack (1942:16, 17), based on U. S. Soil Conservation Service figures for 1937. My figures do not total 100 per cent, since they omit income from certain minor sources. Thompson and Joseph's figures for 1942 (1944:25, 134 n., 135 n.) throw the balance much more heavily toward stock and away from agriculture. These figures are not used, since they contain serious internal inconsistencies.

[10] Cf. Beaglehole (1937:48–50) and Thompson and Joseph (1944:25). Stephen (1936:69) gives examples of the use of prayer sticks for the well-being of livestock.

[11] The statement about the division of labor is based on Beaglehole (1937:18–19).

[12] The analysis of the sociopolitical organization is based on Titiev (1944:59–69, 103–141), except as noted.

The Psychosocial Analysis of a Hopi Life-History

Kinship relations of some sort can be established with virtually all Hopi and, if it appears desirable, can be extended to other Pueblo Indians and even to the Navaho. Clans are grouped in unnamed phratries. A clan is composed of one or more traceable matrilineal lineages. The senior woman of the senior lineage of a clan is a person of considerable significance; she heads the clan and holds the clan fetish. A clan also possesses a kiva—an underground ceremonial chamber, used as a place of ceremonial retreat and men's lodge. The male clan leader is also an important figure. He is selected from among the brothers or the sons of the senior woman. The clan is also an important landholding unit, as will be seen. There is clan and phratry exogamy. In addition, there is no marrying into the father's clan, and rarely is there marrying into the father's phratry. Thus, the clan unites individuals in a solidary unit, allocates land, and, through the senior woman and the male clan leader, has an important control function in the society.

The religious societies, which are linked to clans in a rather complicated fashion, are responsible for putting on the ceremonials of the annual cycle. Most of them are for men; a few are for women. Sometimes, though not always, the same man is the leading male of the clan, leader of the ceremonial group tied to that clan, and head of the kiva in which the society meets. (The situation, however, is often more complex than that.) The leader of a society picks his own successor from among his sister's sons, usually on the basis of ability, and trains the man he selects (Titiev 1944:25). The procedure is the same for the selection of the Village chief from the appropriate clan (the Bear clan).[13] This means that, in general, the positions of Village chief, leader of a religious society, and male leader of a clan descend not only within particular clans but in certain family lines within each clan.[14] That is, while the top offices of Hopi society are

---

[13] Although Stephen says that the Village chief of Walpi is chosen "prescriptively" from among the sons of the eldest sister of the incumbent (1936:951), he also indicates that the sons of other sisters are considered (op. cit., 1020).

[14] When E. C. Parsons (1933:23) speaks of descent of the headship of society *"not in the clan as a whole, but in a maternal family or lineage in the clan"* (italics hers) she is not making precisely this point. Her "lineage" is equivalent to Titiev's "clan." The terms "phratry," "clan," "lineage," and "household" are used in this study as Titiev (1944:44–58) defines them. Any different usage in a quotation will be noted.

not completely ascribed by birth,[15] they are at any rate rigorously circumscribed thereby. They can only be achieved by a man who is born into the "correct" family of a particular clan. Even though there are important exceptions to this rule, especially if a society is in danger of dying out (E. C. Parsons 1936: xxxvii), this limitation on achieved status is a factor of considerable significance, as will be shown.

The membership of a religious society is made up of men from a number of clans, including the clan which provides the leadership. A man joins a ceremonial society by selecting a ceremonial father from that society. Membership in the initiation societies of childhood (Powamu and Katcina) and manhood (Wowochim, Singers, Agave, and Horn), however, is usually determined by the parents' choice of the ceremonial father, a selection in which the child has no voice (Dennis 1940:71, 75). The two childhood initiation societies are mutually exclusive, and so are the adult initiation societies. Beyond that, a man may theoretically belong to as many societies as he wishes—at least he may at Oraibi. It is probable, however, that responsibilities in any one society are time-consuming enough to prevent a man from joining many.[16] Initiation into a society may also result from trespass and from disease. Each society is conceived of as causing and curing a disease, the particular disease being termed the "whip" of the society. If a man trespasses on the secret activities of a society he may fall ill with that disease, but he can ward off this danger by initiation into the society. A man who is cured of sickness by a society joins it.

All Hopi, men or women, are members of one of the two childhood initiatory societies, Powamu or Katcina, which have other major responsibilities beyond initiation, as do the adult initiation societies, to which men alone belong. There are three women's societies; a woman may belong to one or more of them. Men hold important ceremonial offices in them, but in spite of the Hopi belief that the presence of women—their "smell"—is disliked by supernaturals, women take the majority of roles in these ceremonies. As in most areas of Hopi life, there is no taboo against menstruating women.

[15] The terms are used as in Linton (1936:115).
[16] I am indebted to Dr. W. W. Hill for this suggestion.

Some of the religious societies are more "important" than others, since their ceremonies are viewed as being more vital to the total ceremonial round.

Thus, crosscutting the groupings and ties based on clanship are those of the religious societies, to which all men and some women belong. The leaders of these societies are figures of authority and prestige. The members of a religious society form a solidary unit and achieve relative prestige according to the status of their particular society.

As has been said, chieftainship in Oraibi resides in the Bear clan. The most important village officials are the headman of the Parrot clan and the headman of the Pikyas clan; the Tobacco chief, normally of the Rabbit clan; the Crier chief, leader of the Greasewood clan; and the War (police) chief, of the Badger or the Coyote clan. Although they assist the Village chief, their principal functions are in their own clans and societies. The Village chief has important functions in the allocation of land, as will be shown later.

For handling recalcitrants there are few sanctions except public opinion. The principal problems which might require adjudication are land disputes, claims of farmers for reparation for destruction of crops by herds, and failure to respond to the pleas for public-work groups. The War chief was a more effective executive in earlier days, when his prestige and power were reinforced by his role as a leader of war parties.

Thus, the factors which make for a certain fragility of the total Hopi social structure are the weakness of the central political organ and the fact that relationships of solidarity and authority are stronger within the clan and the religious society than they are between clan and society members and the central governing body. On the other hand, the crosscutting network of lines of obligations, solidarity, and authority formed by the clan and the society make for general cohesion: every individual is oriented to several types of structures in the total system. Furthermore, the Hopi are bound together by the recognition that the total round of ceremonies is essential for the well-being of the community. Although this factor is integrative in this sense, it must be pointed out that when a split does occur and the ceremonial cycle is disrupted, individuals are likely to experience feelings of loss of religious protection from the calamities of drought, crop failure, and disease.

THE CLAN AND THE HOUSEHOLD[17]

Further consideration of the clan and the household and their internal differentiation is required to lay bare the skeleton of the social organization.

The kinship system is of the Crow type. An individual is a member of his mother's clan and is a "child" of his father's clan but not a member of it. A number of individuals are classified in the same category of relationship—though this does not imply that they are treated absolutely identically, without any regard for personal feelings or degree of lifelong intimacy. Thus, the same term is used for own mother, mother's sister, mother's mother's sister's daughter, and in fact all members of the clan whom one's mother calls "sister." Within the clan, the children of all women whom one calls "mother" are one's "brother" and "sister." In addition, all persons whose fathers are members of the same clan call one another "brother" and "sister." For a woman, all children of her clan "sisters" are termed "children"; and for a man, all children of his clan "brothers" are "children." All women of the father's clan below the grandparental generation are "paternal aunts." There are many other relationships structured by this system which need not be elaborated here.

A unit of central significance within the clan is the household or group of households. This is composed of a woman, her daughters, sometimes her daughters' daughters, the unmarried sons of these women, and the husbands of all married women. Thus, such a household contains a group of closely related women who have grown up in the same family and have always worked together. The husbands of these women, on the other hand, are drawn from a variety of different groups and retain ties, of major significance, to their clan of birth and the household in which they grew up. They have no particular ties to one another, except when brothers or clan brothers marry sisters. In fact, a

[17] This section, except as noted, is based on Titiev (1944:7–29).

The Psychosocial Analysis of a Hopi Life-History 89

man ordinarily refers to his mother's, rather than his wife's, home as his own. To the end of his life he returns to his mother's, and later to his sister's, home on feast days. (The sister will ordinarily continue to live in her mother's home after the mother's death.)

Thus, a man is strongly oriented toward his own clan. In addition, his relationship with his sister throughout life is one of warmth and affection, uncomplicated by avoidance or respect patterns. To a degree he is an outsider in his wife's family, and his children are members of her clan, whereas his sister's children belong to his clan. Under these circumstances, his disciplinary rights regarding his own children are weak, and those toward his sister's, strong. Toward a sister's son, then, the mother's brother is the chief disciplinarian and source of punishment. As has been pointed out, he may also be the source to which the younger man looks for the inheritance of ceremonial office.

A sister takes a warm interest in her brother's children, in addition to having an affectionate relationship with the brother himself. Paternal aunt and nephew are linked by a very positive bond, which is strongly tinged with sexual joking. The aunt suggests that she would very much appreciate sex relations with her nephew, and her husband makes joking protestations of jealousy. This joking begins very early in the child's life; there may be actual sex contacts later (Titiev 1938:109, 1944:28; D. Eggan 1943:366–67). The aunt's husband, who is called by the same term as the male grandparent, also indulges in harsh practical joking, which the child may reciprocate when he grows old enough to do so. A Hopi's ties to his father's clan members are important and are characterized by warmth, intimacy, and ease.

The child's relationship with grandparents on both sides is a warm one. They are quite indulgent toward him.

The relationship of mother and son is an important one. Toward the child in early life, the mother is quite indulgent, scolding and threatening but seldom punishing, and in general fostering. The male child grows away from the mother through the very early role-patterning of work which occurs in Hopi society: he soon follows his father to the fields. He continues, however, to recognize his mother's key position in the household, a recognition enhanced if she is the senior woman of the clan. As senior woman, she is able to influence her brother's selection of a successor, toward the son she prefers. A mother's advice in the choice of a wife, and her advice in general, carry much weight. Occasionally there is serious strife between mother and son.[18]

The father is the principal preceptor of the male child. From an early age the child accompanies him to the fields and helps him with herding and farming. Nevertheless, the father is not the principal disciplinarian or ceremonial instructor, though he does teach the boy Katcina dancing. With the mother he selects the boy's ceremonial father, in this way determining his son's future society memberships. Thus, there is an important limitation on the possibility of achieving status in accordance with self-set goals.

Between brothers, coöperation is the rule, whether or not they marry into the same clan or household. Even brotherly rivalry over women does not lead to vengeful behavior. Relative seniority is of little moment, except in early life, when the older brother assists in the training of the younger.

Consideration of the attitudes of sister toward sister and mother toward daughter is not pertinent here, since the life-history is that of a man. In brief, these women form a solidary group, but the mother has considerable restrictive power over her daughter. Under circumstances of loss or acute uncongeniality, a mother's sister may substitute for a mother, a close clan sister for a sister, and so on. Extended relationships may be exploited, used, or ignored, according to a wide variety of circumstances.

MARRIAGE[19]

The exogamous rules of marriage have already been mentioned. In addition, a previously unmarried individual should not marry a divorced or widowed person; the spirit of anyone who does so is doomed to a very slow journey to the afterworld. This prohibition is rarely broken. Possibly it helps discourage serious extramarital affairs and thus somewhat reduces the problem of

---

[18] Thompson and Joseph (1944:122) differ somewhat in their view of this relationship.

[19] This section is based on Titiev (1944:30–43), except as noted.

philandering. Although Hopi marriages are usually contracted by the future partners and not by parents, there are many pressures that influence the choice of a partner. The advice of a number of people is of great importance: these include the mother, siblings of opposite sex, and the mother's brother—his advice particularly with regard to his sister's daughter—and relatives in general. Older men who have never married apparently were deterred from doing so by their family's disapproval of all the girls they courted.[20] When pressures of this sort exist, the situation cannot be described as one of unencumbered choice; nor indeed can such choice be expected in a society in which a man must get along not just with his wife but with her entire family. The qualities in a spouse which are valued by both families are industry and a good disposition.

Courtship in Oraibi, and probably throughout the rest of the Hopi towns, normally involves a great deal of sleeping around with various partners. Although tremendous efforts are made to keep these relationships secret, they are almost invariably discovered and the news is circulated. Thereafter, if the relatives of either partner disapprove they exert pressure to discourage the match. If a girl becomes pregnant as a result of such a relationship, she names the "father"—naturally, the particular sleeping mate whom she wants as a marriage partner. Boys also propose directly, even without the social pressure caused by a girl's pregnancy. Parents are aware of the prevalence of nightcrawling (*dumaiya*) and apparently censure it when they discover it. Authorities do not agree about the amount of disapproval of premarital sex activities.[21] In general, it may be said that premarital sex relations are common but are not approved, the burden of disapproval falling on the girl. In the context of the general Hopi attitude toward sex, this suggests that disapproval is closely related to the attitude of the parents toward the particular man in question rather than to ideas of "sin" or to Puritanism.

[20] Titiev (1944:19, 23, 24, 25, 26, 31, 38). In one case he speaks of a girl's having her mother's *permission* to receive the attentions of a particular boy (p. 23).

[21] See Titiev (1944:31), E. and P. Beaglehole (1936:48, 62–63), Thompson and Joseph (1944:60), and Nequatewa (1933:50–51) for differences of opinion. All agree that parents consider premarital sex activities bad, but disagree as to *how* bad.

It is customary for the man to pay the woman when they have dumaiya relationships and also in later adulterous contacts. There is belief in sex witchcraft, practice of which is thoroughly disapproved. Male and female homosexuality exists, though there is some disagreement over its prevalence today.[22]

The actual marriage rites involve considerable distribution of food, in several stages, and last over several months. At first, the bride lives with the groom's family; but later the groom moves into the home of his wife's family, often with some shyness and reluctance. There is no important exchange of durable goods between the families. Cohabitation normally occurs throughout the time of completing the formalities. After marriage a man works for his wife's family.

Divorce is simply accomplished, without formalities, at the wish of either partner. About one-third of the people in one sample had been divorced at least once. This situation has been characterized by E. C. Parsons as a "brittle monogamy." The structural features which permit such fragile marriages are easy to see. There is no property claim to be resolved after divorce. A woman remains secure in her own home; and her unmarried or divorced male relatives, her sons, and her sister's husbands, when it is necessary, do the farm labor until she marries again. For this reason they may object to a woman's divorce. This is one of the few deterrents to divorce. Similarly, a man has a refuge in his mother's or his sister's household, where his labor is welcomed.

Not only are there factors which permit the easy breakup of marriage, but also there are factors which tend positively to bring about divorce. For one thing, during the early years of marriage the loyalties of each partner are still strongly directed toward his own clan. Jealousy is also of great importance. There is no marked sanction against extramarital promiscuity, which occurs with great frequency. But even within the framework of family preferences, marriages are contracted with some empha-

[22] It was more common formerly, according to Titiev (1944:205). Steward (personal communication) considers that it is still quite prevalent. D. Eggan mentions female homosexual behavior but says that it is never a preferred pattern and does not persist after marriage (1943:368); according to E. and P. Beaglehole, however, it is unknown (1936:65).

sis on the sexual preference of the partners. There is always a possibility that while one marriage partner is philandering, the other may still feel a strong sexual attraction toward him (or her), and thus become jealous. Since coöperative hard work is necessary for survival, lack of industry and efficiency on either side will also cause strains. "The most common grounds for separation are stinginess, laziness, violence of temper, and above all, adultery" (Titiev 1944:40).

When there is a divorce, younger children remain with the mother, but the older ones may go with either partner. After the birth of children, marriages tend to become more stable. It is believed that unfaithfulness and quarreling bring about the illness and even the death of young children. This belief forms part of a system of ideas which will be more fully stated below.

Although there are many factors that make marriages unstable and easily broken, the marriage bond is not without strength. During the bitter factional disputes which preceded the split in Oraibi, only about one-sixth of all the household units on which information is available displayed a divided allegiance. At the time of the final break, only four couples separated. Typically husbands followed their wives, but sometimes the reverse was true (Titiev 1944:88–93).

PROPERTY

The two most important nonceremonial types of property are land and herds. In Oraibi at least, the Village chief is "theoretical owner of all the village lands, and all the other clans hold land only on condition of good behavior and the proper observance of ceremonies" (op. cit., 61). The chief's own holdings are large enough for him to be able to allot some of his property to various Soyal officers, including the War chief. Within this framework each clan has its traditional holdings. There is also a portion of "free land," on which an individual can lay out fields with the chief's consent, which is ordinarily obtainable. In theory at least, each man farms a specified area of the lands of his mother's or his wife's clans, though in practice some land descends from father to son. Clan lands are spread around, so that each clan and each individual farms several fields, with different kinds of water supply. With permission of the owner, an individual may farm unused land.[23] Readjustments within the clan on the basis of relative size of households are made without difficulty, though only with regard to use, not ownership (Beaglehole 1937:16). The various rules relating to land use imply the conception that land is clan-owned and inalienable. It is evident that changes in the size of clans may occasion strains, for which there is no traditional remedy. One cause of the Oraibi split was the feeling of the members of the Spider clan that their holdings were too small. The Bear clan not only held more clan land but also, since the chief of the village was of that clan, claimed nominal ownership of the entire village (Titiev 1944:62, fig. 5, 63 n., 75). A conflict between the Pikyas and Patki clans arose from the charge that their landholdings were disproportionate to the importance of the clans.

Herds, which are cared for by the men, are ordinarily passed on, when a man dies, to the members of his clan, though there is also a less marked pattern of transmitting this form of property to the son.[24] An old person has some testamentary freedom, which he sometimes exercises to reward the individual who has cared for him in his old age. Houses ordinarily are passed on through the female line, but in rare cases, a man who has built a house before his marriage may will it to someone or give it away before his death, as he wishes. Farm equipment is often jointly owned by men of the same family, even though they may live and work in different households. The harvest is considered to be the property of a man until he brings it to his wife's home, when it becomes hers. Personal property is inherited in the clan line.

Important Katcina masks and most other ceremonial possessions are owned by the clan. Some of these are controlled by the senior woman of the clan, some by the male leader. The ceremonial property of a society, including the *tiponi,* is usually held in the household of the senior woman of the associated clan. Kivas are also clan-owned. Katcina masks of lesser importance and some ceremonial items are individually owned.

[23] The situation seems to be different on Second Mesa. Cf. Beaglehole (1937:8, 14–17) and Forde (1931:370–71).
[24] The next two paragraphs are based on Beaglehole (1937:10–17).

The Psychosocial Analysis of a Hopi Life-History

There is little information concerning differential wealth, and virtually none relative to the uses of surplus wealth.[25]

BELIEFS AND ETHIC[26]

For the Hopi, the cosmos is a complex, dynamic order in which the parts contribute to the welfare of each other and of the whole by the exchange of services. In this system, man's ritual activities, prayers, and conduct must be correct, to maintain the universe in a harmonious state, particularly with regard to the movement of the sun, growth of crops, rainfall, and animal and human reproduction. In Hopi, the word which means "to pray" also means "to want," "to wish," and "to will" (Kennard 1937:492).[27] There is a belief in foreordination (Thompson, 1945:542), including the conviction that an elder brother will some day come from the east to help the Hopi (Voth, 1905:21, 15, 25, 28; Nequatewa, 1936:105 n, 107 n).

The ideal society is modeled after the ideal universe described above—complex, coöperative, mirroring the natural order and linked to it by elaborate symbolism. In this system the chief of the ranking society, the Village chief, is the keystone, the father of the pueblo, whose particular duty is to concentrate on the wellbeing of the group.

The ideal individual can be summed up by the term *hopi*, usually translated "peaceful." It includes the values: (*a*) strength —physical and psychic, including self-control, wisdom, and intel-

---

[25] Thompson and Joseph (1944:77) mention a family "prominent through its relative prosperity"; this suggests that wealth is one factor in prestige. Elsewhere they indicate considerable differences in economic prosperity of various families (e.g., pp. 68, 69, 72, 75, 81 and 83, all of which involve statements of the economic position of families studied). Cushing considers wealth a means of gaining importance when it is used in constructing a kiva, but Parsons states that the economic factor is not as significant as Cushing's statement would indicate (1922:257 and note).

[26] Discussion of the Hopi ethic is based on Thompson (1945), except as noted. Thompson gives little empirical base for her treatment. It is a synthesis of a large amount of ethnographic material. Although there may be some question whether the Hopi themselves have systematized their beliefs as thoroughly as Thompson's treatment has, there can be little doubt that the beliefs and values she posits are dominant in Hopi society, whatever the difficulties of living up to them.

[27] See Whorf (1941:85-87) for a study of the linguistic aspects of this attitude.

ligence; (*b*) poise—tranquillity, "good" thinking; (*c*) obedience to the law—coöperation, unselfishness, responsibility, kindness; (*d*) peace—absence of aggressive, quarrelsome, or boastful behavior; (*e*) protectiveness—preserving and protecting human, animal, and plant life; (*f*) health. These make up the Hopi "one-hearted," good personality.

In order to contribute maximally to community well-being, the coming of rain, the success of farming, and the like, every individual should live up to the ideal code in action and in thought. If even one person has a "bad heart," rites will fail. That is why the announcement of a ceremonial is accompanied by the Crier's admonition to cease all quarrels (Kennard 1957:492).

The polar opposite of the *hopi* individual is one who is *kahopi* —not Hopi. Such a person may show any or all of the following qualities: "lack of integrity, quarrelsomeness, jealousy, envy, boastfulness, self-assertion, irresponsibility, noncoöperativeness and sickness" (Thompson 1945:545). The extreme development of these characteristics is the witch, the "two-hearted" individual, who is antisocial, lawless, an agent of illness and death.

The concept of the witch requires extensive treatment, since it will be of great significance in the discussion of the life-history.[28] "There are said to be more sorcerers than normal people in each of the Hopi villages, even though ordinary persons may be unable to recognize them in everyday life" (Titiev 1943: 549). There is an international league of witches, both male and female, descended from Spider Woman. Every witch has an animal familiar of some sort; hence his double heart and the name "two-heart."[29] (Op. cit., 550.) There are witches of both sexes. It is believed that there is a witches' society, whose meetings and initiation rites are like those of other societies, with a ceremonial father for each new member. Initiates are taught how to transform themselves into the form of their familiars, and back again. Some people join voluntarily, but children may be

[28] The discussion of witchcraft is based on Titiev (1943), except as noted.
[29] Thompson (1945:544-45), sees the idea of "two-hearted" simply as opposed to "one-hearted." The difference is not of great significance for the present analysis, though it would be valuable if it could be determined whether the idea of hypocrisy and deceit enters into the concept.

initiated before they are old enough to realize the significance of the initiation. It is thus possible for an individual to be a witch for some time without knowing it. Even the parents of such children do not know that the children are witches. The evil activities of witches include inflicting people with sickness or killing them, sending insects to destroy crops, speeding the erosion process and thus destroying farmland, and driving away the rain so as to cause droughts and famine. Most of these actions are performed out of sheer malevolence. But "the Hopi firmly believe that witches can exert harm only on their relatives" (op. cit., 55 n.), and regardless of a witch's intentions, he must kill a relative each year in order to stay alive. Although a witch may pity his victim as a man would pity an animal he killed for food, he must persist in killing his relatives or die.

Many people wear arrow-point amulets or smear their faces with ashes on specific occasions to ward off witchcraft. Once a person has fallen ill, a shaman may be able to cure him. But the shamans most adept at curing—those who can remove substances by sucking—are particularly under suspicion of being witches, and parents fear to call them to cure their children.

There are apparently certain internal contradictions in the system of beliefs regarding witches, and perhaps certain beliefs that vary from mesa to mesa. Thus, though it has been said that a repentant witch will die, it is also said that a shaman is a repentant witch.[30] Don once remarked that shamans had to come to the aid of the sick, to save their own lives (op. cit. 552).[31] It may be, then, that a repentant witch will die *unless* he becomes a good shaman. On Second Mesa it is believed that "a person caught performing magic [witchcraft] would die at the

[30] There is probably a reflection of this notion in Whiting's remark (1939:30) that a medicine man may "enter this profession in order to regain the lost respect of the community."

[31] It must be noted that Don, in addition to being the subject of the life-history, has been an informant—in a few instances the main informant —on points of Hopi ethnography. (See Titiev, 1944:51 *et passim,* and 1943:552.) The legitimacy of using Hopi material, contributed by Don himself, as a background for the analysis of his life might therefore be questioned. Nevertheless, the material he provided has been checked against the word of other informants and is consistent with their information. Rare exceptions, such as Don's emphasis on the Guardian Spirit, are considered in the life-history analysis.

end of four days if he did not admit his wrongdoing and promise to reform" (E. and P. Beaglehole 1936:10). This sort of belief would also reconcile the apparent contradiction.

On Second Mesa it is believed that witches can be *hired* to perform sex witchcraft, malevolent acts against individuals, and acts against the welfare of the whole village, or to cause famine or general illness (Ibid.). Such a belief is not mentioned for Third Mesa and is hard to reconcile with Titiev's previously cited statement, derived from Third Mesa material, that witches can work harm only against their relatives. On Second Mesa there is also a linkage between war magic and witchcraft (Ibid.), not mentioned for Third Mesa.

Although shamans sometimes cure their patients of the effects of witchcraft, they seldom mention the name of the supposed malevolent agent. How shamans learn their skill is not clear; the former medicine society has died out (Titiev 1943:552 n.).[32] Talking about a sorcerer will only prolong his life, and challenging him puts the aggressor in danger. Speaking kindly of him, however, will injure him (E. and P. Beaglehole 1936:9).

Witches are detected in several ways. A shaman may name one; a victim, as he is dying, may cry out the name of the man who is injuring him. But for the most part the identity of the witch is a matter of suspicion. Powerful individuals, including village officials or chiefs, are often targets for such suspicions. So, indeed, are eccentric or aggressive people, or those who inflate their own importance. In times of crisis, village officers are particularly liable to be the objects of such accusations. When Yokioma was claiming power and authority at the time of the Oraibi split, he was accused of witchcraft and accepted the accusation as true. Although no actual killing of witches is recorded, attempts to kill them are not unknown (Titiev 1943: 554 n.). Sometimes, to protect himself from community action, a man has to depend on his reputation as a witch and the threats he makes on this basis.

After death, witches travel to the afterworld at the rate of one step a year, afflicted with hunger and thirst. On arrival they are

[32] A bonesetter trains his own successor—often a sister's son (Whiting, 1939:30).

The Psychosocial Analysis of a Hopi Life-History

put into an oven, from which they emerge as beetles.[33] They never become cloud spirits. To avoid the ordeal, some witches crawl from their graves as bullsnakes and let themselves be killed. If this occurs, they go at once to the afterworld.

Apparently there are Hopi who actually believe that they are witches and really practice witchcraft.[34] These beliefs have important consequences.

> Brought up in an atmosphere of dread and helplessness in the face of evil attacks, they [the Hopi] quickly learn to avoid all appearance of having exceptional ability, and to emphasize moderation in all things. They constantly decry their powers, make frequent professions of humility, and, through fear of arousing the envy or jealousy of the two-hearted, prefer not to seek great honors or to hold high offices. (Op. cit., 556.)

Titiev has speculated that the beliefs about witchcraft may arise from the timidity of the Hopi. It might be possible to develop a theory that Hopi witchcraft beliefs in general were derived either from this timidity or (along the lines of Kardiner's work) from projections of Hopi covert aggression, or from both. But the relationship would appear to be general, rather than specific: it is exceeding doubtful that the entire complex of Hopi witchcraft beliefs could be derived from considering it as a "projective system" (Kardiner 1945:1–46). In this study, beliefs and values will be considered as semi-independent elements of a social system, with causal efficacy of their own (see T. Parsons 1949:151–65). This does not outlaw the possibility that there may be certain *general* correspondences between character structure and belief systems in individuals and groups of individuals, or that the intensity of concern with witchcraft may not fluctuate in relation to other factors.[35]

---

[33] People whose first marriage was to a previously married individual are the only other group punished after death.

[34] Wallis and Titiev (1945:537–39) cite a Second Mesa man who reports that his grandfather and mother's brother told him that they had practiced witchcraft.

[35] E. C. Parsons (1939:1066 n.) notes that Second Mesa and Third Mesa are characterized by more witchcraft than First Mesa, and that there is a general increase in the amount of Hopi witchcraft. Cf. also Parsons (1927: 128; and in Stephen 1936:xl), commenting in the latter on Stephen's infrequent mention of witches. Stephen lived mainly on First Mesa.

Certain features of the witchcraft pattern must be stressed. One is the extreme difficulty of identifying a witch, or of even being sure that one is not a witch oneself. Another is the lack of well-organized and effective modes of countering witchcraft; the only source of help, the shaman or medicine man, is suspect. A third important feature is the tendency for suspicions of witchcraft to increase in times of catastrophe. Finally, in this highly traditionalistic society, innovation and the challenging of authority are peculiarly likely to bring accusations of witchcraft. This reinforces both traditionalism and authority, but in a society with as much ascribed status as Hopi it still further circumscribes initiative.

The concept of the causation of disease is a complex one.[36] There appear to be two dominant elements. On the one hand, the individual's thought or action must be of a character that renders him susceptible to disease. On the other, there may also be some agent of disease: the "whip" of a society, the action of a witch, or other factors, which are about to be discussed. It is felt that by failing to keep proper balance and dying, an individual shows an inadequate sense of community responsibility. For a cure, not only must the afflicting society or a medicine man take appropriate action, but also it is necessary for the sick individual to concentrate on good thoughts and drive out bad ones (Thompson 1945:548 and n.).

Among the "bad" thoughts are thoughts of the dead, the underworld, and the like. They lead to the destruction of will and to susceptibility to illness and death. (Although it is not stated, this idea is compatible with the concept that a lack of concern for the group causes disease, since thoughts of the dead show a greater concern for them than for the living group to which the thinker owes allegiance.) Similarly, being mean or angry will impair the will and tend to bring about premature death. People who do not think good thoughts are particularly susceptible to being harmed by witches. The disturbing thoughts of a person deserted by a mate might cause illness. Also, simply living in a bad atmosphere, surrounded by the quarrels of others, may bring

---

[36] The discussion of disease and death is based on Kennard (1937), except as noted.

sickness and death. That is sometimes the cause of the death of young children. Or even too serious thinking about responsibility may cause death. Another, somewhat different type of situation is that in which an individual whose feelings have been hurt wills himself to die, so as to hurt someone else. Women are particularly prone to do this, and indeed are "meaner" than men (Titiev 1944:23-24).

Although Kennard mentions only what may be termed "will-suicide," the Hopi attitude toward other forms of self-sought death is consistent with his material. Suicides are so strongly disapproved and so rare (Parsons 1939:75) that in the days of Navaho and Mexican warfare, it was customary for a man who wished to kill himself to arrange secretly with the enemy for a skirmish in which he would be killed and the enemy rewarded for killing him. At any rate, such is the tradition. People were not disturbed, apparently, by the fact that sometimes others who had not participated in the bargain were also killed (Nequatewa 1944:45-47; Colton 1936:107 n.; Voth 1905:258 ff.; E. Parsons 1939:75 n.). There are some reports of suicides of aged people (Simmons 1945:229).

There is an idea of natural death, but only the very old are considered to die naturally. Each person, it is felt, has his own road to follow. Normally, his own will keeps him on his path, moving toward health, happiness, and old age; but, as has been said, mental conflict, worry, trouble, or bad thoughts destroy the will and lead to unhappiness, sickness, and even death. Thus, grief for the dead must be avoided, because it lays an individual open to witchcraft attacks. People continually tell each other not to worry, not to grieve—for fear of witches (Titiev 1943:557).

There is fear of contact with a corpse; individuals who carry out the burial rites must afterward undergo purification. Nevertheless, it is the dead who become the Katcinas, gods, cloud spirits, bringers of rain and all that is good. There is no question of a particular individual's turning into a particular Katcina: he simply becomes *a* Katcina. This transformation need not be unduly surprising: it may be that, once the dead have achieved some emotional distance, they lose their dangerously attractive character and become only remote, sacred, kindly, and helpful.

The burial of infants is different from that of adults. The Hopi believe that the dead child returns to the parental house and waits to be reborn into the body of the next child. A boy reappears as a girl, and vice versa. If no other child is born before the mother dies, the spirits of her dead children accompany her to the underworld.

It should be pointed out, then, that a sick or dying individual looks not only to the malevolence of witches or the breaking of taboos for his misfortunes, but also to his inner thoughts, and must blame both the thought and the other cause.

Life Cycle

There is general agreement that Hopi children, at least during the first two years of life, are indulged and are relatively unrestricted (Dennis 1940:83; Goldfrank 1945:519; Thompson and Joseph 1944:51; Titiev 1944:19; and D. Eggan 1943: 362). They are nursed on demand; transition to solid food is gradual; sphincter-control training is mild and is delayed until the second year,[37] and the general attitude is one of indulgence toward these wanted children. A great many relatives participate in indulging the child, chiefly the grandparents, mother's sisters, and paternal aunts. The male infant often receives genital stimulation while nursing and in other situations. A pregnant mother should not nurse. But the mortality rate among infants is high, and after a child's death an older sibling sometimes returns to the breast and may even continue to nurse until his sixth year. Weaning of such a child is sometimes brought about by his age mates' shaming him. The mother puts chili powder or a worm on her breast to discourage nursing. Although an infant is kept on a cradleboard for the first six months or more of life, there is no evidence that this restriction results in any marked frustration or that the learning of locomotor skills is slowed thereby. During his early life, a child is often cared for by an older sister, as well as by the relatives mentioned above.

[37] Enuresis in older children sometimes results in the administration of a cold-water cure by the mother's brother. A good many unoffending age mates of the bed-wetter are apt to be treated at the same time. There is no shaming, however, and the situation is handled seriously, as a cure (Dennis 1940:36–37).

An older child sometimes shows jealousy of a nursing child (E. and P. Beaglehole 1936:39). A more general jealousy among siblings also occurs later, as well as jealousy for the attention of the parent of opposite sex (Dennis 1940:109). Apparently, sibling rivalry is present but is deeply repressed.[38]

From the second to sixth year of a child's life, the general indulgent character of child care continues. By the age of two, the child is toilet-trained and weaned, but he is markedly indulged with regard to food. A sister is likely to care for him outside the home. Male and female role differentiation begins later, but boys and girls are expected to show different emotional character by the age of four. Boys should stop crying by this age, but girls may continue throughout life to cry under stress.

Childhood masturbation is a matter of no concern to Hopi parents.[39] Adults and older children casually play with the genitals of young male children (D. Eggan 1943:365). Children are not formally instructed in sexual matters in childhood, but a child's public imitation of what he saw in the sleeping room creates no disturbance.[40] Children, however, are warned against heterosexual relations. They are told that young girls can bear children, but that the bearing of a child by a young girl would bring the world to an end. Boys are warned that heterosexual relations will bring about premature old age (Dennis 1940:78).

From the age of six the Hopi child is subject to increasing discipline and responsibility. A child's minor aggressive behavior arouses far more concern in Hopi parents than in parents in our society, and requires discipline. Parents and the mother's brother are the principal disciplinary agents. An older sibling who is caring for a child must appeal to the parents tor disciplining if the child fails to obey. Similarly, people of the village who have a complaint against a child may reprove him but must report his misbehavior to parents rather than threaten or command the child themselves. A father is likely to punish for some offense

---

[38] D. Eggan (1943:363–64) and Henry (1947:88, 95). Thompson and Joseph do not discuss the point.

[39] D. Eggan (1943:365) and E. and P. Beaglehole (1936:39). See also Stephen (1938:388–89) for an example of favorable parental attitudes toward infant and child masturbation.

[40] D. Eggan (1943:365). Nevertheless, E. and P. Beaglehole (1936:41) report the case of a girl who was ignorant of the fact of copulation until the age of thirteen.

which is angering him at the moment. For graver discipline, however, the mother will ask one of her brothers to undertake the punishment. As an outsider, the father is glad to step aside and let the clan take over.

Techniques of punishment include scolding—perhaps the most common discipline—ridiculing and teasing, threatening to withhold favors, whipping,[41] pouring cold water on the child or rolling him in the snow, and smoking the child over a fire of green wood, so as to stifle him. This last is considered particularly severe. A mother's brother will sometimes punish a whole group of his sisters' sons when called on to discipline one of them (Dennis 1940:45–46). The effects of this sort of group culpability have nowhere been investigated. Dennis, however, points out the parallel to the ceremonial situation, in which one man's misdeeds affect the entire group (1941:263–64). Other techniques of coercion are those which involve the supernaturals. The mildest of these is the threat that the Katcinas will not bring a child presents at a dance. Usually the presents are withheld until the fourth day of the ceremony, by which time the child has promised to reform. The presents given by Katcinas, of course, are arranged for by the parents.

A more severe form of inculcating the Hopi norms is to threaten the child that the bogey giant Katcinas, Soyoko and Natashka, will come and carry him off and eat him if he is disobedient.[42] The occasional appearance of these figures as Katcina impersonations is used as a particularly awesome method of bringing about an obedient frame of mind.

Before Soyoko is to appear, parents who wish to have their children frightened inform the impersonators about all the misdeeds of the child. Soyoko later repeats these to the child, so that it appears that the supernaturals know all about his behavior. On the third day of the performance, children are kept around the home. Warning Katcinas tell the children to prepare their ransoms (corn products for girls, small animals for boys). The parents then rush to prepare ransom for their children. On the

[41] A child is never whipped at night, for it is believed that a child whipped at night might die (Dennis 1940:46).
[42] The discussion of Soyoko is based on Titiev (1944:216–21).

following day the giants appear—tall, fierce, carrying knives and saws, and full of tales of the child's misdeeds. The child is defended by his relatives. He timidly offers food to the giant, who three times refuses it in favor of carrying off the child himself. Finally, however, he accepts it, and eventually the giants retire to the kiva. There can be no doubt that this procedure is terrifying.[43] In spite of the use of these Katcinas as a part of Hopi discipline, the generalized Hopi feeling against aggression is interestingly exemplified by the ambivalence of the Hopi in their estimates of the value of the Katcina impersonations. Thus, at Oraibi it is felt that though Katcina performances generally contribute to group welfare, the Soyoko performance is likely to be followed by cold winds. At Hotevilla there has been no performance since 1932, because the last impersonator to scare the children fell seriously ill (Dennis 1940:45).

Another Hopi method of socializing and disciplining children which employs supernatural sanctions, one generally agreed to be of crucial importance, is the initiation into the Powamu and Katcina societies. This takes place between the sixth and tenth year of a child's life. Both boys and girls undergo initiation. Afterward, however, only males perform the Katcina dances. Theoretically, until his initiation, the child is ignorant that the Katcina dancers whom he has seen are really only members of his own or other Hopi towns, wearing masks. I say theoretically, but defer discussion of the matter until it becomes relevant in the life-history analysis. There is some evidence that children try to keep from finding out (D. Eggan 1943:372). Since Katcina and Badger clan people have the duty of being Katcina fathers, all children belonging to these clans are initiated into Powamu.

[43] On Second Mesa the child sometimes has to run a race with one of these Katcinas "the little fellow dashing madly to win in the hope that it will save his life" (Titiev 1944:220). Some years ago, perfomances on the top of a kiva in Walpi were designed to demonstrate that the giants actually killed people. Children found even the warning Katcina frightening, according to Stephen, though they tried to put up a good front (1936: 187, 243, 254, 256). It is only fair to add that Titiev records (1944:220) that in 1911, during the last Oraibi Soyoko performance, one girl "threatened to report the So'yoko to the principal of the day school." Even in New Oraibi, where little effort is made to have the children believe in the Katcinas, they do believe in the Soyoko figures, though these never appear in New Oraibi itself (Dennis 1940:90).

For others, their parents decide whether they are to be subjected to the Powamu initiation, which does not have ceremonial whipping, or to the Katcina initiation, in which they are whipped. The more recalcitrant children are normally initiated into the Katcina society. The child's membership is formally determined by his parents' selection of ceremonial parents: a "father" for the boy, a "mother" for the girl. In either case, they should not be closely related to the child.

Since Don was initiated into the Katcina society, stress here will be on that society's rites.[44] The purpose of both initiations is to serve as passage of the initiate into somewhat higher status in the society, to impress the children with the important Katcina secret, and to put before them with all possible firmness the need to abide by the Hopi ethic. The rationale of the whipping of the Katcina society initiation finds expression in the words of a Second Mesa leader of the whippers: "[The children] do not obey their mothers and fathers. We are going to help you old people so that they will mind you." To this the Katcina chief answers, "Of course they do not mind us. But I would rather be on my own children's side than on your side. They do not mind us, but I will take care of my children." He is unsuccessful, however, in persuading the whippers not to proceed, though he does induce them to lay aside willow whips and substitute yucca blades. He then says, "They do not mind us, so we will let you try to make them obey. We will let you force them to keep these things secret." At the close of both ceremonies, Powamu and Katcina, the children are threatened with severe beatings if they reveal what they have learned (Steward 1931:64–65). While the children being initiated into the Katcina society are whipped with yucca blades, the Powamu initiates, who have finished the day before, look on. The children are badly frightened. Boys are whipped nude, struggle to protect their genitals, and some are so badly frightened that they involuntarily urinate, or even defecate (Voth 1901:103–4).

Besides these methods of punishment and coercion, Hopi parents also use various techniques of reward. Praise and ap-

[44] For fuller accounts of both societies, see Voth (1901) and Steward (1931).

The Psychosocial Analysis of a Hopi Life-History

proval naturally form the common day-to-day currency of reward. In addition, gifts from the Katcina dancers are employed. The Katcinas may make presentations at any dance during the half year of their presence in the pueblo, and thus show their approval of the child and their knowledge of his behavior. Parents explain the reason for the gifts. A mother will say to a boy, "You have helped your father in the fields, so the kachinas brought you a nice bow and arrow"; or, "if you are a good boy the kachinas will bring you nice gifts." Or to a girl, "They gave you a kachina doll because you have taken care of your little brother" (Dennis 1940:47). The source of the gift is really some relative, who has made it for a specific child.

After thus considering techniques of reward and punishment, we return to a study of the role of the growing child in society. The period from six to ten is marked by increasing performance of economic activity. After she is ten, a girl spends an increasing amount of time at home and may join one of the women's societies. She may undergo a sort of formal advancement to adult status through a ritual corn-grinding ordeal, though this custom is apparently passing out in most of the Hopi towns. The boy continues to do more and more work in the fields and is absent from his home an increasing amount of the day. His participation in Katcina dances begins about the age of fourteen. By the age of fifteen he is beginning to learn to weave. Courtship usually begins in the sixteenth year or before; this has already been described in some detail. A man may marry before or after the Wowochim initiation, which signalizes full status in the group.

Although little is known of the Wowochim initiation, a few facts are clear.[45] Men alone are initiated. They join one, and only one, of four adult initiation societies—Wowochim, Horns (Al), Agaves (Kwan), and Singers (Tao). The rites are intimately bound up with Masau'u, the god of death, and apparently initiates are ceremonially killed and reborn during the rites. It should be pointed out that adult Hopi are terrified of Masau'u to the degree that the man who impersonates him at night in certain ceremonies is in great fear of meeting the *real* Masau'u and being injured or killed by him. It is safe to say that

---

[45] This paragraph is based on Titiev (1944:130-39).

whatever the character of the initiation—and here the life-history sheds no additional light—it is severe, frightening, and impressive. It seems to build up the young man's attachment to Hopi ceremonialism and to impress him with the force of the community.

IMPLICATIONS

Hopi economic life is uncertain in the extreme and demands hard work from everyone during the agricultural season.

Religious activity aims particularly at the promotion of favorable conditions for agriculture. Failure of ceremonials is attributed to the "bad hearts" of individuals or to the malign influence of witches. This amounts to a universal taboo on aggression in action, speech, and thought, which is quite explicit. It is unlikely that such a taboo can be faithfully observed on all occasions. Nevertheless, not only communal disaster but illness and shortened life are attributed to violation of this taboo. In spite of the ethic described, which is so intimately connected to the Hopi theory of natural causality, there are believed to be a great many people who strikingly fail to live up to it—these are witches. Few effective techniques exist for protection against them.

Little opportunity for gaining many of the positions of prestige is open to a person born outside the families in which office inheres. If he tries to attain such a position he invites accusations of witchcraft.

A great deal of philandering takes place, and one-third of marriages are broken.

Child training revolves chiefly about training toward industry and away from aggression. In this, in addition to action taken directly by relatives, an important part is played by the Katcinas, purportedly supernatural figures, whose link with the parents is revealed in the course of childhood initiation.

Community relations and relations with American society are featured by tension—sometimes slight, sometimes marked.

The adult male is oriented to his family and his clan of birth, and to his wife's family, for whom he has to work.

The analysis of the life-history will revolve about the meaning of these facts to the individual Hopi.

Don's Life

SUMMARY

Don was born in Oraibi in 1890. At the end of the lifehistory he is fifty years of age. He lived through the Oraibi split of 1906, siding with the Friendly (pro-white) group because his family did. He attended school for ten years, three of them away from the Hopi towns, in California. He was initiated into the Wowochim society, married, and had four children, all of whom died in infancy. He finally raised an adopted child to maturity. During his married life he underwent a six-year period of impotence, though prior to this he had numerous extramarital sexual contacts. In spite of infidelity, impotence, early difficulties in making a living, and the death of four children, he and his wife never separated or divorced.

A prestige-driven man, he eventually gained the positions of male leader of the Sun clan, owner of the associated Sun Hill kiva, and ceremonial officer in the Soyal ceremony. He remains an aggressive, prestige-conscious, deeply mistrustful man, who has gradually become convinced that evil in the world is caused by witches, who are to be found everywhere. In recent years his contacts with anthropologists have afforded him much satisfaction.

Don's socialization centered about the problems raised by his insistent aggressive misbehavior toward his elders Although his parents took a role in disciplining, they passed part of this role to relatives, and part to ostensibly supernatural scarers.

In the effort to break him of his bad behavior, virtually the entire battery of Hopi punishment was turned on him. Although it is not absolutely clear from Don's account what relatives meted out what punishment, nor what the sequence was, the general situation was that his parents exhausted their techniques and then turned him over to other relatives for harsher disciplines. In the end, however, none of the punishments did any good, and Don continued to misbehave until the Katcina initiation.

The problem of mistrust.—As early as his sixth year Don was preoccupied with the problem of trust and mistrust. He had "learned to pick out the people whom I could trust" (Simmons 1942:67). Those who treated him kindly, protected him from teasing, or refrained from teasing him are included in the list of trusted individuals accompanying his statement; tacitly excluded are people who teased him or whose primary role toward him was a disciplinary one. It must be remembered that this refers to a time prior to Don's great period of misbehavior and continuous punishment. At the time that Don speaks of, his parents had punished him but little, and his maternal grandfather only twice.

Thus, at the head of the list of those he could trust was his mother; then his father, whom Don liked except for the rare punishments he gave; his maternal grandfather, who favored and taught him; his ceremonial father; his crippled uncle; and his elder sister. He knew that he could always count on his grandfather and on his ceremonial father. He also had a positive attitude toward some people whose personal contacts with him were more remote—some maternal relatives (the village officers mentioned above), who showed interest in him and did not tease him.

Ambivalently regarded were his older brother, who, he felt, was not a very good friend to him, and a paternal aunt who stood up for him when he was teased, but was hot-tempered and unpredictable. Hostiles were to be avoided. There were, of course, in the village, many people of no particular significance to him. Summing up all this, Don says, "I had learned to find my way about the mesa and to avoid graves, shrines, and harmful plants, *to size up people, and to watch out for witches*" (op. cit., 68).

His "grandfathers" were not mentioned as trusted individuals. The role of one of them in breaking him of bed-wetting and in hardening him has already been discussed: Don had serious difficulty in believing that the man's intentions were good; he says that this man was "one of the toughest men I knew" (op. cit., 38). Other "grandfathers" also treated him in like fashion; they also teased him roughly. One of them also made him hug a snowball when he was naked, holding him until he cried. There was no pretense here of discipline: it was a joke, which Don was told he could some day repay. Another time this man tied him like a billy goat to be cut and made a realistic pretense of castrating the four- or five-year-old boy for "trying to make love to my wife" (op. cit., 39). His mother told him afterward that she could not protect him, that a "grandfather" had a right to carry on this sort of joking and teasing, "and that it showed how much he cared for me" (op. cit., 40). This same joking went on all the time, "aunts" pretending they wanted his penis, and "grandfathers"—their husbands—pretending they were furious and intended to castrate him. It took a long time for Don to realize that they were only teasing. Even though this teasing is an "inalienable right" and it is considered bad form for a young man to resent it, it seems that the joke is somewhat lost on a young child (Titiev 1944:29).

Those whom Don failed to include in the circle of trust, then, were the people whose motivations toward him he did not understand—those who disciplined him and claimed to love him, those who treated him very roughly and pretended high regard for him. Furthermore, Don was no stranger to the concealment of aggression. His parents always stopped quarreling when anyone came to the house.

The link between witchcraft beliefs and feelings of mistrust was not as close as it became later. Witches, however, were people to watch out for and avoid. Their power was superior to any weapons known to Don. Evil spirits and Masau'u, the god of fire and death, were two other dangers his grandfather warned him against.

The next element in the pattern of mistrust was Don's growing misgivings about the Katcinas. He knew of them first as supernatural figures who came in answer to prayers, bringing good luck, singing and dancing in the plaza, and giving presents. They afforded some protection from Two-Hearts, "pleased the gods and insured our lives" (Simmons 1942:44). But from his early years on, things happened which made Don think that there was something odd about the Katcinas. Thus, when he was four or five, at Shungopavi he once "saw the Katcinas resting near by. It seemed that they had cut off their heads and laid them to one side. They were eating and were using human heads and mouths like our own. I felt very sad to see those Katcinas without their own heads." (Op. cit., 49.) Don's sadness, it may be surmised, was the beginning of disillusionment.[46] Belief in the Katcinas already required effort and the ignoring of some features of reality. Then, too, the story of the giant Katcinas and their masks gave a further clue.

Whether or not Don's conscious doubts began as early as the fourth or fifth year, they were well developed by his seventh and eighth years. He began to suspect the Katcinas when he observed that he received the same rattles over and over, when the Katcinas stripped them from their legs at the end of a dance to give to the children. He finally refused to accept the rattles because "I concluded that either the Katcinas or my parents were stealing them and giving them back again and again." Although his mother warned him that the Katcinas would be disappointed in his attitude, he "felt offended and ran into the house, leaving the rattles. . . ." (Op. cit., 75.) Then, again, he was disturbed to find his mother making red piki (wafer bread), the kind he always got from the Katcinas and saw nowhere else. Surprised and embarrassed, she said:

> "A Katcina was making piki here, but did not finish. . . . I happened to come in and decided to help." . . . That evening at supper I was still unhappy. . . . My mother . . . finally said, "My son, I told you the truth; the Katcina left that piki and I was finishing it." . . . The next day . . . I did not want any red piki [from the Katcinas]. And to my surprise they gave me not red but yellow piki, and six boiled eggs, all colored! Then I was happy.[47] (Op. cit., 75–76.)

[46] It is possible that Don's doubts began earlier. From the first it was the massive heads which impressed him most strongly. And his mother's saying that the Katcinas had flown away, after she had covered his head with a blanket while they disappeared, seems a thin device.

[47] There is no information, in the literature, relative to the secret making of red or yellow piki. Whiting (1939:15) mentions only that piki of these colors is used on special occasions. From Don's account it appears that he never saw red or yellow piki except as a present from the Katcinas. The colored eggs suggest the possibility of the infiltration of American Easter customs into the area of Katcina presents.

Stephen (1936:363, 387) gives examples of how the giving of Katcina presents is arranged. Although the children are surprised and delighted, the dodges are so obvious that it seems likely that a willing suspension of disbelief is required to maintain credence in the Katcinas.

KATCINA INITIATION[48]

The elements of discipline, mistrust, and suspicions about the Katcinas became connected during the crucial Katcina initiation, at the end of which Don became obedient but at the same time sadly disillusioned and resentful. He was just under nine at this time.[49] Since Tuvenga, his ceremonial father, was too old to act on Don's behalf, this man's nephew, Sekahongeoma, took the role of ceremonial father; his sister was Don's ceremonial mother. Over the protests of Don's mother and his ceremonial mother, Don's father, who had the right to make the decision, insisted that he join the Katcina society instead of the Powamu, which had an easier initiation rite.

> "I want him to join the Katcinas and be whipped. You have complained time after time that you are getting tired of his mischief. So you have no right to back down now. It will do him good to be whipped soundly and learn a lesson. We can pray to the Whipper Katcinas to drive the evil from our boy's mind, so that he may grow up to be a good and wise man. Don't you agree with me?" (Op. cit., 80.)

The two women wept but consented. A stronger form of protest came from Sekahongeoma, who asked four times that the boy be admitted to the Powamu instead.[50] Don's quieter, better-natured brother had been taken into the Powamu. During all this, Don did not cry but smiled. But as the initiation approached, he became more concerned about the flogging.[51] Al-

---

[48] This section is based on Simmons (1942:79–87), except as noted.

[49] Although he refers to himself as being nine years of age, his birthday was in March and the initiation in February. He went to school first in 1899 and participated in his first Katcina dance in January, 1900. A boy dances only after he has been initiated; Don's initiation was therefore in February, 1899. See Simmons (1942:79, 89, 91).

[50] The practice of granting what has been four times requested is current among the Navaho and may be customary among the Hopi. From the context, it appears that Sekahongeoma's request was intended to be as forceful as possible.

[51] Titiev (1946:431) criticizes Thompson and Joseph for saying that children anticipate a whipping during initiation. In this case, at least, it appears that the child not only knew beforehand that he was to be whipped, but he was explicitly told so. Titiev continues by remarking that on Third Mesa there is no whipping in the Powamu initiation. There is variation on this point: on First Mesa Powamu initiates are whipped. See Stephen (1936:200–3), E. C. Parsons (1933:50, 64), Steward (1931:64–65), Fewkes (1903:plate vii); all cited in Titiev (1944:116 n.).

though other boys would tell him nothing after their initiation, he had seen them and knew that "it would be pretty bad." He knew that the boys were struck four times with yucca blades, but he thought he could stand the whipping. "I made up my mind that I would set my teeth to grin and bear it, for other boys had been brave enough to do it." (Op. cit., 80.)

All details of the ceremony need not be given here. After certain rites, during which the boys were wished a long and happy life, a Katcina appeared. He ordered that the children be whipped "to enlighten our hearts and lead us over life's road." (Op. cit., 82.) Other Katcinas made their appearance, and then came the whippers. Some children had begun to cry, but not Don. The whipping followed. Naked and protecting his genitals, Don received four blows from the Ho Katcinas without crying and thought his troubles were over. Four more severe blows, however, drew blood and made him struggle, shout, and urinate involuntarily. His godfather, who had made no effort to take the blows for him, as is sometimes done, finally pulled him away. His ceremonial mother and others in the kiva were upset and angry at the Whipper for giving more than four blows. Don was able to control his sobbing but was too upset and hurt even to watch the other floggings.[52] He did, however, get a little enjoyment out of seeing the Katcinas flog one another. Then the children were warned never to tell uninitiated children what they had seen.

That night Don's bloody wounds stuck to his sheepskin. The next day, "my mother reproached my father for his cruelty." (Op. cit., 83.) His father had requested the double whipping and had told his ceremonial father not to protect him. The wounds caused by the whipping became infected and permanent scars resulted.

The next night came the revelation that the Katcinas were only people of Oraibi. "I recognized nearly every one of them, and felt very unhappy, because I had been told all my life that the Katcinas were gods. I was especially shocked and angry when I saw all my uncles, fathers, and clan brothers dancing as Katcinas. I felt the worst when I saw my own father—and

---

[52] As in many initiations, it is probable that the opportunity to watch one's age mates going through the same ordeal affords some satisfaction.

whenever he glanced at me I turned my face away." (Op. cit., 84.) A worse thrashing than the first was promised to anyone who revealed the secret of the Katcinas to the uninitiated. One child, they were told, was whipped to death for revealing it.

Don's mother now told him how she had arranged that he receive yellow piki instead of red on the earlier occasion when his suspicions were so marked. Thenceforth he received no more presents from the Katcinas, but he did get bows and arrows from his father and from his ceremonial father. "I kept thinking . . . about the Katcinas, whom I had loved." (Op. cit., 84.)

He learned that the real Katcinas had formerly actually appeared at dances, but that they did so no longer:

> . . . since the people had become so wicked—since there were now so many Two-Hearts in the world—the Katcinas had stopped coming . . . and sent their spirits to enter the masks. . . . I thought of the flogging and the initiation as an important turning point in my life, and I felt ready at last to listen to my elders and to live right. Whenever my father talked to me I kept my ears open, looked straight into his eyes, and said, "Owi" (Yes). (Op. cit., 86–87.)

Don, as a consequence of his initiation, had a new ally: his ceremonial father, he was told, could be counted on if his father were to neglect him, and the ceremonial father would never punish him. He also gained a supernatural supervisor: the Sun god[53] appeared to him in a dream and told Don that "he saw and heard everything I did. Although he was kind and polite, I awoke frightened." (Op. cit., 87.) The dream followed a period of praying before sunrise, a duty Don took on himself after initiation.

It was after his initiation that the final element of distrust was introduced into Don's beliefs about witches. He found out that "our closest kin and best friends might be Two-Hearts" (op. cit., 86).

It remains a curious and unexplained fact that even after initiation Don still believed in the giant Katcinas as supernatural figures. When they came into Oraibi he was terrified and

[53] It is tempting to regard this figure as compensation for the loss of the Katcinas.

fled to a kiva to ask protection.[54] Unfortunately, Don says nothing about his reactions when he ultimately learned that the Soyoko, too, were merely masked figures, whose actions were instigated by parents.

ANALYSIS

Don's account shows that two things happened as a result of the initiation. He was transformed from the mischievous boy who dared bring so much punishment on himself, into the boy who kept his ears open and said "yes." But also he suffered from feelings of disillusionment, resentment, and mistrust. From the point of view of personal adjustment, the initiation experience operated as one factor in building up a pattern of mistrust which, it will be seen, was an important element in Don's adult life.[55] The problem arises: How did the initiation bring about these effects?

The initiation experience was not a unique traumatic event which operated as a sole agent in creating Don's reactions. Rather, it was the climax of a long series of experiences. The new elements brought into Don's life by the initiation, and many older attitudes, were now organized into a new product.

On the negative side Don was disillusioned, in a literal sense. He found that the immediate presence of the gods was an illusion fostered by the trickery of the adults of the community, a discovery which shocked and angered him. (That is not to say that Don became an atheist: within a short time he had absorbed the sophisticated point of view that the spirits inhabit the masks when men wear them. Belief in the power of the more distant spirits was strong in his adult life.) The disillusionment, how-

[54] There is no possibility of an error in chronology here: the fact that Don went into a kiva unaccompanied indicates that he had been initiated. At this time the appearance of Soyoko was bound up with the end of Powamu (1901:118), though later Soyoko became somewhat detached from the Powamu and was brought in when needed for discipline. The connection between Powamu and Soyoko continues at First Mesa and Second Mesa (Titiev 1944:118).

[55] The possibility exists that in looking back over this period in his life Don pointed up certain features in accordance with his later experience. If this is the case, it may be said that the earlier events were of less significance in building up feelings of mistrust. The fact remains, however, that in adult life Don was a highly distrustful individual, whatever the relative weighting given to childhood and adult experience.

ever, was not a sudden one. Beginning with his feeling "sad" to see the Katcinas with their "heads" off, and passing through a period of acute conscious doubt, Don had found more and more reason to link the Katcinas with people, particularly with his own parents. (Either his parents or the Katcinas were stealing their presents back; his mother made red wafer bread which he thought only Katcinas gave.) The disillusionment had been long impending, though he had succeeded in staving it off for a time.

In the initiation, however, he had to find out. Not only was he disturbed by the loss of the immediate presence of gods, he was troubled because the Katcinas were not only ordinary men but his own relatives. Worst of all—the thing he could not face— was the fact that among them was his own father. This revelation is the culmination of a sequence of events: first he suspected a link between Katcinas and parents; then he discovered that the Katcinas had been severe at his father's request; last, he found that they were identical with relatives and with his father.

This discovery, together with the newly acquired knowledge that witches were to be found among one's own kin, links up with earlier experience. Don's listing of those whom he could trust was involved with the problem of deciding what were people's real motivations toward him. The people who treated him worst, as he saw it, always claimed to be well-intentioned. His parents had to some degree pushed off the administering of the worst punishments and the making of the worst threats onto other relatives and onto Masau'u, Soyoko, and finally the Katcinas. Now the parents themselves turned out to be the Katcinas. The effect of the initiation, combined with the events which preceded it, and Don's new information on witchcraft, was to confirm his suspicion that things were not what they seemed, that people were unfathomable, untrustworthy, and kept secret their true intentions.

In the Katcina initiation itself, the puzzle remained. What was done to him, he was told, was not aggressively intended but was for his own good. So not only resentment but also mistrust continued. It was impossible for him to fathom true intention.[56]

[56] It is probable that in a society such as Hopi, whose members are forced to conceal their aggressive reactions, the child's observation of his parents' and relatives' behavior is a major factor in building up mistrust.

As for Don's obedience, his discovery that the parents are identical with the Katcinas seems to have made it clear to him once and for all that his parents' solidarity with their own generation surmounted their affection for him.[57] It is true that his parents had previously turned him over to various relatives for punishment, and that in punishing him these relatives had acted as agents for the parents. At other times, however, in toughening Don they operated independently. And the very fact that the parents were unwilling to go as far as other relatives in punishing him indicated that in some degree he could expect leniency from them—could anticipate that their affection would prevent them from treating him as other relatives treated him. Prior to the Katcina initiation, therefore, he was not up against a blank wall of adult solidarity. After the initiation, however, the parents proved to be identical with the agents of punishment—members of the Katcina society.

Thus, the relevation of the Katcina secret, as the culmination of many experiences all pointing in the same direction, operated to produce not only obedience but also mistrust, disillusionment, and resentment.

It is now necessary to discuss the problem of the relationship of Don's experience to general Hopi experience. In this study the understanding derived from Don's case will be compared with more general statements about Hopi culture. The legitimacy of this procedure finds a basis in the ethnological material.

Contact with witchcraft lore, stories or performances of Soyoko, and initiation are universals of Hopi child experience in all except markedly Christianized Hopi families (cf. Dennis 1940:87–92). Therefore it seems fair to assume that the aspects of the behavior of parents and relatives which led to Don's puzzlement and mistrust are general in Hopi society. His experience of course, was atypical in the amount of punishment he received as the worst boy in Oraibi. What emerges from Don's ex-

[57] In other words: the parents' tie with their own generation must outweigh their personal attachment to their children. The speech of the Katcina chief at First Mesa, cited above (Steward 1931:64–65) is an indication of this. After protesting the whipping, the chief finally gives up trying to prevent it, insisting only that yucca be used instead of willow.

The Psychosocial Analysis of a Hopi Life-History

perience and from Dennis' material is a progression of discipline from mildest to most severe, depending on the resistance of the child, until finally aggression against elders was curbed. But the character of the discipline in certain of its universal aspects was always such as to create not only obedience but also distrust, disillusionment, and resentment. Thus, when a parent invoked Soyoko and the Katcinas, the supernaturals always knew about the child's misconduct. Later, when the linkage of supernatural and parent became clear to the child, these unfavorable reactions were likely to result.

Dorothy Eggan's field data, she says, bring out the generalized character of the reaction of disillusionment, both for Powamu and Katcina initiates. She gives a quotation which is said to be typical except for the quality of the English. It is from a girl, and makes a matched pair with Don's words already cited.

> "I cried and cried into my sheepskin that night, feeling I had been made a fool of. How could I ever watch the Kachinas dance again? I hated my parents and thought I could never believe the old folks again, wondering if Gods had ever danced for the Hopi as they said and if people really lived after death. I hated to see the other children fooled and felt mad when they said I was a big girl now and should act like one. But I was afraid to tell others the truth for they might whip me to death. I know now it was best and the only way to teach the children, but it took me a long time to know that. I hope my children won't feel like that" (1943:372 n.).

Since there is no reference to whipping, it is possible that the informant was initiated into Powamu.

Although the data are not all in, it seems extremely probable, from the body of information on children already at hand, that many features of Don's experience in the areas under discussion are common to the experiences of other children. Although the reactions of Hopi children undoubtedly vary in degree, there is no reason to suppose that they vary markedly in kind, in regard to the area of experience which has been treated. This is not to say that *all* aspects of initiation are identical for all children, but only that certain common elements exist. The experience undoubtedly differs in its effects in some respects for boys and for girls, for initiates who experience whipping and for those who do not, and for children who exhibit different amounts of aggressive behavior prior to initiation.

It should be kept in mind throughout that this study is concerned with individuals committed to Hopi religious beliefs and living within the framework of the sociopolitical organization described previously. Although some of the conclusions reached in this investigation *may* apply to Christian Hopi, to Hopi living under village constitution, and to Hopi who have left the reservation, none of them are considered as *necessarily* applying to these Hopi.

MARRIED LIFE

[Shortly after returning from boarding school in California, Don married Irene. (ed.)]

Deaths of Don's children.—The successive deaths of Don's four children created a series of crises in his relations with Irene and her kin. It was not the deaths which were critical, but the community's interpretation of these deaths.

Don was eager for children, but his wife was slow to conceive; the first child, a daughter, was born in 1913, after they had been married two years. Don "was glad it was now plain to everyone that Irene could have a baby and that I could be a father" (Simmons 1942:259). He obeyed all the usual restrictions prior to the birth, and afterward "was careful to raise no arguments with Irene; for such conduct is known to worry a baby and injure its health." Nevertheless, the child became ill. Hopi medicine did not help, and Don was unwilling to try white methods. The child died and Don buried it. He did not tell his wife where the grave was, "fearing that she might feel sad or angry with me sometime, go out there, and wish to die." (Op. cit., 261.) The idea here expressed, that sad feelings and contact with the dead will produce death, is the general Hopi attitude, described earlier.

A cycle of accusations and counter accusations followed. Irene's clan members implied that Don must have done something wrong to have this bad luck. He examined his own conduct and found nothing to blame. Therefore, he knew, someone must be against him. A Hopi doctor corroborated his opinion but would not identify the witch, except to say that it was a close relative of Irene's. Some unfortunate man had thus prolonged his life for four years after Masau'u called him.[58] "No doubt this wretched man had cried alone in the field, wondering what to do; but before others he appeared bright and happy. . . . I burned with anger, but I knew enough to keep my mouth shut and tried to appear cheerful." (Op. cit., 262.)

The enhancement of distrust in Don's adult life appears with great clarity in this passage. The sorcerer cannot be detected, because he is keeping up a cheerful appearance. Don's suspicions cannot be detected, because he, too, aims at concealment of emotion to protect himself. The implications for the entire society are clear: the innocent man knows neither who may be his witch enemy nor who may suspect him, however incorrectly, of witchcraft.

One of Irene's uncles made a deathbed confession that he was a witch; but he said that he was not the one guilty of the infant's death, and accused two of his brothers of being witches. One, he said, had killed the baby. Irene told Don this news. He kept his mouth shut, watched the guilty man, "avoided him as much as possible, but . . . was very polite whenever he was around, hoping thus to gain his pity and soften his spite." (Op. cit., 262.) Similar cases of confession are mentioned from Shungopavi. Wallis' informant from that village had a grandfather who told the informant that he had killed his sister's son by witchcraft, and an uncle who confessed to killing many relatives (Wallis and Titiev 1945:537–539).

More than two years elapsed before the next child was born. Don thought there was something wrong with Irene. On the other hand, her relatives blamed him. It was because of his infidelities, they said, that no more children were born. He considered that the reports of his extramarital activities were grossly exaggerated. Reciprocal feelings of blame led to quarrels and general ir-

---

[58] Titiev states (1943:550), "To prolong his own existence, each sorcerer is obliged to cause the death of one of his relatives annually." This implies that each death prolongs his life one year, rather than the four that Don allows.

ritability for Don and Irene. But they felt that the spirit of the child was waiting to be reborn as a boy[59]; they had frequent sex relations and hoped thus to persuade the spirit to come down from the ceiling and start a new baby. In 1916, when Don was twenty-six, a boy was born. This child also died, and once again Don was convinced that Irene's uncle had caused the death, whereas Irene's relatives were insistent "on the fact that I was unlucky with children." (Op. cit., 270.) Their implication was that Don was to blame in some way.

The next child, too, was slow in coming, though they could hear the spirit chirping in the roof. Don was ready to use love magic—a plant called a "penis plant," which used in moderation would increase sexual relations (Titiev 1944:206, n. 9). It was dangerous, however, and might cause a woman to become promiscuous. At the last moment he decided not to use it, and he was sure that his Guardian Spirit had prevented him from a rash experiment.

Finally, four years after the birth of his son, about 1920, Don's wife bore him a daughter. This daughter, too, died, within four months, in spite of the use of both white and Hopi medicine. For the first time Don openly expressed his accusations against his wife's kin. He turned violently on them and said: "One of you . . . has killed this child. I hope whoever did it will die of the same disease. Examine yourselves from head to foot and uncover your own guilt. I don't want to cry for I am mad" (Simmons 1942:284). Don's grandfather supported him in his accusations in a daring fashion: the evil person might kill Don, he said, but first must kill him (the grandfather). To pit one's power against a witch is a brave act among the Hopi.

Although Don attributed the death to his wife's kin, a lot of blame was directed against Don himself. The people of the village said that he was unfaithful, that his quarrels with his wife had made the babies worry and die, and that his ceremonial duties were carelessly performed. All this disturbed him profoundly.

A sidelight on Don's dilemma is cast by the death of one of

---

[59] Cf. E. and P. Beaglehole (1936:26). It is believed that the spirit of the dead child waits for rebirth in the next child, which will be of the opposite sex. This alternation did occur in Don's case.

The Psychosocial Analysis of a Hopi Life-History

his sister's children. After the sister died, the child was taken to the mission at New Oraibi. It lived only a short time. Don felt that white medical practice was responsible for its death: the navel cord was not bound properly, and the child was circumcised—no wonder it died. He could not depend on white medicine—use of it was the display of the crassest ignorance, he thought—but he believed that witchcraft was stronger than Hopi medicine.

Don's last child, a boy, was born in 1923 or 1924, when Don was thirty-three or thirty-four. Since this was the fourth child, Don hoped that, considering the significance of the fourth try, the underworld would "pity me and let the boy live." Once again Don placed his unfulfilled hopes for greatness on his child. Of this boy, he said that "although we gave him a Hopi name, I called him Alphonso—King Alphonso—and predicted that he would make a good sheepherder, a useful man, and a first-class lover of the girls." (Op. cit., 289.) It is not in his social expectations for the boy that Don's fantasy of greatness is expressed, but in the choice of the name "King Alphonso." Similarly, Don referred to his own succession to the office of chief of the Sun clan as being like that of a king.

This child, too, became ill, and there was an explosive crisis. By this time, Irene's mother was avoiding both Don and his wife, and the Fire clan people were continuing their accusations against Don. They went even farther than before. They not only held him responsible because of his infidelities and incorrect performance of ceremonial duties but "even hinted that I was a "Two-Heart, taking the lives of my children to save my own." (Op. cit., 289.) Irene charged him with being a witch, and he denied it, first to her, and then to her mother and another relative,[60] with Irene present.

[60] Don points out that though this woman, Sequapa, accused him of causing the death of his children by his infidelities, she herself was promiscuous and had been married seven times. He implies that such an accusation came oddly from this woman. Titiev confirms the reputation Don gave her (1944:57 and 40 n., and p. 35 in column headed "Remarried 4, 5, 6, .7, 8" and under heading "Real Coyote"). Farther on (1944: 125 n.), Titiev terms her "notoriously unreliable." By the time Titiev visited Oraibi, Sakwapa, as he calls her, had married again—for the eighth time.

> You women must stand on your feet, look straight into my eyes and speak the truth. You are accusing me unfairly. I am not a Two-Heart and I have never been to their secret meetings. I have no power to defend myself from them. If they wish to kill me they can do it, and eat me too. I am only a common man and not worth very much. I can't even raise my own children. When I am dead, Irene can choose a new husband and get other children. (Op. cit., 289.)[61]

He then argued his case, apparently with such force that the women had nothing to say. Even now he was not sure that his wife believed him. All that she said was, "'I want to keep my baby, but I have lost hope.' . . . I said, 'Irene, I am in an awful fix, out of step and far from my Sun Trail. I don't believe I can save our baby from this trouble.'" (Op. cit., 289–90.)

The reference to the correct trail is evident. The presumable meaning of Don's statement is that, in his frame of mind, his will would be insufficient to save the child. He moved Irene and the baby to his mother's house and rushed for a Hopi doctor the next day, but the child died while he was gone.

> . . . before I was out of sight Irene's old uncle came slyly into my mother's house and had a good chance to shoot another poison arrow into my sick child. . . . In bitterness and sorrow I said, "Now this is the last child that I shall have, for they all die. There are Two-Hearts against me, and it is no use to try any more." Those were wrong words to say, but I . . . felt that mine was a hard life indeed. Long after . . . my anger and grief were more than I could bear. (Op. cit., 290.)

Up to this time Don had tried to contain his grief and rage. Yet this restraint did not save his children. Now he gave vent to his feelings, only to find that to do so was not only ethically bad but dangerous. Don dreamed of his Guardian Spirit, who told him to stop worrying—that he, the Guide, was supporting Don. He told Don that though the Two-Hearts had harmed him, the troubled thoughts which now possessed him because of the death of the children and the accusations of witchcraft would do him no good. The Spirit said, "Brace up, and get back on the Sun Trail. . . . If you don't listen to me, I shall return . . . and judge you. Don't ever get discouraged again or say that you

---

[61] See Titiev (1944:251–52) for examples of conventional humility in speeches, of which this appears to be an example.

are going to die." (Op. cit., 290.) For Don, apparently there was no such thing as righteous anger: his actions and thoughts had brought into jeopardy his support from his Guide. After he told Irene about this dream, she seemed to stop blaming him for the deaths. Although his relations with her improved, Don continued to be not even on speaking terms with her mother.

It can be seen that the death of these four[62] children operated to produce maximal tension between Don and his wife's kin. Mutual mistrust, accusation, and counter accusation resulted finally in an open break between Don and his mother-in-law. The beliefs that infidelity, quarrelsomeness, and slovenly performance of ceremonial duties could cause illness and death, and that the sources of witchcraft were to be sought among the relatives of the ailing children, were responsible for this disruption.

It is conceivable, however, that under other circumstances these same beliefs may serve positive functions for the social system or for the individual, however disruptive they may have been in Don's case. Thus, the Hopi man may be discouraged from some of his philandering, and from quarreling with his wife over minor matters, by the fear of harming his children or, more important, by the fear of being accused of injuring them by such activities. Thus, Hopi theories about the relationship between the father's conduct and the child's health and well-being may possibly serve to maintain what has been shown to be a marital situation tension-ridden and unstable both from the point of view of the social scientist observer and the point of view of the Hopi themselves.

Furthermore, under circumstances less tragic, some of these beliefs may have an expressive function for the Hopi male, since they afford a legitimate opportunity to release aggression against his affinals in the form of mistrust and suspicion. Such aggression is engendered by the man's position as an outsider working for his wife's kin, and it may be released when minor misfortune permits the man to say that someone, probably among his wife's kin, is working against him.

[62] According to D. Eggan (1949:187), Don had *five* children who died. Why he failed to mention one to Simmons is not known.

Although the expressive function of Hopi theories of disease and death has been conceded, this type of approach must not be carried too far. For example, it could be argued that Don simply had an ungovernable amount of hatred for his in-laws, and that the children's death afforded him an opportunity to express it; that in any case he would have sought an opening for a quarrel. The actual course of events does not permit such an interpretation. Don used the first available occasion for a reconciliation with his mother-in-law.

Thus, depending on the situation, Hopi beliefs concerning infidelity, aggression, ceremonial performance, and witchcraft as factors in disease and death operate under some conditions as markedly disruptive, but under other conditions would seem to have potentialities for tension release, or for social control of a difficult relationship. These possible positive functions, however, are themselves fraught with potential tension for everyone concerned.

Don's earlier suspicions of witchcraft disrupted the fabric of his social existence, isolating him from his own grandfather and from his wife's family. By his fiftieth year, Don had suspected his "grandmother," his affinal kin, his grandfather, and finally his own mother, of witchcraft. Disease, in most cases, and death a fortiori created suspicion against the sick or dying, blame of self, and suspicion against others. To die, Don felt, was to will oneself to die, to reject the positive feelings of one's relatives, and to try to disturb them and ultimately to carry them along to the afterlife.

Any hostile feelings outside a very narrow range of permitted aggression created anxiety for his health and for the health of the object of hostility, if he was someone for whom Don had warm feelings. With Nathaniel, who was not a relative, no disastrous social rift occurred. Don had the opportunity to vent anger, though at the expense of considerable anxiety. It is possible that Don's accusations against Nathaniel served as an outlet for many pent-up feelings, that Nathaniel was a scapegoat for Don and for others. More cannot be said without fuller knowledge of Nathaniel's real standing in the community. It seems probable that by pointing out Nathaniel as a witch and standing up to Nathaniel's challenges Don succeeded in allaying

The Psychosocial Analysis of a Hopi Life-History 127

some of the suspicions which existed in Oraibi against Don himself.

The point to be stressed is that witchcraft accusations against neighbors can serve the scapegoating function without disrupting many important relations; such accusations against members of the kin group, however, undermine the most vital relationships that a Hopi has. Yet suspicion is ordinarily directed first against the immediate kin.

The dilemma surrounding aggression, is of central significance for this study. When Don has to contend with aggressive impulses he is faced with a problem which has no satisfactory solution. To express anger is to violate the Hopi moral code. If Don does so he brings social disapproval on himself. He endangers the well-being of the object of his hostility, as in the case of Norman. (This is not true if the object of aggression is himself a witch.) In addition, his own feelings are damaging to himself and may lead to fatal illness. Even when the expression of anger is justified by extraordinary circumstances, such as Don's challenging his affinal kin when they accused him of being a witch, the internal turmoil aroused is apt to be injurious. Don's Guardian Spirit warned him of this after the death of his last child. But holding in such feelings is no better solution. If Don is full of resentment, worry, or rage he is also a prey to disease. He believes that, with few exceptions, neither holding back hostile feelings nor bringing them out can bring anything but danger— danger of illness to himself, danger to the object of his feelings, and danger of social condemnation.

There is no intention in the present study to make any statements about whether or not Hopi society *is* witch-ridden. The intent of the analysis of witchcraft in Don's life is to show that the system of witchcraft beliefs in Hopi culture affords *potentialities* for disruption of interpersonal relations on a wide scale, and for the creation of powerful anxieties in the individual, when the situation is such as to give an opportunity for invoking the system of beliefs. If crops are good, rain is plentiful, health is good, community tensions are low, and white pressures little felt, then witchcraft accusations will be few. If the reverse is true, many openings for such suspicions, fears, and accusations will exist. If the Hopi should tomorrow be converted to Western scientific beliefs concerning meteorology and disease, these opportunities would no longer exist. And if the Hopi should come to believe that all disease and crop failure are the product of the activities of an incomprehensible and unknowable God, whose work is for good but whose immediate intentions are unfathomable, similarly these opportunities would cease. Such an alteration in the system of belief would have manifold consequences for social cohesion and for individual fears.

This is not to say that Hopi beliefs operate *only* to create hostility and fear. Unquestionably they operate also to channelize both. But by helping to create and channelize such apprehensions, these beliefs have consequences for the general well-being of the community.

Nor is it intended to say that witchcraft beliefs are completely disfunctional. They serve as a mode of expressing hostility, as a mode of social control, as a mode of explanation of otherwise incomprehensible phenomena, and, for those who are accused of witchcraft, as a mode of protection. But this particular system of explanations has its particular consequences, and it is these which have been traced in Don's life.

CONCLUSION: APPLICATION OF THE LIFE-HISTORY ANALYSIS

PROCEDURE

It is unnecessary to recapitulate the conclusions that have been reached about Don in the analytical sections of the preceding sections. Now we must face the question: "What is the significance of the findings in this case for an understanding of Hopi individuals and Hopi society?" Some of the logic of the application of the single case for general analysis has already emerged, but it is now necessary to make it more explicit. Clearly, the point of departure cannot be that the course of Don's life or the structure of his personality is typical. Not every Hopi has lost all his children, or has become impotent at some time, or has acted as an informant, or has become Sun chief. Nor does Don represent a determinate point in the distribution of

The Psychosocial Analysis of a Hopi Life-History 129

such personality characteristics as aggression, suspicion, or prestige drive. The generalizations made here must be in such a form that it does not matter if Don is the most extreme in all regards of all men in Oraibi, and Oraibi the most strife-ridden community. (Neither statement is necessarily true.)

To make our generalizations legitimate, we must return to the ethnological material with which we started. We have seen that the system of beliefs and values with which Don operated is that of other Hopi. It follows that their interpretations of certain situations will be similar to his, and the consequences will be similar in range. As W. I. Thomas has said, "If men define situations as real, they are real in their consequences" (Thomas and Thomas 1928:572). The prestige system and the system of role allocation that Don faced are those of Hopi society. The differential locus of responsibility and control in marriage, its tensions, and the strains of relationships to affinals are features of Hopi society. The socialization system that brought Don to conformity is to a significant degree the same for other Hopi. The uncontrollable and unpredictable features of the total environment that affected him—drought and crop failure, disease, infant mortality and other premature deaths—are chronic for all Hopi.

Lastly, relationships with American society, which caused him so much conflict, are features of the situation to which every Hopi must accommodate, though the modes of accommodation are multiple. Education in American schools and attendant value conflicts, the existence of alternatives to Hopi life in American society, American control of the stock program, the tourist trade, missionaries, and the like, are all things in respect to which the Hopi must work out a *modus vivendi*. The intensity and exact nature of the problems thus created will vary in time and will differ for individuals according to personality, social status, sex, and age. But for no Hopi can this sector of life be successfully ignored.

Although in many respects Don is a unique *person,* the beliefs with which he operates, the social system in which he lives, and the human and nonhuman environment he faces are those which our analysis of Hopi society would lead us to expect. Differences between Don's experience and his interpretations of experience, on the one hand, and our expectations on the other, are minute or nonexistent. It follows that *whenever* Hopi face certain situations, then certain typical problems arise for them. How often these problems will arise, precisely what individuals will be affected, or what solutions will be adopted, cannot be decided from this analysis. These are problems for further research. But from the ethnological material and from Don's own life a fairly satisfactory picture of the *range* of possible alternative responses to chronic features of Hopi life has been derived.

We may shift from a consideration of reactions of individuals to a consideration of the *interaction* of a group of people who share these definitions of the situation and participate in the same social system. By so doing we animate our earlier and more static picture of Hopi society. If we add variations in the situation itself—variations in weather, morbidity, mortality, and relations with American society, for example—we can see the effects of a group of individuals operating with a common definition of the situation, in a common social system, under various conditions. It is thus that we arrive at a comprehensive interpretation of the relationship of Hopi beliefs and Hopi action, and finally of Hopi society itself, in its total situation.

Hence, from what has already been said about Don I shall proceed to generalizations about Hopi reactions to recurrent situations, and from these to statements about Hopi society. In doing so, I have no intention of psychological reductionism—of "building up" Hopi society from considerations about the individual. The statements that have been made derive their meaning from the earlier summary of Hopi ethnology. But only by seeing the individual in the social network, only by understanding the range of individual reactions, can we advance to an encompassing view of Hopi society in operation.

The Individual Hopi

THE PRESTIGE-SEEKING MAN

The right to fill certain offices belongs to the senior families of various clans. Among the individuals who might be selected for such offices, some will probably be insufficiently motivated or

The Psychosocial Analysis of a Hopi Life-History

endowed for the exercise of office. The strains which might arise from such a situation are alleviated by the provision for allocating offices to the abler and more strongly motivated individuals within the families which inherit office. Of course, it is possible that some persons acquire offices that they do not want. The life-history gives us no information about such individuals. It can be said, however, that if *every* available Hopi male were unwilling to take *any* office, the society would break down. This situation has not arisen.

The life-history casts light on the other side of this problem—the man who desires prestigeful position but has no legitimate access to it. There are certain alleviations to this situation, also: the prestige that comes from being a good Hopi, and that derived from participation in important religious societies. It is clear from Don's case that these provisions do not make for the alleviation of prestige strains for everyone. It might be argued that individuals like Don are rare. Against this argument it may be pointed out that it is inconceivable that in a society with a great deal of ascribed status, such as Hopi, the combined processes of socialization and selection could bring about a *perfect* correspondence of individual aims and ability on the one hand, and social position on the other. It may be that the example of competitive American society has exacerbated the Hopi situation, but only under the conditions described in Aldous Huxley's *Brave New World* is it possible to avoid the existence of frustrated individuals like Don. Hopi history—the Oraibi split—indicates that such individuals do exist. And whenever they do, whenever a person who wishes a prestigeful position is unfavorably situated by birth, he cannot easily attain it. What are the possible results?

Such a man may simply stifle his wishes, and this doubtless happens. There was a time in Hopi society when a man might find his answer in warfare and the status of "real warrior"[63]—a peculiar, but not a disvalued status. In the old days he might have joined the curers' society, which is now extinct, and even today he might become a curer. But getting the training for such a position is probably difficult. It is not known how curers are

[63] See Titiev (1944:156–63) for a discussion of the warriors' society and the status of "real warrior." See Curtis (1922:65–67) for a possible explanation for the dying out of the warriors' society in recent years.

trained today (Titiev 1943:552 n.); probably they are taught informally by other doctors (F. Eggan, personal communication). The role of curer can perhaps be achieved regardless of birth, but it is regarded with great ambivalence. A curer may eventually find himself a social isolate rather than a man of status, because of accusations of witchcraft. This happened to a Hotevilla doctor, as we have seen.

He might, like Don, achieve a status with anthropologists as an informant, persevering in this course in spite of community opposition, isolation, and accusations of witchcraft. Similarly, he might seek other positions of status with whites on the reservation: teacher, interpreter, government employee. These, too, demand solidarity with Americans and acculturation, and cut a man off from other Hopi. He might seek a position of leadership in the community-council system of acculturated New Oraibi. He might leave the reservation. (The desire for prestige is undoubtedly not the only, or even the main, reason for so doing.) He might become an innovator or inflate his importance by claiming to be a witch. These solutions, too, would cut him off from the very group in which he hoped to attain status.

Lastly, as the history of the Oraibi split and other episodes of that period indicate, he might make a claim to a position not traditionally his, justifying his claim through a reinterpretation of mythology or a complex kinship linkage.[64] This last solution is only likely to succeed if there are other favorable conditions—quarrels over land, factional disputes over policy toward the whites, and the like. Then the claimant will have the backing of interested followers instead of remaining an isolated crank. This is not likely to be a common solution to the prestige problem, but it has been chosen at various times. It demands a willingness to face antagonism and accusations of witchcraft. But Yokioma, a Hopi leader of a schism, did face them, and so did Don as in-

[64] E. C. Parsons (1939:169) has taken a different stand. In the pueblos generally, she says, "Office means work rather than power so that encroachment on others is not a temptation." Although this may be true in many cases, Hopi history gives clear evidence of rival claimants for position, who validate their claims in a variety of ways. Consult Titiev (1944:73–86, 211) for such incidents in Oraibi and Hotevilla. See Stephen (1936:949–52, 1020, 1046–47) and E. C. Parsons' editorial comments (in Stephen 1936:1047–48) concerning possible claimants to the chieftainship at Walpi in 1892–1894.

formant. Once schism starts, the lack of tight political control makes its consequences for social cohesion drastic indeed.

Analysis of Don's motivations and of Hopi social structure indicates, therefore, that if a man is born into the "wrong" place, he can find only a limited number of solutions to the problems raised by his wishes for prestige. None is likely to be completely satisfactory to the individual, and one, the last mentioned, is decidedly disruptive to the group. It is not *how often* such individuals arise that interests us, but *what situations* they may create.

THE PROBLEM OF MISTRUST

It is exceedingly probable that Hopi socialization techniques, effective though they are in producing conformity, leave the individual with a lifelong basis for mistrust concerning the motivations of others. The behavior of joking relatives who claim to be affectionate, parents' fobbing off of responsibility for severe punishment onto other relatives and onto Soyoko, the use of the Katcina figures for rewards and the withholding of rewards, parents' concealment of aggressive feelings in the presence of others, and the initiation experience combine to create in the child's mind a grave difficulty in interpreting the true intentions of others, particularly as regards aggression. This early-created attitude is continually fed by later experience. The concealment of one's own aggression and the inability to detect the evil-intentioned and witches, who are said to conceal their own aggression, make for serious mistrust of others. The nature of witchcraft beliefs, which localize the damaging individual among one's relatives, and more commonly in the more immediate kin group—the very people on whom one depends for emotional security, economic support, and solidarity—put the area of mistrust in the most damaging possible place and tend to bring about a real psychosocial isolation.[65] Although the character structure and life experience of individuals will make for great variations in the amount of such feelings, it is improbable that anyone can escape some situations that mobilize mistrustfulness.

[65] The Navaho, on the other hand, though they do suspect immediate kin of being witches, also direct their hostility and suspicion against vaguer figures—unknown witches from other areas (Kluckhohn 1944:55–56).

THE PROBLEM OF AGGRESSION

The creation of hostility.—In the system of explanatory beliefs, the inevitable misfortunes of Hopi life, such as crop failure, disease, and infant or premature death, are interpreted as due in part to the hostility of others: to their bad thoughts or active practice of witchcraft. (Things would be entirely different if the Hopi believed that their misfortunes came from an unknowable God, from the Devil, from breaking taboos, or from their own bad thoughts alone.) There are other situations, also, that mobilize hostility—the strains of the marital situation and of relationships with affinals, others' accusations of witchcraft or misbehavior, and the like. Thus, though the *amount* of hostility will vary from individual to individual and from situation to situation, there are chronic features of Hopi life that mobilize hostility. This is true of any social order, but in Hopi life hostility arises not only from certain characteristics of interpersonal relations but also out of the interpretations of a variety of natural catastrophes.

The disposition of hostility.—Whatever the origin of hostile and aggressive impulses in any particular case, their existence creates an insoluble problem for any Hopi. If he suppresses them, he may damage himself: both because bad thoughts themselves are harmful—are pathogenic agents, in fact—and because they render an individual particularly susceptible to the effects of witchcraft. Furthermore, simply having aggressive thoughts may damage the object of those thoughts far beyond the conscious intent of the man who holds them. One's own bad thoughts may seriously injure or kill a spouse or a child. Worry or grief may similarly damage the person who is disturbed, and may affect the health of his children. If the bad thinker is a ceremonial participant, his thoughts may damage the whole community. Release of hostility only exacerbates these situations. It hurts the man who releases the hostility, hurts those against whom he releases it, and alienates him from the community, under the opprobrium of being *kahopi,* evil-intentioned, and the like. To express hostility or to conceal it alike may produce accusations of witchcraft, particularly since in a situation in which every man

The Psychosocial Analysis of a Hopi Life-History

knows he conceals certain reactions it becomes very easy to impute those reactions to others.

Consequently, if one is aggressive, or if one has experienced misfortune, the easiest way out is to accuse someone else before one becomes the object of accusations. This process is somewhat curbed by the belief that aggressive behavior toward a witch does not harm the witch but helps him. This and the fear of being damaged by the witch inhibit such accusations, but under severe "provocation" the accusations break through. Thus, cycles of blame and counterblame are set up.

Gossip, on the other hand, since it is not experienced by the gossiper as direct aggression, is a safer outlet and is exceedingly common.

It is not implied that all the Hopi towns and all their component individuals are continually at the boiling point. Nor is it implied that individuals react uniformly to the problem of aggression. The range of responses may run from psychosomatic illness to overt accusations of witchcraft.

Furthermore, the concept of the witch is illuminated by the foregoing. For as the Hopi see it, the witch is the person who escapes the conflict created by aggression. Although he is threatened with ultimate damnation and with possible isolation in this life, he may be aggressive without fearing to hurt himself. Under these circumstances, it is possible that the fantasies about witches have undercurrents of envy, and that a man might find certain attractions in the idea of being a witch. (There are no data for estimating how many people may actually believe themselves to be witches.)

Lastly, it is evident that illness, one's own aggression, and that of others all create great anxiety in Hopi individuals, more than in some other social systems. These situations lead to feelings of helplessness, since protection against witchcraft is slight.

CONFORMITY

In this light, it is clear how the Hopi solve the problem of conformity and of social control, at least in any ordinary crisis. The process of socialization that has been described, culminating in the initiation procedure, provides the foundation for conformity. The dangers of aggression, for oneself and others, and the possibility of social isolation through the gossip of others all direct the individual in nonaggressive, traditionalistic, and coöperative paths.

COMPENSATIONS

The conclusion must not be drawn that life in a Hopi situation is unbearable. It must not be forgotten that adherence to the Hopi way provides insurance for health, economic security, and life; that ceremonial activity is unquestionably a rich and rewarding experience; that under favorable circumstances this way of life may give very considerable security to individuals.

DIFFERENTIAL REACTIONS

Once again it must be emphasized that these conclusions do not tell us *how many* of *what kind* of reactions will occur, nor do they tell us what kind of personalities Hopi have. They entitle us only to say that *whenever* there are prestige-driven Hopi, sick Hopi, aggressive Hopi, those individuals face a particular set of problems to which there is a certain range of responses, some of which reintegrate the individual in the group, and some of which are disruptive of his group relationships.

Hopi Society

Thus far this study has been concerned with the reactions of individual Hopi. Now the question arises: "If a group of people with these reactions lives in the kind of social system that has been described, what are the consequences?"

The Hopi social system is best conceived of as an unstable equilibrium. Its political, economic, and kinship features, its system of beliefs and values, its human and nonhuman environment, and the reactions of individual members to all these features have been examined. The products, taken together, make for a system which operates rather differently under different conditions. Good weather, plentiful crops, a low disease rate, and a minimum of pressures from American society tend to produce coöperation in a social system with minimal means of coercion, conformity to tradition, and feelings of good-will and mutual support. An increase in any area of potential misfortune will start minor cycles of blame, mistrust, and the like, within various groups, but pressures such as gossip and the isolation of deviants will still prevent the breakdown of the system. If, however, individuals arise whose deviance cannot be handled by these techniques, in situations in which it becomes possible for them to mobilize factions, then very serious tensions will arise and perhaps ultimately a town will split. The factions, however, have it in their power to reconstitute new communities. The important fact is that Hopi society has no second line of defense against the innovator, the political dissident, or the like. It is this fact, together with the tendency of Hopi belief to direct blame for catastrophe toward individuals, rather than toward gods or nature, that makes us describe the society as unstable in equilibrium. Under one set of conditions Hopi beliefs and values operate to produce security, conformity, and stability; under another set they produce everything from psychosomatic disease to community fission.[66]

An analogy from American society may dispel this apparent paradox. There are elements in the American value system that emphasize independence, self-sufficiency, responsibility, and enterprise as norms to which individuals should conform. These norms also emphasize the individual's responsibility for his own fate. Under favorable economic conditions these values lead to vigorous effort, enterprise, entrepreneurial activity, and inventiveness. In an economic depression, however, they lead to self-blame, guilt, and depression. Although it is true that the tendency to blame the economic system rather than oneself may increase in an economic depression, the ideology is surprisingly persistent under bad conditions (cf. Lynd 1937:esp. 489–90; and Bakke

[66] For an anthropological interpretation which in several respects parallels that presented here, see Aitken (1930:esp. 372–87). Her views on certain strains in the Hopi social system, on the position of the nonconformist, and on the effects of Hopi beliefs are similar to those developed here. Nelson's novel, *Rhythm for Rain* (1937), presents, in fictional form, a similar interpretation of the different ways that Hopi society operates under favorable and unfavorable conditions.

1940a, 1940b). Similarly, the Hopi react to alterations in their situation in terms of the definition of the situation, cognitive and evaluative, which participation in their society has given them.

It is in the light of this interpretation that various accounts of the Hopi may be seen as complementary rather than divergent. If an observer studies a demoralized Hopi community, he may find witchcraft, suspicion, and hostility to be the more prominent part of the picture. In another Hopi community, under different conditions, coöperation, lack of physical coercion, and peaceful behavior will be more noticeable. Neither aspect will ever be completely absent in any community. Furthermore, the scientist may phrase his problem to concentrate on whichever aspect he wishes. In personality psychology, for example, we may choose the same case to illustrate both the constructive work of the ego and the effects of emotional stress. So, depending on the town selected for study and the problem selected for analysis, either aspect of Hopi society or the interrelationship of the aspects may be profitably examined. It is not a question of which problem is more "correct," nor is it a question of mutually exclusive alternatives. The validity of the present interpretation of the Hopi can be checked by a study of the amount of disruptive or cohesive action in the community. If we find that the community that should be least disrupted is most disrupted, or vice versa, then this interpretation is challenged. With other treatments of the Hopi, a careful evaluation of the body of data employed and the precise form in which the problems are stated tends to show that, by and large, the studies are concerned with different things and different problems and are not actually contradictory. In the context of the interpretation of Hopi society presented here, it becomes possible to see the contribution which each study makes to the understanding of the Hopi, and the way in which the studies fit together.

6 THE BALANCE OF THREAT AND SECURITY IN MESOAMERICA: SAN CARLOS

John Gillin

The cultures of San Carlos may be regarded as systems which provide a balance between the threats and anxieties of life as seen through the local cultural screen, on the one hand, and means and methods available for "handling" such threats. In the following table these patterns of recognized threats and patterns of cultural response are compiled in summary form.

Due in part to the differences in pattern between Indian and Ladino, the members of the two castes are faced with somewhat different problems. The threat to each other, resulting from the caste definition of the situation, has been thoroughly explored by Dr. Melvin Tumin.

Here in general, we may say that the two cultures, as it were, face the threatening problems of their respective situations in somewhat different ways. This may be summarized by a comparison of the two "orientations" or "ethoses," as set out summarily in the following table.

FROM *The Culture of Security in San Carlos,* 1951, by John Gillin, by permission of Middle American Research Institute, Tulane University, and by permission of the author.

TABLE XI
INDIAN AND LADINO ORIENTATIONS OF CULTURE
SAN CARLOS

Item	Indian	Ladino
General	Passive. To effect peaceful adjustment of men to universe, come to terms with universe.	Aggressive. Control universe by man; dominate it.
Nature of universe	Controlled by unseen powers or forces, ongoing, immutable. Man can do nothing to change the powers and the rules by which the universe is operated.	Forces of the universe, including "supernatural," are amenable to human manipulation; God, saints, and other unseen powers have personalities and can be handled on a personality basis.
General response to universe	Man must learn certain patterns of action and attitude to bring himself into conformity with the universal scheme of things. By doing this much punishment may be avoided. Some misfortune is the lot of all men but it may be minimized by carefully learning and following the cultural rules. Force is useless against "God's will," etc.	Every individual has the right to attempt to control the universe, including other men. Human ideas and beliefs are more effective than artifacts. Destructive force even to death, is legitimate and ultimate technique. Even God can be forced to favor the strong.
Individual and group	Individual exists as member of group. Man, not any individual, is highest value. Individual prospers as group prospers. Individual's function is to promote group.	Individual personality has highest value, although this value does not attach to all persons equally. Group exists to promote individual rather than reverse.
Routine	Uninterrupted routine practice of the patterns of life is most satisfying.	Routine boring and dissatisfying. Struggle and oscillation of power is zestful.
Cultural range	Spatially limited. Local community is "the world."	Spatially more expanded. Have kinship, political, eco-

Item	Indian	Ladino
	Although all Indian men have frequently seen other parts of the country on trading trips and during conscript service, they do not identify. Other areas and other peoples and cultures are not actually thought of as a real part of the universe. Temporally limited. No remembered or recorded past, glorious or otherwise. Life goes on in timeless present. Home community contains all goals one can expect to achieve.	nomic ties with other communities. Concept of nationality. Wish to achieve status and power on national scene and even in United States, Europe and other parts of the world. Home town is stepping stone to something better. Temporally more expanded. Historical details and genealogies vague, but strong tradition of glorious past conquest, etc.
Land	Highly valued, but a man must work it with his own hands even though he can pay helpers. Non-agricultural occupations followed to provide money to buy land.	Valued as source of income but personal labor on land is irksome and disgraceful. Control of land, tenants, workmen is means of social and political power as well as economic power.
Material things	Direct approach. Tills milpa, cuts wood, gathers grass, makes pottery, etc. with own hands. Physical weariness from toil accepted as fact of life; carries social approval.	Indirect approach. Things used as instruments or objects of control. Labor disgraceful. Never carries a burden, never walks, never works with hands if avoidable.
Relations to other human beings	Adjustive and permissive. Society unstratified, except by age. Leadership statuses (such as mayor-domo, principal, etc.) thought of as obligations to society. Everyone who follows patterns and precepts receives status sometime during life. No competition or striving for distinction. Envy and competitiveness regarded as anomaly or crime. One category of magical ill-	Ordering and dominating. Social stratification into classes and castes. Statuses of leadership and distinction sharply competitive. Ceremonial politeness to other Ladinos. Domineering behavior toward persons of lower status. Factions and feuds even in same class. Gossip, oaths, insults of aggressive types common. Strong verbal protests. Individual strives for promi-

Item	Indian	Ladino
	ness is envidia, perpetrator of which may be killed with impunity. Leader never gives orders to others, merely imparts superior knowledge. Group decisions by consensus rather than fiat or majority vote. Out-group relations with Ladinos handled by avoidance and submission, within limits.	nence, often assisted by his family. Techniques of overt and indirect aggression cultivated. High status gives right to plan and order subordinates' behavior. Caudillo pattern.
Attitudes toward women and children	Man and woman a cooperative partnership in adjustment to universe. Wives share honors and responsibilities of men in prominent statuses. Bickering between mates uncommon; withdrawal rather than friction in cases of incompatibility. Sex necessary, but natural. Use of sex for exploitation uncharacteristic. Light child discipline.	Marriage important from status point of view. Women's influence indirect. Women do not share with men in public affairs. Man dominates family including wife. Children dependent upon father's status or wealth. Heavier child discipline. Sex used for exploitation of others; sex regarded as necessary for men, not for women.
Religion	General permeation; universe not compartmentalized. Christian deities viewed as a group of saints, etc., and approached by group of humans, not individually. Medicine men have familiar non-Christian spirits. Magical curing, divinations, planting ceremonies, etc., viewed as integral part of life adjustment. Aggression by witchcraft common. Men, grouped into "commissions," cofradías, etc. most active in religion.	Religion compartmentalized and differentiated from secular life. Christian deities approached individually. Individual soul important, especially in "immortal" aspects. Half-belief in magic as a technique when all else fails. Aggression by witchcraft rare. Women most active in religion.

In general, then, the Indian orientation is passive and adjustive, whereas the Ladino attitude toward the universe and other men is aggressive and conflictual. So long as the Indian stays within the framework of his culture, he is less prone to be beset by anxieties and frustrations, which the Ladino culture almost inevitably creates. This seems to be borne out, not only by ethnological material, interviews and life histories, but also the results of Rorschach investigations.[1]

In San Carlos the Rorschach material and observational material alike show what appear to be some fundamental differences, at least in the public, social, or cultural personalities of Indians and Ladinos, respectively. For both castes the range of the culture is distinctly limited and, as might be expected, this is reflected in a relatively restricted personality type in both castes. Neither Indians nor Ladinos show on the adult level much original intellectual ability, freedom in solving problems outside the patterns of the culture, or imagination.

On the Indian side of the line the personality of the typical individual, provided his cultural routine is not interfered with by outside individuals or forces, is relatively more secure and perhaps better integrated than that of the Ladino. In some respects the Indian personality might be considered compulsive. At any rate there is evident what would be called in other countries the compulsive following of the approved patterns of the culture without any strong motivation toward specific rewards, distinctions, prominence, or the like. This is especially evident in the work patterns, and the Indians, male and female alike, follow with the utmost diligence the standard routines, such as milpa work, pottery making, corn grinding, palm braiding for straw hats, and other activity patterns. The same careful following of pattern is likewise evidenced in ceremonial activities, such as fiestas, cofradía ceremonies, magicial cures, and so on. For a great many reasons it seems obvious that the Indian maintains a feeling of personal security so long as he stays within the framework of his culture and is enabled to follow the pathways without deviation which it lays down for him. The adult personality is, on the surface at least, characterized by calmness and com-

[1] Much detailed evidence for the following analysis is presented in Billig, Gillin, and Davidson 1947–48:364 ff.

paratively little affect, or show of emotion, in comparison with the Ladinos. However, the typical Indian personality does not show a neurotic constriction of emotion or the flat schizoid reaction. The abrazo is given, although not with a great show of enthusiasm; patting of the back and the arm, and handshaking are indulged in without any noticeable stiffness. Also, joking is characteristic although always in a restrained manner when the individual is sober. The belly laugh and hearty laughter of any type is uncharacteristic. Likewise there is normally little show of aggressiveness on the part of Indians. That Indians are capable of aggressive actions is shown by many incidents, however. Several cases are on record of Indians attacking each other with sticks or machetes; these cases are always precipitated by some rank breach of the code, such as a man catching his wife with a lover, gross interference on the part of a father-in-law, or something of the sort. Overt aggression usually appears only when the individuals are under the influence of alcohol. That there are aggressive feelings against Ladinos for the restrictions and punishments which the caste system has laid upon the Indians is evidenced by such things as violent attacks made by Indians on certain Ladinos at the time of the 1944 revolution and by the fact that several of the "devils" who are supposed to snatch souls in espanto are called by Ladino names.

Although one would expect that a constricted character structure of this sort, somewhat compulsive and not given to overt expression of emotions, would be the product of an authoritarian type of child-rearing, the fact is that the first five or six years at least of the Indian's life seem to be quite permissive. Children are nursed whenever they cry and they are not expected to develop sphincter control until able to understand language. Babies are not wrapped in constraining clothes or cradles and, in fact, do not ever wear diapers as a general rule. Small children are hardly ever physically punished and are given the utmost freedom to explore their bodies, the furnishings of the house, and their surroundings. However, they are always under supervision either of one of the parents or of an older sibling in order to protect them from accident. But this protection is not given through punishment but simply through removing the child from the source of danger and directing its attention upon some other

The Balance of Threat and Security in Mesoamerica 145

object. For example, if the child crawls toward the fire, he will be lifted up and placed on another part of the floor and given some object to play with, but he will not be spanked or switched. There is no weaning trauma nor, in fact, any other startling experience through which the normal child goes as he emerges from infancy into childhood.

Our Rorschach and observational material indicate that children up to about the age of 18 have a much more out-going type of personality than they develop as adults. They show more imagination than their elders and a much greater readiness to experiment with adjustive techniques not in the pattern. It has been our opinion that part of the constrictive and relatively rigid character structure of the adult is the result of inhibitions inculcated by the caste system rather than the training of early childhood. Boys and girls are inducted into adult patterns gradually and begin to be useful workers in their respective spheres about the age of eight. Motivation based upon respect from others instigates the child to imitate the work patterns of adults, and the adult attitude is that children should not be "forced" but that they should be given responsibilities and allowed to perform activities which are commensurate with their physical and mental development.

It is, I think, noteworthy that what might be considered neuroses within the Indian framework are of two general types which can be interpreted consistently with this view of Indian personality. The principal neurotic manifestation is phrased as espanto or susto (magical fright). It is of importance that from the native point of view this personality upset is believed to be caused by a sudden fright or startle. In other words, the personality can be thrown off balance by any incident which interferes with the smooth performance of the routine patterns. In analyzing a number of cases and cures it also is evident that the person in this condition suffers from heavy anxiety regarding his social relationships, that is, the person with espanto is always out of touch in some way with his fellows and feels that he has lost integration in the social group. The other principal neurotic manifestation is envidia. This literally means envy and is believed to be caused by witchcraft whereby the victim is magically and secretly attacked by someone who is envious of him or otherwise aggressive toward him. In view of the fact that overt aggression is either repressed or constricted in the culture pattern, it is not surprising that anxiety concerning aggression should take the form of fears concerning sub rosa magical attacks. It is also noteworthy that whereas elaborate patterns are available for warding off, curing and carrying out magical attacks, there are no clear-cut patterns of overt aggression in the culture. When an individual attacks another physically, he uses whatever weapon may be at hand, and the attack exhibits a sort of random trial and error flailing about of the arms. This is in contrast to the very careful procedures used in witchcraft.

In summary it seems to be clear that adult Indians at the present time are little adaptable to changes in the situation. By the time they have reached maturity their habit patterns, both overt and non-overt, have been so firmly established that any deviation from the routine tends to upset the personality integration and to create an insecure feeling in the individual. However, the young individuals are quite plastic. The fact that this is so seems to account for the comparative ease with which Indians pass into the Ladino status if they are removed from their Indian cultural environment while young and given an opportunity to learn Ladino patterns, in other communities.

The Ladino personality structure in San Carlos, at least, is also constrictive. This, however, seems to be the result of isolation and of the comparative poverty of local Ladino culture in areas outside its home grounds. In contrast to the manifested personality characteristics of Indians, the Ladinos show much more emotionalism. Not only are likes and dislikes more demonstratively expressed, but the average Ladino is characterized by mood swings which range from depression and helplessness to feelings of high euphoria. Consistent with this is the impression that the typical Ladino is basically much less secure than the typical Indian. He has no feeling of certainty that any of his available culture patterns will produce satisfactions which he expects and he is uncertain about their effectiveness when practiced outside the community. The result is that many Ladinos tend to withdraw from or be hesitant about interaction in the larger world outside, but, since they wish to adjust to the larger world, this produces feelings of frustration and inadequacy. Ladinos are much more aggressive, at least on the overt level, both toward themselves and toward members of the other caste. This aggressiveness can be interpreted in the light of the frustrations which Ladinos face. Furthermore, the Ladinos show a higher percentage of hypochondriasis, psychosomatic ailments, neurotic twitches, and the like. That Ladinos habitually get more drunk more often than do Indians seems to indicate that they find release from anxiety and frustration in alcohol as well as in hypochondriasis and aggressive outbreaks. Many Ladinos resort to cures for relief from magical fright and witchcraft, but do so with an ambivalent attitude. In other words, Ladinos only half believe in these conditions and the measures taken to alleviate them, but this tendency among Ladinos indicates again their willingness to try anything for relief from anxiety of frustration feelings.

Child care among Ladinos is fairly permissive as compared with middle class patterns in Europe or America of 25 years ago, but it is probably more authoritarian than the Indian system. Within the last few years some upper class Ladino families have instituted formula feeding on schedule, rigid cleanliness training, and so on—patterns which have been acquired from the great world outside—but these are not characteristic of the Ladino pattern as a whole up to the present. However, the Ladino child is usually dressed in diapers and underpants, earlier attempts at cleanliness training are instituted by parents, and the authority of the father in particular is more strict. Although small babies are given the breast whenever it is desired, the typical Ladino mother tries to wean her child by the end of the first year and does not permit the child to soil the house once it is able to crawl about. Also the higher one goes in the Ladino class system, the greater is the rigidity of child training.

Ladino children are sent to school at the age of six and subjected to fairly rigid schoolmaster's discipline which emphasizes the value of Ladino life. Proportionately fewer Indian children go to school, but the transition from the Indian home to the schoolroom is more of a trauma for the Indian child than for the Ladino, because the teachers have traditionally taken a negative attitude toward their Indian pupils who are frequently unable to understand or speak Spanish by the time they arrive in school. If the Indian child suffers a greater shock in going to school, he usually escapes from it within a relatively short time. Thus the school discipline has had up to now a relatively insignificant influence on the development of Indian personality patterns, because few Indian children enter school, and most of those who do drop out after the first year or two. With the Ladino, on the other hand, the child goes through the three or four years of elementary school offered locally, and it is the ideal pattern then to send children away to other communities where they can at least get through the sixth year. Thus the typical Ladino is subjected to at least six years of the compulsive type of discipline which has been characteristic of Guatemalan elementary schools up until very recently. At the end of this time most of the Ladinos come back to their home town. Indian children of this age have already worked into the adult patterns which they expect to follow throughout their lives. The boys are helping their fathers in the fields and on pottery-peddling trips. The girls have mastered the techniques of the woman's world. The young Ladino, however, emerging from school is provided with none of the patterns which he will expect to use as an adult, except literacy. The result is that there is a period of adolescent adjustment for Ladinos which does not have a counterpart among the Indians. During this time the girl receives some instruction as to how to manage a house and waits hopefully for marriage. The boy seeks to find a place for himself in the Ladino adult world. Since there is a wider variety of patterns open to the Ladino men than there is to Indians, a certain element of choice is involved here rather than merely the safe road of following one's father's footsteps. Since manual work is not reguarded as desirable for Ladino males, but rather manipulative activities, either in managing agricultural or business enterprises, the adolescent Ladino male is often at loose ends. He is not mature enough to assume the managerial role nor are the patterns whereby he may do so clear, unless he belongs to an established family or is able to develop personal contacts. The rather vague and often unobtainable goals of Ladino culture have been implanted in his thinking by the school and by his fellows. Just as is the case with the Indian youngsters, Ladino youngsters also show more malleability and plasticity than do their elders. By the time a Ladino boy has reached maturity he has either found a place in the local system which usually does not appear to be entirely satisfactory to him, or he has moved outside the community to seek his rewards in the outside world. At any rate those who remain suffer from feelings of anxiety, frustration, and insecurity which we have already mentioned. The high degree of verbosity which many observers have mentioned in connection with Ladino personality traits can, I think, be interpreted as partly related to the comparative insecurity of the real world. Even in a small isolated community like San Carlos, Ladinos are given to living, as one might say, on a partly fanciful level in which argumentation and discussion about ideals and ideas takes up a good deal of time. In rural communities the ideas themselves may be comparatively naïve but they are usually discussed with great affect. As a North American would say, they are taken more seriously than would seem to be justified. Since the culture of the Ladinos does not offer many and sure rewards when their attention is directed primarily toward things, it is perhaps to be expected that fantasy reward on the level of verbalization may serve as a compensation to some extent. If one cannot manipulate things to his own satisfaction, he can at least manipulate ideas or emotions. Thus the Ladino is often a violent partisan when it comes to any matter of opinion or policy.

7 MENTAL DISORDER AND SELF-REGULATING PROCESSES IN CULTURE: A GUATEMALAN ILLUSTRATION

Benjamin D. Paul

The concept of culture, like the proverbial elephant, has been seen from many sides. To some, culture appears primarily as a pattern. To others, it is a process, a frame of perception, a precipitate of history, a mechanism for survival. These are all mutually reconcilable. The particular view depends on one's line of vision and on one's immediate purposes. From where I stand, and for purposes of this meeting, culture can be viewed as a type of "self-correcting" mechanism.

Culture, if it is in working order, lends purpose and direction to the lives of those it serves. All forms of organization, however, are achieved at some price. The costs may be widely distributed throughout the society in the form of strains built into the "typical" personality, or they can be borne disproportionately by a minority of individuals, those typed as "deviants" by their fellows.

My concern here is with the deviant person, and more especially with a process in group behavior which first works in the direction of pushing the individual deeper into deviancy and then, in response to a behavioral signal from the deviant, reverses its direction to bring the disturbed individual back into a better state of balance with society. It is this reversible process which suggests comparison with self-regulating mechanisms, such as the thermostat or the governor of a steam engine.

Abstractly and generally considered, the conception is both

FROM Benjamin D. Paul, "Mental Disorder and Self-Regulating Processes in Culture: A Guatemalan Illustration," 1953, in *Interrelations Between the Social Environment and Psychiatric Disorders,* pages 51–67, Milbank Memorial Fund, by permission of the author and publishers.

Mental Disorder and Self-Regulating Processes

simple and familiar. But its applicability to the socio-cultural sphere remains to be clarified. It is my hope that presentation of a detailed and concrete case will help to communicate the conception of self-regulating forces within culture and possibly stimulate productive comparisons. The case that follows will also raise other problems such as the relation of social role structure to individual deviance in simple societies, and the nature of the interchange between cultural and personality dynamics.

When my wife and I settled down as anthropologists in an Indian village on Lake Atitlán in Guatemala, we made the mistake of hiring the wrong girl as household helper. She soon proved inadequate in many respects, but it was no easy matter to discharge her in view of the fact that her father was an important person whose good will we were eager to preserve. We did manage to dismiss her on some face-saving pretext, proceeding with caution before hiring another girl. After a careful inspection of the field of choice, we selected Maria, the central figure in this case, a person who eventually deserted our household, abandoned her own baby and suffered a psychotic episode.

These unexpected events occurred after Maria had been working with us daily for ten weeks. During this time she had proved herself a good helper in the house, a lively and engaging companion, and a good source of information, if not always a source of good information. We came to know her as well as we knew anyone in the village, recording observations on what turned out to be a pre-morbid period in her life.

Who was Maria? She was a very attractive girl of eighteen, commanding attention even in a village renowned for its beautiful women. She was separated from her husband—her second—at the time she came to work for us and had a nine-month old baby girl. She was the daughter of a man named Manuel, who was, in some ways, an "operator." Manuel and a brother were early orphaned and raised by a kinsman who was a strict disciplinarian and taskmaster. Manuel's brother turned out to be a ne'er-do-well who was living with his seventh wife, and barely eking out a living at the time we arrived. Manuel had enjoyed better fortune. He had married strategically, thereby acquiring a house and land, and had managed to become a shaman, one of about six in the village. Shamanism can be a road to power, and though there was some question as to the legitimacy of his credentials (supernatural signs), he exerted a fair amount of influence in community councils. He was also regarded by some as a man who was lazy, and who sought to escape honest effort in a culture which extols the virtue of diligent labor in the fields. His wife's original inheritance had dwindled somewhat under his mediocre management.

Maria's mother came from one of the wealthy families with a considerable admixture of *ladino* (non-Indian) blood. She was a handsome woman of lighter-than-average complexion, a conscientious housekeeper, and a dutiful wife. But her life was punctuated by violent arguments with her husband, typically touched off by Manuel's habit of coming home drunk from a *fiesta,* and by her complaints that he was dissolving her inheritance in drinking debts. Manuel finally gave up drinking and took to smoking a pipe.

Maria was the oldest of six surviving children. Three children had died in infancy before Maria was born. According to relatives and neighbors, Maria had received much attention and affection as a baby. She was a sickly child, requiring more than ordinary care. When she was old enough to travel, her father took her on trips and to the fields as his traveling companion, a privilege commonly reserved for sons rather than daughters. But later on her father's indulgent attitude changed to one of criticism and punishment. He scolded and beat her for carrying tales ("She was always a great liar and troublemaker"), for her laziness around the house, and for getting into fights with her younger siblings.

Another girl, Juana, was born when Maria was fifteen months old. When Maria came to work for us, Juana was sixteen or seventeen years old. She was married, lived with her husband in her parents' home, and was pregnant with her first child. There was no love lost between Maria and Juana. They had a history of frequent quarrels and had even been rivals for the same beau. While Maria had more attractive features, Juana's lighter skin color carried more prestige. In marked contrast to Maria, Juana was a "good daughter," conforming to cultural expectations which distinguished sharply between the behavior prescribed for men and the behavior prescribed for women. Juana was obedient and respectful toward her parents, worked hard about the house, seldom sought to leave the house for idle purposes, and remained properly reticent in the presence of outsiders.

Some of Maria's traits suggested psychological affinity with masculine rather than with feminine standards. In a community where Maya is the native language, most of the women quickly forget what Spanish they learn as girls in grade school and feel ashamed to use the little they can remember. Men, in contrast, find Spanish useful in their commerce with the outside world. Maria not only had a fair command of Spanish but seemed to take pride in using it. She used her charm to attract men, but her attitude toward them was essentially competitive and hostile. By local standards, she was immodest and aggressive. She was disobedient and resisted authority; at home she was quarrelsome, dominating her younger siblings and engaging in arguments with her father.

Her first marriage lasted only a few months; her husband had accused her of carrying on flirtations with other men. Her second marriage, which had dissolved before we arrived, had been to a culturally marginal man of unstable character. The son of a wealthy family, he had been educated in the capital of Guatemala and had become a schoolteacher, but later lost his job because of excessive drinking. Maria quarreled with her husband and her mother-in-law, the marriage broke up, and she returned with a baby to live with her parents, having no other place to go.

Maria "happened" to be around when we needed a helper. Men and children visited our house freely from the beginning, but women and girls, deterred by fear of public disapproval, tended to keep a polite distance. Maria was one of our first female visitors. She volunteered her assistance about the house and kitchen and immediately began to help us with our Spanish. We thought the decision to hire her was ours, but in retrospect, it seems that Maria in fact selected us.

She was vivacious, gossipy, and an avid informant, but she embroidered nimbly. She was witty and a very clever mimic, but would occasionally lapse into morose silences. She seldom assumed a submissive attitude. When she was corrected in her household duties, she would respond by correcting our Spanish or by withdrawing into dignified silence.

Maria had a flair for the gruesome and the destructive. Once she helped a young man remove a chigger-like insect from his toe. This is done with a needle. She laughed and joked about sticking the needle into his eyes and all over his body. Another time she gave us an account of a celebrated murder that had occurred when she was only a few years old. With the aid of an accomplice, one man had killed another, over a woman. The culprits were apprehended and sent to the penitentiary, where the accomplice eventually died. These were the facts, and Maria presented them, but she allowed her imagination to embellish the story with a wealth of colorful and improbable details. According to her vivid version, the assassin hacked up the body, split the head open, extracted the brain and put it in his pocket. The victim was also shot but wasn't killed until he received the fifth bullet. The accomplice did not merely die during his imprisonment, according to Maria; he was hacked to death, just as the original victim had been.

Maria worked for us part-time, and we paid her weekly. Sometimes she brought along her daughter and let her crawl about our floor. Most of the time the baby was left in the care of her mother or younger siblings. Their house was only a short distance from ours, and Maria could go home to breast-feed the baby. She seemed, in general, to be quite unconcerned about her child.

In our house, where she could escape the protective vigilance of her kinsmen, she had the rare opportunity of meeting the men who came to visit us. This enabled her to carry on conversations and surreptitiously arrange to run away and marry José, one of our informants. Like her previous husband, José was culturally marginal and was hoping to leave his native village when he could find employment in the capital. To disguise their plans, both Maria and José assured us that they wouldn't think of marrying since they were cousins and that their sustained conversations had to do with intrigues involving third parties. One evening when we left Maria alone for a moment, washing the supper dishes, she disappeared, eloping with José to his house. In Maria's village, at the present time, eloping with the boy and leaving the unsuspecting parents is the dominant form of marriage. In this case, Maria found it more convenient to use our house rather than her own as a staging area for the elopement.

Inevitably, Maria's parents learned the facts of the case by the following morning. Manuel, her father, came to our house and asked when we could give him the money he assumed we owed his daughter for the ten weeks of her employment. She apparently had told him that we had not yet begun to pay her. She had told us that her father kept her salary and that she had nothing left to buy essential clothes. In sympathy for her plight, we had presented her a blouse and other items for the Easter holidays.

Following local practices in connection with the elopement pattern, Manuel went to the village court house the day after Maria's disappearance to bring suit against her and José. He wanted to see her punished severely for having caused him anger and humiliation and especially for having abandoned her baby. This was a heartless thing to do to the baby, he contended, and it placed a heavy responsibility on his family, especially since the child was still nursing. The court imposed a fine on the couple, which José's father paid, terminating the court case but not the marriage. Maria returned to live with José and his parents. Her baby was awarded by the court to relatives of the child's real father. They claimed the baby on grounds that they had materially contributed to its support, and they claimed to be able to provide a wet-nurse, a paternal aunt who was then nursing a baby of her own.

People in the village spoke ill of Maria, not so much for eloping from her parents as for deserting her baby. There is no bottle feeding in the village, wet-nursing is regarded as a temporary expedient at best, and it is generally assumed that a baby under one year of age has a poor chance to survive if separated from its mother. Apparently feeling that the baby would be an obstacle in her new marriage, Maria made no effort to keep or regain her. Manuel remained bitter; relationships between Maria and her own family were completely ruptured.

Having alienated nearly everybody else, Maria could still count on José and his parents—but not for long. She promptly antagonized her new mother-in-law, whose name happened to be Juana, the same as the name of Maria's next younger sister. Her mother-in-law charged Maria with indolence and insubordination, and with giving orders to children of the household over whom Maria had no authority.

About a month after their marriage, Maria had a violent argument with José. He accused her of flirting with another man, and she accused him of making overtures to another girl. She reviled José and his parents. He responded by beating her. She in turn suffered a violent attack of *cólera* (rage), a culturally patterned syndrome consisting, according to local conceptions, of a swelling of the heart due to an excess of "bad blood," and consequent symptoms of gasping and suffocation. An attack of *cólera* is nearly always the product of an acrimonious quarrel. It gives the appearance of being a kind of adult temper-tantrum with screaming generally suppressed, and some of the anger directed at the self. The local culture frowns on the expression of overt hostility but nevertheless heated arguments sometimes occur, engendering secondary anxiety which can lead to *cólera*.

Later that night, after the quarrel and the attack of *cólera*, Maria lapsed into a state of unconsciousness which turned out to be the onset of a dissociated episode. Her husband tried to rouse her but could not. He summoned his father, Francisco, but he too was unsuccessful in trying to wake her. In their own words, they found her "cold and stiff as though dead for good." The Maya word *kamik* refers both to death and to unconsciousness, hence the phrase "dead for good" is a Spanish rendering to distinguish death from other losses of consciousness.

José and Francisco were frightened. Francisco shook his son and demanded, "What have you done to her?" He supposed that José might have beaten his wife to death. Francisco then called in a *ladina* (non-Indian) school mistress temporarily residing in the village. The schoolteacher tried some remedies, but without effect. Francisco next summoned one of the village shamans (native medico-magical specialists). The shaman came but was reluctant to try one of his medicines because, as he remarked, "She already looks so serious." He feared she would die, and he did not want to assume any responsibility. He remained in the house, however, and in about two hours Maria showed signs of

Mental Disorder and Self-Regulating Processes 157

life. She began to wail that spirits of the dead were surrounding her and were trying to take her to the realm of the dead. This heightened the fears of those present. The shaman left abruptly, saying that this was not a case for him. Ghosts are not taken lightly by people of this village; their arrival suggests that death is imminent.

Maria was in a state of fugue; she did not respond to overtures and did not recognize what was happening about her. She walked about the house talking and arguing, but only with the spirits. She told the spirits that she did not want to go along.

Realizing that she was *loca* (crazy), Francisco sent for the appropriate shaman. Of the six or seven shamans in the village, only one was qualified by his calling and by experience to deal with insanity. That person, it so happened, was Manuel, Maria's father.

Until this moment, Francisco and Manuel had not been on speaking terms owing to the elopement and the subsequent court case. But that night the breach was speedily remedied. Now in the role of a critical specialist and not in the role of an injured father, Manuel swung into action. He advised that Maria be taken immediately to the neighboring town of Atitlán, regarded as the seat of sorcery, to see a still more powerful shaman, a person who had once cured Manuel of a stubborn illness and had thus become Manuel's mentor in the shamanistic arts.

At two o'clock at night the party set out by canoe—Maria, her father, José, and José's parents. Maria resisted, but she was forcibly taken by the arm. Just before dawn they arrived in Atitlán. Manuel called on the other shaman, and they all paid a visit to the abode of the powerful and dreaded *Maximon*, the master of insanity and black magic. Candles were burned, incense was offered, and the two shamans held conversations with the mystic power, unseen in the darkness of the night.

The seance ended with the diagnosis that Maria had fallen victim to the power of malignant supernatural forces. The cause lay in a history of sinful behavior on the part of any or all of the following: Maria, her father and mother; her husband José, his father and mother. Hence, the first step in the course of treatment was to be a ritual whipping administered to all six by a senior relative. This could be done only by the aged mother of

Francisco, the only living grandparent of the couple. The party returned to the village and asked the grandmother to carry out the whipping. This was to be done as a gesture and as a symbol, and not as an act of corporal punishment. Even though it involved more exorcism than exercise, the old lady refused to cooperate. Like the first shaman who had run out on the case, she feared that someone would die, and did not want to incur any blame. But many other steps were taken. Considerable time, money, and effort were expended by both sets of parents in an effort to placate the threatening spirits. Resort was made to additional shamans and new remedies. The details of the course of cure are not relevant here. The significant thing is that the onset of Maria's illness created a marked change in the pattern of interpersonal activity within her kinship circle and that Maria was aware that not she alone but a group of people were locked in battle with the threatening forces.

Within about a week, Maria had a remission. For awhile she was not as gay as she had been, but she resumed her normal round of activities and no longer suffered from hallucinations. During the six or seven additional months we continued to reside in the village, Maria lived a normal life.

What was Maria's own version of events at the time of her seizure? Several days after the onset of her symptoms, my wife interviewed Maria, visiting her in the home of her own parents. After the night she first experienced hallucinations, she was afraid to remain in the household of Francisco, her father-in-law, for fear of ghosts. "I am afraid to go out of the house," Maria told my wife. "When I go out I feel as though someone were following me. I feel that the spirits are around me." Then virtually without questioning, she gave the following account.

"Saturday night at 11:00 o'clock, I felt that I had left the house of Francisco, that I was walking around strange streets and places, accompanied by spirits of dead women who had come for me. It is absolutely true that I was dead [unconscious] for two or three hours. I didn't feel a thing. My body was completely cold, but my spirit was walking around with the dead.

"They took me to a place where a man brought out a very big book. He looked in it and asked, 'Are you Juana?' and I told him, 'No.' He asked my mother's name and my father's name and other things about me, and then he said, 'No, you are not Juana. Your name is not here, but her name is. You must return. We don't want you here yet.' It wasn't me they wanted but my mother-in-law."

It should be recalled that Maria's sister and her mother-in-law are both called Juana. It is possible that the two persons were merged in Maria's imagery; she had reportedly told another informant that the Juana in her hallucinations was her own sister rather than her husband's mother.

"It was Rosario, the dead sister of my mother-in-law, who took me there, and she was the one who was with me all the time. When I got there, I saw all the dead people whom I had known. They were all there. But the Lord told me to return, that my name was not recorded. Rosario was angry. She had wanted her sister, Juana, called in to confront her dead parents and answer to the charge of stealing all the inheritance which the parents had left. Rosario argued that I should remain, saying 'This one is at least her daughter-in-law. Let her stay.' She was angry.

"Then some of the others [here she names a number of actual women who had recently died in childbirth] wouldn't let me leave. Whenever I tried to pass by in the road, they blocked my path. They said to me, 'You must stay here and help us give milk to the babies.' There were babies all over the ground, without any clothes on, rolling around and playing on the ground. One of the dead women said she was very tired from having nursed the babies and wanted me to stay and help them because there were so many [dead] babies there, but I don't have any milk now." This last statement of Maria's was contrary to fact. According to her own mother, Maria did have milk.

"Finally I didn't want to leave; I wanted to remain there with them, but the father of Juana [José's grandfather] came along the road and beat me with a whip and threw me on the ground and told me to leave." She then recounted how she journeyed home and how her spirit traveled through distant lands for a period of four days under the guidance of Rosario's spirit.

Though she spoke of her spirit as having wandered for four days, Maria actually went to stay in her father's house after the first night of her seizure. This was the first time she had appeared in her parents' home since the evening she had eloped from our house.

But shifting residence had no immediate effect on Maria's condition. According to information that we received from José's sister, for three days "Maria talked out loud, constantly addressing the spirits, protesting that she had no milk, exclaiming that they were trying to take her. When her husband tried to calm her, she would shake off his hand or hit him." According to Maria's mother, Maria was unable to sleep but walked up and down talking to the spirits and intermittently singing and dancing.

The songs she sang were snatches of esoteric, shamanistic incantations she had overheard her father chanting at times when he had come home drunk. Shamans are not supposed to sing their songs or to recite their verses in the presence of children. The words and the tunes are powerful, and capable of bringing disaster to those who sing them without warrant. When Maria's father heard her burst into these songs during the period of her breakdown, he scolded her severely, and ordered her to desist immediately. "This is why you have gone crazy," he told her, "from singing sacred songs that you have no business with."

By the end of a week, Maria was well enough to go out for a walk with her husband. Instead of returning to her father's home, the couple again went to live with José's parents. Maria greeted her father-in-law: "How would you like two laborers who are seeking work and lodging?" To this Francisco replied, "Where are the laborers?" "Why, José and I," said Maria, "I no longer wish to stay in my own father's house." She then offered Francisco a cup of soft drink as a gesture of amity. Francisco hesitated, pointing out that Maria's father might become vexed over the couple's unannounced departure from Manuel's household, especially "since I asked him to do us the favor of curing your illness." Francisco finally consented and accepted the drink after Maria protested that there was nothing wrong with her, that if she were ill she would be in bed. At eight or nine o'clock they all went to sleep.

That same night at one o'clock Maria rose from her bed in a rage and began beating José furiously. His cries aroused his sister's husband who rushed in to investigate, but Maria knocked him to the floor and reached for an axe handle. By this time Francisco appeared in the room. As Francisco reported it, he found Maria climbing over the prostrate brother-in-law and lunging for the latter's testicles. With the aid of his son and son-in-law, Francisco managed to seize Maria and tie her with ropes.

She pleaded for mercy. "I don't want you to kill my son [or son-in-law]," Francisco replied, "So I am going to have you sent away to prison." But her pleas prevailed. She promised never again to misbehave. Thereafter indeed her disturbing symptoms lifted and she resumed her normal activities, continuing to live with José. Of course, "normal" does not preclude occasional quarrels.

How did people in the community explain Maria's strange behavior? Some said the basic fault resided with Manuel, her father—that he had performed unethical acts in the past, and that he was now being punished through his daughter. Others said the fault was Maria's directly. Still others blamed José; others said the sickness was brought on by misdeeds on the part of José's parents. Others thought it to be a combination.

What are the general implications of this case? Let me first raise, in order to dispose of them, two issues which this case does little to resolve. The first issue is this: Do the dynamics of mental disorder remain constant from culture to culture, or do they vary? An easy but equivocal answer is that the psychodynamic *process* is essentially the same, but the *content* (the specific symptoms and manifestations) differs with the cultural milieu. This partly begs the question as to what is content and what is process. In this particular case I should suppose that content refers to the nature of Maria's visual and auditory hallucinations. Perhaps the processes revealed in her behavior fall into place as those characteristic of a "castrating female." Maria was both seductive and hostile towards men; she had met with failure in her effort to escape her culturally-prescribed feminine role, and had finally resorted to a temporary retreat from reality.

The second issue I want to dispose of briefly is this: Do the roots of psychopathology lie tangled in the skein of interpersonal relations, that is, in the social process; or do they reach deeper, originating in hereditary predispositions? Again, the case is necessarily ambiguous in this regard. The data can be so interpreted as to support either view. Maria's social history is certainly an etiological factor, but whether her life experience is the ultimate cause or only the proximate cause must remain an open question. It takes a carefully devised experimental design and not just a case to probe a problem of this kind effectively.

I come now to three general implications that are somewhat more positive. The first of these has to do with the range of role-choice available in a given society. Some authorities say that middle-class women in the United States are torn between competing roles, those of mother, glamor girl, careerist, and the like. There is the wear of indecision arising from excessive latitude of choice, leading to emotional conflict and in some cases to psychopathology. This viewpoint implies that a more unitary, more well defined, feminine role would provoke less anxiety. The case of Maria makes one wonder. The society in which she lived, with its clear definition of the female role, stands as a reminder that the pinch may only be shifted to another foot. There is essentially but one allowed feminine role, the wife-mother-housekeeper role, one that is socially subordinate to the male role. The system works reasonably well for most women in the society. There is no indication that women as a group are more unhappy than men in this Guatemalan village. But in the case of a person like Maria, who was unconventional for reasons of predisposition or socialization or both, the culture provided no role alternatives, no legitimate means of escape into non-domestic activity. Maria tried desperately to evade the demands of her milieu by marrying a succession of culturally marginal men who might have had the means and the motivation to leave the village to live in a less constricting urban environment. In the United States she might have become absorbed in a professional career. In her village she could only rebel, and eventually break with reality when the battle became unbearable. As a matter of fact, Maria did eventually escape from the village. Five years later when we revisited Guatemala, we learned that she and José had moved to Guatemala City and were raising a family.

The second of my concluding points relates to the question of secondary guilt in mental patients. If emotional illness connotes personal inadequacy in the judgment of society and hence also in the self-estimation of the patient, this should arouse secondary guilt, or blaming one's self for being emotionally disturbed. This in turn might aggravate the illness in spiral fashion. If secondary guilt can be a handicap to recovery, then the culture of the Guatemalan village tends to mitigate this particular handicap and thus encourage remission or recovery. Two cultural features permit escape from a sense of secondary guilt. One is the fact that hallucinations are not culturally defined as products of fantasy. Sights and sounds of ghosts are regarded by most normal people in Maria's village not as fears and fancies but as real occurrences. It was never doubted by others that dead women actually surrounded Maria during her illness. Maria thought so at the time, and she continued to think so after recovery. In Maria's village people do not share our quip: "I'm hallucinating again."

The difference between Maria and her kinsmen was that she could see and hear the spirits that were present, while they could not see or hear them. Spirits are believed capable of making themselves selectively visible and invisible. Maria was sick in the eyes of her neighbors not because she imagined visitations, but because she was host to visitations, just as we might consider a person sick because he is host to microbes we cannot see but know to be present on the basis of our cultural information.

The other cultural circumstance that minimizes secondary guilt is the merciful ambiguity of the blameful agent in bringing on Maria's sickness. Spirits are sent for a cause (bad behavior) but who committed the transgression? Was Manuel really the intended target? Some thought he was. If so, was it because he himself had done evil things or was it because of hidden enemies who wished him ill? Both these thoughts were expressed. Was it Francisco? Was it José? Was it Maria herself? Some certainly thought so. Was the malefactor Maria's mother-in-law, Juana? Maria certainly thought so, and some agreed with her. Each judge could cast blame where he would and find cultural justification for his judgment. It is locally believed that supernatural retribution is sometimes ineffective against people with "strong" characters, and that in such cases the punishment is deflected onto more susceptible kinsmen, usually offspring. It is likely that in her own mind, Maria was only an innocent bystander who fell victim to ghostly vengeance directed at someone else in the household. Our culture, having discredited these non-rational escapes, makes it more difficult for the mental patient to avoid a sense of secondary guilt or conscious self-blame.

The last of my three general points reverts to the concept of self-regulation in the socio-cultural process. When a ribbon in a typewriter moves far enough in one direction it trips a hammer and the movement is reversed. A like process appears to have occurred in Maria's human environment. The more she tried to evade the feminine role, the more she was renounced by society. Progressively alienating her parents, her parents-in-law, and finally her husband—her last social prop—she and her society had reached a state of complete mutual rejection. At this point, quantitative saturation brought a qualitative change; unable to proceed further in the same direction, Maria suddenly and dramatically altered her mode of behavior from argument and rebellion to psychological withdrawal. This culturally available act redefined the social situation. She was no longer an active threat to society and its norms; she was now regarded by those about her as the passive target of a more sinister threat, the forces of literal death. Any kinsman might be struck when ghosts are around. Any relative might in fact be to blame. To save themselves, for purely personal reasons if for no others, her relatives had to work for Maria and with Maria to repel the invading spirits. The process of social alienation was now reversed; the ribbon was winding the other way. Community of concern and anxiety is an important form of social solidarity. Groups of relatives who had been at odds with each other—her husband's family and her own family—now came together in common action. From an attitude of scorn and avoidance, her own father switched to one of sympathy and assistance. Once shunned by society, Maria was now the center of attention. She became the center of attention in a very literal sense. It is believed that the soul of anyone who is gravely sick, whether the disease is emotional or organic, is in peril of being seized by were-animals who wait for the weakened patient to be left unguarded. It is therefore necessary for relatives and neighbors to be in constant protective attendance. Maria was under day-and-night vigilance during most of the time that she (and her kinsmen) were in deepest danger.

Maria recovered. I should like to think that the process of redefinition and reversal just described was instrumental in the remission of her symptoms. What differs in Maria's society from our own is not so much the actual process of mental disorder as the *cultural definition* of this process—belief in an external threat and in joint jeopardy. By an abrupt switch in her mode of deviance, Maria was able to trip the cultural lever that set restitutive processes in motion. Having no hospitals to hide her in, the community provided Maria with a key to re-enter their own society.

8 SOME CULTURAL DETERMINANTS OF HOSTILITY IN PILAGA INDIAN CHILDREN[1]

Jules Henry

With the accumulation of well-documented studies of highly contrasted cultures it has become increasingly clear that an adequate discussion of personality in any culture involves a description of the social forms of that culture. The basis on which people are grouped together in household and village, the relationship system that lays the basis for the distribution of food and property; marital arrangements and the mechanisms that determine how and by whom the social ideals may be achieved—all these are included under the term social forms. It is with these factors, or rather with their combined effects, that personality developments show their highest correlation—in children as well as in adults—and it is on the basis of these that I wish to discuss the marked hostility found in Pilaga children.

The Pilaga Indians who were the object of our study during the period September 1936–November 1937 live on a mission near the Pilcomayo River in the Argentine Gran Chaco. They had been there eight months when Mrs. Henry and I arrived.

FROM Jules Henry, "Some Cultural Determinants of Hostility in Pilaga Indian Children," 1940, *American Journal of Orthopsychiatry,* 10:111–22. Copyright, The American Orthopsychiatric Association, Inc. Reproduced by permission of author and publisher.

[1] Presented at the 1939 meeting. I wish to express my gratitude to my colleagues Drs. Benedict, Bunzel, and Linton, and to Dr. David M. Levy, who were kind enough to read this paper and discuss it with me. The field work forming the basis of this study was made possible through a grant from the Columbia University Council for Research in the Social Sciences.

Some Cultural Determinants of Hostility

Although the Pilaga have a few small gardens, they depend for most of their food on wild fruits and fish. For about three months of the year—when there is very little wild fruit and fish—they suffer almost semi-starvation.

The Pilaga live in small villages between which there are strong feelings of hostility and fear of sorcery. The population of our village was 127, of which 37 were children under 15 years. The eight houses of the village were arranged in an irregular ellipse around a central plaza which was used for drying fruit, as a playground for children, and for social gatherings. Our house was near one end of the ellipse and our nearest Indian neighbors lived about ten feet away. When the weather grew too hot to sleep indoors and we moved outside, we were practically sharing sleeping quarters with our neighbors.

None of the Pilaga spoke enough Spanish to make communication in that language worthwhile, but after about six months we were fairly well versed in the Pilaga language and, by the time we were ready to leave, we were almost fluent.

Living as we did in the heart of the community we had an excellent opportunity to observe our subjects. We were on friendly terms with them, and were in and out of each other's houses all day long. The children in particular were constantly with us: they came to visit, played with our toys, clambered all over us, or they just looked on.

The symptoms of conflict in Pilaga children are obvious enough to be noticeable as soon as one enters the community. They are hungry for attention and extremely violent and quarrelsome. Since, from the etiological point of view, a consideration of home environment throws most light on such problems, I shall begin this discussion with an analysis of the Pilaga household.

The Household. The Pilaga think of their villages and households as groups of blood relatives living together in peace and harmony and supporting one another in all things. Actually village and household are made up only in part of blood relatives; villagers and housemates do not support one another in all things, and peace and harmony are maintained in the face of tension and repressed hostility.

Although Pilaga housemates call one another by relationship terms, detailed genealogical analysis of household populations shows that as many as half the members of any one household may not be relatives within the strict genealogical definition of the term. They are people who, having been brought together by a variety of circumstances,[2] feel they are related and even use relationship terms for one another, but among whom there is very little solidarity. In some primitive societies solidarity is strengthened through participation by the people in large ceremonies which are for the common good, or in some economic enterprise in which the total yield is pooled. But among the Pilaga there are no ceremonies for the common good, and even where a number of people engage in a joint enterprise, such as communal fishing or food-gathering, there is no pooling of the yield.

Although the Pilaga live in large households containing many families, the basic cooperating unit is still the simple family and it is this unit that holds food as private property. Some South American Indian tribes which live in "big houses" sheltering many families, have communal meals in which the large households eat together and share all food, but among the Pilaga each family eats separately at its own hearth.[3] Although people distribute most of the food they obtain by their own work to other members of the household, the primary sanction for giving is not praise or expectation of return, but fear—fear of being called stingy, fear of being left alone, and fear of sorcery.[4] In times of scarcity invitations are hardly ever extended to share "potluck." The only expedient open to a hungry person is begging, and begging is accompanied by fear of giving offense.

Anywhere in times of scarcity the problem arises as to who is to get what there is. In many societies this situation is met

[2] The factors most powerful in establishing these agglomerates are: 1) actual relationship; 2) arrival of individuals to join married-in siblings; 3) scattering of village populations due to village decomposition upon the death of a chief.

[3] In times of great scarcity the family with food frequently places its pot in a conspicuous place—usually outside the house—as a tacit invitation to the less fortunate. This, however, is not a true invitation and is accepted with reluctance. True invitations are rarely given. A true invitation is a shout to the guest or a visit to his house by the host in order to fetch him.

[4] One who gives also receives from others, but food is also given away to those from whom returns are neither expected nor received.

by some system whereby certain relatives, such as an uncle or a cousin, for example, are the people traditionally accepted as the ones to receive what there is. But among the Pilaga there is no such system. There is only the idea that everything must be shared among all relatives,[5] and since frequently no account is taken of the fact that there may not be enough to go around, considerable resentment is engendered.

Thus there develop within Pilaga society two closely related cycles of feeling which produce great tension and hostility.[6] The first cycle is: reluctance to share is accompanied by reluctance to beg. Reluctance to beg leads to exclusion from sharing, which produces resentment and, in turn, leads to reluctance to share. The second cycle develops in part from the physical fact of scarcity and the inefficient mechanism for distribution. These result in exclusion from sharing, which again produces resentment.

In this way Pilaga customs of food distribution strengthen hostility to a degree rare among primitive societies.

The Cultural Position of Pilaga Women. Although the general lack of dependability and warmth within the household would in any case furnish a very unsatisfactory environment for children, the total situation is made even more difficult because the status of Pilaga women is in so many ways inferior to that of the men.

The Pilaga women provide only the wild fruits, while the men supply the much more highly valued fish, game and cultivated vegetables. Economically, therefore, women are contemptible to the Pilaga.[7]

---

[5] I speak here of relationship in its broadest sense as conceived by the Pilaga.

[6] Actual outbursts are rare, and it is this fact of repression that aggravates the situation, not only from the psychological but also from the legal point of view, for if the withholding person were roundly insulted he would hesitate before being stingy.

[7] During the summer months the older men are drunk almost continuously on beer made from the wild fruits which the women provide. Yet, although the women obediently go for many gallons of water to make this beer, often walking miles to get it; although they provide firewood to heat it, they do not touch a drop of it. Mate, too, is largely consumed by the men; and although the women love tobacco, generally the only time they get a chance to smoke is when the ethnologist gives them some tobacco.

Pilaga women are considered "weak things" and female infanticide was practiced until about ten years ago. Even today when a female child is born its mother may be anxious lest the father ask to have it killed. Women's disabilities, however, extend even further, for status and achievement are not measured in terms of things that women can do. The most desirable wealth is not pots and ponchos—objects of female manufacture—but live-stock, which were obtained in war, and articles of White manufacture.[8]

Pilaga women are even deprived of whatever consideration they might receive as child-bearers, for it is believed that the man's orgasm projects a complete homunculus into the woman, and that it merely grows in her until it is big enough to come out.

Finally the Pilaga woman has no part in that which above all things is the way to prestige in Pilaga culture—warfare.

Pilaga women show considerable hostility to the men and say the men are "no good." In the courting dances the women have the upper hand and maltreat the men unmercifully. By tradition the woman picks her partner and he will be her lover for the night. Since there are few women and many men,[9] the men must wait patiently and endure all. The women beat the men and jerk them around by the hair violently enough to almost throw them.

Marriage Arrangements. The environment which is rendered difficult for children by the lack of solidarity among members of the household and by the special disabilities of women is made still worse by Pilaga marriage regulations.

Because of incest taboos a woman usually chooses her husband from a different village. He is thus an outsider. This arrangement whereby a man leaves his own village in order to live among his wife's people is called matrilocal residence in anthropological parlance, and in many primitive societies where

[8] Nowadays these things can be obtained by working for Whites part of the year, but since an Indian woman receives only half of the pay of a man the old pattern is perpetuated.

[9] The general numerical superiority of the men is increased by the women's reluctance to dance for fear of the men and fear of the hordes of violent little boys who attack them.

Some Cultural Determinants of Hostility 171

it exists it operates to give maximum security to the woman while cutting the ground from under the man. This occurs most frequently where there is great solidarity between the girl and her group and where the girl and her group hold all rights in the land.[10] Among the Pilaga, however, where there is no great solidarity among members of the same household and village, and where the rights in a few little patches of land are held only by the few older men who care to trouble themselves with gardening, the situation is reversed. Far from being in any way dependent on their wives' kin, husbands are great assets to the household, for they take the place of the young men who marry out and they provide the highly valued animal foods. The wife has no property rights of any importance[11] and no great personal backing in her own village. So, too, the woman becomes particularly dependent on her husband because he is one of the few people from whom she can take food and property without fear of his resentment.

What actually happens in Pilaga society is that both husband and wife show some rather extreme signs of insecurity.[12]

To a young husband his wife's village, like most villages other than his own, is one toward which he has always had a marked conscious hostility, and the men and women of strange villages are always felt to be sorcerers. For months after he has entered his wife's village the husband is scarcely visible. At the crack of dawn he is off to his mother's house, if it is not too far away, and he only returns to his wife at night. If he remains with his wife during the day he often stays indoors, lying down.

Pilaga wives, on the other hand, tell many stories of husbands who beat their wives[13] when they find them visiting even in another part of the same household. If a group of gossiping women detect a distant movement in the bush they are in a mild panic of fear of their husbands and scuttle back to their fires. Over and over again the Pilaga women warned Mrs. Henry

---

[10] Or in some other important property, such as cattle, for example.
[11] She owns only her personal belongings.
[12] The extreme symptoms of the man wear off in the course of a year.
[13] Once a child has been born to him a man begins to take a more active part in village life. Nevertheless he still spends most of his time in his wife's section of the house. Women never lose their fear of being beaten for visiting.

to run home when they saw me coming in the distance. "Go! Run! He'll beat you!" It made no difference to them that she assured them that I was not "fierce" and that I never beat her.

In our society important motivating forces behind marriage are love and economic advantage. Among the Pilaga, however, emotional bonds do not play a very important role, and in early youth economic considerations do not loom large. Certain factors do, however, make marriage desirable to the young people. Although the unmarried women in a household will fetch water for a young man and provide him with vegetable food and even with some firewood, once the women are married the products of their labor go to their husbands and children, and the unmarried young men become increasingly uncomfortable. Although there is premarital sexual freedom the young men are eager to marry because since they outnumber the young women they find it difficult to obtain sexual partners. Young women, on the other hand, need never lack for lovers, and they are not so eager to marry as the young men. Yet ultimately they must marry in order to avoid becoming beggars.[14]

The lack of large economic stakes on both sides, however, and the absence of deep emotional attachments makes early marriage so unstable that it has about it very much the air of a casual affair. Since no Pilaga child can be born without a father the pregnancies resulting from these unions must be aborted.[15] Among the young women abortions and threats of abortion are so frequent that one could almost say of a first child that it is just an unperformed abortion.

Thus far the examination of Pilaga institutions has shown: 1) that the household fails to provide adequate security; 2) that food sharing, the mechanism for insuring solidarity among individuals, develops considerable tension among them; 3) that women suffer important disabilities; 4) that marriage itself contributes to the emotional insecurity of both husband and wife, and 5) that the great instability of early marriage acts as a constant threat to early pregnancies.

Still other disturbing factors develop from situations that are correlated with pregnancy and lactation rules.

---

[14] Parental pressure is important too, for the parents want the husband as a fisherman.
[15] The Pilaga have no contraceptive techniques.

Pregnancy and Lactation. Traditionally a Pilaga woman must go to her husband's village[16] as soon as she becomes pregnant, and the husband takes this opportunity to demand that she go there. This may precipitate a severe conflict, for it is now the girl's turn to be afraid of the sorcerers in her husband's village.

Nenarachi, our next-door neighbor is a case in point. When she became pregnant her husband made the usual demand— that she follow him to his village. For a long time she refused until he at last beat her. Next day she went with him. When we went to visit her in her husband's village, the change that had come over her was shocking. When we saw her there the first time she was watching a tatooing. Now, since women are the tatooers, a tatooing is an event which is always of the greatest interest to them. They watch the work with expert eye and laugh and talk a great deal. Not so Nenarachi. She sat stony and sad. When Mrs. Henry asked Nenarachi whether she was happy in her husband's village she whispered, "No. I will never be happy here." She was afraid of sorcerers and told Mrs. Henry so. About six weeks later she left her husband, and we were delighted one morning to see Nenarachi back in our village.

But now there was talk of an abortion. "Who would take care of the child?" said the Pilaga. So for a week or so there were rumors that Nenarachi was going to "throw away her child," but at last one night her husband returned. He told us that his relatives had insisted that he come back so that "the child would not be killed."

Thus the conflict arising out of residence rules for the pregnant woman may result in a threat to the life of the child.

As time goes on and second and third children are born Pilaga marriages become more stable. Nevertheless there is still another factor that acts as a constant threat to marital relationships and makes the position of the mother particularly difficult.

From the time she is six months pregnant until her baby can run about, sexual intercourse is taboo to the Pilaga mother, for the Pilaga believe that were a woman to have intercourse when she was "big" the child in her womb would die; and if she were to give birth to a second child before the first could run about

---

[16] She may never return to her own village, or she may return after her child is born or even sooner.

then the first child would die. Pilaga women will not nurse two of their own children at once, and they believe that if a child is weaned before it can run about it will not eat.

Now, a long taboo on intercourse during pregnancy and lactation is found in many parts of the primitive world. In many cultures where it occurs, however, the difficulties arising from it are solved through the institution of polygyny. The Pilaga woman, however, will not tolerate a co-wife. An important factor in female opposition to a co-wife may be seen in the matrilocal residence rule. Since the population of Pilaga villages makes it very unlikely that a man could find two wives in one village, he would have to spend his time between two villages, and hence his contributions of food and game would be divided. As a matter of fact although polygyny among the Pilaga is rare, in the few cases that do occur, the wives are, with rare exception, in separate villages. Even were it possible for a man to find two wives in one village his contributions would most likely be divided between two families—all the more so since female infanticide makes it very unlikely that two marriageable sisters could be found in one household. When, in addition to these factors, we consider the lack of solidarity between Pilaga households, it becomes clear that the whole idea of a co-wife must be intolerable to a Pilaga woman.[17] Therefore, although she may be willing to let her husband have affairs she will fight both her husband and the other woman if an affair becomes serious.

Factors Affecting the Desirability of Children. The Pilaga woman occupies an inferior position in her culture, and, like her husband, she is reared in an atmosphere of insecurity and tension. This tension is heightened by fear of her husband and by the anxiety which the taboo on intercourse injects into her life. Her marriage represents to her the sacrifice of her freedom to economic necessity.

For the young wife a first child is at least a partial guarantee of economic security, for pressure is brought to bear to keep the couple together in order to preserve the child. To all women, however, a baby is equally a threat, for the taboo on intercourse

[17] The preponderance of males over females is another factor that makes polygyny difficult.

sends their husbands out in search of adventure. Finally, infants interfere with their mothers' work, and not only do some women object to having children because of it, but actually contemplate abortions.[18]

To the young husband the baby represents his most secure tie to his wife, and at all times it is evidence of a man's "good work," for he alone is responsible for its being. So too, once a child is born to him a man's marriage has more the appearance of a stable union and he begins to acquire status in his wife's village. On the other hand the presence of the baby implements the taboo on intercourse, and some men say, although none too seriously, that they are jealous of their newborn infants.

Thus a number of cultural factors operate to make babies both desirable and undesirable.

The Development of the Child's Personality. Thus far the discussion of Pilaga institutions has shown that there are a great number of factors making for insecurity, and that although a child is, to a certain extent, desirable in many cases, the desire is far from whole-hearted.

When the baby at last comes into the world it is received with great warmth, but as time passes it is gradually rejected. The initial warmth is followed by gradual withdrawal, until by the time a third sibling is born the first gets practically no attention at all beyond receiving the necessities of life.

Since a complete discussion of the developmental picture is beyond the scope of this paper I shall limit myself to a brief description of the child's life until the birth of a second sibling.

When the baby is very young it is the object of constant attention. At the first whimper it is nursed by its mother, or in her absence, sometimes by its grandmother. It is bathed and kept free of lice, and its mother carefully plucks out its eyelashes to make it beautiful. She kisses it over and over again, rubbing her mouth violently on the baby's in an ecstasy of pleasure. The baby is passed around from hand to hand and people in the house and visitors take turns mouthing it. But as time passes, as the baby's personality begins to develop, and as the baby becomes more and more interested in the things around it, it gets

---

[18] We have no instances of the abortion of a second pregnancy in a married woman who is living with her husband.

less and less attention from everyone, for the adults regard the child's expanding interests as a rejection.

The withdrawal of attention takes place by almost imperceptible degrees, and is evident at first only in the mother's increased slowness in stopping her work to nurse her weeping baby, and in a diminishing of the mouth rubbing.

At about the eighth month of the infant's life two important factors operate with particular vigor to undermine the child's security. These factors are his mother's work and the absence of solidarity within the household. In order to gather in the crops of wild fruits the child's mother must spend hours away from home. She often cannot take the child with her, for the distance she has to go is too great and the baby too heavy to carry in addition to her burden of wild fruit. In some primitive communities where similar conditions exist the mother can leave her child with some other woman who will suckle it if it grows hungry or weeps. Among the Pilaga, however, this does not occur because there is so little solidarity within the household and because the reluctance to take food from others forces all of the able-bodied women and many of the weak and the aged out to look for food. Often, therefore, the baby is left with an old and feeble (sometimes blind) grandparent who can do little for it.

The period of greatest suffering for the baby begins, however, when it can walk a little. This is the time when it begins to explore the world outside the house.[19] Now, alone, outside the familiar circle of its housemates, the child is afraid. Little children tear past at breakneck speed, screaming, or tumble about on the ground in violent play. Strangers walk by. The baby bursts into tears, but its elders are slow to reassure it.

During the period when the baby is investigating the outer world it is almost continuously in tears. Not only is it frightened by contact with strangers, but its mother leaves it more and more alone as she goes about her work. Formerly she had left the baby alone for hours; now she leaves it alone for a whole day. It eats a little pounded corn or drinks a little honey water, but the baby is hungry, and by evening it is so wrought up that when its tired mother comes home it cannot wait to be picked up but has a tantrum at her feet.

[19] The babies are often encouraged by their mothers to go outside.

Some Cultural Determinants of Hostility

Although as the Pilaga child grows older he receives the breast less often, partly because he eats other things, partly because he is busy playing, and often because his mother is away working, he can still have access to her breast frequently. He is still very much the object of his mother's attention, and he spends many hours sitting on her thighs as she parts his hair looking for lice. Once a new sibling appears, however, this is radically changed. Though his mother may nurse him even while she is in labor, when the new child is born the older sibling is absolutely denied the breast. Not only this, but the attention his mother and father once gave him is now directed to the new baby. Formerly when he wept he was given the breast and comforted by his mother. Now he is told to "Be quiet" and sent to play outdoors or to a relative, who may afford him some casual comfort in the form of a morsel of food.

This situation leaves the older sibling stunned. He wanders disconsolately about near the house and whimpers continually, apparently without cause. When he comes home it is not infrequently to try out little schemes for doing away with the new baby, and his mother must be very watchful lest he injure the new sibling. Naturally this only intensifies the situation, for the mother's redoubled attention serves to isolate the older sibling even more.

In some cultures the shock of rejection may be somewhat lessened through a marked change in the status of the older sibling, or through some device whereby he is given considerable prestige or made to feel important. In other cultures again, the older sibling becomes the care of some special relative who takes the child everywhere and is a constant companion. Among the Pilaga, however, these things do not occur. The Pilaga have no device for giving status of prestige to anyone below the rank of chief, and one of the outstanding facts of Pilaga life is that no one troubles himself much about a child with a younger sibling. In view of the foregoing discussion of Pilaga social structure we can readily understand why no one other than the parents should bother much about the child, but why fathers should show such indifference is another matter. It is not that all Pilaga fathers are completely indifferent to the child who has just been weaned. Indeed, some fathers take them visiting, buy them gifts, and even delouse them. But their interest in the child never extends to the play and fondling that is typical for the responsive father in our society. Over and over again among the Pilaga the picture is of the apathetic father who suffers his little child to squat between his knees. There is good reason, in the social arrangements in this tribe, as we have seen for the jealousy of their infants which Pilaga fathers explicitly remark upon, and warmth does not develop between fathers and children.

Thus, without status and deprived of warmth, the Pilaga child remains a poor hostile little flounderer for a number of years until he at last begins to take his place in the adult economic activity.

Dr. David M. Levy has described earlier the doll experiments performed by Mrs. Henry and me. They amplify and confirm in a clear-cut way the results of our long day-by-day observation of the Pilaga children, viz., that feelings of hostility toward parents and siblings are intense enough to show themselves in the patterns Dr. Levy has already demonstrated as typical for similar situations in our own culture. That is to say, the day-by-day and experimental play behavior of the children is characterized by destructive attempts against the parents and siblings, by attempts at restitution, and by regression.[20]

Discussion

RUTH BENEDICT, Ph.D.: There are two separate problems raised by Dr. Henry's paper, and, in general, by anthropological investigations in other cultures. 1) Are hostility and sibling rivalry, as described on the basis of studies on our own culture, facts of human nature to be detected in any social milieu, however different from ours? 2) How are we to interpret the presence of maximum interpersonal hostily in some cultures and minimal in others; and can cross-cultural studies throw any light on the factors that foster it in some societies and minimize it in others?

In regard to the first problem, the conclusion seems warranted that *hostility* is a potentiality of human nature in the sense that

[20] It is not yet clear, however, that there is evidence of self-punishment in day-by-day behavior.

Some Cultural Determinants of Hostility

it is always relevant to investigate it. In Dr. Henry's extremely hostile Pilaga situation, the theoretical bearing of his investigations seems to me to be that the behavior shown is in detail analogous to the behavior described from our own society. There is regression, destructive behavior directed toward parents and siblings, and attempts at restitution, all of which can be described in the formulations applicable to studies made in New York City. The most important problem under this head that is suggested by cross-cultural information is whether the sibling situation is universally as dynamic in producing hostility as it is in our own culture. There are societies with very considerable hostility in most personal relationships but in which the relationship of siblings is conspicuously warm and endures throughout life. It would be well worth investigating what the mechanics of hostility are in such societies, and how the sibling situation is isolated from the more general hostility.

The second question: how are we to interpret the presence of maximal interpersonal hostility in some societies and minimal in others, and can cross-cultural studies throw any light on the factors that foster it in some societies and minimize it in others, should be clearly differentiated from the first question. This second question is of particular importance to members of this association, which has a strong interest in therapeutic considerations, and besides, is of acute social importance. For instance, if our knowledge were confined to the Pilaga, the correlate of their marked hostility might be thought to be scarcity of food. The Pilaga, like so many primitive peoples, have annually a long "hungry time" and are acutely hungry. This correlation with markedly hostile societies, however, does not hold when a long series of different societies are examined. A whole array of primitive cultures meet such conditions by sharing food which at other times is less communal. That is, famine often, instead of producing tension in a society, draws its members more closely together in that they meet it by pooling all resources. The Pilaga have no such social mechanisms; societies which do have them do not present the Pilaga picture of hostility. The correlation of hostility is not with scarcity economy, but with non-cooperative cultural mechanisms. This is clear in their attitude toward property. Property institutions among the Pilaga are based on rights of private possession even of the basic necessities of life, and their mechanisms of distribution include no honorable rights of hospitality, and no reciprocal exchanges which advance prestige. The hungry can only beg, and beg shamefully. This is rare among primitive peoples, but it occurs in several parts of the world, always associated with marked hostility. Dr. Henry has described the frustration and hostility generated by other Pilaga cultural institutions.

This instance from the Pilaga can be generalized. The indication from cross-cultural studies is that minimal interpersonal hostility, also, is correlated with certain cultural institutions, political and economic as well as forms of the family and methods of child-rearing. The social institutions of such cultures make it possible for an individual to advance the general welfare of the society at the same time and by the same act that advances his own prestige or security. That is, such societies have cultural institutions which make a reality of the old *laissez faire* slogan which is today in such bad repute: private advantage is public gain. In such societies, any productive activity is a gain to the whole society and is rewarded with honor and prestige, but the corn or fish or venison is distributed throughout the community by mechanisms which contribute to the individual's own prestige. Any acquisition of a wife is a gain to the whole community, which is thereby strengthened, but the individual's advantage is equally served. The social institutions of such societies make it possible for a man to live honorably and without disaster so long as he is guilty of no asocial act, and he will not be singled out for humiliation before his fellows unless he is lazy or a reprobate. Conversely, he has no experience of a situation in which he can obtain a personal advantage at the expense of another member of his society.

These very general indications of the way in which human experience is patterned by the institutions of the culture can be greatly expanded, and should be studied in detail by joint field investigations of psychiatrists and anthropologists. Psychoanalysis has contributed immeasurably to the demonstration that human attitudes and behavior must be studied in relation to that individual's life experience. With the growing recognition that an individual's experiences are so greatly determined by the cultural

Some Cultural Determinants of Hostility 181

institutions of his society, it is of great importance to test the conclusions arrived at on the basis of behavior moulded by our own cultural institutions. Such study has great bearing on theoretical interpretations of our own cultural findings, for if hostility is amenable to great development under some social conditions and becomes vestigial under others, hostility as found in any one social milieu, e.g., our own, cannot be a fixed datum to be explained, for instance, by inevitable frustrations the organism undergoes in the process of socialization, but must be studied in relation to the environmental factors that foster it. If extreme changes in the virulence of interpersonal hostility, also, take place in a generation or two, clearly this cannot be due to biological changes, which do not occur so rapidly. It is clear from Dr. Henry's case of the Pilaga that extreme hostility is not merely a function of high civilization as such, nor of the mechanization of industry, nor yet of the institution of capitalism. It is not a price which we in our culture are paying for great social progress, and which we might, therefore, pay willingly. It is a condition which arises at any level of society when certain social institutions occur, institutions which are not specific either to complex or to simple societies. The problem is of equal theoretical and practical importance.

Part III AFRICA AND OCEANIA

9 THE INTERNALIZATION OF POLITICAL VALUES IN STATELESS SOCIETIES

Robert A. LeVine

The purpose of this paper is to suggest the following proposition: To understand and predict the contemporary political behavior of African peoples who were stateless prior to Western contact, one must take account of the traditional political values involved in their local authority systems, particularly since such values continue to be internalized by new generations after their society has come under the administration of a modern nation-state. Most anthropological students of stateless societies have concentrated their attention on the total-society level, analyzing the structure of inter-group relations in the absence of a central authority. In my opinion, a concept such as "segmentary society," which is at the total-society level of analysis, is an inadequate tool for the investigation of political variation and adaptation in African societies. To illustrate this point, I shall compare political behavior in two East African societies having segmentary lineage systems: the Gusii of Kenya, among whom I did field work,[1] and the Nuer of the Sudan, on whom four excellent monographs have been published by two independent field workers (Evans-Pritchard 1940, 1953, 1956; Howell 1954).

The Nuer and Gusii are similar in many aspects of indigenous socio-political organization. First of all, the two societies resemble each other in size and scale. The Nuer population is about

FROM Robert A. LeVine, "The Internalization of Political Values in Stateless Societies," 1960, *Human Organization,* 19:51–58, by permission of the author and the Society for Applied Anthropology.

[1] In 1955–1957 on a Ford Foundation Fellowship and with the assistance of the author's wife, Barbara B. LeVine.

350,000, that of the Gusii, 260,000. Among the Nuer, there are fifteen so-called tribes, within which compensation for homicide could be collected; the Gusii have seven such units based on the same principle. Both societies lacked superordinate political structures and were, in that sense, "stateless." There were no permanent positions of leadership with substantial decision-making power, and no formal councils. The major social groups within the tribes of both societies were patrilineal descent groups, each of which was associated with a territory and was a segment of a higher-level lineage which contained several such segments. Lineage structure is similar in many details for Nuer and Gusii: a lineage is named after its ancestor; its segments derive from the polygynous composition of the ancestor's family and are named after his several wives or their sons; the growth of lineages from polygynous families and their progressive segmentation are regular features of the system. Although Gusii lineages are more highly localized than Nuer ones, in both societies lineage segments and the territorial units associated with them engaged in armed aggression against segments of the same level. Two segments of equal level within the tribe would combine to fight a different tribe, but would conduct blood feuds against each other at times. This multiple-loyalty situation, plus the effect of mutual military deterrence, resulted in the maintenance of a certain degree of order which Evans-Pritchard has called "the balanced opposition of segments." Thus, in comparing Nuer and Gusii, it is possible to hold constant major structural variables in the precontact political systems.

There are also many similarities in the conditions which the Gusii and Nuer faced in coming under colonial administration. For both peoples, serious administration began in a punitive expedition brought on by an attempt to assassinate the District Commissioner (the Nuer succeeded in killing a D.C., while the Gusii only wounded the first one sent to rule them). British-led forces conducted the punitive expedition in both cases, and the aims of the early administrators were identical: to establish law and order on the pattern of British colonies elsewhere. This meant the abolition of feuding and warfare, and the establishment of chieftainship and native courts for the peaceful settlement of

The Internalization of Political Values

disputes. A major difference in the exposure of the two societies to British administration is chronological. The Gusii came under colonial rule in 1907, while the Nuer were not conquered until 1928. This twenty-year lag must be borne in mind as the analysis proceeds, so that the extent to which it contributes to the sharpness of the contrast may be assessed. With this qualification, it may be said that a comparison of political changes in Nuer and Gusii societies has the advantage of using groups which are matched on pre-existing political structure (in gross aspect) and on the nature of the political institutions introduced.

Contemporary Political Behavior

The contemporary political behavior of the Nuer and Gusii will be compared on two points: the adjustment of individuals to leadership roles in the introduced judicial system and the tendency of the traditional blood feud to persist or die out under British administration. Howell, writing in 1954 of the Nuer courts, states:

> . . . there is still everywhere a reluctance to give anything in the nature of a judgement. In many disputes, where the rights of one or another of the disputants are abundantly clear, a rapid and clear-cut decision might be expected. This is rarely forthcoming . . . (Howell 1954:230-31).

He goes on to say with respect to sentencing:

> . . . although Nuer chiefs and court members may be aware of the value of punishment, they are still reluctant to inflict it, especially as they are often subjected to recriminations by their fellows when the case is over. A fixed penalty (which they desire) absolves them from this and throws the responsibility on the Government. (Op. cit.:236.)

It is clear from these statements that Nuer judges do not relish their positions of authority over their fellow men, whose disapproval they fear. They attempt to avoid using the authority of their offices by making indecisive verdicts and by demanding that the government set fixed penalties for offenses. By contrast, the government in Gusiiland has never had any trouble finding men willing to deliver judgment on their fellows. If anything,

Gusii chiefs and judges have, from the early days of administration, tended to err on the side of arbitrariness and severity. Some of them may be charged with favoritism and accepting bribes but not with vacillation. Gusii Tribunal Court presidents complain of the puny sentences they are empowered to inflict. Location chiefs, who act as constables and informal courts of first instance, go far beyond their formal powers, incarcerating young men for insolence to their fathers, threatening legal sanctions against husbands who neglect their wives, punishing their personal enemies with legal means at their disposal. Gusii judicial leaders do not fear the adverse opinions of their fellow men because they know that their judicial authority is respected and even feared by the entire group. Chiefs and Tribunal Court presidents are the most powerful individuals in Gusiiland; immoderate criticism of them to their faces is considered impolite as well as simply unwise.

The second point of comparison concerns the persistence of the blood feud in the face of an established court system for the peaceful settlement of disputes. Howell states of the contemporary Nuer:

> Spear-fights between rival factions are not uncommon, and the blood-feud is still a reality among the Nuer despite severe deterrents applied by the Administration. Casualties are sometimes heavy, and most Nuer bear the marks of some armed affray . . . it would be a mistake to believe that the Nuer do not frequently use in earnest the spears and clubs which they keep always at their sides. (Op. cit.:39.)

Howell also mentions occasional "extensive hostilities" when "the intervention of State police armed with rifles is sometimes necessary" (op. cit.:66). He relates an incident in which he, as District Commissioner, intervened prematurely in a developing feud and

> . . . was publicly and most soundly rebuked by the elder statesmen of the area, and was told that such matters should be left to the chiefs themselves.

The Nuer chiefs, though, are sometimes "unwilling or afraid to intervene and restrain their fellows."

The Internalization of Political Values

The Gusii situation is strikingly different. Despite the persistence of ill feelings between lineage segments, the blood feud was replaced by litigation in the early days of British administration. Nowadays the only occasion on which overt group aggression occurs is at the funeral of a childless married woman whose death is attributed to the witchcraft of her co-wives. People from her natal clan attempt to destroy her belongings so they will not be inherited by her "murderers," and they may even attack her husband for his complicity in the affairs leading to her death. Significantly, however, women are usually the aggressors on such occasions, which are more likely to result in a court case than an all-out brawl. Fights are normally personal and show little tendency to involve groups of individuals. The Gusii, long reputed to be among the most litigious of Africans in Kenya, utilize assault charges in court as an alternative to physical aggression.[2] Soon after one individual insults or threatens another, they are both on their way to chief or court to lodge assault charges. Two-thirds of the vast number of assault cases are dismissed, most of them on the grounds that there is no evidence that assault has taken place. The Gusii are so eager to involve a higher authority in their quarrels that victims of alleged assaults would relate their stories to me and show me their injuries if I happened to meet them on their way to the chief.

To summarize to this point: Nuer judicial leaders are more uneasy about making decisions and inflicting punishments on their fellow men than are their Gusii counterparts. Nuer men continue to practice the blood feud after twenty years of colonial rule, while the Gusii have a strong tendency to resolve their conflicts in court. The hypothesis that these differences are due to the twenty-year head start which Gusii political acculturation had, can be rejected on the grounds that the present tendencies of rulers and ruled in Gusiiland manifested themselves in the early years of British administration.

[2] Phillips, writing in 1944, states, ". . . Comments on the intensely litigious disposition of the Kisii are to be found in official reports for at least thirty years past. . . ." He goes on to cite 1942 court records to show how much more litigation was brought by the Gusii (Kisii) than by their Nilotic neighbors, the Luo, p. 31.

Political Values

Can these differences in the political behavior of the Nuer and Gusii be related to more general differences in their political values? It is instructive in this connection to examine their values (as expressed in behavior) concerning authority and aggression. Both Evans-Pritchard and Howell use the words "democratic," "egalitarian," and "independent" in characterizing Nuer behavior. Evans-Pritchard also mentions the Nuer possession of "a deep sense of their common equality," (1940:134) and states, "There is no master and no servant in their society, but only equals. . . ." Both investigators give detailed accounts of the Nuer avoidance of using the imperative mode of speech, and the anger with which a Nuer reacts to an order which is not couched in terms of polite request. Nuer men refused to help a sick Evans-Pritchard carry his equipment when he was leaving the field because his way of asking them to do it was not euphemistic enough (op. cit.:182). They refuse to be ordered about by other Nuer or by Europeans, and they also exhibit little deference to persons in political roles. Referring to the Nuer leopard-skin chiefs, Evans-Pritchard states:

> . . . The chiefs I have seen were treated in everyday life like other men and there is no means of telling that a man is a chief by observing people's behavior to him (op. cit.:176).

Howell says of the contemporary situation:

> . . . though the Nuer have a proper respect for the authority of their District Commissioner, no one could argue that this in any way curbs their blunt methods of expressing approval of his decisions, or more often, disapproval. . . . He is addressed by his "bull-name," greeted as an intimate by men and women of all ages, praised, but often severely criticized, by the chiefs (1954:3).

In characterizing the Gusii attitude toward authority, one finds it necessary to use terms such as "authoritarian" which connote dominance and submission. Command relationships are a part of everyday life and are morally valued by the Gusii. A higher-status person has the right to order about persons of lower status, and this right is not limited to a functionally specific relationship.

The Internalization of Political Values

The contemporary location chief, for example, is surrounded by lackeys ready to do his bidding, and these lackeys have considerable command power over the populace in matters unrelated to the governing of the location. The chief, or someone in his immediate family, can stop anywhere in his location and order a man he does not know to do a personal favor for him, and it will be done. Schoolteachers, by virtue of their prestige; traders, by virtue of their wealth; elders, by virtue of their age; and sub-headsmen, by virtue of their political position, all have the privilege of telling other people what to do, and they use this privilege to pass onerous tasks on to persons of lower status. Orders are given in imperative terms and often in harsh tones, yet this is considered normal and proper conduct. Europeans are accorded considerable command power, whether or not they are government officials. Deferential behavior to persons of higher status is also pronounced among the Gusii and this was the case in the past as well as today. Traditionally, local community decision-making was dominated by the elders and the wealthiest individuals of the area; the local lineage was an age-hierarchy in terms of deference and dominance. Old men enjoy relating tales of the awe in which people held Bogonko, a nineteenth-century hero and leader of the Getutu tribe. It is said that when he walked out of his home area people fled from their houses until reassured that he would do them no harm. Songs in praise of his wealth, power, and accomplishments were composed. When he attended his grandson's wedding, woven mats were laid down so that he should not have to walk on cow dung. A soft voice and downward glance constitute traditionally proper demeanor for someone talking to an elder, chief, or other figure of importance. It is significant that some of the major political leaders of contemporary Gusiiland started out as servants to the major figures of their day, and that uneducated men with political aspirations often want to be cook or chauffeur to a chief. Gusii leaders are deferential to the District Commissioner and do not often contradict him.

The Gusii, then, appear to have authoritarian values while the Nuer are extremely egalitarian. This difference in values is manifest if one examines community or family relationships in the two societies. Nuer village life is characterized by economic mutuality, and an ethic of sharing surplus goods so intense that it is impossible for a man to keep such goods as tobacco if his supply exceeds that of his neighbors; they simply take it from him (Evans-Pritchard 1940:183–84). Among the Gusii, who live in scattered homesteads rather than villages, each homestead tends to be an independent economic unit; communal sharing is not considered desirable and the privacy of property is guarded. Although Gusii men, like Nuer, eat at each other's places, they have a greater tendency to congregate at the homestead of a wealthy man, who can afford to feed them well and who dominates them economically and politically to some extent. Both Nuer and Gusii are formally patriarchal in family organization. The available evidence indicates that the Gusii *paterfamilias* is much more powerful vis-à-vis his wives and sons than his Nuer counterpart. Among the Nuer, men do not beat their wives; sons can go off to live with their maternal uncles; and the eldest sons can curse their parents. Among the Gusii, wives are frequently beaten; sons can find no refuge at their mother's brothers'; and only parents may curse their children. Thus, the contrast between egalitarian and authoritarian values can be found in many spheres of Nuer and Gusii life.

Values concerning aggression are also of interest here. The Nuer have been described as "truculent" (op. cit.:134) and "easily roused to violence" (op. cit.:181).

> A Nuer will at once fight if he considers that he has been insulted, and they are very sensitive and easily take offense. When a man feels that he has suffered an injury . . . he at once challenges the man who has wronged him to a duel and the challenge must be accepted (op. cit.:151).

No such code of honor obtains among the Gusii, who consider it preferable to avert aggression whenever possible. Gusii men tend to be quiet and restrained in interaction and, although enemies try to avoid meeting one another, when they are forced into contact they will be civil and even friendly, although they have been backbiting or sorcerizing one another covertly. This is summed up in the proverb, "Two people may be seen together but their hearts do not know one another." Another proverb epitomizes Gusii avoidance behavior toward persons of a quarrelsome disposition: "A biting snake is pushed away with a stick." Serious crimes of violence are committed almost exclusively by intoxicated individuals. Thus the Gusii preference to avoid interpersonal aggression, and to resolve it in the courts when it comes to a head, contrasts sharply with the Nuer tendency to settle quarrels by fighting.

Using the classification of political systems proposed by Fortes and Evans-Pritchard (1940:5–6) or the revision of it proposed by Southall (1956:241–63), the Nuer and Gusii both fall into the same class, that of stateless segmentary societies. Yet, as has been shown above, they are poles apart in terms of political values which are significantly involved in their contemporary political situation.[3] If authority values were the criteria of classification, the Nuer would probably fall with societies like the Masai, whose political organization is based on age groups (Fosbrooke 1948), or with the Fox Indians, whose opposition to the concentration of power and authority was expressed in their political, religious, and kinship organization and their resistance to European domination (Miller 1955). The Gusii, in terms of authority values, might be classed with African kingdoms or with smaller-scale and less stratified chiefdoms in which inequalities in the allocation of authority were cherished rather than reviled. The corporate lineage is sometimes thought of as an inherently egalitarian institution, but, as the Gusii case indicates, it is also flexible enough to be able to develop in a non-egalitarian direction with an emphasis on generational status differences and a recognition of seniority based on wealth.

Certain aspects of Nuer and Gusii sociopolitical organization which would be considered peripheral under the Fortes-Evans-

[3] There is the question of why the political values of the Nuer and Gusii are so different. One possible hypothesis is an ecological one: the environment of the Nuer in the swampy upper Nile region necessitates local community cohesion and mutuality while tending to isolate one community from another. The Kenya highlands, where the Gusii live, provides an abundant agricultural base, with much less need for local cooperation and allows more contact between relatively distant parts of the society. This is consistent with the facts that the Nuer have more than twice as many tribal units as the Gusii, although their population is far from twice as large, and that, for the Gusii, the whole society is the maximal lineage, descended from Mogusii, while, for the Nuer, maximal lineages are components of the total society. Thus, Nuer social organization and values seem adapted to an environment which forces the cohesion of small groups but prevents that of large ones, while Gusii social organization and values seem less constrained by the physical environment.

Pritchard scheme indicate the divergent tendencies of the two societies. The Nuer have an age-set organization which, while it is not an important factor in their political life, nonetheless exhibits some degree of group organization based on relationships of equality. The Gusii have no organized group of peers. In the nineteenth century, Getutu, largest of the seven Gusii tribes, developed a hereditary chieftainship which resulted in some centralization of judicial power in that tribe. The chieftainship later bifurcated along lines of lineage segmentation but the leadership tradition remained strong in Getutu and is so today. This development, although limited to one part of Gusii society, was a movement in a distinctly authoritarian direction, especially when compared to temporary leadership movements among the Nuer. It is probable that, if the Gusii had lived in an area which contained a centralized chiefdom, they would have, as the Uganda-Congo tribes described by Southall did, voluntarily accepted its domination for the authoritarian order it offered. This is speculation and cannot be verified. But one thing seems certain from the above, and that is that classifying political systems on the basis of their predominant political values, particularly those concerning authority, yields insights into them which cannot be obtained by a scheme based purely on the broad outlines of political structure. The authority structure of cohesive groups within stateless segmentary societies has been neglected by investigators in favor of the structure of lineages and their relation to territorial units.[4] It is time that this situation be remedied by closer attention to problems in the allocation and exercise of authority.

CHILDHOOD EXPERIENCE

The contrasting values of the Nuer and Gusii described above indicate differing means of making decisions and different paths of action concerning the settlement of disputes, in short, basic

[4] The most recent example of this is the volume entitled, *Tribes Without Rulers: Studies in African Segmentary Systems,* Middleton and Tait 1958, in which six political systems are described with a minimal treatment of problems of internal authority. Leach 1954 represents an approach taking greater account of authority values.

The Internalization of Political Values

differences in the political systems of the two groups. In stateless societies with segmentary lineages, decisions are made mostly at the level of the local community and local lineage group, where permanent solidary bonds exist. The extended family as minimal lineage is a unit in the local political system, and its authority structure tends to resemble that of larger units. This resemblance has been made explicit for the Nuer and Gusii. Since the extended family functions both as a political unit and as an institution for the care and training of the young, the individual's induction into the political system actually begins in early childhood. His socialization into the authority structure of the family leaves him with values and role expectations which are adaptive in sociopolitical units above the family level. Because of this connection between the early family environment of the child and the political system, it is reasonable to expect differences in the early learning experiences of typical individuals in Gusii and Nuer societies. Psychological theory and research suggest two aspects of childhood experience as particularly relevant to the learning of values concerning authority and aggression: parent-child relations and aggression training. It should be possible to develop some theoretical expectations about these aspects for the Nuer and Gusii, and to check the available evidence for confirmation or disconfirmation.

1. PARENT-CHILD RELATIONS

Several investigators in the fields of social and developmental psychology, among them Frenkel-Brunswik (1955 and in Adorno 1950:359–60), Riesman, and Whiting, have proposed the general hypothesis (based on psychoanalytic theory) that the individual's attitudes toward authority are a function of his early relationships with his parents. The factors often held responsible for the development of such attitudes are: a) the authority structure of the family, i.e., the extent to which family authority is concentrated, in hierarchical fashion, or equally distributed among its members. In a family in which authority is concentrated, the child is held to develop authoritarian or rigid absolute values, and where it is equally shared, he internalizes egalitarian, group-oriented, and cooperative values. b) The closeness and warmth of the relationship between the child and the parent with most authority in the household. In particular, Frenkel-Brunswik found that American men scoring high on the F (authoritarianism-ethnocentrism) scale characterized their fathers as "distant," "stern," and "with bad temper," while those scoring low said their fathers had been "warm" and "demonstrative." (Op. cit.:359–60.) This finding appears to have had a major influence on thinking in this field of study. c) The degree to which the discipline administered is severe, with physical punishment most important. It is held that the child who has been beaten by a powerful parent will grow up submissive to arbitrary authority and to cherish a non-egalitarian ideal. The comparison of the Nuer and Gusii on these characteristics will be limited to (b) and (c), since (a) has been described above.

The father-son relationship is the appropriate category for studying childhood antecedents of authority values among Nuer and Gusii since both groups are strongly patrilineal, with men occupying all positions of authority in the kinship and political systems. Furthermore, residence at marriage tends to be patrilocal in both societies, so that many men live in close proximity to their fathers until the latter die. For the father, the father-son relationship is one between lineage-mates and is, therefore, likely to reflect the authority values which characterize his relations with other members of his lineage. For the son, the relationship represents his induction into the authority system of the minimal lineage, of which he is likely to remain a member as an adult, and it probably serves also as a prototype for other intralineage authority relationships. Concerning the Nuer, Evans-Pritchard states:

> . . . the father also takes an interest in his infant children, and one often sees a man nursing his child while the mother is engaged in the tasks of the home. Nuer fathers are proud of their children and give much time to them, petting and spoiling them, giving them titbits, playing with them and teaching them to talk: and the children are often in the byres with the man. I have never seen a man beat his child or lose his temper with him, however aggravating he may be. When a father speaks crossly to his child, as he does if, let us say, the child goes to the edge of a river or among the cattle, where he may be injured, it is evident that the child is not afraid of his loud words and obeys from affection rather than fear (1953:137).

Among the Gusii, fathers rarely take care of infants, as most mothers have daughters or sisters aged five to eleven who are charged with the responsibility of caretaking in her absence. If there is no such child caretaker (*omoreri*), the mother's co-wife or mother-in-law helps her out in this regard, but the father's role in infant care is minimal. Nor do fathers spend much time with their children, play with them, or act otherwise nurturant. On the contrary, the Gusii father tends to be aloof and severe, being called in by the mother primarily when the child needs to be disciplined. Fathers threaten their sons with punishment, and administer harsh beatings with wooden switches, explicitly intending to make the sons fearful and therefore obedient. The mother and older siblings help to exaggerate the punitive image of the father by warning the child of the dire paternal punishments which await him if he does wrong. At the end of his son's initiation ceremony the father ritually promises not to beat him any more, as an acknowledgement of his maturity. Most Gusii men recall a thrashing by the father for neglect of cattle-herding as one of their outstanding childhood experiences.

The patterns of father-son relations in Nuer and Gusii childhood experiences conform to the expectations generated by psychological hypotheses. The Nuer, who as adults have egalitarian values, grow up with warm, demonstrative fathers who do not beat them physically. The Gusii, who exhibit authoritarian behavior as adults, have experienced, as children, fathers who are remote, frightening, and severely punitive. This indicates the possibility that the difference in values concerning authority between Nuer and Gusii is related to the concomitant difference in early father-son relations.

2. AGGRESSION TRAINING

Psychologists have done considerable research on childhood antecedents of aggressive behavior. One of the most recent and comprehensive research studies on the topic is that of Sears, Maccoby, and Levin on the child-rearing patterns of 379 American mothers. They found a positive relationship between the mother's permissive attitude toward the aggressive behavior of her child and the degree of his aggressiveness. The more permissive the mother, the more aggressive the child (1957:259). Although no direct relationship between the aggressive behavior of an individual as a child and his aggression as an adult has been established, it is possible to use the above finding as a hypothetical basis for predicting that the Nuer, who are more aggressive and who set a high value on physical aggression, will be found to permit more aggressive behavior in their children than the Gusii, who tend to disvalue aggression and seek to avoid it. Evans-Pritchard states of the Nuer:

> . . . From their earliest years children are encouraged by their elders to settle all disputes by fighting, and they grow up to regard skill in fighting the most necessary accomplishment and courage the highest virtue (1940:157).
>
> . . . A child soon learns that to maintain his equality with his peers, he must stand up for himself against any encroachment on his person or property. This means that he must always be prepared to fight, and his willingness and ability to do so are the only protection of his integrity as a free and independent person against the avarice and bullying of his kinsmen. (Op. cit.:184.)

With the Gusii, on the other hand, parents do not encourage their children to fight but rather to report grievances to the parents. Adult disapproval of fighting is so strong that most children learn at an early age not to fight in the presence of parents or other adult relatives. When they are by themselves, herding cattle, however, boys do engage in physical aggression against one another. If a boy is hurt badly or beaten by a boy he does not know well, he will run to a parent, usually the mother, who will question him about it and then angrily cross-examine the other children involved. Mothers describing this procedure said that they "make a case," using the expression for conducting a trial. If the mother concludes that her own child was at fault, she will warn him and tell him he got what he deserved. If she concludes that the fault lay with someone else's child, she will loudly complain to the parents of the aggressor and demand that he be punished and controlled in the future. I have seen this happen and believe it is the normal procedure. When injury to a child is serious or permanent, an actual assault and damages litigation is initiated with the local elders. Older boys are warned against fighting on the grounds that they will involve their parents in lawsuits. Thus, as predicted on grounds of a psychological hypothesis, Nuer parents are permissive toward the aggression of their children and, in fact, actively encourage it, while Gusii parents do not tolerate fighting but promote reliance on adult intervention for the settlement of disputes.

This finding suggests that there may be a relationship between the difference in values concerning aggression on the part of Nuer and Gusii adults, and the concomitant difference in aggression-training of children in the two societies.

Discussion

Since Nuer and Gusii are both segmentary lineage societies, a theory which uses total-societal structures (acephalous segmentary lineages, central state organization, etc.) as the sole means of differentiating one political system from another would be hard put to explain why their contemporary patterns of political behavior under British rule are divergent. I have attempted to explain the divergence in terms of differing values, institutionalized in their political systems and internalized by individuals as they grow up in the family.

The Nuer, whose present-day judicial leaders shrink from passing judgment on and penalizing their fellow men, are seen as having an egalitarian ethic manifested in many aspects of their life, including community and family relations. In their early years, Nuer boys are treated in a nurturant and non-punitive way by their fathers, a pattern which personality theorists have hypothesized as antecedent to the learning of egalitarian values. The persistent feuding of the Nuer is part of a wider value-orientation favoring personal aggressiveness in which honor is easily offended and violence begun on trifling provocation. On the childhood level, Nuer individuals grow up in a mileu of adults who permit and encourage their fighting, and it is suggested here that this promotes the development of aggressive behavior patterns.

The Gusii, whose present-day judicial leaders are only too willing to pass judgment on and to punish members of their own group, are characterized by authoritarian values exhibited in many facets of interpersonal behavior on the local and family levels. Gusii fathers are emotionally distant from and physically punitive toward their young sons, which may be a necessary prerequisite for the internalization of authoritarian values. The tendency of Gusii men to disvalue aggression, attempt to avoid it, and to resolve aggressive conflict in court whenever possible is paralleled by the tendency of parents to express disapproval of childish aggression and to encourage children to report fighting to their elders. This child-training experience probably serves to inhibit overt aggressiveness in the individual and to strengthen litigiousness as an alternative behavior pattern.

By virtue of their greater willingness to submit to hierarchical authority and their greater inhibitions concerning the expression of aggression, the Gusii were able to make a more rapid and "satisfactory" adaptation to a colonial administration which required these very characteristics of them than were the Nuer, whose values concerning authority and aggression were contradictory to the demands of the British government. If and when the Nuer accept the idea of decision-making and peaceful conflict resolution at the level of the total society, they are likely to develop leadership patterns which are less autocratic than those of the contemporary Gusii, but their intergroup antagonisms and preference for local autonomy may block the acceptance of large-scale political integration.

It is not suggested here that child-training variables are independent determinants of political behavior but rather that they are shaped and selected by the functional requirements of local authority systems, just as any social group trains its members to conform to the rules which help maintain it. Thus child training may be *cause* with respect to the behavior of individuals, but is *effect* with respect to the traditional values which aid in the maintenance of social structures. If a pattern of child training is operating effectively, it is producing individuals whose personal values conform to the social values of the groups in which they participate as adults. Furthermore, the analysis presented here does not suggest that value-influenced child rearing practices are the only, or even the most important determinants of political behavior. Since the Gusii and Nuer are matched on two important sets of independent variables, i.e., the traditional struc-

The Internalization of Political Values

ture of group affiliations and the nature of the colonizing power, it has been possible to detect in clearest form the influence of other variables such as child training. My claim is that these latter variables account for some of the cross-cultural variance in political behavior, but not for all of it. While the validity of the analysis presented here is by no means established, it has, at the very least, the advantage of differentiating between two societies whose outward forms of political organization are similar. Furthermore, the aspects of childhood experience in which differences were found were not selected on an impressionistic basis but were investigated because of the indications from psychological theory and research that they are antecedents to personal behavior concerning authority and aggression. The differences in childhood experience conform to the expectations generated by psychological research. Finally, the theoretical approach used here is consistent with the hypothesis of Bruner based on research among American Indians:

> That which was traditionally learned and internalized in infancy and early childhood tends to be most resistant to change in contact situations (1956:194).

This hypothesis lends plausibility to the persistence, under British administration, of those traditional Nuer and Gusii political values which are internalized in the early years of life.

It has not been the purpose of this article to launch an attack on the study of political structure as such, but to add to it a new dimension which, hopefully, will increase its explanatory power by bringing it simultaneously closer to the realities of contemporary politics and to the findings of behavioral sciences other than social anthropology. In line with this aim, it is possible to draw two conclusions from the above study which bear on the comparative analysis of political behavior.

Conclusions

1. An invariant correspondence between sociopolitical organization at the total-society level and values concerning authority should not be assumed to hold cross-culturally. In the particular

case of stateless societies, it is fallacious to assume synonymity between the balanced opposition of equal segments and egalitarian political values, or to assume that corporate lineages are

FIGURE 4

Total Society Organization

		Stateless Societies			States		
		Multikin Villages and Bands	Segmentary Lineages	Age and Associational Groups	Segmentary States	Federative States	Centralized States
Degree of Concentration of Authority Within Local Units	Very High						
	High						
	Low						
	Very Low						

inherently egalitarian. The notion that sociopolitical organization at the total-society level varies concomitantly with authority values should be treated as an hypothesis to be tested empirically. For this purpose, the unit of comparison should be a relatively universal decision-making unit such as the local community. The degree of concentration of authority[5] within local units could be rated for a large number of societies which would also be classified according to their total-society organizations (see diagram). If the hypothesis is valid, then most societies would fall in the cells on the upper-right and lower-left of the chart, i.e., stateless societies would prove to have a low concentration of authority within their local units and states would prove to have a high concentration of authority in comparable units. It would also be possible to compare the authority structures of stateless

[5] In actual research this would have to be broken down into a number of specific variables, but elaboration of the concept is beyond the scope of this paper.

The Internalization of Political Values

societies having different types of total-society organization, as well as the local authority systems of states of different kinds of central organization. If there were no significant correlations between total society organization and local authority structure, then the influence of other variables on local authority structure would assume high priority for future research.

2. All societies have authority structures and values concerning the allocation of authority. In stateless societies, the proper unit for the analysis of such phenomena is not the total society, where we are likely to mistake lack of a central political hierarchy for egalitarianism, but the maximal decision-making unit (or some cohesive subgrouping within it). Most often this unit corresponds to the village, but it may be a cluster of villages, a hamlet or neighborhood, or even a domestic group such as the polygynous extended family. The local decision-making unit provides adult individuals with a model for behavior toward incipient authority structures in the wider society, and it is simultaneously the model from which the child learns values concerning authority. This dual function is likely to continue even after national administration has drastically altered the nature of total-societal political organization by bringing it under state control. For this reason, the analysis of authority and other political values at the local level is most likely to yield valid predictions about contemporary political behavior in newly introduced governmental institutions.

10 SEX ETHOS AND THE IATMUL *NAVEN*[1] CEREMONY

Gregory Bateson

DESCRIPTION OF THE *Naven* CEREMONIES

The outstanding feature of the ceremonies is the dressing of men in women's clothes and of women in the clothes of men. The classificatory *wau* dresses himself in the most filthy of widow's weeds, and when so arrayed he is referred to as *"nyame"* ("mother"). Two classificatory *waus* were arrayed for the *naven* of the young man in Palimbai who had made a large canoe for the first time in his life. They put on the most filthy old tousled skirts such as only the ugliest and most decrepit widows might wear, and like widows they were smeared with ashes. Considerable ingenuity went into this costuming, and all of it was directed towards creating an effect of utter decrepitude. On their heads they wore tattered old capes which were beginning to unravel and to fall to pieces with age and decay. Their bellies were bound with string like those of pregnant women. In their noses they wore, suspended in place of the little

FROM *Naven*, second edition, by Gregory Bateson with the permission of the publishers, Standford University Press. Copyright 1958, by the Board of Trustees of the Leland Stanford Junior University, and by permission of the author.

[1] This is based upon Bateson's study of the Iatmul, a tribe located on the Sepik River in New Guinea. The purpose of the complicated *naven* ceremony is for a large number of people to celebrate the first achievement of a young boy. (editor)

Sex Ethos and the Iatmul Naven Ceremony

triangles of mother-of-pearl shell which women wear on festive occasions, large triangular lumps of old sago pancakes, the stale orts of a long past meal.

In this disgusting costume and with absolutely grave faces (their gravity was noted with special approbation by the bystanders), the two "mothers" hobbled about the village each using as a walking stick a short shafted paddle such as women use. Indeed, even with this support, they could hardly walk, so decrepit were they. The children of the village greeted these figures with screams of laughter and thronged around the two "mothers", following wherever they went and bursting into new shrieks whenever the "mothers", in their feebleness, stumbled and fell and, falling, demonstrated their femaleness by assuming on the ground grotesque attitudes with their legs widespread.

The "mothers" wandered about the village in this way looking for their "child" (the *laua*) and from time to time in high-pitched, cracked voices they enquired of the bystanders to learn where the young man had gone. "We have a fowl to give to the young man." Actually the *laua* during this performance had either left the village or hidden himself. As soon as he found out that his *waus* were going to shame themselves in this way, he went away to avoid seeing the spectacle of their degraded behaviour.

If the *wau* can find the boy he will further demean himself by rubbing the cleft of his buttocks down the length of his *laua*'s leg, a sort of sexual salute which is said to have the effect of causing the *laua* to make haste to get valuables which he may present to his *wau* to "make him all right".[2] The *laua* should, nominally at least, fetch valuables according to the number of times that the *wau* repeats the gesture—one shell for each rubbing of the buttocks.

The *wau*'s gesture is called *mogul nggelak-ka*. In this phrase the word *mogul* means "anus", which *nggelak-ka* is a transitive verb which means "grooving", e.g. *ian nggelak-ka* means to dig a ditch. The suffix *-ka* is closely analogous to the English suffix, -ing, used to form present participles and verbal nouns.

[2] This is the pidgin English translation of an Iatmul phrase, *kunak-ket*. The suffix *-ket* is purposive; and the word *kunak* means to "make ready", "repair", or "propitiate".

This gesture of the *wau* I have only seen once. This was when a *wau* dashed into the midst of a dance and performed the gesture upon his *laua* who was celebrating the *wau*'s ancestors. The *wau* ran into the crowd, turned his back on the *laua* and rapidly lowered himself—almost fell—into a squatting position in such a way that as his legs bent under him his buttocks rubbed down the length of the *laua*'s leg.

But in the particular *naven* which I am describing, the two *waus* did not find their *laua* and had to content themselves with wandering around the village in search of him. Finally they came to the big canoe which he had made—the achievement which they were celebrating. They then collapsed into the canoe and for a few moments lay in it apparently helpless and exhausted, with their legs wide apart in the attitudes which the children found so amusing. Gradually they recovered and picked up their paddles, and sitting in the canoe in the bow and stern (women sit to paddle a canoe, but men stand), they slowly took it for a short voyage on the lake. When they returned they came ashore and hobbled off. The performance was over and they went away and washed themselves and put on their ordinary garments. The fowl was finally given to the *laua* and it became his duty to make a return present of shell valuables to his *wau* at some later date. Return presents of this kind are ceremonially given, generally on occasions when some other dances are being performed. The shells are tied to a spear and so presented to the *wau*.

In more elaborate *naven,* especially those in which women play a part, there is a classificatory spreading of ritual behaviour not only to cause the classificatory relatives of the actual *laua* to perform *naven* for him, but also to cause persons not otherwise involved to adopt *naven* behaviour towards other individuals who may be identified in some way with the actual *laua*. For example, the characteristic *naven* behaviour of the elder brother's wives is the beating of their husband's younger brother when his achievements are being celebrated. Owing to the classificatory spreading of the *naven* not only does the boy who has worked sago get beaten by his elder brother's wives, but also the boy's father's elder brothers' wives get up and beat the father. Further, men other than the performing *waus* may take the opportunity to make presentations of food to their various *lauas*.

Before attempting to account for the details of the ceremonial, we may conveniently summarise the *naven* behaviour of the various relatives:

Wau (mother's brother) wears grotesque female attire; offers his buttocks to male *laua;* in pantomime gives birth to female *laua* who looses his bonds; supports himself on the adze presented by her; presents food to *laua* of either sex and receives in return shell valuables; acts as female in grotesque copulation with *mbora*. These ceremonial acts may be performed either by own *wau* or classificatory *wau*—most usually the latter.

Mbora (mother's brother's wife) wears either grotesque female attire or (probably grotesque) male attire; dances with digging stick behind her head; takes male part in mimic copulation with *wau;* like *wau* she presents food to the hero of the *naven* and receives valuables in return.

Iau (father's sister) wears splendid male attire; beats the boy for whom *naven* is celebrated; steps across his prostrate *mbora;* participates in mimic contest between *mbora* and *iau* in which the former snatch the feather headdress from the latter.

Nyame (mother) removes her skirt but is not transvestite; lies prostrate with other women when the homicide steps across them all.

Nyanggai (sister) wears splendid male attire; accompanies the homicide, her brother, when he steps across the women; he is ashamed but she attacks their genitals, especially that of *tshaishi;* weeps when *wau* displays anal clitoris.

Tshaishi (elder brother's wife) wears splendid male attire; beats husband's younger brother and her vulva is attacked by his sister.

Tawontu (wife's brother, i.e. *wau* of ego's children) presents food to sister's husband (*lando*) and receives valuables in return. *Tawontu* may, I believe, rub his buttocks on *lando*'s shin, when the latter marries *tawontu*'s own sister.

Sex Ethos and *Naven*

The most important generalisation which can be drawn from the study of Iatmul ethos is that in this society each sex has its own *consistent* ethos which contrasts with that of the opposite sex.

Among the men, whether they are sitting and talking in the ceremonial house, initiating a novice, or building a house—whatever the occasion—there is the same emphasis and value set upon pride, self-assertion, harshness and spectacular display. This emphasis leads again and again to over-emphasis; the tendency to histrionic behaviour continually diverts the harshness into irony, which in its turn degenerates into buffooning. But though the behaviour may vary, the underlying emotional pattern is uniform.

Among the women we have found a different and rather less consistent ethos. Their life is concerned primarily with the necessary routines of food-getting and child-rearing, and their attitudes are informed, not by pride, but rather by a sense of "reality". They are readily co-operative, and their emotional reactions are not jerky and spectacular, but easy and "natural". On special occasions, it seems, the women exhibit an ethos modelled upon that of the men, and it would appear that certain women are admired for what we may describe as Iatmul-masculine characteristics.

If we return at this point to the problems presented by the *naven* ceremonies, we see these problems in a new light. The elements of exaggeration in the *wau*'s behaviour appear, not as isolated oddities, but as patterns of behaviour which are normal and ordinary in Iatmul men. This answer may seem rather uninteresting but it involves a major generalisation about cultural behaviour, and in science every step is a demonstration of consistency within a given sphere of relevance. We might perhaps have studied this consistency more fully but the answer would still have been of the same type. To pursue the matter further we should be compelled to shift to some other scientific discipline, e.g. to the study of character formation.

In the case of the women, with a double emphasis running through their ethos, their *naven* behaviour can be completely classified as consistent either with their everyday ethos or with their special occasional pride. All the behaviour of the mother is patterned upon submission and negative self-feeling. Her action in lying naked with the other women while her sons steps over them, and the cliché "that so small place out of which this big man came", are perfectly in keeping with the everyday ethos of Iatmul women, and constitute a very simple expression of her

Sex Ethos and the Iatmul Naven Ceremony   209

vicarious pride in her son. Thus the problem of the mother's behaviour, like that of the *wau*'s exaggerations, may now be referred to other scientific disciplines.

In the behaviour of the transvestite women, the father's sister and the elder brother's wife, we may see an expression of the occasional pride such as women exhibit on the rare occasions when they perform publicly with men as an audience.

Examination of Iatmul ethos has accounted for the tone of behaviour of the various relatives in *naven,* but there are many details which cannot be thus summarily dismissed. Consider the *wau:* his buffooning is normal, but that is no reason why he should dress as a woman in order to be a buffoon, and, as we have seen above, the structural premises within the culture, whereby the *wau* might regard himself as the *laua*'s wife, are still not a dynamic factor which would compel either the community or the *wau* to emphasise this aspect of the *wau-laua* relationship. We have still to find some component of the *naven* situation which shall act in a dynamic way to induce transvesticism.

I believe that we may find an answer to this problem if we examine the incidence of transvesticism in European society. In the *naven,* the phenomenon is not due to abnormal hormones nor yet to the psychological or cultural maladjustment of the transvestites; and therefore in looking for analogous phenomena in Europe we may ignore the aberrant cases and should examine rather the contexts in which some degree of transvesticism is culturally normal.

Let us consider the case of the fashionable horsewoman. Her breeches we may perhaps regard as a special adaptation, and she will say that her bowler hat is specially designed to protect her head from overhanging trees: but what of her coat, tailored on decidedly masculine lines? She wears feminine evening dress at the hunt ball, and her everyday behaviour is that of a culturally normal woman, so that we cannot explain her transvesticism by a reference to her glands or abnormal psychology.

The facts of the matter are clear: a culturally and physically normal woman wears, in order to ride a horse, a costume unusual for her sex and patterned on that of the opposite sex; and the conclusion from these facts is equally obvious: since the woman is normal, the unusual element must be introduced by the act of riding a horse. In one sense, of course, there is nothing exceptional in a woman's riding—women have ridden horses for hundreds of years in the history of our culture. But if we compare the activity of riding a horse with other activities which our culture has decreed suitable and proper for women, we see at once that horse-riding, which demands violent activity and gives a great sense of physical mastery,[3] contrasts sharply with the great majority of situations in a woman's life.

The ethos of women in our culture has been built up around certain types of situation and that of men around very different situations. The result is that women, placed by culture in a situation which is unusual for them but which is usual for men, have contrived a transvestite costume, and this costume has been accepted by the community as appropriate to these abnormal situations.

With this hint of the sort of situation in which transvesticism may be developed, we may return to Iatmul culture. First let us consider the contexts in which partial transvesticism occurs, namely, in the case of women who take part in spectacular ceremonies. Their position is very closely analogous to that of the horsewoman. The normal life of Iatmul women is quiet and unostentatious, while that of the men is noisy and ostentatious. When women take part in spectacular ceremonial they are doing something which is foreign to the norms of their own existence, but which is normal for men—and so we find them adopting for these special occasions bits of the culture of the men, holding themselves like men[4] and wearing ornaments which are normally only worn by men.

[3] In Freudian phrasing the act of riding a horse might be regarded as sexually symbolic. The difference between the point of view which I advocate and that of the Freudians is essentially this: that I regard such sexual symbols as noses, flutes, *wagon,* etc., as symbolic of sex ethos, and I would even see in the sexual act one more context in which this ethos is expressed.

[4] In theatrical representations, humorous journalism and the like, there is a common belief that the postures, gestures, tones of the voice, etc., of the horsewoman are to some extent modelled on those of men, and we might see in this an analogy with the proud gestures of the transvesite and semi-transvestite Iatmul women. I am uncertain, however, to what extent these postures, etc., of the horsewoman occur in real life, and whether they are not perhaps imaginary.

Sex Ethos and the Iatmul Naven Ceremony

Looking at the *naven* ceremonies in the light of this theory we can recognise in the *naven* situation conditions which might influence either sex towards transvesticism. The situation may be summed up by saying that a child has accomplished some notable feat and its relatives are to express, in a public manner, their joy in this event. This situation is one which is foreign to the normal settings of the life of either sex. The men by their unreal spectacular life are perfectly habituated to the "ordeal" of public performance. But they are not accustomed to the free expression of vicarious personal emotion. Anger and scorn they can express with a good deal of over-compensation, and joy and sorrow they can express when it is their own pride which is enhanced or abased; but to express joy in the achievements of another is outside the norms of their behaviour.

In the case of the women the position is reversed. Their cooperative life has made them capable of the easy expression of unselfish joy and sorrow, but it has not taught them to assume a public spectacular role.

Thus the *naven* situation contains two components, the element of public display and the element of vicarious personal emotion; and each sex, when it is placed by culture in this situation, is faced by one component which is easily acceptable, while the other component is embarrassing and smacks rather of situations normal to the life of the opposite sex. This embarrassment we may, I think, regard as a dynamic[5] force which pushes the individual towards transvesticism—and to a transvesticism which the community has been able to accept and which in course of time has become a cultural norm.

Thus the contrasting ethos of the two sexes may be supposed to play and to have played in the past a very real part in the shaping of the *naven* ceremonies. It has provided the little push which has led the culture to follow its structural premises to the extremes which I have described. When the women take part in spectacular ceremonial other than *naven,* the structural premises which might justify complete transvesticism are lacking, and the

---

[5] Such metaphors as this are of course dangerous. Their use encourages us to think of ethos and structure as different "things" instead of realizing as we should that they are different *aspects* of the same behavior. I have let the metaphor stand *pour encourager les autres.*

women content themselves with wearing only a few masculine ornaments.

Lastly we may consider the adoption of widow's weeds by the *wau* and the wearing by the women of the best masculine ornaments obtainable. The former is no doubt a buffooning expression of the men's distaste for the women's ethos. We have seen that the context of mourning is one in which the differing ethos of the two sexes contrasts most strongly and most uncomfortably, and the wearing of a widow's weeds by the *wau* is clearly on all fours with the men's trick of caricaturing the dirging of the solitary widow as she paddles her canoe to her garden. In shaming himself he is, incidentally, expressing his contempt for the whole ethos of those who express grief so easily.

The women on the other hand have no discernible contempt for the proud male ethos. It is the ethos appropriate to spectacular display, and in the *naven* they adopt as much of that ethos as possible—and even exaggerate it, gaily scraping the lime sticks in their husbands' gourds till the serrations are quite worn away. Here it would seem that their joy in wearing masculine ornaments and carrying on in the swaggering ways of men has somewhat distracted them from the business in hand—that of celebrating the achievement of a small child. Apart from the one incident in which the women lie down naked while the hero steps over them, the *naven* behaviour of the women is actually as irrelevant as that of the men. Thus the presence of contrasting ethos in the two sexes has almost completely diverted the *naven* ceremonial from simple reference to its ostensible object.

Nevertheless, since *naven* behaviour is the conventional way in which a *wau* congratulates his *laua* upon any achievement, there is no doubt that this behaviour, distorted and irrelevant as it may seem to us, is yet understood by the *laua* as a form of congratulation.

11 AN INVESTIGATION OF THE THOUGHT OF PRIMITIVE CHILDREN, WITH SPECIAL REFERENCE TO ANIMISM

A PRELIMINARY REPORT

Margaret Mead

INTRODUCTORY

This is a brief and preliminary report of an investigation into the thought of primitive children with particular attention to the problem of animism. It was conducted during the winter of 1928–29 among the Manus people of the Admiralty Islands, Mandated Territory of New Guinea, where I worked as a Fellow in the Social Sciences, of the Social Science Research Council. Some reference has been made to these results in my book on the education of Manus children (1930), and in my article on "The Primitive Child." (1931) I plan to defer full and detailed publication until after I have repeated this experiment among another primitive people. In the meanwhile, since the subject is one of interest to a group of investigators, it seems desirable to publish a summary report of my findings to date.

THE PROBLEM

During the last fifteen years two originally unrelated lines of investigation have tended to converge, investigations in child psychology and investigations and speculations concerning the mentality of primitive man. The assumption of M. Lévy-Bruhl

FROM Margaret Mead, "An Investigation of the Thought of Primitive Children, with Special Reference to Animism," 1932, *Journal of the Royal Anthropological Institute*, 62:173–90, by permission of the author and the Royal Anthropological Institute.

(1926, 1928) that the savage was prelogical, and the assumption of M. Piaget that the thought of the young child differed not only in degree but in kind from the thought of the adult, and was thereby more closely related to the thought of the savage than to the thought of the civilized man, gave rise to some very interesting problems. Was it true that there survived in the thought processes and in the institutions of primitive man a type of mentality which was found to be characteristic of young children in civilization? The findings of Rasmussen (1920), Sully (1926 [sic. 1903? Ed.]), and more especially Piaget (1926, 1928, 1929, 1930) (although his two latter volumes had not appeared in 1928) were strongly suggestive that there were important parallels between the phenomena which the anthropologist had described as animism and the observed spontaneous thought of young children. At the same time this parallelism was essentially inconclusive. The investigator merely compared a series of experiments or recorded observations upon civilized children with a type of thought which could be inferred from the myths and institutions of primitive man. Such a comparison was suggestive only.

A number of problems immediately presented themselves. Was this type of child-thought which confused cause and effect, imputed personality or spirit to inanimate objects and insisted upon an anthropomorphic interpretation of the universe, characteristic of all children of a certain age, or only of children who had been subjected to a particular set of environmental conditions? Was this type of thought a function of immaturity of intellectual development, or was the disappearance of this type of thinking in older individuals a function of a particular type of education peculiar to western civilization? Would this type of thought, granting that it were a universal aspect of the child mind, tend to continue and develop in a favourable environment, and was this the explanation of the parallels which could be drawn between primitive institutions and children's spontaneous sayings?

This was essentially a problem which could never be completely solved within the confines of western civilization, hinging as it did upon the differences in cultural *milieu* between advanced and primitive cultures.[1] Like all problems which in-

[1] The word primitive will be used throughout this paper to refer to those peoples who are completely without the benefits of written tradition.

volve the problem of the effect of social environment, results of experimentation and investigation within one social setting can never be positively definitive, but merely suggestive.

In 1928 I was awarded a fellowship to investigate this particular problem among a primitive people of Melanesia. The exact choice of the Manus tribe of the Admiralty Islands was made upon the basis of various practical considerations quite irrelevant to the problem. Recorded Melanesian cultures all showed a rich institutionalized animism which promised well for an investigation anywhere within the Melanesian area.

The problem was phrased as follows: Was the thought of primitive children characterized by the type of animistic premise, anthropomorphic interpretation and faulty logic, which had been recorded for civilized children, or was this type of thought a product of special social environment? If such thinking were characteristic of the primitive children investigated what was the result of attaining intellectual maturity in an atmosphere congenial to such thought, rather than under the influence of an education informed by the spirit of western science?

The Setting

The Manus people are a tribe of lagoon-dwelling fishermen, who live on pile-built houses in the southern lagoons of the Admiralty Islands. They are a brown-skinned, frizzy-haired people of medium stature, approximating somewhat more closely to the Micronesian than to the Melanesian type. They have no sort of political organization beyond a hereditary war leadership in each village; the society is held together by the intricate bonds of kinship and affinal obligations. A Government station has been established in the Admiralties since 1912, and the majority of the men under thirty-five have spent two or three years as indentured labourers on a plantation or schooner or in the police force. The women do not go away to work and speak no pidgin English, the language of the work boy. No mission has yet been established on the south coast, and the people were, without exception, pagan. Brief descriptions of the salient aspects of the culture are contained in *Growing Up in New Guinea,* and will not be repeated here.

All the work was done in the village of Peri during the six months of December to June, 1928–29. I worked throughout this period in collaboration with my husband, Dr. R. F. Fortune, who was making an investigation of the general culture. This circumstance made it possible for me to shorten materially the time which must be consumed in getting an understanding of the general outlines of a primitive culture before any special problem can be isolated and studied. I learned the Manus language, and all work with the children was conducted in it. The Manus language is a simple Melanesian language; a month is sufficient to get a good working knowledge of it; it is strikingly lacking in idiomatic refinements or delicate nuances.

In the village of Peri there were 210 people, of whom 87 were young people under or just at puberty. Actual ages were unknown, and only approximations based upon the people's knowledge of relative age could be used. Division into small age-groups was, in any event, impracticable because of the small number of cases. Of the group specially studied, there were twenty-two children, eleven boys and eleven girls between the approximate ages of two and six, and nineteen children, ten boys and nine girls between the approximate ages of six and twelve.

These forty-one children were studied under the following conditions:

(*a*) With their parents and their brothers and sisters in their own homes, in canoes, or in other houses during ceremonies.

(*b*) At play in groups in the shallow lagoons.

(*c*) At play in groups on the three small coral rubble inlets which constituted the only level ground in the village.

(*d*) At play on the wide verandahs of our house which had been built of native materials and with only slight modifications of the native style of architecture.

(*e*) Within the large living room of our house. Here play was sometimes random on rainy days, but more often devoted to drawing. I provided them with a large square table, 8 feet square and a foot and a half high, at which they could kneel and draw. The room also contained a number of low cedarwood boxes upon which the children could sit, or beside which they could kneel and draw. The floor was composed of narrow strips of split timber with wide cracks in between, corresponding exactly to the floor of a native house. The room also contained a high table, three chairs, shelves curtained with a native mat, a "children's shelf," which contained odd bits of coloured paper, string, crayons, pencils, etc. There were a few books on high shelves, a few small photographs on the walls, and a glass Chinese chimes hung from the central rafter. The children became perfectly familiar with the entire room, and entered and left it without permission from me. They were sent out by the older boys at meal times and during the siesta hour, and sometimes went to sleep on the floor or curled up on a box.

They learned to take me very much for granted, accepting the original situation which I down that I liked children, that I wanted as many children as possible to come to my house and stay as long as they liked. I never interfered in any way with their behaviour unless a situation seemed actually dangerous. Although I sometimes took part in their games, I more often claimed to be engaged in my own affairs, and they became accustomed to having me write or typewrite, or apparently read in their midst. Dr. Fortune worked in another house.

Environments *b, c* and *e* were all combined within easy access of our house, as the lagoon playground extended around it on three sides, and it abutted on one of the small islets on the fourth side. The children were in the water one minute, up on the island the next, sprawling on the veranda or romping through the house the minute after.

It should be remarked that Manus children are accustomed to going wherever they like about the village, and are in no fear of adults. The Manus men delight to humour and play with the children, so that my indulgence was in no sense out of character either to the children or to their parents. The children were originally attracted to the house by curiosity, in the wake of the adolescent boys and girls who did the house work, and by presents, balloons, balls, etc., which I dealt out day by day. Later they came to draw, and they came also from a quickly established habit of rendezvous.

Methods

As the existence of a primitive culture was in itself an experimental condition I utilized this fact as much as possible by observation of the children in normal social situations. In order to provide a more controlled situation and also in an attempt to elicit types of material which did not appear under ordinary observational methods, directly experimental methods were used. The methods employed fall under the following heads:

(*a*) Observation of a group of children, or of a child and an adult, or a group of children and adults, etc., in some ordinary social situation.

(*b*) Collection of spontaneous drawings.

(*c*) Interpretation of ink blots.

(*d*) Definite stimuli in the form of questions designed to provoke animistic responses.

(*a*) I handled this material in the form of running notes, with time records in two-minute intervals for certain types of play groups. It included questions from children to adults, children's responses to adult commands, explanations, etc., children's subterfuges, children's responses to situations of emotional stress, such as quarrels, severe illnesses, accident, fear displayed by adults, strangers in the village; birth and death; children's responses to storm, cyclone, animals, fish, birds, shadows, reflections, scenes between pairs of age-mates, between elder and younger children, between fathers and children, between mothers and children, between children and infants.

As these observations were all directed towards two particular ends, the definition of the type of child behaviour characteristic of children within the Manus culture, and the analysis of the thought of Manus children with a view to comparing it with the animistic thought said to be characteristic of children in western civilization, I proceeded as follows. Any particular type of situation, *e.g.* a child's behaviour when threatened by its parents with supernatural punishment was observed each time it occurred until a type response was discerned; from that time on, each situation

An Investigation of the Thought of Primitive Children

of the same type was observed, but not recorded in detail if it bore out the type findings based upon previous observations. All deviants or contradictions of the type-finding were recorded in detail. When a series was obtained the deviants were analysed and the deviating child investigated to determine whether special features of the child's family background, mentality, or temperament accounted for the deviation.

This method is possibly inferior to the laborious recording by a staff of stenographers of every response made by every child over many months. But one investigator attempting to cope with the difficulties of field-work in a primitive community in the few months allowed by climate and field funds, cannot hope to duplicate the voluminous methods of modern nursery school research. Such an investigator must confine himself to an attack upon the core of the problem and use methods like those outlined above to shorten field labour whenever possible. This method is open to less objection in a primitive culture than in a heterogeneous civilized society, because of the homogeneity of the subject's experience. The number of standardized type responses is far greater in a primitive society than in a civilized one.

(*b*) Drawings were collected to the number of 32,000 over a period of five months. No child had ever used a pencil and paper before. Any attempts at drawing had been confined to one game, outlining a shadow on soft soil with a sharpened stick used as a stylus. This game was only played by the older children and had never, so far as I could judge, been used to make original drawings instead of outlines. At least such use was not known to the group of children which I studied. As beginning drawing with the very young children would have involved actual instruction in the use of a pencil, I decided that a situation more closely analogous to the normal imitative educational situation could be produced if the older children were permitted to draw first and the younger ones led to imitate them. Five boys of about fourteen years of age were given pencil and paper and simply told to "draw," *taro we,* literally "to make a mark." They had seen us write and they had seen some half dozen Government officials write in record books. The brightest of the group, Kilipak, said, "Let's draw a human being." He and one other boy, Tamapwe, provided leads of this sort which the other three followed. The next day the next younger group, after having crowded about the older boys' elbows, were given pencils, until finally the youngest children were drawing without having received any instruction from me. I never passed any judgment upon the children's work, with the exception of a very generalized "That's splendid! That's fine!" type of encouragement to the younger children.

A definite regimen of behaviour was set up. When a child finished a sheet of paper, or tired of drawing with a half completed sheet, he must bring it to me. I wrote the name and date on the corner, and the interpretation of each picture on the paper. This procedure was standardized by the older children also; the older ones spontaneously explained their drawings; when the smaller ones failed to explain their unintelligible scrawls the older children insisted upon an explanation; this very simply became translated into a fixed rule. In this way the drawings bore most completely upon the problem under investigation.

For the drawing I used the large standard sheets of coarse-grained buff paper, and the children were given their choice between lead pencils and crayons. The crayons, although coloured, were never popular, and only selected when all the available pencils were in use; then most of the small children would select black crayons in preference to coloured ones. This seemed to be accounted for in terms of a preference for a sharp point and a lack of appreciation of colour. Only the fourteen- and fifteen-year-olds after four months of drawing hit on the idea of using the coloured crayons for realistic effects, and this was confined to drawing canoes and boats which they are accustomed to seeing painted.

(c) The interpretation of the ink blot test was used as a more controlled way of handling the children's responses. I made my own set of ink blots; they averaged about an inch and a half in greatest dimension, blue on a white surface. The child was shown one at a time and asked *"Tito ko no pwa tcha?"* "What is this like?"

The response was recorded without comment. If a child was slow or shy, I added an encouraging phrase or so: *"e ki la,"*

An Investigation of the Thought of Primitive Children

"come on," or *"Oi tu pa sani, ne?"* "You understand, don't you?"

(*d*) I also presented the children with a series of problems, utilizing in several cases situations which originally occurred spontaneously. These problems were:

(1) The attribution of malicious intent to a canoe which had drifted from its moorings. *Ndrol tasitan muan, ne? i tu wek.* That canoe is bad, isn't it? It's drifting.

(2) The attribution of personality to Chinese glass chimes. This was of the type which can be purchased in Woolworth's, rectangular pieces of glass suspended by slender cords from a supporting ring, and a piece of paper suspended from the whole so that the slightest wind will agitate the paper and cause the glass pieces to tinkle against each other. This was hung from a cross-beam of our house.

In this experiment I utilized an adult magical concept in an attempt to assimilate the chimes to native ideas of the supernatural. I said the chimes was a *ramus*, a property-getting charm. Manus adults have a variety of such charms, shells to be worn in the ear or hung on a betel bag, shell crescents with which food is magically crisscrossed, bird claws which are worn hanging down the back, elaborate constructions of grass and pig's tusks on the front house post, special drumsticks which, when used, make people bring the drummer the property for which he is asking—all these and others fall under the category of *ramus*, charms which cause other people to give you what you ask. It is a thoroughly magical concept, operating automatically without any intermediary. When I hung the chimes up I did so in the presence of adults, and remarked, "There is my *ramus*. It is crying out for Manus things which I want to take away with me to my own country." The adults accepted this explanation at once. One remarked, "What kind of property does it want?" Another said, "Is it asking for fish?" And a third said, "It is calling for beadwork."

In presenting it to the children I used this same conceptualization: "This is my *ramus*. It cries for native property. What do you think it is crying for now?"

I listened also for spontaneous comment upon the little chimes, which tinkled for the next three months whenever the wind blew.

(3) Presenting them with a dancing doll of the type which is constructed of paper so that arms, legs and the whole body have a tremendous extensibility like the paper chains made for Christmas trees. When these dolls are suspended they can be manipulated by very slight jerks of the string.

(4) The attribution of malicious intent to a pencil. When a child had made a drawing which he considered bad and had shown his displeasure by remarking on it: "*Tito muan,*" "this is bad"; or "*Io no tu taro we ka pwen,*" "I just drew, that's all," *i.e.* without definite intent to produce any result (this was a most frequent alibi). I would then seize the opportunity to say, "*Pensil muan, ne. Pensil ne po mangas wiyan pwen,*" "The pencil is bad, isn't it? The pencil doesn't do good work."

(5) The problem of how the writing on the paper was made by my portable typewriter. This was a question in which the children took a tremendous spontaneous interest from the start. They would gather around the typewriter for an hour patiently trying to analyse the mechanism. I have listed this problem under posed problems, because the typewriter itself was an artificial situation which I had introduced into their environment.

(6) The problem of the Japanese paper flowers which open out when placed in water. An atmosphere of expectation was engendered; I remarked that something most important was about to take place; enjoined most careful attention and dropped one of the paper pellets into a bowl of water, and simply recorded the comments. This problem and No. 3 had to be posed to one child after another in immediate succesion to prevent intercommunication. It was, therefore, of a type which it was impracticable to use often, as I did not have the necessary assistance to segregate the children who had taken the test from those who had not. It meant persuading adults to act as warders in what seemed to them a meaningless piece of behaviour. Complicating the native social situation in this way is always of doubtful value, as it is impossible to estimate accurately the repercussions in other departments of native social life.

An Investigation of the Thought of Primitive Children

These six problems contained the following elements:

(1) Personalization through ascription of motive to a moving inanimate object. This was a less extreme form of personalization than No. 4, for a canoe is less amenable to control than a pencil.

(2) The personalization of an instrument producing mechanical or rhythmical sounds.

(3) Presentation for explanation of an object in human form which made apparently voluntary dancing motions.

(4) Personalization through ascription of motive and separate will power to a pencil. This problem contained the additional element of offering an acceptable alibi for failure in execution.

(5) A mechanical device of such complexity that the connection between the visible movements of my fingers on the typewriter keys and the writing had to be deduced without any knowledge of the principles involved.

(6) An appearance of greatly accelerated but natural growth, or, alternatively, the presentation of an appearance of wonderful transformation from a pellet into a flower.

Results

(a) Observations of Spontaneous Behaviour

As the investigation was designed to discover and record spontaneous animistic thought as expressed in the conversation, games, etc., of children, I expected this aspect of the investigation to yield the most interesting results. The results, however, were virtually negative. I found no evidence for spontaneous animistic thought in the uncontrolled sayings or games of these Manus children during five months of continuous observations, alone or in groups, when they were unconscious of being observed at all.

Before going further it is necessary to distinguish between what I am calling "spontaneous animism" and a child's acceptance of animistic categories which are explicit or implicit in the linguistic concepts of its elders. When an English-speaking child refers to a ship as "she," he is not being spontaneously animistic, he is merely conforming to a recognized category of gender. But when a child draws a picture of a steamboat, setting the steamboat on end, inserting a face in one end, and attributing human activities to the steamboat,[2] this is spontaneous animistic thought, although it may be, as I shall suggest later, rooted in a traditional linguistic usage. Similarly a child who talks to a dog, or a horse, or a cat, or a parrot, is not necessarily animistic, but is merely imitating traditional adult behaviour. On the other hand, an English-speaking child who has long conversations with a toy engine or with a tree has spontaneously attributed personality in a way which transcends the traditional pattern of its group. Similarly a child who says his prayers and asks God to make him a good boy and not let it rain to-morrow is showing no childish or spontaneous animism, while a child who invents an imaginary playmate, holds long conversations with the playmate and reports sayings and adventures of this imaginary playmate, is indulging in a type of thought which may, with due reservations upon how much stimulation the child has received from others, be called spontaneous, and non-traditional.

Therefore, I do not class it as spontaneous animism when a Manus child says, "The ghost of the wife of Pondramet married the ghost of Sori last night." In saying this the child is merely repeating a piece of gossip, as he would say, "A woman in the village of Rambutchon has had a baby." The Manus adults believe that the ghosts of the dead live all about them in the village; they are continually in communication with these ghosts through diviners and mediums, and marriages and quarrels on the ghostly plane are often reported by mediums. The children accept the alleged presence of the ghosts in general, and parrot their parents' comments. Only if a child spontaneously elaborated the idea of ghosts, talked with them, saw them, invoked them for his private ends, would I class remarks upon the ghosts as spontaneous.

So when a Manus child calls a pig by name and tells it to come and eat, which is exact reproduction of adult behaviour, I do not call this spontaneous. But had a Manus child ever been seen conversing with a dog or commenting upon a dog's feelings or even

[2] Fortune, R. F., "On Imitative Magic" (MS). Reproduction of a drawing by Priscilla Heale.

An Investigation of the Thought of Primitive Children   225

addressing a remark to a dog, this would indeed have been spontaneous, for Manus dogs are unnamed and never spoken to in words. The natives control them entirely by kicks, cuffs, and a low guttural call.

Also when a Manus child explained a woman's sickness by saying she had a snake in her belly, this was merely repeating a doctor's diagnosis, and from the child's point of view was a statement of fact, although the adults knew that the terrific distortion of the woman's abdomen was from no natural snake, but from a supernatural snake.

Similarly with the treatment of the concept of the *tchinal* or mischievous land devil, in the persons of whom the water-dwelling Manus people caricature and express their fear and distrust of their land neighbours. The adult describes the *tchinal* to the child in an attempt to intimidate him from wandering about at night and to explain to him why his presence is inconvenient when the parent goes to the market at the edge of the land. *Tchinals* have extraordinarily long arms, protruding teeth, hair which hangs matted over their eyes. Their fingernails are as long as their fingers, and they will pursue and eat men. If a child reported having seen a *tchinal,* or added more and personal detail to this traditional picture, or showed special fear of a special *tchinal* whom he declared to inhabit a special spot, only in such cases would these be declared to be evidences of spontaneous animistic thought.

To summarize, I considered strictly traditional behaviour, whether expressed in language or belief, as insufficient proof that a child spontaneously attributed personality to natural phenomena, animals or inanimate objects, or created imaginative non-existent personal beings.

I found no instance of a child's personalizing a dog or a fish or a bird, of his personalizing the sun, the moon, the wind or the stars. I found no evidence of a child's attributing chance events, such as the drifting away of a canoe, the loss of an object, an unexplained noise, a sudden gust of wind, a strange deep-sea turtle, a falling seed from a tree, etc., to supernaturalistic causes. This is the more remarkable when it is realized that if a stone falls suddenly in the bush near an adult, he will usually mutter, "a spirit," and the common explanation of the loss of any small object such as a knife, if the explanation of theft is rejected, is that a spirit took it. In adult theory spirits put ideas into peoples' minds, are responsible for any insane or unreliable behaviour—in the native idiom a spirit "twists the neck" of the unfortunate demented person. Also spirits send turtles to their mortal wards, or guide the feet of their wards to the turtles, and it is angry spirits which send cyclones to injure a sinning man's house. Furthermore, the adults believe that one spirit was recently turned into a crocodile, and that carved crocodiles can talk. So in this case the children not only did not construct new and spontaneous explanations to account for the behaviour of natural phenomena, animals or unexplained sounds or motions around them, but they actually largely neglected the stock explanations provided by the culture.

The evidence of observation was confirmed by the evidence from the drawings. There were no animals acting like human beings, no composite animal-human figures, no personified natural phenomena or humanized inanimate objects in the entire set of drawings. If a shark was drawn it was drawn either as a mere representation, as accurately as possible, or as part of a scene in which a man was spearing a shark. The sun and moon were not spontaneously selected as subject-matter for drawing; when I asked the children to draw them the sun was indicated by a circle, the moon variously as a crescent and a circle. There was no humanization.

The treatment of spirits was equally scant. I shall discuss this topic under two heads: (1) The treatment of the child's individual guardian ghost, and (2) the treatment of the subject of the general spirit population of the village.

(1) Little boys from the age of five or six, with a few exceptions in households where there are several children, have a guardian ghost assigned to them. This is usually either the spirit of a dead male child or a child born on the spirit plane. Occasionally a spirit of a grandfather who has been supplanted by some younger and more recently deceased ghost, will be given to the male child of the house. In theory this ghost goes everywhere with the child to protect him from all spiritual dangers, notably from the malicious attack of other ghosts. In order to appreciate the children's treatment of these guardian ghosts of theirs it is necessary to describe briefly the relationship between

An Investigation of the Thought of Primitive Children

an adult male and his Sir Ghost (*i.e.* the special deceased male relative whose skull is hung in his house and upon whom he relies for protection).

A man communicates with his Sir Ghost through a medium, or a diviner. Through the medium he asks his Sir Ghost's opinions, and receives long and detailed replies. Through his divining bones, or those of another diviner, he asks his Sir Ghost questions which can be answered by signs meaning yes or no. If he is not a bone diviner he may still consult his Sir Ghost by asking him a question, spitting on a betel leaf and watching which side of the leaf the juice runs down. Before this latter type of communication a man may chat aloud amiably with his Sir Ghost for several minutes. Similarly a man gives his Sir Ghost verbal orders to accompany other members of his household on dangerous expeditions. If asked, a man can tell at once where his Sir Ghost is.

All this the children have seen and heard. But to their own guardian ghosts they pay no such attention. Most of them can tell the name of their ghosts, but not always the relationship. No child claimed to have seen his ghost, nor knew of any other child who had ever seen his ghost. Only one child had ever talked with his ghost, and he, Bopau, was regarded as aberrant by his companions. No child was ever heard to ask his ghost to do anything for him, such as help him win a race, etc. When I questioned the older children, aged twelve to fourteen, in more detail on the subject of the helpfulness of their ghosts, they all expressed great scepticism. "Probably he wouldn't be there." "There is no use talking to him. I think he isn't there." "No, don't ask him. Do it yourself."

Also the boys never boast of having spirits when the girls do not, although the men make just this point against the women.

Against this background of general sceptical lack of interest, little Bopau stood out strongly. He was the case which deviated from type; if my observations and conclusions were correct the reasons why Bopau took a creative interest in his ghost where the others did not, should complement my findings in the other cases. This they did. Bopau was an orphan. His father had been dead only two years, and although Bopau lived in the house of his father's younger brother, he was not beloved there. His dead father, Sori, was the Sir Ghost of this younger brother, Pokenau.

Pokenau had assigned to Bopau a spirit-child of no importance named Malean. But Bopau claimed that Sori, his father, was his ghost, and that Sori talked with him and he with Sori. He rejected the ghost assigned to him. He was a lonely, shy, unloved child, compensating for his loneliness by imaginary intercourse with his ghostly father.

(2) In the treatment of spirits in general the children show very little interest. There are only half a dozen drawings which are said to be ghosts rather than human. These had no distinguishing ghostly attributes. The children hear a good many reports of ghostly activity, some of which they remember. When a child is ill a séance is held over it. Often the child himself, even a child of thirteen or fourteen, does not know the spiritual diagnosis of the sin which has caused his illness. (It is never his sin, but always a transgression of some older relative.) They go to sleep during séances, imitate ghostly whistles to frighten their elders, and use the argument which their parents use to them, *"Kor e palit,"* "the village is ghost-ridden," *i.e.* dangerous, to keep unwanted younger children from accompanying them on some expedition, and the younger children soon learn to answer, *"Kip e aua,"* "You are lying." The children play no games involving the ghosts.

The question of the children's treatment of the *tchinals,* land devils, differs somewhat in accordance with adult habit. The ghosts are an important constituent of the adult world; adults obviously act most of the time with reference to ghostly wishes; the names of ghosts are always on adult lips. With the *tchinals,* however, it is different. The parents threaten the children with them if they go to a slightly distant islet to play, yet the parents go carelessly to that islet. The parents speak of the wishes of ghosts, but never discuss *tchinals* among themselves. The children accept the concept of the *tchinal* with good humour, but slight real belief. Once I saw them playing a game of seizing each other and shouting, "I am a *Sir Tchinal.* I eat men." This only happened once, however. In their drawings they adopted the habit of branding any drawing of a human being which was a failure as a *tchinal.* Analysis of the drawings of the group and of individuals revealed that there was no style of depicting a *tchinal;* it was simply a faulty or accidentally grotesque attempt at drawing a human being. Even the traditional aspects of the

An Investigation of the Thought of Primitive Children

tchinal, the long matted hair and the long fingernails, did not appear in the drawings. The children not only failed to elaborate imaginatively upon the traditional concept, but they even neglected to utilize some of the salient traditional features.

One other point deserves special mention here, the question of reflections in water. The adults believe that if the image of a Manus falls in fresh water, part of his soul stuff will remain there, in the power of a fresh-water demon, and magical rites are necessary to recover the soul. The elders avoid taking children to the mainland because the children will not take this belief seriously, but instead enjoy peering over the edge of the canoe at their shifting images in the fresh water. This is a case where the children actually reject the concept that the image is an inextricable part of the personality, a prelogical concept which should have been, on the old hypothesis, particularly congenial to the immature mind.

(B) THE EVIDENCE OF THE DRAWINGS

This has already been touched upon in the discussion, and can be merely summarized here. The drawings showed no personalization of inanimate objects or animals or natural phenomena. They showed only a few drawings which were said to be ghosts, although the ghosts occupy fully a third of adult thought and conversation; the drawings of ghosts contained no special features; many faulty attempts at depicting the human form were classed as *tchinals*. There were no scenes of *tchinals* eating men or *tchinals* turning into other things, such as occur in the tales. There were no scenes in which ghosts killed men or stole their soul stuff, or any other scenes depicting the traditional intercourse between ghosts and men. There were no drawings of skulls, although a skull, the bodily abode of the ghost, hung from the rafters of almost every house in Peri. The only scenes which were drawn were strictly realistic—fights, games of ball, boat races, scenes of fishing for turtle or shark.

(C) THE INK BLOT TEST

The ink blot test also provided no results which indicated a tendency to spontaneous animistic thought on the part of the children. The children's responses could be divided into three groups which have no correlation with either age or sex.

(1) Children who genuinely tried to discover what the ink blot was meant to be, and having hit upon an answer gave it with conviction and sometimes with an explanatory detail showing which part of the blot convinced them that their interpretation was correct. Most numerous group.

(2) Children who began by an attempt to discover the proper interpretation, but whose interest soon wavered, and who then offered the same explanations in more or less regular alternation throughout the series. So the replies would be dog, pig, man, pig, dog, man, etc.

(3) Children to whom the ink blots suggested so little that they had to look about them for suggestions, and then named the ink blot after a pot, or an article of furniture. Least numerous group.

A few children followed the pattern already established in their drawings; when the ink blot showed too little resemblance to the object named they would add "of a *tchinal*." So Popoli said "a house . . . hym . . . I think it is the house of a *tchinal*." All the children gave only one answer; they did not permit their imaginations to play with the material. Once a child had said, "That is a crocodile," he accepted the ink blot as a depiction of a crocodile, and turned away from it without further interest. The most intelligent children scrutinized the drawings most carefully, and in a few cases failed to find any close counterpart within their own experience. They then suggested things of which they had heard but never seen, "a cassowary," "a telephone" (of which a work boy had brought home the tale), "part of a foreign canoe," "a horse." The replies did not show a high standard of community response. For example, No. 8 was interpreted as head of a man, island, bird, bird, stone, rat, ball, tattoo mark, pig, mirror, cloud, pepper leaf, tree trunk, a whirlwind, I don't know, human being, a snake, head of a man, human being, mirror, head of a man, pig, pig, pig, verandah, pig, tree, etc.

(D) DEFINITE STIMULI

Space does not permit my reporting here in full the answers to the six experimental situations. In this preliminary report I shall merely quote one set of answers for twenty children, and give the type answer for the other five tests.

(1) The attribution of malicious intent to a canoe which had drifted away. The stimulus question, "That canoe is bad, isn't it? It has drifted away."

Answers

Girls between three and six years of age

Masa. No; Popoli[3] didn't fasten it.
Kawa. No; the punt (used to fasten canoes with) slipped.
Maria. No; it wasn't fastened.
Pwailep. No punt.
Ngalowen. Popoli is stupid; he didn't fasten it right.
Sāpa. No; no punt to fasten it.
Itong. No; it wasn't fastened right.
Molung. Not fastened.
Saliko. I can fasten a canoe; Popoli can't.
Alupwa. No; no fastening; no punt.

Boys between three and six years of age

Bopau. No punt through the outrigger.
Mee. No punt; bad Popoli.
Ponkob. The canoe floats. No punt, no punt, no punt.
Pokus. No; where's the punt?
Pope. No; no punt; it floats away.
Topal II. Popoli didn't fasten it; Popoli will lose his canoe.
Salemon. It will float away; there is no punt in it to fasten it.
Tchokopal. No; I fasten my canoe, my canoe, my canoe. Then it does not drift.
Pomitchon (aged six). Popoli is a stupid boy; he doesn't know how to fasten a canoe; when I fasten a canoe, it doesn't drift; I understand.

---

[3] The name Popoli is used throughout for the child who did not fasten the canoe properly. Actually different names occurred as the experiment was repeated under different circumstances.

THE GLASS CHIMES

(2) The children know very little of the *ramus* concept beyond applying the name to the wrappings and pigs' tusks on house posts, which are stationary *ramus*. Their interest was not caught by the word. They turned instead immediately to studying what made the sound. The type answer for the children of five or six was: "The wind winds the paper. It shakes the strings. Then the glasses hit and it sounds." The type answer for the younger children was of this order: "The paper moves. It pushes. It sounds," or "The wind winds. The glass hits. It sounds."

(3) The dancing doll.—The responses here were of two types. Some of the youngest children responded first by imitating the loose-jointed movement of the doll. Only afterwards did they speculate on the source of movement. The older children wanted to manipulate the doll at once. Younger child's type response, after imitative dance for a minute: "She pulls the string. It's dancing." Older child's type response: "Let me pull the string and shake it. Let me make it dance."

(4) The attribution of malicious intent to the pencil.—Younger child's response: "I drew it." "I made it." "I made it badly." Older child's type response. "No, I didn't make it right," this of one's own work. Bystander comment: "No, she did it wrong." "No, she is stupid. She doesn't know how to draw right."

(5) The typewriter.—This was a more complicated problem and mainly interesting for method of attack. The children's first question was: "How does it work?" Then followed a series: "She hits those white things, there." "When she hits them those things jump." "There's a string under there." "No, a stick which moves when she hits the white things, and then the stick moves and pushed the other thing (type) up." "Then it hits the black cloth and that makes the mark." "Why?" "There's a mark there," points to type. This was typical for the age of five–six. The younger children watched without comment.

(6) The Japanese paper flowers. Younger child's typical response: "The water gets inside and makes it bigger, like a hibiscus" (the Manus have no general word for flower). Older child's

typical response: "It's rolled up. The water loosens it. It's like a hibiscus, isn't it?"

In evaluating the accuracy of this response it should be borne in mind that these children have spent their lives in the water, and understand the action of water far better than civilized children.

Discussion of Results

The results of these various lines of investigation show that Manus children not only show no tendency towards spontaneous animistic thought, but that they also show what may perhaps legitimately be termed a negativism towards explanations couched in animistic rather than practical cause and effect terms. The Manus child is less spontaneously animistic and less traditionally animistic than is the Manus adult. This result is a direct contradiction of findings in our own society, in which the child has been found to be more animistic, in both traditional and spontaneous fashions, than are his elders. When such a reversal is found in two contrasting societies, the explanation must obviously be sought in terms of the culture; a purely psychological explanation is inadequate.

There are two alternative explanations, both of which involve a cultural determinant, which may be offered in the light of the Manus evidence. The contention that a tendency to spontaneous animistic thought is a function of immature mental development must, of course, be dismissed. It may, however, be argued that the human mind possesses a tendency towards animistic thought, and also a tendency towards non-animistic practical observations of cause and effect relationships. Proceeding upon this premise, the argument would be that in modern society the methods of education now in vogue tend to discourage the animistic tendencies of the human mind, until such tendencies are almost entirely suppressed, while in Manus the system of education tends to discourage the practical non-animistic thought processes so that the growing individual becomes progressively more animistic and less matter-of-fact in his thinking. This theory recognizes a psychological substratum tending towards animistic thought, and allows culture only a suppressive, non-creative rôle.

An alternative explanation would disallow the contention that the human mind had a universal tendency towards animistic thought, and limit this tendency as an idiosyncrasy of some human minds only. It would further propose that animistic tendencies of individual adult minds had left their impress upon the human language and human institutions in such a way that an individual born within a human society had a set of animistic conceptions and premises ready-made for his acceptance. Upon this theory children born into our society would first be made animistic by their culture, and then, through later processes of education this animistic tendency would be criticized and in large measure eliminated.

Before considering these alternative possibilities further it is necessary to enquire what evidence can be derived from Manus culture. Here again it will be necessary to summarize briefly and leave fuller statement for more extended publication. Analysis of the Manus culture, including the language, religious beliefs, mythology, folk beliefs and methods of education, leads me to the following conclusions.

The matter-of-fact nature of Manus child-thought is dependent upon the following conditions:

(1) The fact that the Manus language is a bare simple language, without figures of speech, sex gender or rich imagery.

(2) The fact that the Manus child is forced at a very early age to make correct physical adjustments to his environment, so that his entire attention is focussed upon cause and effect relationships, the neglect of which would result in immediate disaster in terms of severe punishment.

(3) The fact that the adults do not share the traditional material of their culture with their children.

These three factors in the situation deserve some further explanation. The Manus language belongs to the Austronesian stock, but it is conspicuously bare, and lacking in metaphor. In the course of hundreds of texts recorded by Dr. Fortune only three similes were found. The use of verbs which apply to the specifically human action of persons to describe the action of

An Investigation of the Thought of Primitive Children

inanimate objects is also absent. The wind winds. The sun does not smile or waken. There is only one third person pronoun for all genders. The language provides the child with no stimulating leads to spontaneous animistic thought.

Compare this condition with the wealth of metaphor and animistic suggestion in English. Children are taught the distinctions between he, she and it, and then find the moon personalized as "she," and ships described in animistic terms which would bewilder a Manus adult. Children are taught poetry in which natural phenomena and animals are continually personalized in language and ascribed behaviour. That is, where the Manus language provides no linguistic base for spontaneous animism, the English language does.

The second reason, the enforced physical adjustment of the child, is also very important. As I have described the physical education of Manus children at some length elsewhere (1930: chapter III) I shall not go into detail here. Suffice it to say that Manus children are taught the properties of fire and water, taught to estimate distance, to allow for illusion when objects are seen under water, to allow for obstacles and judge possible clearage in canoes, etc., at the age of two or three. Matter-of-fact adjustment which permits of no alibis, for a child is punished for awkwardness or physical failure, forces the children's thought along practical lines. Furthermore, the material environment offers no mechanical complexities such as elaborate machines, beyond the comprehension of the child, and so conducive to animistic speculation. The simple mechanical principles upon which a Manus native builds and navigates his canoes, or builds his house, present no mysteries. The child is not discouraged from an attempt at matter-of-fact understanding by explanations which he cannot follow, nor does the adult find the attempt at explanation too difficult and fall back upon fanciful explanations like the example in which a mother told a child who had already spent hours exploring the internal structure of a piano that the sounds were made by little fairies who stood on the wires and sang.[4] Also the Manus adult is careful not to discourage children in their efforts towards a physical control of their environment.

[4] Quoted by Susan Isaacs (1931:130).

Children are never told they are "too little," "too weak," "not old enough" to do anything. Each child is encouraged to put forth its maximum effort, in terms of its individual capacity always, and not in terms of invidious comparison with other children.[5] It is never intimidated. If a child attempts something beyond its capacity it will be diverted, but not openly discouraged. The child is therefore not constrained to manufacture alibis in terms of seven league boots or imaginary playmates who possess the skill and adult licence denied to him. A child's attention is always concentrated upon what he can do now, not upon what he is unable to do. It is unnecessary to labour comparisons with the educational methods of our own society, methods in some measure imperative because of the dangerous mechanical complexity of modern life, in some part merely the result of traditional attitudes towards precocity.

The third reason suggested to explain the Manus child's lack of animistic thought is the peculiar educational attitudes of the Manus in respect to their non-material culture. Children are taught early and painstakingly how to walk, swim, climb, handle a canoe, shoot a bow and arrow, and throw a spear accurately. They are taught to talk. But they are not given any instruction in the social and religious aspects of adult life, beyond occasional threatenings with ghosts or *tchinals,* which, occurring only in this particular context, the children soon learn to recognize as bogies only. Children are told no stories of any kind, nor are they expected to be interested in stories, which are for "men and women, not for children." As myths play a very slight part in Manus life, and are seldom told—the average adult cannot tell more than four or five complete tales—the children do not overhear them. They are not required to conform to the will of the ghosts; when they are ill it is for an adult sin, and they are neither told nor expected to understand the intricacies of the religious life. They are permitted at ceremonies, but take no part in them, regarding all social, economic and religious ceremonial as tiresome things which adults do, but from which children are exempt. If they were actively shut out from adult life their curiosity might

[5] I have discussed this individual standard of education in an article published in the *18th Annual Report of Schoolmen's Week,* 1931.

be stimulated; as it is they are prevailingly indifferent. Thus it is that they learn very late, near puberty for girls, often past puberty for boys, the religious concepts of the Manus, concepts which would be a rich background for spontaneous animism if taught them as children, as our children are taught traditional theology, myths and fairy tales.

Within the Manus culture itself it is, therefore, possible to find explanations of the differences between Manus child-thought and Manus adult-thought. The language offers no stimuli, the method of education fixes the children's attention along antithetical lines; the adult culture, which provides each generation grown to maturity with a set of traditional animistic concepts, provides the children with no background for animistic constructs. Contrasting conditions occur in our own society, the language is richly animistic, children are given no such stern schooling in physical adjustment to a comprehensible and easily manipulated physical environment, and the traditional animistic material which is decried by modern scientific thinking is still regarded as appropriate material for child training.

Upon the strength of one experiment, in one native culture, it is possible to draw only negative conclusions. Animistic thought cannot be explained in terms of intellectual immaturity. Further research will be necessary to determine whether animism must be regarded as a tendency of all human minds which may be stimulated or suppressed by educational factors or merely as an idiosyncrasy of some human minds, which has become crystallized in the language and institutions of the human race.

12 IFALUK GHOSTS: AN ANTHROPOLOGICAL INQUIRY INTO LEARNING AND PERCEPTION

Melford E. Spiro

It was not very long ago that a book describing the culture of a primitive society would include the description of its belief system in a chapter devoted to "superstitions" and cognate phenomena. The belief in ghosts, for example, was attributed either to the innate (and inferior) character of the "primitive mind," or to the prescientific stage of primitive culture. The rise of scientific anthropology, however, has led to a conception of primitive religion which excludes the term *superstition* from the anthropological lexicon. But however relativistic the anthropologist may be, he cannot escape the problem of accounting for the seemingly irrational character of many of the beliefs and rituals he observes; and though he may not wish to use the invidious term "superstition" to characterize these beliefs, he is called upon to explain their existence and persistence.

The traditional explanation of such beliefs has been that they are culturally determined. According to the concept of cultural determinism, the individuals within any society are "molded" by the predetermined pattern of their culture, so that if a belief in ghosts is part of the society's cultural heritage, the members of the society, being the "carriers" of this heritage, will willy-nilly believe in ghosts (see White 1949).

Recently, however, the concept of cultural determinism has come under careful scrutiny. It has become evident that this

FROM Melford E. Spiro, "Ghosts: An Anthropological Inquiry into Learning and Perception," 1953, *Journal of Abnormal and Social Psychology*, 48:376–82, by permission of the author and the American Psychological Association.

concept, although useful as a short-hand notation, has unfortunate implications which lead to over-simplified and mechanistic notions concerning the relationship between cultural heritage and human behavior. The mere existence of an institution as part of the cultural heritage is *not* a sufficient condition for its acceptance by members of the society. On the contrary, the acquisition of culture is a process in which the "external" cultural heritage is internalized (learned) by the individual, and this process involves considerable resistance, conflict, and tension (Spiro 1951).

Since anthropology has no learning theory of its own, it has turned to psychology for its "laws" of learning, with the hope that these laws, developed in the laboratory, could explain the process of cultural learning. It is the thesis of this paper that social scientists may have been too hasty in accepting the experimental laws of learning because some cultural phenomena, at least, cannot be explained by current learning theories. This thesis will be developed in connection with the belief in malevolent ghosts in a South Seas society.

IFALUK AND ITS GHOSTS

Ifaluk[1] is a tiny atoll in the Central Carolines (Micronesia) inhabited by about 250 people, whose culture reveals few indications of acculturation (Burrows and Spiro 1953). Its subsistence economy consists of fishing and horticulture, the former being men's work, the latter women's. Politically, the society is governed by five hereditary chiefs, who are far from "chiefly," however, in appearance or behavior. Descent is matrilineal and residence is matrilocal. Though clans and lineages are important social groups, the extended family is the basic unit for both economic and socialization functions. It is particularly important to stress, in relationship to this discussion, that Ifaluk is notable for its ethic of nonaggression and for its emphasis on helpfulness, sharing, and cooperation as typical and expected forms of interaction (Burrows 1952; Spiro 1950).

[1] The field work on which this section of the paper is based took place in 1947–48, as part of the Coordinated Investigation of Micronesian Anthropology (CIMA), and was sponsored by the Pacific Science Board of the National Research Council and the Office of Naval Research.

Ifaluk religion asserts the existence of two kinds of supernaturals, high gods and ghosts. The former, though important in myths, do not play an important role in daily life, whereas the latter do. Ghosts are of two varieties, benevolent and malevolent. The former are the immortal souls of dead, benevolent mortals; the latter are the immortal souls of dead, malevolent mortals.[2] One's character in the next world is not a result of reward or punishment for activity in this world; it is, rather, a persistence in time and space of one's mortal character.

Malevolent ghosts, called *alus,* delight in causing evil. They are responsible for any immoral behavior committed by the Ifaluk, and they cause illness by the indiscriminate possession of any member of their lineage. Benevolent ghosts, on the other hand, attempt to help the people; with their assistance the human may exorcise the malevolent ghosts. In all ages and for both sexes, the malevolent ghosts are the most feared and hated objects in Ifaluk (Spiro op. cit.:67–71). Consequently, most of Ifaluk ceremonial, and much of their unceremonial, life is preoccupied with the *alus.*

Our problem is to account for the existence and persistence of this "irrational" and "punishing" belief. The theory of cultural determinism can explain why it is that the belief in *alus,* rather than the belief, say, in Satan, is part of Ifaluk culture; but it does not explain why this belief, despite its irrational and punishing character, is acquired anew by each generation. It seems, moreover, that current learning theories are equally incapable of accounting for the learning of this belief.

Alus AND LEARNING THEORY

It is difficult to see how Hullian learning theory, because of its conception of "learning" is capable of accounting for any belief. "Learning," writes a distinguished Hullian learning theorist, is

---

[2] This scheme presents us with a knotty problem. Since the people agree that there are no malevolent Ifaluk and since ethnographic observation confirmed the native contention, and since—so the people maintain—the same condition existed in the past, whence are derived these malevolent ghosts?

"... the observed behavioral changes that occur with practice" (Spence 1950). Learning theory, therefore, is concerned with "... formulating the laws relating the behavioral changes which occur with practice to the particular environmental (stimulus) conditions, past and present, that play a role in these changes" (Spence 1947:1).

It is apparent that a learning theory that is concerned with *changes* in *behavior* cannot deal with belief systems in general and with the belief in the *alus* in particular, which involve the *acquisition of knowledge*. (It is unimportant whether the knowledge is true or false. The statement that the universe is populated by malevolent ghosts is false from the standpoint of a transcultural science. It is true from the point of view of the Ifaluk, and they can confirm its truth value by abundant evidence.)

Even the Tolmanian theory, with its cognitive emphasis, is of little assistance, for Tolman's "cognition" is a limited concept, referring to that knowledge which enables the organism to choose one behavioral response among several when experiencing a "demand" (1934).

Perhaps we are too formalistic and are ignoring the heuristic value of the experimental laws of learning, even though the definitions of "learning" seem to preclude their applicability to such cultural phenomena as religious beliefs. Aside from a suggestive paper by Tolman (1949) and a stimulating chapter by Lewin (1942), the theoretical application of learning theory to human social learning has been restricted to the Hullian derived theory of Miller and Dollard (Dollard and Miller 1950; Miller and Dollard 1941).[3]

Defining "learning" as the connection of a response and cue-stimulus, and conceiving of "response" in broad terms so as to include covert and symbolic—as well as overt—behavior, Miller

[3] Since the above was written, Tolman has contributed an essay on human learning to *Toward a General Theory of Action*, by Talcott Parsons and Edward A. Shils (Eds.), but the author has not had an opportunity to study it carefully. In a pioneering work, Whiting (1941) has analyzed the socialization process in a New Guinea society in terms of the Hullian system, with considerable success. The gaps in his analysis may derive from the pioneering nature of the work or from theoretical difficulties inherent in the system. The data presented in this paper would seem to support the latter hypothesis.

and Dollard explain this connection by the constructs of "drive" and "reward." In attempting to analyze the belief in *alus* in terms of these concepts, this author found that they did not apply. It is apparent, on a priori grounds, that the learning of this belief does not involve a primary drive; and an analysis of the nature and functions of this belief, as well as the conditions in which it is learned, fails to reveal what secondary drive might be involved. This belief does have important adaptive and adjustive consequences (Spiro 1952), but to identify the consequences of the belief with the drive for its learning would leave us in a most vicious circle.

If the learning of this belief does not presuppose a drive variable, it follows, from the Hullian learning theory, that its learning has no reinforcement value ("reinforcement" being defined as the lowering of drive intensity). This deduction is empirically confirmed. The belief in the *alus,* as we have already pointed out, is highly punishing for it means living in fear of evil creatures who cause illness and death.

Since the belief in these *alus* is fear-provoking, this belief may be viewed as a secondary drive and, indeed, it does serve to initiate a number of behavior patterns (rituals, ceremonies, taboos, etc.). Drives are learned, according to Dollard and Miller, by a typical conditioning process in which a neutral cue-stimulus, when associated with an unconditioned stimulus, elicits the same response as the latter. Hence, fear drives are learned by an association of a neutral stimulus with an unconditioned fear-eliciting stimulus (Dollard and Miller op. cit.: 69). But the fear of the *alus* is not learned in this way. Ifaluk children are not taught about the *alus* in a formal, nonaffective manner; rather the cognitive and affective aspects of the belief are learned as part of a unitary learning process. A strange noise is heard on the roof of the house, a stone is thrown at a woman while bathing, a tree falls on a young child, a person becomes ill—and the cause is attributed to the activity of an *alus.*

Our analysis, if correct, has led us into an intriguing paradox. As social scientists we are committed to the postulate that beliefs are learned, but we seem unable to account for the belief in evil ghosts by the laws of learning. It is our hypothesis that this paradox may derive from a misplaced confidence in the postulate of interspecific psychological equivalence that seems to underlie the current theories of learning (see Thorpe 1950), a postulate which makes possible the "reduction" of human learning to the relatively simple models used in infrahuman animal learning (see Irving 1949). This postulate is based on the preassumption that learning is "automatic" (Hall 1943:69) and "mechanistic" (Boring 1946). The crucial role played by symbolization, particularly language, in human behavior (Cassirer 1944; Goldstein 1940) renders this a doubtful methodological assumption when applied to human social learning.[4] Since human social learning is primarily cultural learning, and since cultural activity is primarily symbolic activity, we should proceed with extreme caution before we apply unqualifiedly the learning principles derived from infrahuman *a*cultural behavior to human cultural behavior. Hilgard puts the matter judiciously in writing: *"Only if the process demonstrable in human learning can also be demonstrated in lower animals is the comparative method useful in studying it"* (Hilgard 1948:329, italics his).[5]

Although Hull may be correct in insisting that animal learning

[4] Tolman seems to agree with this position, although he states that "everything important in psychology . . . can be investigated in essence through the continued experimental and theoretical analysis of the determiners of rat behavior at a choice point in a maze," he excludes from this generalization "such matters as involve society and words" (1938:34).

[5] It is an interesting commentary on the nature of our culture, and one that would make a fascinating subject for the sociology of knowledge, that animal behavior has become the model for the study of human behavior. In a strange historical dialectic the anthropomorphism of primitive peoples has found its "antithesis" in the zoomorphism of many experimental psychologists. It is equally strange that some sociologists and anthropologists have been willing to accept this interpretation of human behavior and society. The sociologists, whose rigorous sampling techniques have made them wary of generalizing from one statistical universe to another within the same species (from lower- to middle-class populations, for example), are prepared to generalize from one species to another (rats and humans, for example). Anthropologists use animal societies as foils for the understanding of human societies because of the limited amount of socially acquired and socially transmitted learned behavior patterns in the former. If the bulk of the cultural behavior with which anthropology is concerned is not found in animal societies because infrahuman animals cannot learn these distinctively human behaviors, how can anthropologists learn about human social learning from them? For an incisive critique of the use of animal models in human psychology, see Allport (1947).

be viewed as the "mere interaction" of organism and environment it is difficult to view organism and environment as sufficient conditions for human social learning. A learning theory which does not emphasize the concepts of personality and of cultural heritage as necessary conditions in human learning and as independent variables in the learning process, is not adequate to the task of accounting for this type of learning.[6] Humans bring to any learning situation a fund of attitudes, norms, values, and beliefs—derived from their cultural heritage—on the basis of which they perceive, select, and respond (consciously and unconsciously) to their environmental (physical and cultural) stimuli. Hence, humans acquire beliefs concerning ghosts, for example, not as biological organisms in an objective environment, but as personalities (biosocial organisms) in a culturally constituted environment (see Hallowell 1951).

Alus AND PERCEPTION THEORY

If stimuli (including culturally-given belief systems) are differentially perceived—hence, differentially responded to—as functions of differential cultural experience, it is necessary to know how the Ifaluk perceive the *alus* if we are to understand why they acquire this belief.

The selectivity of perception is a function, among other things, of the perceiver's frame of reference which, in turn, derives from his previous experience. Individuals who have perceived their world as threatening will be disposed to believe in the existence of threatening objects or persons—malevolent ghosts, for example—for such a belief falls within their frames of reference. But individuals who have perceived their world as secure will not be so disposed, for there is nothing in their experience which corresponds to this belief. Where we find a culturally patterned belief, we may be sure that the members of the society share a

---

[6] Lewin, of course, took full account of these variables in his emphasis on such concepts as "ego-involvement" and the social field (1935, 1942). Allport has long expressed dismay at the exclusion of the ego from psychology (1943). The importance of the cultural heritage has been stressed most forcibly by Kroeber (1948).

common frame of reference within which this belief is perceived. And it follows that the experiences which have given rise to this frame of reference have occurred within certain culturally patterned contexts.

Frames of reference, then, are learned in the process of interaction with other individuals in which the nature of one's world is inferred from the perception of it. This inference then functions as a "hypothesis," as Bruner and Postman term it (Bruner 1951; Postman 1951), in future transactions with the environment. By "hypothesis," writes Postman:

> ... we mean, in the most general sense, expectancies or predispositions of the organism which serve to select, organize, and transform the stimulus information that comes from the environment. A given sensory input has not only energy characteristics which trip off a series of organized reactions in the nervous system, but it has cue or clue characteristics as well—it carries *information* about the environment. It is with respect to these information characteristics of stimuli that hypotheses operate (op. cit.:249).

Since the *alus* are conceived of as threatening and terrifying objects, we must discover what experiences lead the Ifaluk to develop the hypothesis that their world is threatening and, therefore, predispose them to believe in these threatening ghosts. Since this belief is already strongly held by the young children, such a hypothesis must arise in the early experiences of the Ifaluk young children.

The first threatening experience, which begins at birth and continues for the duration of infancy, is the daily washing of the infant at dawn in the cold water of the lagoon. That this immersion is painful and threatening is an inference drawn from three kinds of data. First, the water at dawn is very cold, so that even adults refuse to enter it until after sunrise. Second, the contrast between the infant's previous activity—sleeping, wrapped in a blanket, between its parents—and the sudden awakening and immersion in the cold water must be particularly painful. That this is so is indicated by the great crying and wailing of the infants during the entire bathing. Finally this is the one activity over which the infant has no control. An Ifaluk infant, with this one exception, is the master of his environment. His slightest cry elicits an adult response of attention and care. The Ifaluk premise that infants are utterly helpless creatures leads to the conclusion that their every whim must be satisfied and that they must never suffer pain. The mother, for example, may not leave her house for the first three months after the baby's birth, so as to ensure her constant attendance upon it. She must sit by its cradle and, at its first cry or other indication of discomfort, she takes it into her arms, gives it the breast, or attempts other pacifying techniques. The baby is fed on demand. After the first three months the mother may leave the infant's side only if another adult takes her place. Only after he can walk and talk is the mother, or her surrogate, allowed to leave the baby alone, and only then are any disciplines, including toilet training, instituted. Until then the baby is never restrained, even when his activities are destructive, and his needs are seldom frustrated. This is an infant-centered culture, *par excellence* (see Burrows and Spiro, op. cit.). Thus the experience of the morning bath stands in sharp contrast to the typical experience of the infant. Not only does he suffer pain in the bathing experience, but all his cries, which are so remarkably efficacious in achieving his ends in other situations, are of no avail in this one.

Now the infant not only responds to these quite different stimulus situations in overt and observable ways, but—it is our hypothesis—he also learns something about the nature of his world from his perception of these situations. This learning, to be sure, is of a primitive, kinesthetic type, in which a pleasure-pain rhythm is set up in the organism as integral to its experience. Certain expectations are created in the infant with respect to the satisfaction or the frustration of its desires; and a frame of reference, or hypothesis concerning the nature of its world is emerging —a hypothesis that its world is both satisfying and threatening.

This infantile hypothesis is reinforced by a much more threatening experience of childhood. The birth of a sibling means that the heretofore indulged child is relatively ignored, and his place is now taken by the younger sibling as the object of indulgence. The older child is now left to shift for himself emotionally; many of his cries go unheeded and many of his needs are frustrated. Thus, the Ifaluk infant, whose frustration tolerance is, understandably, amazingly low, is exposed to a highly threatening experience—the apparent loss of parental love. It is little wonder that Ifaluk parents say that a child becomes "ill" at the birth of a sibling. And it is also little wonder that a study of those children whose positions had been "usurped" by a new sibling revealed that no fewer than 58 per cent, and as many as 96 per cent, displayed the following behavior characteristics: fighting and attacking, willful disobedience, destruction of property, temper tantrums, eating problems, night terrors, thumb-sucking, crying and whining, shyness, and "negativism" (Spiro 1950:99 ff.). We may conclude, assuming that the clinical inferences drawn from such symptoms are valid, that the children perceive this situation as highly threatening. And again, it is our hypothesis that the children not only respond to this situation in certain observable ways but that they learn something about their world from their perception of this situation. What they learn serves to reinforce their "hypothesis" derived from the infantile experience—that the world, among its other characteristics, is threatening.

We may now state our thesis more clearly. The Ifaluk child learns to perceive his worth in terms of such dichotomies as pleasure-pain, security-insecurity, assurance-threat. This bipolarization of his world forms the basis for his "hypotheses" concerning his world. These "hypotheses" he brings to any learning situation, and it is on the basis of these "hypotheses" that he will accept or reject any cultural belief, including the belief in ghosts. As Postman has written:

> We can conceive of the perceptual process as a cycle of hypothesis-information-trial and check of hypothesis-confirmation or nonconfirmation. In any given situation the organism is not indifferently ready for the occurrence of any or all types of objects. Rather the organism expects, is *eingestellt* for a limited range of events. Into the organism which is thus "tuned," information is put by sensory stimulation. This information serves to (1) broaden or narrow the range of hypotheses or (2) confirm or deny specific hypotheses. If the information confirms the hypothesis, a stable perceptual organization is achieved (op. cit. 251).

If we examine the Ifaluk belief in ghosts benevolent and the malevolent alike, we discover a number of isomorphisms between this belief and the culturally patterned childhood experiences we have discussed. (*a*) Just as there are many adult figures in the child's life who care for him (all the people in his extended family dwelling), so there are a number of *alus*. (*b*) Just as these adults both protect and harm the child, so *alus* protect (prevent and cure illness) and harm (cause illness). (*c*) Just as the primary harming adults are females (it is the mother, or his sisters, who bathes the infant, and who rejects the child the most severely), so the most vicious malevolent ghosts are female. (*d*) Just as those who cause the pleasure and pain of childhood are the (living) relatives of one's lineage, so the *alus* who cause pleasure and pain are the (dead) relatives of one's lineage. (*e*) Just as the adults inflict pain indiscriminately on all children (whether one is good or bad, he is "rejected" upon the advent of a new sibling), so the malevolent *alus* cause illness and death indiscriminately (the good and the bad alike are attacked by the *alus*). (*f*) Just as the consequence of adult protection is security and the consequence of adult rejection is anxiety, so the consequence of *alus* protection (prevention or cure of illness) is security, and the consequence of *alus* attack (illness) is anxiety.

It is our thesis, then, that the Ifaluk child accepts the culturally-given belief in ghosts because this belief is in accord with his previous experiences. The Ifaluk child has learned to perceive his world as both threatening and gratifying and, hence, he can give ready assent to a belief which postulates the same kind of a world. This public belief confirms, in a real sense, his own private "hypothesis" concerning the nature of his world. And since this public belief is culturally sanctioned, carrying with it the authority of tradition and of social approval, it adds ever greater cogency to his own private "hypothesis."

The Psychodynamics of Belief and the "Truth" of Tradition

Thus far we have offered a hypothesis for the acquisition of the belief in *alus,* but this hypothesis does not account for its persistence in adulthood. Learned beliefs, like other learned responses, are subject to extinction unless they are reinforced by practice. Beliefs, which constitute the cognitive affirmation of experience, must, in turn, be confirmed by experience. For the nature of this confirmation of the belief in *alus* we turn to the psychodynamics of this belief.

The ethic of nonaggression is the supreme value in Ifaluk. Not only is the overt expression of hostility forbidden, but its very sensation is viewed as shameful. (This is inconsistent, of course, with the belief that hostility is caused by *alus*.) Nevertheless, the people do have hostile drives (see Spiro op. cit.: ch. 3), and this hostility may help to explain some of the anxiety —if the anxiety theory of Freud (1936) and Mowrer (1939) is correct—which is characteristic of the Ifaluk personality structure. Now anxiety is not only learned, but it in turn serves as a drive for the learning of behavioral techniques which will reduce its intensity (Dollard and Miller op. cit.:ch. 5). The Ifaluk have learned to reduce the intensity of their anxieties by projecting their hostilities onto the *alus*.

Ifaluk belief asserts that men are intrinsically good, that they are not responsible for hostile thoughts or acts, but that hostility is caused by the *alus*. Thus, the belief allows the people to reject their own hostile drives as being "ego-alien," and to project them onto the *alus*. This resolution of anxiety by the projection of hostility not only serves to confirm the validity of their belief, but at the same time, it perpetuates the belief by re-creating the image of these malevolent ghosts.

With this in mind, we may resolve an unresolved paradox concerning this belief: the *alus* are conceived of as the ghosts of evil people, but according to both the Ifaluk and ethnographic observation there are no evil people in Ifaluk. If so, how can there be *alus*? Our analysis, however, has revealed (by implication) that there are evil people in Ifaluk.

First, the Ifaluk child knows "evil" people. His parents who bathe him in cold water and who "reject" him when he needs them—they surely are evil.

But the adults, no less than the children, experience evil people, and this experience continues throughout life. *The evil person that the adult experiences is himself,* for everyone who experiences hostile drives within himself is evil. Thus, psychologically viewed, the tradition is true. There are evil people in Ifaluk, all of whom experience aggressive drives; and the *alus* do have their origin in the souls of evil people, as the projection of the evil (aggressive drives) in their own souls.

SUMMARY

The acquisition of the Ifaluk belief in malevolent ghosts, it has been our thesis, cannot be explained by either traditional theories of cultural determinism or of learning. This belief, we have attempted to demonstrate, is learned by the child according to certain principles of perception and cognition. However irrational the belief in malevolent ghosts may appear to us, it is not irrational for the Ifaluk child. On the contrary, it is a pragmatic, cognitive truth; a truth that publicly confirms his own personal experiences. This belief continues to persist in adulthood, because it is re-created by the psychodynamics of Ifaluk personality functioning.

13 PSYCHOLOGICAL WARFARE AND THE JAPANESE EMPEROR

Alexander Leighton and Morris Opler

During the war, whether or not we should attack the Emperor in our propaganda directed at Japan was an important practical issue. It was hotly disputed with strong feelings on both sides of the question.

At present and in the future our policy in regard to the Emperor and the Imperial Institution remains of practical importance in our dealings with Japan. This was highlighted at the time of the surrender when the Japanese informed us they were prepared to accept the Potsdam Declaration, but wanted clarification regarding what would happen to the Emperor. This was the only question asked. It is therefore important for all of us as citizen critics of our Government's foreign policy to understand the cultural and psychological significance of the Emperor.

On a wider scale, the phenomenon of the Emperor illustrates the working out of some of those basic assumptions regarding human and cultural nature derived from psychiatry and anthropology.

1. *Research Findings:* From our preliminary work in morale analysis, we concluded that the Japanese soldiers' attitudes toward the Emperor represented an exceedingly strong and enduring constellation of beliefs and feelings. As a consequence, it was thought not only useless and wasteful to attack this symbol, but

FROM Alexander Leighton and Morris Opler, "Psychiatry and Applied Anthropology in Psychological Warfare against Japan," 1946, *American Journal of Psychoanalysis,* 6:20–34, by permission of the authors and the publisher.

actually dangerous, since such attacks could well serve to increase enemy resistance and determination. On the positive side, it seemed to us that resistance both in battle and on the home front could be lowered by a clear and repeated statement declaring that the fate of the Emperor and the Imperial Institution after an Allied victory would be up to the Japanese.

It was subsequently found that throughout the war no matter how their morale deteriorated in other respects, in this faith and belief the Japanese remained steadfast. After the end of hostilities, surveys in Japan revealed that the overwhelming majority of the civilian population were strong in their devotion to the Emperor. (See Morale Division Report of U. S. Strategic Bombing Survey, Government Printing Office.) In fact, next to the food question, the greatest fear of the Japanese seemed to be that the Allies might bring some harm to him. Even the Japanese communists, whose policy is to dispense with the Imperial Institution, recognized the strength of the popular feeling and at one time accepted the fact that they must compromise with it. Said one of them:

"If the majority of the people fervently demands the perpetuation of the Emperor, we must concede to them. Therefore we propose as a suggestion that the question of maintaining or disposing of the Emperor be decided after the war by plebiscite. Then, even if the outcome of the plebiscite is the perpetuation of the Emperor such an Emperor must be one who does not possess power."

A Japanese peer who is a member of the Social Democratic party told Leighton that he believed the Emperor should be outside of politics, but when the question of abolition was raised, said "No, it would be too lonely without him."

2. *The Nature of Human Beliefs:* To understand these attitudes, let us consider first the general nature of human belief and sentiment.

All people everywhere have systems of belief and among all people everywhere these beliefs show certain common characteristics.

For one thing, beliefs often have a *logical basis*. That is they have components based on and supported by observation combined with reasoning. This is true not only of scientific and scholarly thought, but of everyone's common daily experiences about the house, in the office, and at play. Nor is it true only of our culture, for the jungle native in his hunting and the Japanese peasant in his planting have hundreds of beliefs based on experience and reasoning.

Beliefs also have a *social and cultural basis*. The individual maintains his ideas not only through reasoning, but from the precept and example of his fellows and from the pressure of their opinions. This involves the things which in any given society "everybody knows" without the need of proof or even demonstration, and he who questions them is made to feel either a fool or guilty. In actual fact, beliefs dominated by this characteristic may or may not be true and they may or may not be logical. Their chief quality is their social and cultural nature.

That the world is flat, that it is a crime against God to use anesthetics, that swine are unclean, that Holy Water has power, that corn pollen will make a man healthy and lucky, that vitamins are what we all need, that cannibalism is evil, that free competition will solve the world's economic difficulties—all these are examples of beliefs which exhibit a large element of the cultural component.

Still another support for belief lies in the *emotional balance within the individual, in his personal aspirations, anxieties and conflicts*. Beliefs primarily of this order may be socially shared and they may have a logical structure, but their main characteristic is their role as ideas which enable the individual to feel better about something which would otherwise produce an unpleasant or distressful state of emotions. Many of the neurotic convictions that are familiar to psychiatrists are of this type. However, they are by no means confined to neurotics, and are part of the equipment with which people of all types and nations make their way through life.

Beliefs, then, among all the various groups of people of the world show elements that are logical, cultural and tied to intrapersonal balance and sense of security. Any given belief will probably have all three elements inherent in it, but their relative proportions may vary greatly.

Beliefs also show varying degrees of strength. Those which have the *greatest tenacity and resistance to change are the fundamental assumptions regarding values, man's place in life, the nature of the world and the nature of the supernatural.* Although influenced and, within limits, modifiable by reason, they are profoundly *emotional rather than logical,* are felt with certainty rather than thought through and are largely *cultural and concerned with the intrapersonal balance.* They lie close to the roots of human motive, to the sense of protection in the storms of the world. They enable thousands, even millions of people to act together in common understanding and with a feeling of mutual belonging where otherwise there would be strife and confusion; they protect the conscious self from devastating doubts and uncertainties and provide a sense of compensation for such adverse influences in life as the inevitability of death and the loss sooner or later of all things held dear. The logical content of these beliefs does not matter nearly so much as their ability to fulfill these functions. In times of stress, human dependence on such beliefs has a tendency to become greater, at least for a time and may be affirmed even at the price of life itself.

3. *Belief in the Emperor:* If these assumptions are true, it should be possible to estimate the strength of a system of belief by examining its cultural prevalence and its relationship to the sense of individual security (the intrapersonal balance).

As already noted, the greatest number of references to the Emperor from all Japanese sources during the war were expressions of faith, devotion, loyalty, and declarations concerning his importance. For example:

"From childhood on I was taught that the Emperor is of divine origin and that if capable I may become the premier of my nation, but never could I be Emperor."

"The Emperor is the father of the whole nation, a living god."

"I saw two Japanese soldiers worn out with wounds and hunger. One of them called to the section leader and asked to be killed, as he could not keep up with the retiring force. He asked that he be remembered to his family and said, 'Long live the Emperor!' ('Tenno Heika, banzai!'). The section leader then shot him through the head."

"A Japanese soldier stated that the morale in his unit was very high in spite of their hopeless situation. All the men were deeply

Psychological Warfare and the Japanese Emperor 255

instilled with the spirit of undying loyalty to the Emperor and were resigned to their fate."

"A good many people will unhesitatingly fight an invading army, even with nothing more than bamboo poles, if the Emperor so decrees. They would stop just as quickly if he so decreed."

In a diary was found this entry: "In order to do our best for the Emperor, we must deny ourselves and our families. One's faith then becomes a thing exalted in the world. We achieve immortality by casting aside our petty temporal lives and becoming a member of the Fraternity of the Spirits of Dead Heroes. Our spirits and bodies are not merely our own; they are rather for the gods who created the world to use and dispose of. We live by the grace of the Emporer. For people who live in this belief, life is worth while, living has a purpose."

A poem from a diary:

"The shield of our Emperor's domain, this Iwo Jima,
Upon our honor we hold this ground, We, the Defenders."

It should not be supposed from these quotations that every Japanese died willingly with "Long live the Emperor" on his lips. Our records revealed that many others called for their mothers or other loved ones instead. Nevertheless the number of references to the Emperor at a time of reverse, last effort or self-destruction indicates that he was one of the important supports in Japanese morale.

Why were loyalty to the Emperor and faith in him so strong? Can an explanation be found in terms of the concepts that have been outlined regarding the nature of strong belief?

In part the answers are already evident in the quotations given above.

To begin by summarizing, it may be said that for the Japanese the Emperor symbolizes the fundamental assumptions regarding values: the nature of the world, the nature of the supernatural and man's place—those things which among all peoples are strongly felt and extremely resistant to change because of their intimate connection with the sense of security, the sense of orientation and the hope of fulfilling of aspirations.

The extent of the belief in the Emperor was found to be so

wide as to constitute a non-logical, cultural type of faith strongly reinforced in any one individual by the sheer pressure of the whole society. It would be impossible for one to reject it without stepping outside almost all the ideas and value systems that are Japanese; and since most Japanese are not members of any other society except their own, this would mean a kind of isolation that few human beings except psychotics and extreme mystics can endure.

However, the symbol also has wide latitude in the way it can be interpreted and this permits a strong personal identification with the Emperor on the part of people who are very different from each other. A close scrutiny of Japanese comments on the Emperor and a checking of these against the point of view of the speaker in regard to other matters reveals that to the expansionists and militarists he was the strong war leader bent on liberating the East from Western domination; to those who were or became opposed to war, the Emperor was steadfastly a man of peace deceived by the warmakers in Japan; to the partisans of democracy, he was and still is a democrat at heart; to the simple and uneducated he wielded supernatural powers; to the sophisticated he symbolized the highest ideals of a way of life. Such flexibility in the interpretation of the Emperor's significance was made possible by the degree to which he was shielded by custom and etiquette from direct contact with public affairs and by the manner in which he was surrounded by subordinates who took responsibility for error. In this he resembles the "sacred chiefs" usually found in the Pacific Islands. In Samoa and Tonga, the sacred chief did not engage in the mundane but, occupying the highest position of prestige, left politics and administration to a secular chief.

The Emperor, then, is all ideal things to all men and the symbol of each individual's successful tussle with and relief from his insecurities.

The structure of the Japanese family is another source of the faith in the Emperor displayed by adults. The rigid hierarchy and other restrictive aspects of the Japanese family have been described; less often stressed, though just as important, is the tremendous sense of security, and the strong feeling of belonging that also exists in this unit. The Japanese father is not so much the autocrat who demands, as he is the recipient of honors which others strive to give, feeling their worth in terms of their success and faithfulness in this giving. When failures occur, it is less often the father who chastises the offender than it is the other members of the group, and all feel the adverse opinion of the neighbors. The child who grows out of this setting into adult life and becomes aware of the larger society of the nation is ripe for a counterpart of the father in these adult relations. He finds it in the Emperor who is endlessly spoken of as the Father of his people. To him each can give and feel that this giving contributes a worth-while purpose to life.

Through all of this runs the religious aspect of the Emperor symbol. Here, as in the case of the Emperor's "real intentions," there is much room for interpretation so that he can fulfill the needs of very different sorts of persons, including Christians as well as Buddhists and those who belong to Shinto sects. However, the distinction between religion and everyday life so often formalized in Western thought, is much more fluid in the East, and this is true of the Japanese. Filial respect and devotion shade off into religious devotion to dead ancestors who are considered to be deities watching over their descendants. All men are potential deities to be revered after death, but the greater the man, the greater the god he will be. The Emperor with his line of ancestors stemming from the founders of the nation has the greatest potentiality of living men. Because of his frequent ceremonial communication with the departed imperial ancestors he is a symbolic bridge between the living and these mighty dead of the past. This parallels on a grander scale the ties between living and dead and the feeling of continued fellowship and intercourse that goes on in each Japanese household before its family shrines.

The Emperor symbol therefore plays a major role. It serves as a bond between the living members of Japanese society, it is a repository of national ideals, it links those alive and those departed, and it assures each Japanese a place in the afterlife.

Thus a man who might otherwise be lost in a chaotic universe and appalled by his littleness, helplessness, and temporariness finds meaning and security in believing he is a part of something far greater than himself that spans the natural and the supernatural world.

Such a system, like all such systems is full of logical contradictions. How, for example, can the Emperor be supremely divine and yet fooled by his advisers? These considerations are logical enough from an outsider's point of view, but are inconsequential in context, for the strength of the belief lies in its cultural force and in its meaning and service in the emotional life of man.

Although it is hard to find any exact parallel in our culture to the Japanese feeling for the Emperor, the difference is one of degree and combination rather than of kind. Almost all of us have symbols in which we believe with the same strength as that displayed by the Japanese toward the Emperor. With us, however, these beliefs are not so widely shared and differ more among various groups of people. Nor, as a rule, do we combine so many things in any one symbol. However, if we could imagine a symbol that represented together the flag, the constitution, a religious ideal and our feelings for the family we might get some insight into the Japanese attitude.

It is perhaps now clear why the analysts early came to the conclusion that it was not profitable to attack the Emperor in psychological warfare. At best, it seemed wasteful since dialectics in leaflets stood little chance of penetrating such a culturally and emotionally rooted non-logical system of belief. One cannot successfully attack with logic that which is not grounded in logic.

At worst, it seemed probable that attacks on the Emperor would remind the people of their allegiance and tighten their grip on their belief at a time when other aspects of morale might be giving away. There would be renewed determination and death would seem to them preferable to submission before an enemy who vilified the values that were at the foundation of existence. Better to lose one's life than to lose all hope.

Our view was frequently countered with the argument that the present form of Emperor belief was recent and to a large extent the product of militarist propaganda. Without raising the question of validity in this statement, it did not seem to us that either item was necessarily correlated with the strength or weakness of a belief system. It is not the "real" facts, but what a

Psychological Warfare and the Japanese Emperor 259

people *think* their history is that counts in matters of this sort. In this particular case, the Japanese thought of the Imperial System as having great antiquity. This was much more significant than whether or not it actually had such ancient history.

In regard to the use of the Emperor by militarists in their propaganda, ruling classes everywhere have commonly employed religious and other beliefs in this manner and such action cannot be assumed to signify weakness in the belief systems themselves.

America no longer has to deal with the question of psychological warfare against Japan but there is the problem of developing a peaceful way of life in that nation and many think that the key is re-education. An understanding of the Emperor is necessarily important in this connection. He is still there, still functions as a symbol in the lives of the people, and is now credited by many of them with having saved Japan by stopping the war.

However, even though his influence is still strong and even though our analysis indicated that during the war there was nothing the Allies could do to shake this faith, it does not follow that the beliefs about the Emperor will continue changeless in the future or that we are powerless to influence the direction of change. On the contrary, as a result of emotional upheaval due to defeat, the impact of the American troops in Japan and conscious efforts on the part of American officials to influence Japanese thought through press, radio and movies, some alteration is exceedingly likely to occur. America's opportunity is on a scale and with a force that is far different from that which existed when we were outside Japan hurling in both leaflets and bombs.

This does not mean, however, that the change will necessarily be what America wishes or that a shift away from faith in the Emperor will make for peace. In this matter we are very likely to assume more than is warranted, and for an interesting reason.

The Emperor is a symbol to us as well as to the Japanese and we give to this symbol a measure of uncritical belief. Instead of representing security and high aspirations, however, the Emperor to us stands for oppression, cruelty, and a whole constellation of related evils. This is in part the result of war-time propaganda and in part the result of a cultural pattern that represents monarchs as a primary source of social evil. Its historical origin in successive generations of individuals and groups fleeing oppression in Europe is interesting, but not relevant here. The main point is that the pattern, while not undisputed, has been and is a prevalent one reaching far into the folklore of the mountains, the bottom lands and the prairies. As Huck Finn put it, "All kings is mostly rapscallions . . . Take 'em all around, they're a mighty ornery lot. It's the way they was raised."

Added to this, due to conflicts in our family and social life, we may have intrapersonal motives for wanting to crush and punish authoritarian symbols, motives related to our own struggles, insecurities, and aspirations.

It is therefore very easy for us to look on the Emperor as a kind of sore in the social body of Japan and to believe that if it is cut out everything will be satisfactory. Because he is called Emperor, we project into him attributes of tyrants. In a sense, this projection is similar to that exhibited by the Japanese, only in our case he symbolizes evil instead of good.

It is therefore worthwhile to be on guard against illusions and to ask ourselves what changes we want in the Emperor system and why, and to be sure that they are really related to peace and not merely serving personal emotional catharsis.

It is possible that belief symbols such as the Emperor can serve the welfare of men, self-government and good international relations just as well as they can serve home front oppression and overseas aggression. The Society of Friends and the Knights Templars both professed Christianity, and so did both the killers and the killed at St. Bartholomew. A Saracen at the time of the Crusades might have thought that the only way to stop these invasions was to eliminate Christianity. Now, however, we may wonder if he had his finger on the cause or only on a particular mode of expressing an aggression that came from other sources.

14 THE RELATION OF GUILT TOWARD PARENTS TO ACHIEVEMENT AND ARRANGED MARRIAGE AMONG THE JAPANESE[1]

George De Vos

This paper, based on research materials gathered in Japan, suggests certain interpretations concerning the structuring of guilt in Japanese society. Especially pertinent are Thematic Apperception Test (TAT) materials in which the subjects invent stories about a series of ambiguous pictures, which were taken from

FROM George De Vos, "The Relation of Guilt Toward Parents to Achievement and Arranged Marriage Among the Japanese," *Psychiatry*, 23:287–301, 1960. Copyright, The William Alanson White Psychiatric Foundation, Inc. Reprinted by special permission of The William Alanson White Psychiatric Foundation, Inc. and the author.

[1] The author is indebted to Hiroshi Wagatsuma for his able assistance and collaboration in the analysis and interpretation of basic materials. The materials on which the following interpretations are based were obtained by the author as a member of a large interdisciplinary project in cooperation with the Human Relations Interdisciplinary Research Group of Nagoya under the direction of Dr. Tsuneo Muramatsu, Professor of Psychiatry, Nagoya National University. This research, which is continuing in Japan under Professor Muramatsu's direction, was sponsored in part by the Center for Japanese Studies of the University of Michigan, the Foundation Fund for Research in Psychiatry, and the Rockefeller Foundation. The author, who takes full responsibility for the views expressed in the present paper, based on material from a single village, participated in the Human Relations Interdisciplinary Research Group as a Fulbright research scholar in Japan from September, 1953, to July, 1955. Subsequent research on these psychological materials in the United States was assisted in various stages by a faculty research grant from the University of Michigan, the Behavioral Science Division of the Ford Foundation, and the National Institute of Mental Health. The Human Relations group hopes to be able to make more definitive statements than those of the present paper upon completion of its analysis of comparable primary material taken from three villages and two cities.

Niiike, an agricultural village of central Honshu. It is possible to obtain from the stories involving themes of achievement and marriage relationships indirect verification of hypotheses concerning the nature of internalization of the Japanese social sanctions that have been influenced by the traditional neo-Confucian ethics sustained by the dominant samurai class in the past.

A central problem to be considered is whether the Japanese emphasis on achievement drive and on properly arranged marriage may possibly have its motivational source in the inculcation of shame or guilt in childhood.[2] It is my contention that this emphasis is not to be understood solely as a derivative of what is termed a 'shame' orientation, but rather as stemming from a deep undercurrent of guilt developed in the basic interpersonal relationships with the mother within the Japanese family.

The characteristic beliefs, values, and obligatory practices that provide emotional security and are usually associated in the West with religious systems and other generalized ideologies—and only indirectly related to family life (Kardiner 1939:89–91)—are related much more directly to the family system of the tradition-oriented Japanese. The structuring of guilt in the Japanese is hidden from Western observation, since there is a lack of empathic understanding of what it means to be part of such a family system. Western observers tend to look for guilt, as it is symbolically expressed, in reference to a possible transgression of limits imposed by a generalized ideology or religious system circumscribing sexual and aggressive impulses. There is little sensitivity to the possibility that guilt is related to a failure to meet expectations in a moral system built around family duties and obligations.

[2] This paper will not discuss subcultural variations. Niiike village is representative of a farming community that has well internalized the traditional, dominant values held by the samurai during the Tokugawa period (about 1600–1868). Other local rural traditions emphasize other values. For example, material from a fishing community wherein the status position of women is higher than in the farming community considered shows far different results in the projective tests. Women are perceived in TAT stories as more assertive, even aggressive, toward their husbands. Guilt is not expressed in stories of self-sacrificing mothers. Love marriages are accepted and not seen in the context of remorse, and so on. A comparison of the attitudes of the farming village with those of the fishing village is presented in detail in De Vos and Wagatsuma, 1961.

Piers and Singer, in distinguishing between shame and guilt cultures, emphasize that guilt inhibits and condemns transgression, whereas shame demands achievement of a positive goal (1953; cf also French, n.d.). This contrast is related to Freud's two earlier distinctions in the functioning of the conscience. He used *shame* to delineate a reaction to the ego ideal involving a goal of positive achievement; on the other hand, he related *guilt* to superego formation and not to ego ideal. A great deal of Japanese cultural material, when appraised with these motivational distinctions in mind, would at first glance seem to indicate that Japanese society is an excellent example of a society well over on the shame side of the continuum.

Historically, as a result of several hundred years of tightly knit feudal organization, the Japanese have been pictured as having developed extreme susceptibility to group pressures toward conformity. This strong group conformity, in turn, is often viewed as being associated with a lack of personal qualities that would foster individualistic endeavor.[3] In spite of, or according to some observers because of, these conformity patterns, which are found imbedded in governmental organization as well as in personal habits, the Japanese—alone among all the Asian peoples coming in contact with Western civilization in the nineteenth century were quickly able to translate an essentially feudal social structure into a modern industrial society and to achieve eminence as a world power in fewer than fifty years. This remarkable achievement can be viewed as a group manifestation of what is presumed to be a striving and achievement drive on the individual level.

Achievement drive in Americans has been discussed by Riesman, among others, as shifting in recent years from Puritan, inner-directed motivation to other-directed concern with conformity and outer group situations (1950). Perceived in this framework, the Japanese traditionally have had an other-directed culture. Sensitivity to 'face' and attention to protocol suggest that the susceptibility to social pressure, traced psychoanalytically, may possibly derive from underlying infantile fears of abandonment.

---

[3] See, for example, Lafcadio Hearn's statement that Japanese authoritarianism is that of "the many over the one—not the one over the many" (1905:435 *ff.*).

Personality patterns integrated around such motivation, if culturally prevalent, could possibly lead to a society dominated by a fear of failure and a need for recognition and success.

Intimately related to a shift from Puritan patterns in America were certain changes in the patterns of child-rearing. Similarly, it has been observed in Japan that prevailing child-rearing practices emphasize social evaluation as a sanction rather than stressing more internalized self-contained ethical codes instilled and enforced early by parental punishment. In spite of some earlier contentions to the contrary based on a few retrospective views (e.g. Gorer 1943) the child-rearing patterns most evident in Japan, in deed, if not in word, manifest early permissiveness in regard to weaning and bowel training and a relative lack of physical punishment.[4] There is, moreover, considerable emphasis on ridicule and lack of acceptance of imperfect or slipshod performance in any regard. There is most probably a strong relationship between early permissiveness and susceptibility to external social sanctions. In line with the distinctions made between shame and guilt, the Japanese could easily be classified as shame oriented and their concern over success and failure could be explicable in these terms. Somehow this formula, however, does not hold up well when reapplied to an understanding of individual Japanese, either in Japan or in the United States.[5] Emphasis on shame

[4] See, for example, the empirical reports by Lanham (1956) and Edward and Margaret Norbeck, (1956). A forthcoming publication by Edward Norbeck and George De Vos, "Culture and Personality: The Japanese," will present a more comprehensive bibliography, including the works of native Japanese, on child-rearing practices in various areas in Japan.

[5] The five clinical studies of Japanese-Americans in Seward (1958) consistently give evidence of depressive reactions and an inability to express hostile or resentful feelings toward the parents. Feelings of guilt are strongly related to an inability to express aggression outwardly, leading to intrapunitive reactions. Feelings of worthlessness also result from the repression of aggressive feelings. The Nisei woman described by Norman L. Farberow and Edward S. Schneidman in Ch. 15 (pp. 335 ff.) demonstrates the transference to the American cultural situation of certain basic intrapunitive attitudes common in Japan related to woman's ideal role behavior. The Kibei case described by Marvin K. Opler in Ch. 13 (pp. 297 ff.) well demonstrates a young man's perception of the manifest "suffering" of Japanese women. The case described by Charlotte G. Babcock and William Caudill in Ch. 17 (pp. 409 ff.) as well as other unpublished psychoanalytic material of Babcock's, amply demonstrates the presence of deep underlying guilt toward parents. Such guilt is still operative in Nisei in

sanctions in a society does not preclude severe guilt. While strong feelings of anxiety related to conformity are very much in evidence, both in traditional as well as present-day Japanese society, severe guilt becomes more apparent when the underlying motivation contributing to manifest behavior is more intensively analyzed. Shame is a more conscious phenomenon among the Japanese, hence more readily perceived as influencing behavior. But guilt in many instances seems to be a stronger basic determinant.

Although the ego ideal is involved in Japanese strivings toward success, day-by-day hard work and purposeful activities leading to long-range goals are directly related to guilt feelings toward parents. Transgression in the form of 'laziness' or other nonproductive behavior is felt to 'injure' the parents, and thus leads to feelings of guilt. There are psychological analogs between this Japanese sense of responsibility to parents for social conformity and achievement, and the traditional association sometimes found in the Protestant West between work activity and a personal relationship with a deity.[6]

Any attempt to answer questions concerning guilt in the Japanese raises many theoretical problems concerning the nature of

---

influencing occupational selection and marriage choice. Seward in a general summary of the Japanese cases (p. 449) carefully points out the pervasive depression found as a cohesive theme in each of the cases. She avoids conceptualizing the problems in terms of guilt, perhaps out of deference to the stereotype that Japanese feel 'ashamed' rather than 'guilty.' She states, "Running through all five Japanese-American cases is a pervasive depression, in three reaching the point of suicidal threat or actual attempt." Yet she ends with the statement, "Looking back over the cases of Japanese origin we may note a certain cohesiveness binding them together. Distance from parent figures is conspicuous in all as well as inability openly to express resentment against them. In line with the externalization of authority and the shame-avoidance demands of Japanese tradition, hostility is consistently turned in on the self in the *face-saving devices* of depression and somatic illness." (Italics mine.)

[6] Robert Bellah (1957), perceives, and illustrates in detail, a definite relationship between prevalent pre-Meiji Tokugawa period ethical ideals and the rapid industrialization of Japan that occurred subsequent to the restoration of the Emperor. A cogent application of a sociological approach similar to that of Max Weber allows him to point out the obvious parallels in Tokugawa Japan to the precapitalist ethical orientation of Protestant Europe.

internalization processes involved in human motivation. It is beyond the scope of this paper to discuss theoretically the complex interrelationships between feelings of shame and guilt in personality development. But the author believes that some anthropological writings, oversimplifying psychoanalytic theory, have placed too great an emphasis on a direct one-to-one relationship between observable child-rearing disciplines culturally prevalent and resultant inner psychological states. These inner states are a function not only of observable disciplinary behavior but also of more subtle, less reportable, atmospheric conditions in the home, as well as of other factors as yet only surmised.

Moreover, in accordance with psychoanalytic theory concerning the mechanisms of internalizing parental identification in resolving the Oedipal developmental stage, one would presume on an a priori basis that internalized guilt tends to occur almost universally, although its form and emphasis might differ considerably from one society to another. This paper, while guided by theory, is based primarily on empirical evidence and a posteriori reasoning in attempting to point out a specifically Japanese pattern of guilt. Developmental vicissitudes involved in the resolution of Oedipal relationships are not considered. Concisely stated, the position taken in this paper is as follows:

Guilt in many of the Japanese is not only operative in respect to what are termed superego functions, but is also concerned with what has been internalized by the individual as an ego ideal. Generally speaking, the processes involved in resolving early identifications as well as assuming later adult social roles are never possible without some internalized guilt. The more difficult it is for a child to live up to the behavior ideally expected of him, the more likely he is to develop ambivalence toward the source of the ideal. This ideal need not directly emphasize prohibited behavior, as is the case when punishment is the mode of training.

When shame and guilt have undergone a process of internalization in a person during the course of his development, both become operative regardless of the relative absence of either external threats of punishment or overt concern with the opinions of others concerning his behavior. Behavior is automatically self-evaluated without the presence of others. A simple dichotomy relating internalized shame only to ego ideal and internalized guilt to an automatically operative superego is one to be seriously questioned.

Whereas the formation of an internalized ego ideal in its earlier form is more or less related to the social expectations and values of parents, the motivations which move a developing young adult toward a realization of these expectations can involve considerable guilt. Japanese perceptions of social expectations concerning achievement behavior and marriage choice, as shown in the experimental materials described in this paper, give ample evidence of the presence of guilt; shame as a motive is much less in evidence.

Nullification of parental expectations is one way to "hurt" a parent. As defined in this paper, guilt in the Japanese is essentially related either to an impulse to hurt which may be implied in a contemplated act, or to the realization of having injured a love object toward whom one feels some degree of unconscious hostility.

Guilt feelings related to various internalization processes differ, varying with what is prohibited or expected; nevertheless, some disavowal of an unconscious impulse to hurt seems to be generic to guilt. In some instances there is also emphasis on a fear of retribution stemming from this desire to injure. Such seems to be the case in many of the Japanese. If a parent has instilled in a child an understanding of his capacity to hurt by failing to carry out an obligation expected of him as a member of a family, any such failure can make him feel extremely guilty.

In the following materials taken from the rural hamlet of Niiike,[7] an attempt will be made to demonstrate how guilt is often related to possible rebellion against parental expectations. Two possible ways for the male to rebel are: (1) Dissipating one's energies in some sort of profligate behavior rather than working hard, or neglecting the diligence and hard work necessary for obtaining some achievement goal. (2) Rejecting arranged marriage by losing oneself in a marriage of passion, a so-called "love marriage."

[7] See the comprehensive, five-year study of this village by means of various social science disciplines by members of the Center for Japanese Studies of the University of Michigan (Beardsley, Ward, Hall 1959).

In women, guilt seems related to becoming selfish or unsubmissive in the pursuit of duties involved in their adult role possibilities as wife and mother. This could mean, as in the case of men, refusal to accept the parents' marriage arrangement, or, after marriage, failure to devote oneself with whole-hearted intensity, without reservations, to the husband and his purposes and to the rearing of the children. Failure to show a completely masochistic, self-sacrificing devotion to her new family is a negative reflection on the woman's parents. Deficiencies in her children or even in her husband are sometimes perceived as her fault, and she must intrapunitively rectify her own failings if such behavior occurs. TAT stories taken from the Niiike sample bring out in both direct and indirect fashion evidence to support these contentions.

The Relation of Guilt to Achievement

The Japanese mother has perfected the technique of inducing guilt in her children by quiet suffering. A type of American mother often encountered in clinical practice repeatedly tells her children how she suffers from their bad behavior but in her own behavior reveals her selfish motives; in contrast, the Japanese mother does not to the same extent verbalize her suffering for her children but lives it out before their eyes. She takes on the burden of responsibility for her children's behavior—and her husband's—and will often manifest self-reproach if they conduct themselves badly. Such an example cannot fail to impress. The child becomes aware that his mother's self-sacrifice demands some recompense. The system of an obligation felt toward the parents, aptly described by Ruth Benedict, receives a strong affective push from the Japanese mother's devotion to her children's successful social development, which includes the standards of success set for the community (1946). As discussed in a previous paper, the educational and occupational achievements of Japanese-Americans also show this pattern, modified in accordance with American influences (Caudill and De Vos 1946).

The negative side of accomplishment is the hurt inflicted on the parent if the child fails or if he becomes self-willed in marriage or loses himself in indulgence. Profligacy and neglect of a vocational role in Japan—and often in the West as well—is an attack on the parents, frequently unconsciously structured.

The recurrence of certain themes in the TAT data, such as the occurrence of parental death as a result of disobedience, suggests the prevalence of expiation as a motive for achievement (Wagatsuma 1957). Themes of illness and death seem to be used not only to show the degree of parental, especially maternal, self-sacrifice, but also seem to be used as self-punishment in stories of strivings toward an ideal or goal with a single-minded devotion so strong that its effects may bring about the ruin of one's health.

These attitudes toward occupational striving can also be seen in the numerous examples in recent Japanese history of men's self-sacrifice for national causes. The sometimes inexplicable—to Western eyes at least—logic of the self-immolation practiced in wartime by the Japanese soldier can better be explained when seen as an act of sacrifice not resulting only from pressures of group morale and propaganda stressing the honor of such a death. The emotions that make such behavior seem logical are first experienced when the child observes the mother's attitude toward her own body as she often exhausts it in the service of the family.

To begin the examination of TAT data, the relation of guilt to parental suffering is apparent in certain TAT stories in which the death of the parent follows the bad conduct of a child, and the two events seem to bear an implicit relationship, as expressed in the following summaries (*W* indicates a woman, *M* a man):[8]

W, age 16, Card J13: A mother is sick; her son steals because of poverty; mother dies.

M, age 41, Card J6GF: A daughter marries for love against father's will; she takes care of her father, but father dies.

[8] The TAT cards used in the Japanese research were in most instances modifications of the Murray cards, with changed features, clothing, and background to conform to Japanese experience. The situations in the original Murray set were maintained. New cards were added to the modified set to elicit reactions to peculiarly Japanese situations as well. The numbers given for the stories used illustratively in this paper refer to modified cards resembling the Murray set with the exception of J9 and J11, which represent original Japanese family scenes.

W, age 22, Card J6GF: A daughter marries against her father's opposition, but her husband dies and she becomes unhappy.

M, age 23, Card J18: A mother strangles to death the woman who tempted her innocent son; the mother becomes insane and dies. The son begs forgiveness.

In such stories one may assume that a respondent first puts into words an unconscious wish of some kind but then punishes himself by bringing the death of a beloved person quickly into the scene.

One could also interpret such behavior in terms of cultural traditions. Punishing or retaliating against someone by killing or injuring oneself has often actually been done in Japan in both political and social arenas. Such self-injury or death became an accepted pattern of behavior under the rigid feudal regime where open protest was an impossibility for the suppressed and ruled. Numerous works on Japanese history contain accounts of the severe limitations on socially acceptable behavior and spontaneous self-expression.

Understanding the 'emotional logic' of this behavior, however, requires psychological explanations as well as such valid sociological explanations. This "moral masochistic" tendency, to use Freud's terminology, is inculcated through the attitudes of parents, especially of the mother. Suffering whatever the child does, being hurt constantly, subtly assuming an attitude of "look what you have done to me," the Japanese mother often gains by such devices a strong control over her child, and by increasing overt suffering, can punish him for lack of obedience or seriousness of purpose. Three of the above stories suggest that a mother or father is 'punishing' a child by dying. Parents' dying is not only the punishment of a child, but also more often is the final control over that child, breaking his resistance to obeying the parental plans.

This use of death as a final admonishment lends credence to a story concerning the Japanese Manchurian forces at the close of World War II. The young officers in Manchuria had determined to fight on indefinitely, even though the home islands had surrendered. A staff general was sent by plane as an envoy of the Emperor to order the troops to surrender. He could get nowhere with the officers, who were determined to fight on. He returned to his plane, which took off and circled the field, sending a radio message that this was the final directive to surrender. The plane then suddenly dived straight for the landing field, crashing and killing all on board. The troops then promptly surrendered.

It is not unknown for a mother to threaten her own death as a means of admonishing a child. In a therapy case with a delinquent boy, the mother had threatened her son, with very serious intent, telling him that he must stop his stealing or she would take him with her to the ocean and commit double suicide.[9] The mother reasoned that she was responsible and that such a suicide would pay for her failure as a mother, as well as relieve the world of a potentially worthless citizen. The threat worked. For the man this kind of threat of possible suffering becomes related to the necessity to work hard in the adult occupational role; for the woman, it becomes related to working hard at being a submissive and enduring wife.

In other of the TAT stories the death of a parent is followed by reform, hard work, and success. Examples of these stories are:

W, age 16, Card J7M: A son, scolded by his father, walks out; the father dies; son works hard and becomes successful.

M, age 39, Card J5: A mother worries about her delinquent son, becomes sick and dies; the son reforms himself and becomes successful.

M, age 54, Card J13: A mother dies; the son changes his attitude and works hard.

W, age 17, Card J7M: A father dies; son walks out as his mother repeatedly tells him to be like the father; when he meets her again, she dies; he becomes hard-working.

W, age 38, Card J9: Elder brother is going to Tokyo, leaving his sick mother; his sister is opposed to his idea; his mother dies; he will become successful.

M, age 15, Card J6M: A son becomes more thoughtful of his mother after his father's death; he will be successful.

[9] Reported in unpublished material of a Japanese psychiatrist, Taeko Sumi.

Emphasis on hard work and success after the death of parents clearly suggests some expiatory meaning related to the "moral masochistic" attitude of the mother in raising her child. The mother's moral responsibility is also suggested by other stories, such as a mother being scolded by a father when the child does something wrong, or a mother—not the father—being hurt when the child does not behave well. The feeling experienced by the child when he realizes, consciously or unconsciously, that he has hurt his mother is guilt—because guilt is generated when one hurts the object of one's love. The natural ambivalence arising from living under close parental control supplies sufficient unconscious intent to hurt to make the guilt mechanism operative.

The expiatory emphasis on hard work and achievement is also evident as a sequel in TAT stories directly expressing hurt of one's mother or father:

M, age 17, Card J11: A child dropped his father's precious vase. The father gets angry and scolds the mother for her having allowed the child to hold it. The child will become a fine man.

M, age 53, Card J18: A child quarreled outside; his mother is sorry that his father is dead. The child makes a great effort and gets good school records.

M, age 24, Card J11: A mother is worrying about her child who has gone out to play baseball and has not yet come back. When he comes home he overhears his mother complaining about his playing baseball all the time without doing his schoolwork. He then makes up his mind not to play baseball any more and to concentrate on his studies.

Although the realization of having hurt one's parents by bad conduct is not stated in the following story, it is another example of the use of working or studying hard—obviously as the means to achievement—to expiate possible guilt:

W, age 17, Card J3F: A girl worries about the loss of her virginity, consults with someone and feels at ease. She studies hard in the future.

In the same context, if one fails to achieve, he has no way to atone. He is lost. The only thing left is to hurt himself, to extinguish himself—the one whose existence has been hurting his parents and who now can do nothing for them. Suicide as an answer is shown in the following stories:

> *M, age 57, Card 3BM* [original Murray card]: A girl fails in examination, kills herself.
>
> *W, age 32, Card J3F:* Cannot write a research paper; commits suicide.

On the level of cultural conditioning, the traditional teaching of *On* obligations enhances the feeling of guilt in the child, who is repeatedly taught by parents, teachers, books, and so forth, that his parents have experienced hardship and trouble and have made many sacrifices in order to bring him up. For example, financial strain and, significantly, ill health because of overwork may haunt the parents because of this child. Of course the child did not ask for all this sacrifice, nor does he consciously feel that he has intentionally hurt the parents, but there seems no way out; all this suffering takes place somewhere beyond his control, and he cannot avoid the burden it imposes. Certainly the child cannot say to himself, "I did not ask my parents to get hurt. Hurt or not, that is not my business," because he knows his parents love him and are also the objects of his love. What can be done about it then? The only way open to the child is to attain the goal of highest value, which is required of him; by working hard, being virtuous, becoming successful, attaining a good reputation and the praise of society, he brings honor to himself, to his parents, and to his *Ie* (household lineage), of which he and his parents are, after all, parts. If he becomes virtuous in this way, the parents can also receive credit. Self-satisfaction and praise from society go to them for having fulfilled their duty to *Ie* and society by raising their children well. The pattern repeats itself; he sacrifices himself masochistically for his own children, and on and on.

My assumption is, therefore, that among many Japanese people such a feeling of guilt very often underlies the strong achievement drive and aspiration toward success. If this hypothesis is accepted, then it can easily be understood that the death of a parent—that is, the culmination of the parent's being hurt following some bad conduct of a child—evokes in the child a feeling of guilt which is strong enough to bring him back from delinquent behavior and to drive him toward hard work and success. This is what is happening in the TAT stories of parental death and the child's reform.

GUILT IN JAPANESE MARRIAGE RELATIONSHIPS

The feeling of *On* obligations generated in the family situation during childhood is also found to be a central focus in Japanese arranged marriages. This feeling of obligation is very pronounced in women. In a sense, a woman expresses her need for accomplishment and achievement by aiming toward the fulfillment of her roles as wife and mother within the new family she enters in marriage. The man does not face giving up his family ties in the same way. Interview data suggest that for a Japanese woman, failure to be a dutiful bride reflects on her parents' upbringing of her, and therefore any discord with her new family, even with an unreasonable mother-in-law, injures the reputation of her parents.

Marriages which go counter to family considerations and are based on individual passion or love are particularly prone to disrupt the family structure; they are likely to be of rebellious origin, and any subsequent stresses of adjustment to partner and respective families tend to remind the participants of the rebellious tone of the marriage and, therefore, to elicit guilt feelings.

The TAT stories give evidence of guilt in regard to both types of "unacceptable" marriage behavior—they show the wife's readiness for self-blame in marriage difficulties with her husband, and they express self-blame or blame of others, on the part of both men and women, for engaging in possible love marriages.

THE WIFE'S SELF-BLAME IN DIFFICULTIES WITH HER HUSBAND

Of the stories involving discord between a man and his wife, several indicate a woman's feeling herself to be wrong in a situation which in America would be interpreted as resulting from the poor behavior of the husband. There are no cases of the reverse attitude—of a man's being blamed in an even slightly equivocal situation.

Four of five such stories are given by women. The man's story involves a need for reform by both partners, who are united in a love marriage and therefore apparently conform to the guilt pattern of such marriages, which I shall discuss shortly. In summary, the four women's stories are:

W, age 26, Card J3F: A wife quarreled with her husband when he returned from drinking. She leaves her house to cry, feels guilty for the quarrel.

W, age 54, Card J4: A husband and wife quarrel because the former criticized her cooking. The wife apologizes to him.

W, age 37, Card J4: A husband and wife quarrel, and after it the wife apologizes to her angry husband.

W, age 22, Card J5: A husband comes home very late at night; the wife thinks it is for lack of her affection and tries hard; he finally reforms.

Such attitudes also seem to be reflected in other test data, such as the "Problem Situations" material[10] collected in Niiike village. It is especially interesting to note that a husband's profligacy can be attributed by women to the wife's failure. It seems that the husband's willfulness—as is also true of a male child—is in some instances accepted as natural; somehow it is not his business to control himself if he feels annoyed with his wife. The wife nonetheless has to take responsibility for her husband's conduct. In one therapy case of a psychotic reaction in a young wife, the mother-in-law blamed the bride directly for her husband's extramarital activities, stating, "If you were a good and satisfying wife, he would have no need to go elsewhere."[11]

In connection with this point it may be worth mentioning that on the deepest level probably many Japanese wives do not 'give' themselves completely to their husbands because the marriage has been forced on them as an arrangement between the parents

---

[10] This test included items specifically eliciting a response to a hypothetical disharmony between wife and mother-in-law. In such cases the results indicate that the wife often sees herself as to blame for failing in her duty as a wife. She "should" conduct herself so as to be above reproach.

[11] Described by the Japanese psychiatrist, Kei Hirano.

in each family. Wives often may not be able to adjust their innermost feelings in the marital relationship so as to be able to love their husbands genuinely. They may sense their own emotional resistance, and believe that it is an evil willfulness that keeps them from complete devotion as dictated by ethical ideals of womanhood. Sensing in the deepest level of their minds their lack of real affection, they become very sensitive to even the slightest indication of unfaithful behavior by the husbands. They feel that the men are reacting to the wives' own secret unfaithfulness in withholding. They cannot, therefore, blame their husbands, but throw the blame back upon themselves. They may become very anxious or quickly reflect upon and attempt to remedy their own inadequacies—as when their husbands happen to be late in getting home. Another hypothetical interpretation is that, lacking freedom of expression of their own impulses, Japanese women overidentify with male misbehavior; hence, they assume guilt as if the misbehavior were their own.

This propensity for self-blame in women is not necessarily limited to the wife's role. In the following story a younger sister somehow feels to blame when an older brother misbehaves.

> *W, age 17, Card J9:* An elder brother did something wrong and is examined by the policeman; he will be taken to the police station, but will return home and reform. The younger sister also thinks that she was wrong herself.

One might say, in generalization, that the ethical ideal of self-sacrifice and devotion to the family line—be it to father or elder brother before marriage, or to husband and children after marriage—carries with it internalized propensities to take blame upon oneself and to express a moral sensitivity in these family relationships which no religious or other cultural sanctions compel the men to share.

LOVE MARRIAGES AND OTHER HETEROSEXUAL RELATIONSHIPS

Of the Niiike village TAT stories involving marriage circumstances,[12] 13 directly mention an arranged marriage and 24

[12] A total of 80 persons gave 807 stories; 33 persons gave one or more stories involving marriage circumstances.

Guilt Toward Parents Among the Japanese

mention a love marriage. While 9 of the 13 arranged marriage stories show no tension or conflict between the people involved, only 2 of the 24 stories mentioning love marriage are tension-free. The rest all contain tension of some kind between parents and child or between the marriage partners. In other words, many of the men and women in Niiike who bring up the subject of love marriage still cannot see it as a positive accomplishment but rather see it as a source of disruption. As mentioned, love marriage carried out in open rebellion against the parents is punished in certain stories by the death of a beloved person.

M, age 41, Card J6F: They are father and his daughter. The mother has died. The daughter is sitting on a chair in her room. The father is looking in, and she is turning around to face him. He is very thoughtful of his daughter, and as she is just about of age [for marriage], he wants to suggest that she marry a certain man he selected. But she has a lover and does not want to marry the man her father suggests. The father is trying to read her face, though he does know about the existence of the lover. He brought up the subject a few times before, but the daughter showed no interest in it. Today also—a smile is absent in her face. The father talks about the subject again, but he fails to persuade her. So finally he gives in and agrees with her marrying her lover. Being grateful to the father for the consent, the daughter acts very kindly to him after her marriage. The husband and the wife get along very affectionately also. But her father dies suddenly of apoplexy. The father was not her real father. He did not have children, so he adopted her, and accepted her husband as his son-in-law. But he died. He died just at the time when a baby was born to the couple.

W, age 22, Card J6: The parents of this girl were brought up in families strongly marked with feudal atmosphere—the kind of family scarcely found in the present time. So they are very feudal and strict. The daughter cannot stand her parents. She had to meet her lover in secret. She was seeing her lover today as usual, without her parents knowing it. But by accident her father came to find it out. She was caught by her father on the spot. When she returned home her father rebuked her severely for it. But she could not give up her lover. In spite of her parents' strong objection, she married him. [*Examiner:* Future?] The couple wanted to establish a happy home when they married. But probably she will lose her husband. He will die—and she will have a miserable life.

There are a number of stories about unhappy events in the lives of a couple married for love. Many of these are found in response to Card 13 of the TAT, which shows a supine woman, breasts exposed, lying on a bed. A man in the foreground is facing away from the woman with one arm thrown over his eyes. A low table with a lamp is also in the room. Since responses to this card bring out in clear focus some basic differences between guilt over sexuality in Americans and in the Japanese, it will be well to consider them in some detail. Card J13 in the Japanese series is a modification of the original Murray TAT Card 13, with furniture and facial features altered.

Comparing Japanese and American responses to Card 13, it is obvious that while Americans rarely express remorse in connection with a marriage, the Japanese of Niiike express remorse in a heterosexual situation *only* in the context of marriage. In Americans, Card 13 is apt to evoke stories of guilt related to intercourse between partners not married to each other with the figure of the woman sometimes identified as a prostitute, or sometimes as a young girl. When the figures are identified by Americans as married, the themes are usually around the subject of illness. In contrast, in the sample of 42 stories given in response to this card in Niiike village, not one story depicts a theme of guilt over sexuality between unmarried partners. Remorse is depicted only when it is related to regret for having entered into a love marriage.

Most of the Japanese stories given about this card fall into one of three categories: sex and/or violence (10 stories); marital discord (10 stories); and sickness or death (20 stories). Some striking differences in themes are related to the age and sex of the subjects.

Card 13: Sex and/or violence.—Six stories involve themes of extramarital sexual liaison. In three, the woman is killed by the man. Five of the six stories are given by men, who were with one exception under 35 years of age, and one is given by a woman under 25. The young woman's story depicts a man killing a woman because she was too jealous of him. One young man sees a man killing an entertainer who rejects him. Another sees a man killing a woman who was pursuing him "too actively." Another young man gives the theme of a student and a prostitute.

Guilt Toward Parents Among the Japanese

In this story the man is disturbed by the prostitute's nakedness, not by his feelings of guilt over his activity.

The man over 35 sees the picture as depicting disillusion in a man who unexpectedly calls on a woman with whom he is in love, only to find her asleep in a "vulgar" fashion. As is true in the stories of other men over 35, which pertain to marital discord, the man is highly censorious of the woman's position on the bed. The Japanese woman is traditionally supposed to be proper in posture even when asleep. To assume a relaxed appearance reflects a wanton or sluttish nature.

Japanese men are apt to split their relationships with women into two groups: those with the wife and those with entertainers. Other evidence, not discussed here, supports the conclusion that for many men genuine affection is directed only toward maternal figures. Conversely, little deep affection seems freely available toward women perceived in a sexual role. Moreover, the Japanese male must defend himself against any passivity in his sexual relationship, lest he fall into a dependent relationship and become tied. By maintaining a rude aloofness and by asserting male prerogatives, he contains himself from involvement.

Men can resort to a violent defense if threatened too severely. Younger women especially tend to see men as potentially violent. Three women under 35 see a man as killing a woman, in two cases his wife. In addition to the jealousy mentioned before, the motives are the wife's complaint about low salary (a man must be seen as particularly sensitive about his economic prowess if such a complaint results in murder), and regret for entering a love marriage. The latter story, which follows, is particularly pertinent to understanding how guilt is related not to sexuality per se but to becoming "involved."

> *W, age 22:* He got married for love with a woman in spite of oposition by his parents. While they were first married they lived happily. But recently he reflects on his marriage and the manner in which he pushed his way through his parents' opposition—and the present wife—he wishes his present wife would not exist —he attempts to push away the feeling of blame within his breast. One night on the way home he buys some insect poison and gives it to his wife to drink and she dies. What he has done weighs on his mind. He gives himself up to the police. He trust-

fully tells his story to them. He reflects on how wicked he has been in the past. He completes his prison term and faces the future with serious intent.

This story indirectly brings out a feeling of guilt for attempting to carry out a love marriage. Since such a marriage is psychologically forbidden fruit, the tasting of it brings upon the transgressor punishment, much like what happens for sexual transgressions out of wedlock in the fantasies of some more puritanical Westerners.

Card 13: Marital discord.—The nature of the stories concerning marital discord is unique to the Japanese. Seven of the 21 Niiike men giving stories about Card 13 mention marital discord. Five of these men and all three women giving such stories are between 35 and 50 years of age. The men tend to see the marriage as ending badly, whereas the women are more optimistic about seeing the discord resolved. Both sexes usually place the blame for the discord on the women.

As in one of the stories mentioned previously, the men take a cue for their stories from the position of the woman in the bed. Rather than seeing the woman as ill, as do many of the women responding to this card, the men use the woman's posture as a basis for criticizing her. One of the chief complaints found in these stories is that such a woman obviously does not take "proper care" of her man. The following stories bring out the nature of some of the feelings leading to the castigation of the wife for "looseness" and lack of wifely concern for her husband. The man, too, is castigated in some of the stories, but not with the strength of feeling that is turned toward the woman.

M, age 39: This is also very difficult for me. What shall I say— I can't tell my impressions—what shall I say—it seems to me that they do not lead a happy life. The man often comes back home late at night, I suppose. But his wife does not wait for her husband. She has decided to act of her own accord, I suppose— he is back home late again, and his wife is already asleep. He thinks it might be well to speak to her. I suppose there is always a gloomy feeling in this family. Well, if they lead a peaceful life, such a scene as this would never occur. It is customary that a wife takes care of her husband as she should when he comes home —and afterward she goes to bed. But, judging from this picture, I suppose this wife wouldn't care a bit about her husband. Such a family as this will be ruined, I think. They should change their attitude toward each other and should make happy home. [*Examiner:* What about the future?] They will be divorced. It will be their end. [*Examiner:* Do you have anything to add?] Well, I expect a woman to be as a woman should be. A man also should think more of his family.

M, age 41: This is also—this man is a drunkard, and his wife also a sluttish woman. And the man was drunk, and when he came back his wife was already asleep—and, well—finally, they will be ruined. They have no child. They will become separated from each other. This wife will become something like *nakai* or a procuress. The husband will be held in prison—and the husband will kill himself on the railroad tracks. And—the wife will work as a *nakai*, and after contracting an infectious disease will die. An infectious disease which attacks her is dysentery. They worked together in a company and were married for love. That is their past. [*Examiner:* What does it mean that they will be ruined?] He became desperate. He became separated from his wife, so that he became desperate. If a man committed a bad thing, nobody cares for him. He could not hope for any help, so that he killed himself.

M, age 35: Well, this man and woman married for love. The woman was a café waitress and married the man for love. But they have not lived happily, so the man repents the marriage very much. Well, this man used to be a very good man, but he was seduced by the waitress and lost his self-control, and at last he had a sexual relationship with her. Afterwards, he becomes afraid that he has to think over their marriage. If their married life has any future at all, I hope they maintain some better stability. But if this woman doesn't want to do so, he needs to think over their marriage, I suppose.

The latter story especially brings out strong feelings of guilt related to an attempt to carry out a love marriage. The story directly depicts the guilt as being related to losing self-control and becoming involved with an unsuitable woman, not with the sexual activity per se.

Implied, too, is the criticism that any woman who would make a love marriage is not really capable of being a very worthy wife. Therefore, in addition to depicting guilt for going counter to the parents in a love marriage, Card 13 indicates the potential avenue for projecting guilt on to the woman who is active enough to enter a love marriage. Such a woman's conduct obviously does not include the proper submissiveness to parental wishes and attention to the needs of her spouse.

This castigation of the woman is therefore directly related to an expectation that the wife rather than being a sexual object should be a figure fulfilling dependency needs. The man sees his wife in a maternal role and is probably quick to complain if his wife renders him less care and attention than were rendered him by his mother. Since the wife-mother image tends to be fused in men, there is little concept of companionship per se, or sharing of experience on a mutual basis. Also, the wife's acting too free sexually excites aspects of sexuality toward the mother that were repressed in childhood. The wife-mother image cannot be conceived of in gross sexual terms. It is speculated by some that the mistress is a necessity to some men, because their sexual potency toward their wives is muted by the fused wife-mother image. Certain free sexual attitudes on the part of the wife would tend to change the mother image of her to a prostitute image and cause castigation of her as morally bad.

One may say that this fusion of images has a great deal to do with the conflict often arising between the young bride and her mother-in-law. The mother-in-law's jealousy is partially due to her fear of being directly replaced in her son's affection by the bride, since they are essentially geared to similar roles rather than forming different types of object relationship with the man. The wife becomes more intimate with the husband after she becomes a mother, and essentially treats him as the favorite child.

These sorts of attitudes were present in Hirano's case, mentioned previously, wherein a woman's psychotic episode was precipitated by her mother-in-law's attacks, including the interpretation that the dalliance of her son with other women was further proof of the wife's incompetence. It was interesting to note that during the wife's stay in the hospital the husband was able to express considerable feeling of concern for her. There was no doubt that he loved her. In effect, however, this feeling was more for her as a maternal surrogate than as a sexual partner. His mother knew she had more to fear from the wife in this respect than from liaisons with other women, with whom the husband never became too involved. He, on the other hand, had no manifest guilt for his sexual activities—in effect, they were approved of by his mother in her battle with the wife.

Card 13: Sickness or death of wife or mother.—In six instances (five women, three of them teen-agers), Card 13 is interpreted as a mother-son situation with the mother either sick or dead. The son is pictured specifically as working hard or studying; in one story the son steals because they are so poor. The younger girls especially seem to need to defend themselves from the sexual implications of the card by inventing a completely desexualized relationship. Unable to make the card into a marital situation, much less a more directly sexual one, some fall back on the favored theme of a sick mother and a distraught, but diligent, son. Emphasis on studying hard suggests the defensive use of work and study to shut out intrapersonal problems. Diligent work to care for the mother is again unconsciously used to avoid any feelings related to possible guilt. The way out is the one most easily suggested by the culture. Seeing Card 13 as a mother-son situation is rare in American records, even in aberrant cases.

Seeing Card 13 as illness or death of a wife is the most characteristic response of women; fourteen women, most of them over 35 years of age, gave such stories. Six men, including four of the five in the sample over 50, selected this theme. The middle-aged women were strongly involved in their stories about the death of a wife. Such stories were the longest of any given to the card. In sharp contrast to the derogatory stories directed toward the women by the men, the women use respectful concepts, such as *Otoko-naki* (manly tears), in referring to the men. On certain occasions it is expected that "manly tears" are shed. Although a man is usually expected not to cry freely when sober, the death of a wife is an occasion on which he is expected to cry. Much emphasis is placed on the imagined love felt toward the wife by a husband, on his loneliness, and on his feeling of loss because of the absence of wifely care. Concern with potential loneliness and possible loss of such care is certainly reflected in the fact that the older men in most instances select similar themes. The women in all but one case see the wife as dead or dying; the man is frequently seen as remarrying. Conversely, the men are more optimistic about recovery of a wife from illness and more pessimistic about remarriage if she does not recover.

One woman constructs a story of the noble self-sacrifice of a sick wife who commits suicide so as not to be a burden to her husband. This type of story, which recalls many sentimental novels written in Japan, is considered very moving by the Japanese, since it is supposed to reflect the degree of devotion of a wife for her husband and his goals and purposes. Tears are brought to the eyes of the older members of a *Kabuki* audience when such a story unfolds. To the Westerner, the stories seem to be excessively masochistic and overdrawn. The Japanese ethical ideal of the self-sacrificing role of woman is here emphatically displayed.

The foregoing materials from a farming village, which other evidence suggests is deeply imbued with traditional attitudes, are consistent with the interpretation that the potentiality for strong guilt feelings is prevalent in the Japanese. Such feelings become evident when there is failure in the performance of expected role behavior. Guilt, as such, is not as directly related in the Japanese to sexual expression as it is in persons growing up within cultures influenced by Christian attitudes toward sexuality. As first pointed out by Benedict, there is little pronounced guilt or otherwise negatively toned attitude directed toward physical expression of sexuality per se (op. cit.). Rather, there is concern with the possible loss of control suffered by becoming involved in a love relationship that interferes with the prescribed life goals of the individual.

From a sociological standpoint, Japanese culture can be considered as manifesting a particularistic or situational ethic as opposed to the more universalistic ethic built around moral absolutes found in Western Christian thought.[13] This evaluation can be well documented, but does not mean that the Japanese evidence a relative absence of guilt in relation to moral transgressions. Whereas the applicability of the more universalistic Western ethic in many aspects may tend to transcend the family, the

---

[13] See Talcott Parsons (1951:175), for a description of the particularistic achievement pattern. This category suits traditional Japanese culture very well.

Japanese traditional ethic is actually an expression of rules of conduct for members of a family, and filial piety has in itself certain moral absolutes that are not completely situationally determined even though they tend to be conceptualized in particularistic terms. This difference between family-oriented morality and a more universalistic moral system is, nevertheless, a source of difficulty in thinking about guilt in the Japanese.

Another reason for the failure to perceive guilt in the Japanese stems from the West's customary relation of guilt to sexuality. Missionaries in particular, in assessing the Japanese from the standpoint of Protestant moral standards, were often quoted as perplexed not only by what they considered a lack of moral feelings in regard to nonfamilial relationships, but also—and this was even worse in their eyes—by a seeming absence of any strong sense of 'sin' in their sexual relationships. It seems evident that the underlying emotional content of certain aspects of Christianity, in so far as it is based on specific types of repression and displacement of sexual and aggressive impulses, has never appealed to the Japanese in spite of their intellectual regard for the ethics of Christianity. Modern educated Japanese often recognize Christianity as advocating an advanced ethical system more in concert with modern universalized democratic ideals of man's brotherhood. As such, Christianity is favored by them over their more hierarchically oriented, traditional system with its rigidly defined, particularistic emphasis on prescribed social roles. To the educated Japanese, however, the concept of sin is of little interest in their attitudes toward Christianity. The lack of interest in sin is most probably related to the absence of childhood disciplines that would make the concept important to them.

Traditional Western disciplinary methods, guided by concern with the inherent evil in man, have been based on the idea that the child must be trained as early as possible to conquer evil tendencies within himself. Later, he learns to resist outside pressures and maintain himself as an individual subject to his own conscience and to the universalist laws of God. The traditional Western Protestant is more accustomed in certain circumstances to repress inappropriate feelings. 'Right' thoughts are valued highly and one generally tries to repress unworthy motives toward one's fellow men. Justice must be impartial and one must not be swayed by the feelings of the moment or be too flexible in regard to equity.

In Japanese Buddhist thought one finds a dual concept of man as good and evil but in Shinto thought, and in Japanese thinking about children generally,[14] the more prevailing notion is that man's impulses are innately good. The purpose of child training is merely the channeling of these impulses into appropriate role behavior.

The definitions of proper role behavior become increasingly exacting as the child grows and comes into increasing contact with others as a representative of his family. As such, he learns more and more to be diplomatic and to contain and suppress impulses and feelings that would be disruptive in social relations and put him at a disadvantage. He is not bringing a system of moral absolutes into his relations with others any more than the usual diplomat does in skillfully negotiating for the advantage of his country. The Japanese learns to be sensitive to 'face' and protocol and to be equally sensitive to the feelings of others. He learns to keep his personal feelings to himself as a family representative. It would be just as fallacious to assume, therefore, that the Japanese is without much sense of guilt, as it would be in the case of the private life of a career diplomat.

The fact that so much of conscious life is concerned with a system of social sanctions helps to disguise the underlying guilt system operative in the Japanese. This system, which severely represses unconscionable attitudes toward the parents and superiors, is well disguised not only from the Western observer but also from the Japanese themselves. The Westerner, under the

[14] It is significant that the Japanese usually use Shinto ceremonials in regard to marriage and fertility, and to celebrate various periods in childhood whereas Buddhist ceremonials are used mainly in paying respect to the parents—that is, in funerals and in memorial services at specified times after death. It must be noted that the material in this paper does not include any reference to fear of punishment in an afterlife; although present in traditional Buddhism in the past, such feelings are not much in evidence in modern Japan. Relatively few modern Japanese believe in or are concerned with life beyond death. (See De Vos and Wagatsuma 1959 especially pp. 13 *ff.*) It is my contention that fear of punishment either by the parents, society, or God is not truly internalized guilt. Insofar as the punishment is perceived as external in source, the feeling is often fear or anxiety, as distinct from guilt.

tutelage of Christianity, has learned to 'universalize' his aggressive and other impulses and feel guilt in regard to them in more general terms. The modern Japanese is moving toward such an attitude, but is affected by the traditional moral structure based on the family system, or if expanded, on the nation conceived of in familial terms.

Lastly, some difficulty in perceiving Japanese guilt theoretically, if not clinically, is due to the fact that psychoanalysis—the psychological system most often consulted for help in understanding the mechanisms involved in guilt—tends to be strongly influenced by Western ethical values. Psychoanalytic writers, in describing psychosexual development, tend to emphasize the superego on the one hand and concepts of personal individuation and autonomy on the other. A major goal of maturation is freedom in the ego from irrational social controls as well as excessive internalized superego demands. In understanding the Japanese this emphasis is somewhat out of focus. Maturational ideals valued by the traditional Japanese society put far more emphasis on concepts of 'belonging' and adult role identity.

In studying the Japanese, it is helpful, therefore, to try to understand the nature of internalization of an ego ideal defined in terms of social role behavior. Concern with social role has in the past been more congenial to the sociologist or sociologically oriented anthropologist,[15] who in examining human behavior is less specifically concerned with individuation and more concerned with the patterning of behavior within a network of social relations.

However, the sociological approach in itself is not sufficient to help understand the presence or absence of a strong achievement motive in the Japanese. It is necessary to use a psychoanalytic framework to examine the psychological processes whereby social roles are internalized and influence the formation of an internalized ego ideal. The ideas of Erikson, in his exploration of the role of "self-identity" in the latter stages of the psychosexual maturation process, form a bridge between the psychoanalytic systems of thought and the sociological analyses which cogently

[15] This approach is also evident in the theorist in religion. Also, the recent interest in existentialist psychiatry is one attempt to bring in relevant concepts of "belonging" to the study of the human experience.

describe the place of role as a vital determining factor of social behavior (Erikson 1956). The avenue of approach taken by Erikson is a very promising one in understanding the Japanese social tradition and its effect on individual development.

Part IV EURASIA

15 FAMILY SYSTEM AND THE ECONOMY: CHINA

Francis L. K. Hsu

The situation-centered world is characterized by ties which permanently unite closely related human beings in the family and clan. Within this basic human constellation the individual is conditioned to seek mutual dependence. That is to say, he is dependent upon other human beings as much as others are dependent upon him, and he is therefore fully aware of his obligation to make repayment, however much delayed, to his benefactors. The central core of Chinese ethics is filial piety, which defines the complex of duties, obligations, and attitudes on the part of children (sons) toward their fathers and mothers. Why do sons owe filial piety to their parents? Because of their "indebtedness" to the elders who brought them forth and who reared them to maturity. Since the kinship structure, no matter how widely extended, is built on expanded consanguine and affinal relationships represented in the parent-child triad, all members in it are either at the receiving or the giving end of a human network of mutual dependence.

The individual enmeshed in such a human network is likely to react to his world in a complacent and compartmentalized way; complacent because he has a secure and inalienable place in his human group, and compartmentalized because he is conditioned to perceive the external world in terms of what is

FROM Francis L. K. Hsu, *Clan Caste and Club,* 1963, D. Van Nostrand and Co., pp. 1–3, and from *Americans and Chinese,* Copyright 1953 by Henry Schuman, Inc. A revised edition of the latter will be published by Doubleday and Company, Inc. under the title, *Conflict of Cultures.* Reprinted by permission of D. Van Nostrand and Co., and of Doubleday and Company, Inc., and the author.

within his group and what is outside it. For what is within his group and what is outside it have drastically different meanings for him. As he generalizes from this basic assumption, there are quite different truths for different situations throughout his life's experiences. Principles which are correct for one set of circumstances may not be appropriate for another at all, but the principles in each case are equally honorable.

The good situation-centered Chinese, in fact, tends to have multiple standards. The prisoner's standards are not his jailer's, and the man's are not the woman's. Because he enjoys within his primary kinship group a security, continuity, and permanency that he cannot find outside it, the situation-centered Chinese has a greater feeling of certainty about life than does an average individual in many other societies and therefore is more likely to be complacent. Since double or multiple standards of morality and conduct are normal, they present the individual with no inner conflict. The individual feels no resentment against conforming and no compunction about behaving differently under contrasting sets of circumstances. He may be taught charity as a personal virtue, to improve his fate and that of his ancestors and descendants, but he will have no necessary compulsion or desire to champion the cause of the oppressed as a whole or to overthrow the privileged position of all oppressors. The primary guide for his behavior is his place, the place of his primary group in the accepted scheme of things, and the knowledge of how to better that place; but he will have little sense of the justice or injustice of intergroup relations as a whole or any desire to change them. Consequently the Chinese society through history has tended to be remarkably static, for it lacked *internal* impetus to change.

The individual-centered world is characterized by temporary ties among closely related human beings. Having no permanent base in family and clan, the individual's basic orientation toward life and the environment is self-reliance. That is to say, he is conditioned to think for himself, to make his own decisions, and to carve out his future by his own hands and in his own potentialities. Emerson expressed the essence of this view eloquently. "The nonchalance of boys who are sure of a dinner, and would disdain as much as a lord to do or say aught to con-

Family System and the Economy: China

ciliate one, is the healthy attitude of human nature. . . . He cumbers himself never about consequences, about interests; he gives an independent, genuine verdict. You must court him; he does not court you." Again, "Whoso would be a man, must be a nonconformist. He who would gather immortal palms must not be hindered by the name of goodness, but must explore if it be goodness. Nothing is at last sacred but the integrity of your own mind" (1841).

The individual brought up under this pattern will find being dependent intolerable, for it ruins his self-respect; but he will find having others dependent upon him no less problematic, for this position generates resentment on their part. Yet after struggling free of parental and other yokes, the individual finds that he is without anything or anyone positive to live for. He is, therefore, likely to be beset with the problem of the meaning of life. He tries to achieve this meaning by conquering the material universe, by militantly propagating his belief in his god or Utopia, or by exploiting or aggressively improving his fellow human beings in his own or other societies. Because he is not tied down by his primary groups, he finds the whole world his oyster; but because he has no permanent ties with his fellow human beings except those which he constructs with his own efforts, he is likely to view life and the environment in terms of unilineal absolutes. So that he may have something permanent to hold on to, the world is either absolutely good or absolutely evil, entirely romantic or entirely miserable, wholly for him or wholly against him. If the world is not all as he desires it, then it should be changed by his own hands. He tends to harbor universalism in a love or hatred hard to come by among his situation-centered Chinese brethren. At any given point of time the individual may be forced by circumstances to conform to a multiplicity of standards or organizational requirements, but because of the inner conflict such conformity generates, these very standards and requirements will be ammunition for individual rebellion and group reform or revolution. Consequently, throughout history the Western society, of which America is one of the latest versions, has tended to be remarkably dynamic, for it has great *internal* impetus for change.

Two Approaches to Economic Life

The Chinese bureaucracy has long been the road to economic as well as social betterment. One of the basic reasons why the Chinese looked to places in the bureaucracy for their income was that Chinese commerce and industry were so rudimentary that bureaucratic positions offered the most lucrative jobs in the entire society. This seems surprising when we recall that the Chinese have long produced some of the world's most beautiful goods, including Shang bronzes, Han jades and Ming vases. Such items today add splendor and prestige to every important museum and a vast number of homes the world over. Furthermore, the Chinese society has been one of the very few in history to enjoy a continuous civilization for over three millennia, and within this time it has been blessed by longer periods of internal stability and peace than those known to the majority of mankind. Why did the Chinese not achieve an extensive development of their economy? This puzzle has aroused much speculation, most of it divorced from the basic realities of Chinese life. But if we apply the results of our analysis thus far we must conclude that Chinese economic life has been restricted by the same factors which underlie other characteristics of their social life, government and religion.

We have seen that mutual dependence is the outstanding Chinese characteristic, and that this deep-seated tendency to rely upon other persons, especially those within the primary groups, produces in the Chinese a sense of social and psychological security. Given this anchorage and a concept of the supernatural that derives from it, the Chinese feels little compulsion to seek other forms of material or psychological comfort. The self-reliant American, however, strives to eliminate from his life both the fact and the sense of reliance upon others. This unending struggle to be fully independent raises the threat of perpetual social and psychological insecurity. A close parental bond is severed early in life; the marriage which replaces it is unstable; heroes come and go; class affiliation is subject to a constant struggle to climb from one level to another; and the alliance

Family System and the Economy: China 295

with God, though less ephemeral than the preceding relationships, is nevertheless affected by the same divisive forces. For, given the ideal of total self-reliance and its concomitant version of a God who helps those who help themselves, Americans seek their final anchorage in harbors other than men or the supernatural.

It seems to me that these are the basic factors differentiating the economic life of the Chinese from that of the Americans.

THE CHARACTERISTICS OF THE CHINESE ECONOMY

Viewed from any angle, Chinese business has long shown itself to be a stable thing, without expansive or aggressive designs. Take manufacturing for example. In addition to bronzes, jades and vases, a myriad of other products and skills have made China famous: rugs, lacquer work, embroidery, silk, porcelain screens, cloisonné, ivory work, teakwood furniture, brass objects, silver and gold ornaments, fireworks and boats. It was for some of these items of commerce that Western explorers and traders have since ancient times undertaken hazardous trips to the East. But significantly few Chinese have ever made comparable attempts to seek a market for their goods in the West.

The majority of these products and many others whose listing could be extended almost endlessly are manufactured in homes or small family shops. The average Chinese craftsman usually handles the manufacturing processes of a single product from the beginning to the end. His hours are long, his efficiency is low, and his returns are meager.

The personnel of a typical Chinese handicraft shop consists of a master, his wife, one or more of his children, one or two journeymen and one or two apprentices. The physical plant often is no more than two rooms, one fronting on the street. The back room is the living quarters of the master and his family. During the day the front room is the workshop and sales department, the manufacturers doubling as salesmen, and at night it serves as the living quarters for the journeymen and apprentices. The master and the journeymen usually take their meals together, while the master's wife and children dine in the kitchen. The apprentices act as servants for all.

The craft guilds are not only local in character, having no ties with their counterparts in other communities, they also have as members both the owners and their employees. For, although the guilds fix prices, wages and the terms of apprenticeship and although their officers work to settle disputes within the craft or with other guilds, their primary concern is the protection of localized interests against encroachment by political authority from beyond the local scene. Further, they stabilize the relationship between employers and employees as well as between one shop and another instead of promoting competition or strife among these parties.

The workmanship, ingenuity and artistry that go into many Chinese products amaze most Westerners, but these goods are today still being produced with tools and methods that the Chinese have inherited from a time unknown. Consequently, the products of contemporary Chinese craftsmen bear close resemblance to many of their ancient antecedents, and changes in styles have occurred, if at all, only once in several generations.

This does not mean that the Chinese have been wholly devoid of new ideas in the field of production. The Chinese commonly are credited with the invention of gunpowder, printing and paper, but it is not generally known that they were probably the first to utilize the assembly line. The principle of the assembly line was employed as early as the 16th century in porcelain manufacturing plants supervised and operated by the imperial government. In such plants, some workers specialized in making the base, some in glazing, others in painting a decorative figure, while still others specialized in coloring the edges. Every teapot, cup or plate thus went through a number of specialized departments before its completion. But this idea was never extended to other industries nor extensively accepted by private manufacturers of porcelain.

What is true of Chinese handicraft industries is equally true of Chinese commerce. Although Westerners think of the Chinese as good merchants, commerce has never been of great importance in China nor, as a rule, have its practitioners been highly esteemed. Nevertheless commercial activities have flourished in local communities and between different regions of the country.

Family System and the Economy: China

But the bulk of China's trade has always been carried on by family enterprise.

Generally speaking, in addition to that typical of the craft shop, we may differentiate between three kinds of selling in China. The first is the periodic market found in a Chinese village or small town. These markets may be held in the towns or villages themselves or at a short distance from them in an area traditionally agreed upon. They may occur at intervals varying from once every three days to once a year. They may last for one day, several days, or several weeks. Though the periodic market is especially prevalent in southwest China, it is not rare elsewhere. Wherever held, these markets attract hundreds of men, women and children. They stream to the market place carrying everything from fruit to furniture. A vendor's place of business may be a table, a tent, or a spot on the ground. Others, of course, merely come to buy. At day's end the seller of fruit may carry home a piece of furniture that he has purchased with his earnings, while those who came empty-handed may return wealthier but without goods, having profited by reselling commodities bought in the market. And, as with markets throughout the world, many persons come solely to look, inquire about prices, and visit with their friends and have a good time in general.

The largest of these periodic markets is held in Tali, Yunnan province. This begins during the third lunar month and usually lasts several weeks. My last visit to this market was in 1942. Then, as in the dim past, buyers and sellers were drawn there not only from nearby places, but they also came from a number of southern provinces and Tibet. Many aboriginal groups came in caravans, having camped all along the route. Present were jugglers, tight-rope walkers, magicians and diviners. The market was like an industrial fair in the United States, except that the exhibitors represented no one but themselves and all buying and selling were done then and there.

The second type of retail commerce takes place in city and town shops. These range from one-room affairs, very much like the craft shops described before, to establishments employing thirty, forty or even a hundred persons. Occasionally a firm may have two or more branches in different parts of the same community or in two or three other cities. The smaller businesses are family affairs but the larger ones have stockholders, a managerial group, clerks and apprentices learning the trade. Goods at such well-established firms are never subject to haggling, a practice found only among traders at bazaars, periodic markets and peddling stands. Western visitors thinking otherwise have often created situations acutely embarrassing to themselves and the merchants. Most of the old retail houses in China have signboards which read as follows:

> "Whether you are nine or ninety
> We sell at fixed prices."

The reason for this is much deeper than a desire to rise above the bargaining of the itinerant peddler. The majority of these establishments conduct much of their business, as do the craft shops, with long-term customers. All important customers are known personally to the management. In these firms a typical business transaction takes place as follows: Upon entering, the customer is received by the manager, who sits on a long bench near the entrance. The two of them sit down and, while drinking tea served by an apprentice, they chat about the weather, the market, and local affairs. Eventually the customer may say that he wishes to look at a certain kind of cloth, and the manager asks one of the clerks to show him the goods, either on the counter or near where they sit. The customer examines the goods, and, if satisfied, the transaction is completed. He may pay cash or have the amount charged; if the latter the clerk makes an entry in the purchaser's account. Whichever the case, there are no receipts. Finally the customer may stay to have lunch or dinner with the manager and the assistant manager.

This manner of doing business may be described as friendship before trade. Therefore most regular patrons of any shop expect to receive some token of appreciation on each of the three annual festivals when bills have to be paid. Even with the majority of customers, who may only be acquainted with or unknown to the management and who deal directly with the clerks, business is done on the basis of good will and local respectability. No firm can expect to continue in business if, by unilateral action, its prices, which are often fixed by the guilds, fluctuate wildly or if it goes back on its word.

The third variety of business is conducted by independent entrepreneurs who transport goods from one part of China to another and distribute them to retailers on a wholesale basis. This has never been an easy task in China, and has always called for a liberal use of wits, energy and initiative, especially in the days before railroads and insurance. The entrepreneur not only personally selects and oversees the packing of commodities, but he also accompanies the goods from their point of origin to their destination. He may not only have to direct the loading and unloading from one type of transportation to another, but he must negotiate with local officials and police for passage through their locality and even with bandits for certificates of safe conduct. If he knows of a market for goods that are not available, he may commission a number of individual craft shops or families to produce the desired commodities. He furnishes the capital necessary for purchasing raw materials and often advances a part of the wages. Nowadays many of these men also provide hand-operated machines to the workers they commission. Hosiery knitting in Hopei province is even an example. Studies made by the Nankai University at Tientsin show that a sizable group of merchants maintain this relationship with a large number of rural households. The merchants furnish the yarn, the hand-operated machinery and an advance in wages, which are on a piece basis, and then collect the finished products for sale in urban markets. How extensive this type of enterprise may be is unknown, but it is to be found in all parts of the country.

In many instances Chinese entrepreneurs—principally those dealing in such staples as rice, salt or tea—became extremely wealthy. In the third century B.C. a businessman became the most successful government administrator of his time. District records speak of local merchants who counted their fortunes in millions of cashes.[1] Nevertheless the basic characteristic of

---

[1] The Chinese "cash" was a metal disk which usually had a square hole in its center to permit stringing. This ancient medium of exchange was discontinued during the 1920's in favor of coins of the Western model.

Chinese commerce is the same as that of her manufacturing: the absence of expansionist designs. The role of commercial guilds is indicative. While these guilds may be more imposing structures than those of the craftsmen and, as a whole, are better endowed, their functions are not at all different from the manufacturers' guilds. Their mission is to hold the line and to protect the merchants from excessive government exploitation, not to encourage or chart trade expansion. Like other guilds, they too are organized by locality and by trade. The salesmanship of their members, who are preoccupied with filling needs as they occur and holding their customers by friendship and good will, is as much in keeping with this approach as advertising on the American model is not. These businessmen feel no call to study retailing procedures, do exact cost accounting, or hold conventions to improve sales methods or promote new products.

Consequently, most manufacturers and merchants have been satisfied with a profit that would seem unreasonably low to Americans. What, we must therefore ask, keeps them from wishing to increase their returns? One answer is to apply the oft-reiterated East-West myth: the Chinese are more spiritual and therefore less interested in profit than Americans. This is completely false. Any American who has had business experience with Chinese merchants can tell us that they try to obtain all the profit they can. There is nothing spiritual about them in this regard.

But if we abandon the misconceived spiritual-material dichotomy and look into the very real contrast in the two people's patterns of human relationship we come closer to explaining the relative stability of the Chinese economy. The key fact is that, both within the shop and without it, the Chinese owner and his workers can find satisfactions that are not available to their Western counterparts. Within the shop the human relationship is like that of a family. Authority is in the hands of the master and his wife, while obedience is expected of the apprentices. The journeymen are like the big brothers or uncles who come in between. Outside the shop the ambition of the master and his wife is to be able to buy a piece of land, rebuild the family home, and thenceforth enjoy the company of their

Family System and the Economy: China

fellow townsmen. The ambition of the apprentices and other workers is in the same direction.

The question may be raised, if the master and his wife can achieve their sense of social and psychological importance through shop ownership which, if it is at all profitable, brings other benefits, will not all merchants, assuming the same attitude, necessarily compete? Won't this force an all-round increase in business efficiency, scale of operation and the exploitation of new markets with new products? The answer is no. With a cultural emphasis on mutual dependence, the ceiling of competition is lowered in every sphere of endeavor. The individual Chinese desires the glory, wealth and leisure which accompany success, but in his desire to climb he sees nothing wrong in settling for a position where he benefits by association, however marginal, with the more successful. He might become a servant in the big house; as a servant he shares the social importance of the big house. He might become a secretary to an important person; as secretary he is far more fortunate than others who do not occupy a similar position. His daughter might marry into the family of a prominent person; as a relative of such a man he is treated by the rest of the community with more deference and respect than if he were not. Even making the successful one his "dry father" or a "sworn brother"[2] are all legitimate signs of his own success.

It has been plausibly argued for some time that commerce and industry cannot develop in a society where the majority of the people derive no more than a bare living from small farms. This observation appears to fit the condition of China where at least 75 percent of the population live on farms and where even most of the so-called urban population have their roots in the villages or exist as absentee landlords. Such a picture is perhaps adequate for descriptive purposes, but it does not explain why

[2] The term "dry father" is literal in its meaning and implies the same role as that of the American godfather, with the exception that the relationship between the parties concerned is not established in a church or temple. A "dry father" and his "dry son" have about the same privileges and responsibilities as a natural father and son except that the younger man has no right to automatic inheritance. The relationship of "sworn brothers" is similar to that of the "dry father" and "dry son" except that it is between persons of more or less equal standing.

those who have profited from commerce and industry, like all Chinese who have attained a degree of success in any endeavor, desire to go back to their home community and invest in farms.

The physical environment of the average Chinese farmer would have no attraction for Americans. For one thing, the majority of Chinese farms are small, so small that with their present technological equipment only about seven percent of them are suitable for optimum production. Though farms tend to be larger in the north than in the south, it remains true that four-fifths of the Chinese agriculturists derive their livelihood from farms that are less than five acres in extent.

For another thing, farming methods remain primitive—tools are crude and animal power, much less mechanical assistance, is virtually unavailable. The average farmer toils twelve to fourteen hours a day during the summer. His winter work day is not much shorter because he must undertake other labors to eke out a living.

Both in the north and in the south, the women, when they do not go into the field, raise silk-worms, pigs and chickens, tend fruit trees or vegetable gardens or weave. The products of these efforts supplement the family income directly or are sold or bartered in periodic markets.

The smallness of the farm and the primitive methods of land exploitation result in a third feature: poverty. At least one-third of the Chinese farmers exist on a calorie count that is below the minimum number for subsistence. Further, in spite of the high rate of interest, which averages 32 percent per year, more than one-third of the farmers covered in one nationwide survey had to obtain credit not, in the main, for productive purposes, but to purchase food and to meet ceremonial expenses (Buck 1937:439). The preceding figures relate to owners and tenants. The lot of the farm laborer is even worse.

Logically these features would seem to favor vigorous competition in agricultural pursuits and an exodus of persons from the farm into industry and commerce with a consequent expansion of these latter fields, thus producing a better balanced and more prosperous general economy. There is also the frequently propounded and widely accepted theory that military aggression often is rooted in over-population. In the recent past the Ger-

Family System and the Economy: China

mans and the Japanese spoke of the need for living space as a *raison d'être* for their actions. Even pacific nations, such as the United States and Switzerland, have lent a sympathetic ear to this argument. And bookshelves are crowded with works which support this thesis, a recent example of which is Josui de Castro's *The Geography of Hunger* (1952).

But in China necessity has been neither the mother of invention nor the father of aggression. For many centuries China has been over-populated, land has been scarce, agriculture has been arduous, and malnutrition and even starvation have been the lot of untold millions. But instead of producing an inventive or even commercially aggressive spirit, these facts have induced in the people who inhabit the villages an even greater desire to stay where they are in spite of the fact that it has meant a further reduction of their already low standard of living.

This shows itself in several related ways. Perhaps the most pervasive evidence is the people's sentimental attachment to land, which often overrides all considerations of personal economic welfare. For to the Chinese, his land is not merely an investment. It is life itself. Accordingly, there is almost no sacrifice he is not prepared to make an order to avoid selling his land. When in dire need he is more likely to mortgage his land than to sell it, even though mortgage payments over the years often run much higher than the actual price of the land.[3]

When a land transaction does occur in China the scene is marked by a most revealing contrast of moods: for the seller's family the event is like a funeral, often marked by tears; for the buyer's family it is like a wedding, usually colored by laughter. For the same reasons the sale of land cannot be final unless endorsed by the seller's grown-up sons and sometimes even by his brothers who are no longer living under the same roof with him. Furthermore, very often he can sell his land to someone who is not related only if his clansmen do not wish to buy.

The people's desire to remain where they are shows itself

[3] Pearl S. Buck, in her great novel *The Good Earth,* has, in my view, captured this Chinese sentimental regard for land as no other author has ever done. The protagonist, Wong Lung, even after having become wealthy, rigidly opposed the attempts of his modern educated sons to liquidate the family's landed property and move into the city.

also in the large surplus of labor which remains on the land, especially in the south and southwest. During the many years of civil strife and the seven years of war against Japan, when the military demand for manpower was greatest, Chinese farms and city firms which needed help never experienced any hardship. The migratory laborers did not all come from the ranks of the landless. Many originated from farms which are too small to maintain the number of people who must live on them. For this reason, though *each acre* of Chinese land produces 50 percent more rice or 15 percent more wheat (the two staple foods of the Chinese) than its American counterpart, *each farmer* in China produces less than one-fourteenth the annual average yield of the American farmer.

Why does such an abundant labor force stay on the small farms? The usual explanation is that, instead of instituting a system of primogeniture in inheritance, the Chinese never abandoned the principle of equal division. Thus, either before or after the death of the parents, property is distributed equally among all the sons. This, it has been alleged, is why large numbers of Chinese have failed to migrate to areas adjacent to China and why also they have not proved aggressive colonizers of Mongolia, Manchuria, Formosa, the southwestern provinces and the coastal islands.

But obviously not all Chinese in a particular community own land. If the equal division principle affected those whose parents left some inheritance, what became of those others whose parents left nothing? More important, however, is the fact that of those people who did migrate to the frontier regions, a very substantial number of them periodically returned to their old home towns or retired there after they had made their "fortune." Others sought at least to strengthen their ties with their ancestral communities through donations to clan temples, hospitals and schools.

The pattern of Chinese emigration to the South Seas, Europe and America is even more revealing. In the first place, the majority of these emigrants, like their countrymen who went to Manchuria or southwest China, tend to maintain their home ties and a desire to retire to their ancestral villages. In the second place, all emigrants had their origin in a few coastal counties of China. Most of the Chinese who settled in Europe came from

Family System and the Economy: China

a few counties in Chekiang province; most of those in the South Seas came from a few counties in Fukien and Kwangtung provinces; and the ancestors of 90 percent of the Chinese in Hawaii were inhabitants of one county in Kwangtung province, while the forebears of over 90 percent of the Chinese in the continental United States came from four adjacent counties in the same province. Admittedly the early contacts of the inhabitants of these coastal provinces with the West had something to do with it. Then, too, some European emigrants to the United States and elsewhere have also acted like the Chinese with reference to their countries of origin, sending gifts, endowing schools and performing other good works. But early Western influence was by no means confined to the relative few coastal counties from which some Chinese emigrated.

Again, if we look at China's history we cannot escape the conclusion that the attachment of the Chinese to their ancestral communities is matched by their reluctance to leave them. European emigrants may entertain a sentimental regard for their homelands, but this has not prevented their coming to America by the millions. At the heights of China's dynastic powers, in Han (202 B.C.–200 A.D.), in T'ang (618–906 A.D.), in Yuan (1260–1368 A.D.) and in Ming (1368–1644 A.D.), the Chinese could have followed their conquering armies to many alien lands from Korea to Persia and eastern Europe and become the pioneers of new domains. But they did nothing of the kind.

Thus equal division of inheritance and the reluctance to emigrate, instead of being cause and effect, are actually common expressions of the same pattern—the pattern of mutual dependence within the primary groups. This pattern is so deeply embedded and so satisfying socially and psychologically that the individual is prepared, almost without reflection, to forego material rewards that may be obtainable elsewhere. His material welfare is relatively less important to him than his place of respect among his primary social relations.

CHINESE GOVERNMENT AND CHINESE ECONOMY

The preceding analysis, it seems to me, clarifies the relationship between the Chinese government and the Chinese economy. Chinese ruling houses, as we have observed, favored agriculture over commerce. They often went so far as to suppress the latter. The rulers never dared to challenge private ownership of land among the farmers, but they have always taken liberties with merchant wealth through special levies, commandeering, or outright confiscation. Because the agricultural tradition was of ancient vintage, its sanctity was respected by the tradition-bound government. Nor did the people, secure in this tradition, seek any change. But, for this same reason, the people did not develop an expanding and powerful industrial and commercial economy. And this, the absence of a countering force, permitted the government to assume an autocratic attitude in respect to these endeavors while permitting the agriculturist to proceed without interference.

Since the Chinese look to control over men as the principal source of wealth, there is a definite and traceable continuity that runs from the mutual dependence of parents and children, among relatives, between masters and disciples, between friends, and between big bureaucrats and small bureaucrats to that between the government as a whole and the people as a whole. For security in their old age, parents do not look to property ownership so much as they do to the filial piety of their sons. In the same way, the measure of a dynastic regime's success was not the extent to which it developed the country's natural resources but the degree to which it secured its subjects' obedience and insured their protection. In all cases the balance of power depended upon socially or politically defined relationships, not upon economic rights. A father has power over his son no matter how much money the son can command. The father's power comes from his paternal position. In the same way the emperor "owned" his subjects no matter how wealthy they became. The founder of a dynasty usually achieved his position by the sword, but his successors lorded over their charges merely because they occupied the throne.

This autocratic behavior of the Chinese government was somewhat modified between 1929 and 1937 under the Nationalist regime of Chiang Kai-shek. This was the period, the reader will recall, when Chiang's regime was at the summit of its power and popularity. It was during this period too that China's modern commerce and industry reached their highest development since the time China's doors were knocked open by the West. A combination of three factors forced a modification of the traditional relationship between China's government and her economy.

First, much of China's commercial and industrial wealth was centered around or deposited in the banks located in the foreign concessions and the International Settlement in Shanghai. Though some banks were Chinese, most were foreign-owned, and because of extraterritorial privileges the Nationalist government, though powerful, had no means of reaching this wealth by laws that it could design.

Second, in its attempt to consolidate its power over the vestigial warlords and the upcoming Communists, the Nationalist government had to depend upon foreign supplies of arms which it could not manufacture within the country. These foreign arms had to be bargained for through the regular channels and procedures of foreign trade which only the financiers and the commercial people could handle.

Third, the Nationalist government, in its bid for international prestige and assistance, had to gain the confidence of the Western countries. As commerce and industry are of primary importance in these Western countries, the Nationalist government could not secure their confidence unless it showed a certain degree of respect toward its own merchants and industrialists. Consequently, industrial and commercial interests were more respected and favored by the Nationalist government than by any previous regime in China's history. In return, it was more ardently supported by these interests than was any previous regime. The relationship between the Nationalist government and the commercial and industrial community was so close that the Japanese militarists, in support of their expansionist schemes, launched repeated propaganda attacks charging the Nationalist government with a "subversive alliance with the Chekiang financial lords."

When the ravages of war destroyed the bases of the Chinese commercial and industrial interests in the coastal provinces, the Nationalist government lost no time in reasserting its never questioned supremacy over them. The pattern was so much a part of the Chinese tradition that the readjustment occurred without significant popular protest.

AMERICAN ECONOMIC ATTITUDES

Our purpose here is not to plow over the ground so thoroughly covered in numerous accounts of the structure of American business and agriculture. It is the attitude of the self-reliant American toward his economic activities that we shall investigate here. But absolute self-reliance is an unattainable ideal. As explained earlier every individual has two environments—the external and the internal—and these he must balance in a way that provides him with emotional security. This security is made up of a sense of self-importance and a feeling of purposefulness. The Chinese, who retains his primary ties to which he relates all subsequent bonds, finds his security in human relationships. The American, who regards all human relationships as subject to severance or to being repatterned when personally convenient, must seek security outside the human fold. And since his God helps him who helps himself, the one remaining source of security is the acquisition of material comforts or the conquest of the physical environment in other ways.

American economic activities assume, therefore, a number of characteristics that are foreign to the Chinese scene. There is a divisiveness which, though restrained in politics and religion because the individual fears non-conformity, is unbridled in economic matters because of the free enterprise tradition. Too, there is a constant change in production procedures and product styles, thereby introducing new kinds of goods and services or giving new appearances to the old. Intense competition makes such changes indispensable because the very existence of a manufacturing concern, and even the retail or service enterprises it supplies, depends upon its determination to expand. It was for this reason that, when asked the secret of success, one of the leading business women in the United States said, "Beat last year's record." To assist them in reaching this goal, commercial and industrial firms must enroll advertisers to inform prospective consumers how necessary to their welfare is a new service or goods of whose existence, much less necessity, these consumers are perforce ignorant until the campaign begins. "Give me any product," I heard an advertising executive say, "and I can make it sell."

And although the American entrepreneur's efforts are directed toward maximizing his profit so as to achieve more material comfort, his ultimate satisfaction lies elsewhere. Many a Chinese has been puzzled by the unfaltering zeal of wealthy American industrialists and businessmen for whom greater monetary returns can have little material meaning. We do not have to cite the careers of the most famous, but just consider the case of any one of the nine vice-presidents of General Motors, each of whom, in the year 1949 alone, reportedly received a bonus of from $227,450 to over $500,000. From the Chinese point of view any one of them could stop worrying about profit right then and there. Most wealthy bureaucrats or merchants have always chosen to retire early in life. The characteristic Chinese attitude is summed up in the saying, "When currents are swift, bravely stop at the suitable moment."

The careers of H. H. Kung and T. V. Soong are interesting in this connection. Both are millionaires whose wealth was derived from political power. But following Chiang's mainland defeat, both men chose a life of ease and silence in the United States. Neither has participated in any of the activities, such as those of the China Institute or the Committee for Free Asia, aimed at promoting faith in the Nationalist administration.

The majority of Chinese bureaucrats would have stopped long before Kung and Soong did. For to the Chinese, money is important to obtain the needed comforts of life, but little more. The successful American who has more money than he needs to insure the comforts of living nevertheless continues his quest because money is the most significant sign of his importance—his control over things.

Here the American faces a dilemma. He has greater control over more things than anyone else on earth. But such control is not as a rule emotionally satisfying unless it leads to closer or more permanent relationships with men. In obedience to the ideal of self-reliance, it is precisely this need—common to all mankind and an inevitable consequence of human life, into whatever society a man may be born—that the American has sought to deny.

For all human beings begin life in a state of dependence. The child's physical needs are supplied by his elders. As the once completely dependent individual grows progressively more independent and moves beyond this first set of relationships, the pattern that he has learned in these formative years becomes the basis of his reactions to the wider society and the other individuals who compose it. All humans—Americans or Eskimos, Chinese or Hottentots—have a compelling need to be in the company of other human beings, not only to avoid temporary loneliness but because they seek human relationships which embody the surety of those they once shared with their parents or guardians.

The Chinese, by retaining permanently a close relationship with those persons he has known in infancy and childhood, meets easily the need for intimate human association. He therefore feels little compulsion to extend his control over the physical world, since he achieves a sense of self-importance and purposefulness by the direct route available to him in the primary groups. His self-importance is assured through his seniority and the respect due him. His purposefulness perpetuates itself because his kinship and communal obligations and responsibilities never end. The American, however, follows a circuitous path in his search for emotional security. He strives to separate himself from his previous ties, but his conquest of the physical environment is propelled, consciously and unconsciously, by his search for the same rewards sought by the Chinese. Yet when he has arrived at a position where he possesses much more than is needed for his material comfort, he is rudely awakened by the temporary and superficial nature of his relationship with other men. To strengthen his sense of self-importance and to ensure his place among his fellows he intensifies his acquisitive activities and creates more devices for his security and safety.

For this reason legal provisions to protect personal and property rights are much better developed in America than in China, and insurance and pensions are a necessity in one nation and unknown in the other. And for the same reason, despite a colossal and ubiquitous banking system, lonely "Silas Marners" regularly make the front pages when their hoarded wealth is discovered after their unnoticed death. Finally, these compulsions are at the root of the American economic system which, according to Dr. Harold Moulton, president of the Brookings Institute, "will give coming generations a standard of living eight times as high as the one we now enjoy."[4]

The effect of these compulsions is evident where everyone's problems of daily existence are concerned. Because of it the parent-child relationship often takes on the same business-like appearance, and the parents' chief hope during a son's schooling is that high grades and the right social contacts will result in a lucrative job upon graduation; the marital bond, though secured in Western tradition by love and God, is increasingly defined in terms of legal rights and material support; the success of the government is measured by projects and jobs well done; and devotion to God is practically equated with imposing church houses, large budgets, and multitudinous club activities.

[4] Quoted in an editorial in the *Chicago Sun-Times,* Jan. 21, 1952.

16 MODAL PERSONALITY AND ADJUSTMENT TO THE SOVIET SOCIO-POLITICAL SYSTEM[1]

Alex Inkeles, Eugenia Hanfmann, and Helen Beier

Two main elements are encompassed in the study of national character.[2] The first step is to determine what modal personality patterns, if any, are to be found in a particular national population or in its major sub-groups. In so far as such modes exist one can go on to the second stage, studying the interrelations between the personality modes and various aspects of the social system. Even if the state of our theory warranted the drafting of an 'ideal' research design for studies in this field, they would require staggering sums and would probably be beyond our current methodological resources. We can, however, hope to make progress through more restricted efforts. In the investigation we report on here we studied a highly selected group from the population of the Soviet Union, namely, former citizens of Great Russian nationality who 'defected' during or after World War II. We deal, furthermore, mainly with only one aspect of the complex interrelations between system and personality, our sub-

FROM Alex Inkeles, Eugenia Hanfmann, and Helen Beier, "Modal Personality and Adjustment to the Soviet Socio-Political System," 1958, *Human Relations*, 11:3–22, by permission of the authors and the Tavistock Institute of Human Relations.

[1] Revised and expanded version of a paper read at the American Psychological Association Meetings in San Francisco, Sept. 1955. Daniel Miller read this early version and made many useful comments. The authors wish to express their warm appreciation for the prolonged support of the Russian Research Center at Harvard. Revisions were made by the senior author while he was a Fellow of the Center for Advanced Study in the Behavioral Sciences, for whose support he wishes to make grateful acknowledgement.

[2] For a discussion of the basic issues and a review of research in this field see Alex Inkeles and Daniel J. Levinson (1954).

Modal Personality and Adjustment to the Soviet System 313

jects' participation in and adjustment to their Communist sociopolitical order.[3] We find that certain personality modes are outstanding in the group, and believe that we can trace their significance for our subjects' adjustment to Soviet society.

SAMPLE AND METHOD

An intensive program of clinical psychological research was conducted as part of the work of the Harvard Project on the Soviet Social System.[4] The Project explored the attitudes and life experiences of former Soviet citizens who were displaced during World War II and its aftermath and then decided not to return to the U.S.S.R. Almost 3,000 completed a long written questionnaire, and 329 undertook a detailed general life history interview. The individuals studied clinically were selected from the latter group. Criteria of selection were that the interviewee seemed a normal, reasonably adjusted individual who was relatively young, had lived most of his life under Soviet conditions, and was willing to undertake further intensive interviewing and psychological testing.

The group studied clinically included 51 cases, forty-one of whom were men. With the exception of a few Ukrainians, all were Great Russians. Almost half were under 30, and only 8 were 40 or older at the time of interview in 1950, which meant that the overwhelming majority grew up mainly under Soviet conditions and were educated in Soviet schools. Eleven had had a minimum education of four years or less, 22 between four and eight years, and 18 advanced secondary or college training. In residence the group was predominantly urban but if those who had moved from the countryside to the city were included with

[3] For analysis of another aspect of the psychological properties of this group, see Eugenia Hanfmann (1957).

[4] The research was carried out by the Russian Research Center under contract AF No. 33(038)–12909 with the former Human Resources Research Institute, Maxwell Air Force Base, Alabama. For a general account of the purposes and design of the study see: R. Bauer, A. Inkeles, and C. Kluckhohn (1956). The clinical study was conducted by E. Hanfmann and H. Beier. A detailed presentation is given in the unpublished report of the Project by E. Hanfmann and H. Beier (1954).

the rural, then approximately half fell in each category. As might be expected from the education data, the group included a rather large proportion of those in high-status occupations, with 11 professionals and members of the intelligentsia, 7 regular army officers, and 9 white-collar workers. Sixteen were rank-and-file industrial and agricultural workers, and five rank-and-file army men. In keeping with the occupational pattern but running counter to popular expectations about Soviet refugees, a rather high proportion were in the Party (6) or the Young Communist League (13). Again running counter to popular expectations about refugees, the group was not characterized by a markedly high incidence of disadvantaged family background as reflected either in material deprivation, the experience of political arrest, or other forms of repression at the hands of the regime. Ten were classified as having been extremely disadvantaged, and 15 as having suffered minor disadvantage.

All of the Soviet refugees have in common their 'disaffection' with Soviet society. The clinical group included mainly the more 'active' defectors who left Soviet control on their own initiative, rather than the 'passive' who were removed by force of circumstance. Thirty-four had deserted from the military[5] or voluntarily departed with the retreating German occupation armies. In general, however, the clinical group was not more vigorously anti-Communist than the other refugees. They overwhelmingly supported the principles of the welfare state, including government ownership and state planning, and credited the regime with great achievements in foreign affairs and economic and cultural development. They refused to return for much the same reasons given by other refugees: fear of reprisal at the hands of the secret police, because of former oppression, opposition to institutions like the collective farm, or resentment of the low standard of living and the absence of political freedom. In psychological adjustment, finally, they seemed to reflect fairly well the tendency toward adequate adjustment which characterized the refugees as a whole.

[5] This was in part a result of our selection procedure. The larger project was particularly interested in post-war defectors, almost all of whom came from the Soviet military occupation forces in Germany. Half of the men fell in that category.

Modal Personality and Adjustment to the Soviet System 315

With regard to the parent refugee population, then, the clinical group was disproportionately male, young, well educated, well placed occupationally and politically, and 'active' in defecting.[6] In its internal composition, the sample was also unbalanced in being predominantly male, but otherwise gave about equal weight to those over and under 35, in manual vs. white-collar occupations, from urban or rural backgrounds, with education above or below the advanced secondary level.

Each respondent was interviewed with regard to his childhood experience, some aspects of his adult life, and his adjustment to conditions in a displaced persons' camp. Each took a battery of tests which included the Rorschach, TAT, a sentence-completion test of 60 items, a 'projective questions' test including eight of the questions utilized in the authoritarian personality study, and a specially constructed 'episodes' or problem-situations test. We regard the use of this battery of tests as a matter of special note, since most attempts to assess modal tendencies in small-scale societies have relied upon a single instrument, particularly the Rorschach. The various tests differ in their sensitivity to particular dimensions or levels of personality, and differentially reflect the impact of the immediate emotional state and environmental situation of the subject. By utilizing a series of tests, therefore, we hope that we have in significant degree reduced the chances that any particular finding mainly peculiar to the special combination of instrument, subject, and situation will have been mistakenly interpreted as distinctively Russian. In addition the use of this battery enables us to test our assumptions in some depth, by checking for consistency on several tests.

Each test was independently analysed according to fairly standard scoring methods, and the results were reported separately.[7] In reporting their results, however, each set of analysts

[6] The young post-war defectors on the whole did prove to be less stable and more poorly adjusted. Apart from this issue of adjustment or 'integration', however, they shared with the rest of the sample much the same range of outstanding personality traits. Therefore, no further distinctions between that group and the rest are discussed in this paper. See E. Hanfmann and H. Beier (*op. cit.*).

[7] On the 'Episodes Test' a detailed report has been published, see Eugenia Hanfmann and J. G. Getzels (1955). A brief account of results on the Projective Questions has also been published in Helen Beier and

made some observations on the character traits which seemed generally important to the group as a whole. Further, in drawing these conclusions the analysts made use of a criterion group of Americans matched with the Russian sample on age, sex, occupation, and education. The availability of such test results posed a challenge as to whether or not these general observations, when collated and analysed, would yield any consistent patterns for the group as a whole.

To make this assessment we selected the eight major headings used below as an organizing framework. We believe that they permit a fairly full description of the various dimensions and processes of the human personality, and at the same time facilitate making connections with aspects of the social system. These categories were, however, not part of the design of the original clinical research program,[8] and were not used by the analysts of the individual instruments. While this circumstance made for lesser comparability between the tests, it acted to forestall the slanting of conclusions to fit the analytic scheme. The statements in the conclusions drawn by the analysts of each instrument were written on duplicate cards, sorted, and grouped under all the categories to which they seemed relevant. The evidence with regard to each category was then sifted and weighed, and where there were ambiguous findings the original tables were re-examined for clarification. Relevant impressions based on the interviews were also drawn on. Similarities and differences between those in our sample and the matching Americans aided in grasping the distinctive features of the Russian pattern. On this basis a characterization of the group was developed under each heading of the analytic scheme.

It should be clear that the sketch of modal personality characteristics presented below is not a simple and direct translation

---

Eugenia Hanfmann (1956). The other results were described in the following as yet unpublished reports of the Project, which may be examined at the Russian Research Center: Beier (1954), Rosenblatt *et al.* (1953), Fried (1954), Fried and Held (1953), Roseborough and Phillips (1953).

[8] The basic categories were suggested to A. Inkeles by D. J. Levinson in the course of a seminar on national character, and are in part discussed in Inkeles and Levinson (*op. cit.*). They were somewhat modified for the purpose of this presentation.

of particular test scores into personality traits. Rather, it is an evaluative, summary statement, following from the collation and interpretation of conclusions drawn from each test, conclusions which were in turn based both on test scores and on supplementary qualitative material. The word modal should not be taken too literally in this context. We have relied on some test scores when only a small proportion of the sample manifested the given response or pattern of responses, if this fits with other evidence in developing a larger picture. In stating our findings we have been freer with the evidence than some would permit, more strict than others would require. We attempted to keep to the canons of the exact method, without neglecting the clinical interpretations and insights. In this way we hoped to arrive at a rich and meaningful picture of the people studied, a picture that would provide an adequate basis for an analysis of their adjustment to the socio-political system.

BRIEF SKETCH OF RUSSIAN MODAL PERSONALITY CHARACTERISTICS

1. CENTRAL NEEDS[9]

Since all human beings manifest the same basic needs, we cannot assert that some need is unique to a given national population. Among these universal needs, however, some may achieve greater strength or central importance in the organization of the personality, and in this sense be typical of the majority of a given group.

Probably the strongest and most pervasive quality of the Russian personality that emerged from our data was a need for *affiliation*. By this we mean a need for intensive interaction with other people in immediate, direct, face-to-face relationships, coupled with a great capacity for having this need fulfilled through the establishment of warm and personal contact with others. Our subjects seemed to welcome others into their lives

---
[9] See H. Murray (1938). We do not strictly follow Murray in our use of the 'need' terminology.

as an indispensable condition of their own existence, and generally felt neither isolated nor estranged from them. In contrast to the American subjects, the Russians were not too anxiously concerned about others' opinion of them and did not feel compelled to cling to a relationship or to defend themselves against it. Rather, they manifest a profound acceptance of group membership and relatedness. These orientations were especially prevalent in test situations dealing with relations between the individual and small face-to-face groups such as the family, the work team, and the friendship circle.

Closely linked with the need for affiliation is a need for *dependence* very much like what Dicks (1952) spoke of as the Russians' 'strong positive drive for enjoying loving protection and security', care and affection. This need shows not only in orientation towards parents and peers, but also in the relations with formal authority figures. We did not, however, find a strong need for submission linked with the need for dependence, although Dicks asserts it to be present. In addition there is substantial evidence for the relatively greater strength of *oral* needs, reflected in preoccupation with getting and consuming food and drink, in great volubility, and in emphasis on singing. These features are especially conspicuous by contrast with the relative weakness of the more typically compulsive puritanical concern for order, regularity, and self-control. However, our data do not permit us to stress this oral component as heavily as does Dicks, who regards it as 'typical' for the culture as a whole.

Several needs rather prominent in the records of the American control group did not appear to be of outstanding importance in the personality structure of the Russians. Most notable, the great emphasis on *achievement* found in the American records was absent from the Russian ones. Within the area of interpersonal relations our data lead us to posit a fairly sharp Russian-American contrast. Whereas the American records indicate great strength of need for *approval* and need for *autonomy,* those needs were rather weakly manifested by the Russians. In approaching interpersonal relations our American subjects seemed to fear too close or intimate association with other individuals and groups. They often perceived such relations as potentially

Modal Personality and Adjustment to the Soviet System 319

limiting freedom of individual action, and therefore inclined above all to insure their independence from or autonomy within the group. At the same time the Americans revealed a strong desire for recognition and at least formal acceptance or approval from the group. They are very eager to be 'liked', to be regarded as an 'all right' guy, and greatly fear isolation from the group. Finally we note that certain needs important in other national character studies were apparently not central in either the American or the Russian groups. Neither showed much need for dominance, for securing positions of superordination, or for controlling or manipulating others and enforcing authority over them. Nor did they seem markedly distinguished in the strength of hostile impulses, of desires to hurt, punish, or destroy.

2. MODES OF IMPULSE CONTROL

On the whole the Russians have relatively *high awareness* of their impulses or basic dispositions—such as for oral gratification, sex, aggression, or dependence—and, rather, *freely accept* them as something normal or 'natural' rather than as bad or offensive.[10] The Russians show evidence, furthermore, of *giving in* to these impulses quite readily and frequently, and of *living them out*. Although they tended afterwards to be penitent and admit that they should not have 'lived out' so freely, they were not really punitive towards themselves or others for failure to control impulses. Of course, this does not mean complete absence of impulse control, a condition that would render social life patently impossible. Indeed, the Russians viewed their own impulses and desires as forces that needed watching, and often professed the belief that the control of impulses was necessary and beneficial. The critical point is that the Russians seemed to rely much less than the Americans on impulse control to be generated and handled from within. Rather, they appear to feel a need for aid from without in the form of guidance and pressure exerted by higher authority and by the group to assist them in

[10] Such a statement must of course always be one of degree. We do not mean to say that such threatening impulses as those toward incest are present in the awareness of Russians or are accepted by them more than by Americans.

controlling their impulses. This is what Dicks referred to as the Russians' desire to have a 'moral corset' put on his impulses. The Americans, on the other hand, vigorously affirm their ability for *self*-control, and seem to assume that the possession of such ability and its exercise legitimates their desire to be free from the overt control of authority and the group.

In this connection we may note that the review of individual cases revealed a relative lack of well-developed *defensive structures* in many of the Russian subjects. Mechanisms that serve to counteract and to modify threatening feelings and impulses—including isolation, intellectualization, and reaction formation—seem to figure much less prominently among them than among the Americans. The Russians had fewer defenses of this type and those they had were less well established.

3. TYPICAL POLARITIES AND DILEMMAS

Within certain areas of feelings and motives individuals may typically display attitudes and behavior that belong to one or the opposite poles of the given variable, or else display a preoccupation with the choice of alternatives posed by these poles. Such preoccupation may be taken to define the areas of typical dilemmas or conflicts, similar to the polarized issues, such as 'identity vs. role diffusion' and 'intimacy vs. isolation', which Erikson (1950) found so important in different stages of psychological maturation.

In our Russian subjects we found a conscious preoccupation with the problem of *trust vs. mistrust* in relation to others. They worried about the intentions of the other, expressing apprehension that people may not really be as they seem on the surface. There was always the danger that someone might entice you into revealing yourself, only then to turn around and punish you for what you have revealed. Another typical polarity of the Russians' behavior is that of *optimism vs. pessimism,* or of faith vs. despair. One of our projective test items posited the situation that tools and materials necessary for doing a job fail to arrive. In responding to this item our Russian subjects tended to focus on whether the outcome of the situation will be good or bad for the actor, while the Americans at once sprang into a plan of action for resolving the situation. Finally, we may include under the typical polarities of the Russians' attitude that of *activity vs. passivity,* although in the case of this variable we found little indication of a sense of a conscious conflict. However, the subjects' choice of alternatives in the projective tests tended to be distributed between the active and the passive ones, while the Americans' preference for the active instrumental response was as clear-cut and strong as was their generally optimistic orientation.

The pronounced polarities of the Russians' orientation lend support to Dicks' assertion that 'the outstanding trait of the Russian personality is the contradictoriness—its ambivalence' (*op. cit.*). Two qualifications, however, must be kept in mind. First, the strength of our Russian subjects' dilemmas may have been greatly enhanced by the conditions of their lives, both in the Soviet Union and abroad. Second, the American subjects also show some involvement in problematic issues, though they were different from the Russian ones. Thus the problem of 'intimacy vs. isolation' or 'autonomy vs. belongingness', to which we have already alluded, seemed a major dilemma for Americans whereas it was not such an issue for the Russians.

4. ACHIEVING AND MAINTAINING SELF-ESTEEM

In their orientations toward the self, the Russians displayed rather low and *unintense self-awareness* and little painful self-consciousness. They showed rather high and *secure self-esteem,* and were little given to self-examination and doubt of their inner selves. At the same time they were not made anxious by examination of their own motivation or that of others, but rather showed readiness to gain insight into psychological mechanisms. The American pattern reveals some contrasts here, with evidence of acute self-awareness, substantial self-examination, and doubting of one's inner qualities.

We were not able to discern any differences between Americans and Russians in the relative importance of *guilt* versus *shame* as sanctions. There were, however, some suggestive differences in what seemed to induce both guilt and shame. The Americans were more likely to feel guilty or ashamed if they failed to live up to clear-cut 'public' norms, as in matters of etiquette. They were also upset by any hint that they were inept, incompetent, or unable to meet production, sports, or similar performance standards. The Russians did not seem to be equally disturbed by such failures, and felt relatively more guilty or ashamed when they assumed that they had fallen behind with regard to moral or interpersonal behavior norms, as in matters involving personal honesty, sincerity, trust, or loyalty to a friend. These latter qualities they value most highly and they demand them from their friends.

5. RELATION TO AUTHORITY[11]

Our clinical instruments presented the subjects with only a limited range of situations involving relations with authority. These did not show pronounced differences in basic attitudes between Russians and Americans, except that Russians appeared to have more fear of and much less optimistic expectations about authority figures. Both of these manifestations might, of course, have been mainly a reflection of their recent experiences rather than of deeper-lying dispositions. Fortunately, we can supplement the clinical materials by the life history interviews which dealt extensively with the individual's relations with authority. A definite picture emerges from these data. Above all else the Russians want their leaders—whether boss, district political hack, or national ruler—to be warm, nurturant, considerate, and interested in the individuals' problems and welfare. The authority is also expected to be the main source of initiative in the inauguration of general plans and programs and in the provision of guidance and organization for their attainment. The Russians do not seem to expect initiative, directedness, and organizedness from an average individual. They therefore expect that the authority will of necessity give detailed orders, demand obedience, keep checking up on performance, and use persuasion and coercion intensively to insure steady performance. A further

[11] Relations to authority may be thought of as simply one aspect of a broader category—'conceptions of major figures'—which includes parents, friends, etc. We have included some comments on the Russians' perceptions of others under 'cognitive modes' below.

Modal Personality and Adjustment to the Soviet System 323

major expectation with regard to the 'legitimate' authority is that it will institute and enforce sanctions designed to curb or control bad impulses in individuals, improper moral practices, heathen religious ideas, perverted political procedures, and extreme personal injustice. It is, then, the government that should provide that 'external moral corset' which Dicks says the Russian seeks.

An authority that meets these qualifications is 'good' and it does what it does with 'right'. Such an authority should be loved, honored, respected, and obeyed. Our Russian subjects seemed, however, to expect that authority figures would in fact frequently be stern, demanding, even scolding and nagging. This was not in and of itself viewed as bad or improper. Authority may be, perhaps ought to be, autocratic, so long as it is not harshly authoritarian and not totally demanding. Indeed, it is not a bad thing if such an authority makes one rather strongly afraid, make one 'quake' in expectation of punishment for trespassing or wrongdoing. Such an authority should not, however, be arbitrary, aloof, and unjust. It should not be unfeeling in the face of an open acknowledgment of one's guilt and of consequent self-castigation. Indeed, many of our subjects assumed that authority can in fact be manipulated through humbling the self and depicting oneself as a weak, helpless person who needs supportive guidance rather than harsh punishment. They also assumed that authority may be manipulated by praise or fawning, and seduced through the sharing of gratificatory experiences provided by the supplicant—as through the offer of a bottle of liquor and the subsequent sharing of some drinks. Russians also favor meeting the pressure of authority by evasive tactics, including such devices as apparently well-intentioned failure to comprehend and departures from the scene of action.

Throughout their discussions of authority our respondents showed little concern for the preservation of precise forms, rules, regulations, exactly defined rights, regularity of procedure, formal and explicit limitation of powers, or the other aspects of the traditional constitutional Anglo-Saxon approach to law and government. For the Russians a government that has the characteristics of good government listed above justifies its right to rule by virtue of that performance. In that case, one need not fuss too much about the fine points of law. By contrast, if government is harsh, arbitrary, disinterested in public welfare—which it is apparently expected to be more often than not—then it loses its right to govern no matter how legal its position and no matter how close its observance of the letter of the law.

6. MODES OF AFFECTIVE FUNCTIONING

One of the most salient characteristics of the Russian personality was the high degree of their *expressiveness* and emotional aliveness. On most test items the Russian responses had a stronger emotional coloring, and they covered a wider range of emotions, than did the American responses. Their feelings were easily brought into play, and they showed them openly and freely both in speech and in facial expression, without much suppression or disguise. In particular they showed a noticeably greater *freedom and spontaneity in criticism* and in the expression of hostile feelings than was true for the Americans. There were, further, two emotions which the Russians showed with a frequency far exceeding that found in the Americans—*fear,* and *depression* or despair. Many of the ambiguous situations posited in the tests were viewed by them in terms of danger and threat, on the one hand, and of privation and loss, on the other. Undoubtedly this was in good part a reflection of the tense social situation which they had experienced in the Soviet Union, and of their depressed status as refugees, but we believe that in addition deeper-lying trends were here being tapped. These data provide some evidence in support of the oft-noted prevalence of depressive trends among the Russians.

7. MODES OF COGNITIVE FUNCTIONING

In this area we include characteristic patterns of perception, memory, thought, and imagination, and the process involved in forming and manipulating ideas about the world around one. Of all the modes of personality organization it is perhaps the most subtle, and certainly in the present state of theory and testing one of the most difficult to formulate. Our clinical materials do, however, permit a few comments.

In discussing people, the Russians show a keen *awareness of*

Modal Personality and Adjustment to the Soviet System

the 'other' as a distinct entity as well as a rich and diversified recognition of his special characteristics. Other people are usually perceived by them not as social types but as concrete individuals with a variety of attributes distinctly their own. The Russians think of people and evaluate them for what they are rather than in terms of how they evaluate ego, the latter being a more typically American approach. The Russians also paid more attention to the 'others'' basic underlying attributes and attitudes than to their behavior as such or their performance on standards of achievement and accomplishment in the instrumental realm.

Similar patterns were evident in their perception of interpersonal situations. In reacting to the interpersonal relations 'problems' presented by one of the psychological tests they more fully elaborated the situation, cited more relevant incidents from folklore or their own experience, and offered many more illustrations of a point. In contrast, the Americans tended more to describe the formal, external, characteristics of people, apparently being less perceptive of the individual's motivational characteristics. The Americans also tended to discuss interpersonal problems on a rather generalized and abstract level. With regard to most other types of situation, however, especially problems involving social organization, the pattern was somewhat reversed. Russians tended to take a rather broad, sweeping view of the situation, *generalizing* at the expense of detail, about which they were often extremely vague and poorly informed. They seemed to feel their way through such situations rather than rigorously to think them through, tending to get into a spirit of grandiose planning but without attention to necessary details.

8. MODES OF CONATIVE FUNCTIONING

By conative functioning we mean the patterns, the particular behavioral forms, of the striving for any valued goals, including the rhythm or pace at which these goals are pursued and the way in which that rhythm is regulated. In this area our clinical data are not very rich. Nevertheless, we have the strong impression that the Russians do not match the Americans in the vigor of their striving to master all situations or problems put before them, and to do so primarily through adaptive instrumental orientations. Although by no means listless, they seem much more *passively accommodative* to the apparent hard facts of situations. In addition, they appeared less apt to persevere systematically in the adaptive courses of action they did undertake, tending to backslide into passive accommodation when the going proved rough. At the same time, the Russians do seem capable of great bursts of activity, which suggests the bi-modality of an *assertive-passive pattern* of strivings in contrast to the steadier, more even, and consistent pattern of strivings among the Americans.

To sum up, one of the most salient characteristics of the personality of our Russian subjects was their emotional aliveness and expressiveness. They felt their emotions keenly, and did not tend to disguise or to deny them to themselves, nor to suppress their outward expression to the same extent as the Americans. The Russians criticized themselves and others with greater freedom and spontaneity. Relatively more aware and tolerantly accepting of impulses for gratification in themselves and others, they relied less than the Americans on self-control from within and more on external socially imposed controls applied by the peer group or authority. A second outstanding characteristic of the Russians was their strong need for intensive interaction with others, coupled with a strong and secure feeling of relatedness to them, high positive evaluation of such belongingness, and great capacity to enjoy such relationships. The image of the 'good' authority was of a warm, nurturant, supportive figure. Yet our subjects seemed to assume that this paternalism might and indeed should include superordinate planning and firm guidance, as well as control or supervision of public and personal morality, and if necessary, of thought and belief. It is notable, in this connection, that in the realm of conative and cognitive functioning orderliness, precision of planning, and persistence in striving were not outstandingly present. Such qualities were rather overshadowed by tendencies toward over-generalizing, vagueness, imprecision, and passive accommodation. Countering the image of the good authority, there was an expectation that those with power would in fact often be harsh, aloof, and authoritarian. The effect of such behavior by authority is alienation of loyalty. This fits rather

Modal Personality and Adjustment to the Soviet System 327

well with the finding that the main polarized issues or dilemmas were those of 'trust vs. mistrust' in relations with others, 'optimism vs. pessimism', and 'activity vs. passivity', whereas the more typically American dilemma of 'intimacy vs. isolation' was not a problem for many Russians. Though strongly motivated by needs for affiliation and dependence and wishes for oral gratification—in contrast to greater strength of needs for achievement, autonomy, and approval among the Americans—our Russian subjects seemed to have a characteristically sturdy ego. They were rather secure in their self-estimation, and unafraid to face up to their own motivation and that of others. In contrast to the Americans, the Russians seemed to feel shame and guilt for defects of 'character' in interpersonal relations rather than for failure to meet formal rules of etiquette or instrumental production norms. Compared with the Americans, however, they seemed relatively lacking in well-developed and stabilized defenses with which to counteract and modify threatening impulses and feelings. The organization of their personality depended for its coherence much more heavily on their intimate relatedness to those around them, their capacity to use others' support and to share with them their emotions.

RELATIONS OF MODAL PERSONALITY AND THE SOCIO-POLITICAL SYSTEM

In the following comments we are interpreting 'political participation' rather broadly, to cover the whole range of the individual's role as the citizen of a large-scale national state. We therefore include his major economic and social as well as his specifically political roles. This may extend the concept of political participation too far for most national states, but for the Soviet Union, where all aspects of social life have been politicized, it is the only meaningful approach. Specifically, the questions to which we address ourselves are as follows.

Assuming that the traits cited above were widespread among the group of Great Russians studied by our project, what implications would this have for their adjustment to the role demands made on them by the social system in which they participated?

To what extent can the typical complaints of refugees against the system, and the typical complaints of the regime against its own people, be traced to the elements of non-congruence between these personality modes and Soviet social structure?

A full answer to these questions would involve us in a much more extensive presentation and a more complex analysis than is possible here. We wish to stress that our analysis is limited to the Soviet socio-political system as it typically functioned under Stalin's leadership (see Bauer *et al.,* 1956, and Fainsod 1953), since this was the form of the system in which our respondents lived and to which they had to adjust. To avoid any ambiguity on this score we have fairly consistently used the past tense. We sincerely hope that this will not lead to the mistaken assumption that we regard the post-Stalin era as massively discontinuous with the earlier system. However, to specify in any detail the elements of stability and change in post-Stalin Russia, and to indicate the probable effects of such changes on the adjustment of Soviet citizens to the system, is beyond the scope of this paper. As for the personality dimensions, we will discuss each in its relations to system participation separately, rather than in the complex combinations in which they operate in reality. Only those of the personality traits cited above are discussed that clearly have relevance for the individual's participation in the socio-political system.

Need Affiliation. Virtually all aspects of the Soviet regime's pattern of operation seem calculated to interfere with the satisfaction of the Russians' need for affiliation. The regime has placed great strains on friendship relations by its persistent programs of political surveillance, its encouragement and elaboration of the process of denunciation, and its assignment of mutual or 'collective' responsibility for the failings of particular individuals. The problem was further aggravated by the regime's insistence that its élite should maintain a substantial social distance between itself and the rank-and-file. In addition, the regime developed an institutional system that affected the individual's relations with others in a way that ran strongly counter to the basic propensities of the Russians as represented in our sample. The desire for involvement in the group, and the insistence on loyalty, sincerity, and general responsiveness from others, received but little opportunity for expression and gratification in the tightly controlled Soviet atmosphere. Many of the primary face-to-face organizations most important to the individual were infiltrated, attacked, or even destroyed by the regime. The break-up of the old village community and its replacement by the more formal, bureaucratic, and impersonal collective farm is perhaps the most outstanding example, but it is only one of many. The disruption and subordination to the state of the traditional family group, the Church, the independent professional associations, and the trade unions are other cases in point. The regime greatly feared the development of local autonomous centers of power. Every small group was seen as a potential conspiracy against the regime or its policies. The system of control required that each and all should constantly watch and report on each other. The top hierarchy conducted a constant war on what it scornfully called 'local patriotism', 'back-scratching', and 'mutual security associations', even though in reality it was attacking little more than the usual personalizing tendencies incidental to effective business and political management. The people strove hard to maintain their small group structures, and the regime persistently fought this trend through its war against 'familieness' and associated evils. At the same time it must be recognized that by its emphasis on broad group loyalties, the regime probably captured and harnessed somewhat the propensities of many Russians to give themselves up wholly to a group membership and to group activity and goals. This is most marked in the Young Communist League and in parts of the Party.

Need Orality. The scarcity element that predominated in Soviet society, the strict rationed economy of materials, men, and the physical requirements of daily life seem to have aroused intense anxieties about further oral deprivation that served greatly to increase the impact of the real shortages that have been chronic to the system. Indeed, the image of the system held by most in our sample is very much that of an orally depriving, niggardly, non-nurturant leadership. On the other hand, the regime can hope to find a quick road to better relations with the population by strategic dumping or glutting with goods, which was to some extent attempted during the period of Malenkov's ascendancy, although perhaps more in promise than reality.

Need Dependence. The regime took pride in following Lenin in 'pushing' the masses. It demanded that individuals be responsible and carry on 'on their own' with whatever resources were at hand, and clamored for will and self-determination (see Bauer 1952.) Clearly, this was not very congruent with the felt need for dependent relations. At the same time the regime had certain strengths relative to the need for dependence. The popular image of the regime as one possessed of a strong sense of direction fits in with this need. Similarly it gained support for its emphasis on a massive formal program of social-welfare measures, even if they were not too fully implemented. This directedness has a bearing also on the problem of submission. Although the regime had the quality of a firm authority able to give needed direction, it did not gain as much as it might because it was viewed as interested in the maximation of power *per se*. This appears to alienate the Russian as he is represented in our sample.

The Trust-Mistrust Dilemma. Everything we know about Soviet society makes it clear that it was extremely difficult for a Soviet citizen to be at all sure about the good intentions of his government leaders and his immediate supervisors. They seemed always to talk support and yet to mete out harsh treatment. This divided behavior pattern of the leadership seemed to aggravate the apparent Russian tendency to see the intentions of others as problematical and to intensify the dilemma of trust-mistrust. On the basis of our interviews one might describe this dilemma of whether or not to grant trust as very nearly *the* central problem in the relations of former Soviet citizens to their regime. The dilemma of *'optimism vs. pessimism'*, of whether outcomes will be favorable or unfavorable, presents a very similar situation.

The Handling of Shame. The regime tried exceedingly hard to utilize public shame to force or cajole Soviet citizens into greater production and strict observance of the established rules and regulations. Most of our available public documentary evidence indicates that the regime was not outstandingly successful in this respect. Our clinical findings throw some light on the reason. The regime tried to focus shame on non-performances, on failures to meet production obligations or to observe formal bureaucratic rules. To judge by the clinical sample, however, the Rus-

Modal Personality and Adjustment to the Soviet System 331

sian is little shamed by these kinds of performance failures, and is more likely to feel shame in the case of moral failures. Thus, the Soviet Russian might be expected to be fairly immune to the shaming pressures of the regime. Indeed, the reactions of those in our sample suggest the tables often get turned around, with the citizen concluding that it is the regime which should be ashamed because it has fallen down in these important moral qualities.

Affective Functioning. The general expansiveness of the Russians in our sample, their easily expressed feelings, the giving in to impulse, and the free expression of criticism, were likely to meet only the coldest reception from the regime. It emphasized and rewarded control, formality, and lack of feeling in relations. Discipline, orderliness, and strict observance of rules are what it expects. Thus, our Russian subjects could hope for little official reward in response to their normal modes of expression. In fact, they could be expected to run into trouble with the regime as a result of their proclivities in this regard. Their expansiveness and tendency freely to express their feelings, including hostile feelings, exposed them to retaliation from the punitive police organs of the state. And in so far as they did exercise the necessary control and avoided open expression of hostile feelings, they experienced a sense of uneasiness and resentment because of this unwarranted imposition, which did much to color their attitude to the regime.

Conative Functioning. The non-striving quality of our Russian subjects ties in with the previously mentioned characteristics of dependence and non-instrumentality. The regime, of course, constantly demanded greater effort and insisted on a more instrumental approach to problems. It emphasized long-range planning and deferred gratification. There was a continual call for efforts to 'storm bastions', to 'breach walls', 'to strive mightily'. With the Russian as he is represented in our sample, it does not appear likely that the regime could hope to meet too positive a response here; in fact it encountered a substantial amount of rejection for its insistence on modes of striving not particularly congenial to a substantial segment of the population. Indeed, the main influence may have been exerted by the people on the system, rather than by the system on them. Soviet official sources have for many years constantly complained of the uneven pace at which work proceeds, with the usual slack pace making it necessary to have great, often frenzied, bursts of activity to complete some part of the Plan on schedule, followed again by a slack period. It may well be that this pattern results not only from economic factors such as the uneven flow of raw material supplies, but that it also reflects the Russian tendency to work in spurts.

Relations to Authority. In many ways the difficulties of adjustment to the Soviet system experienced by our subjects revolved around the gap between what they *hoped* a 'good' government would be and what they *perceived* to be the behavior of the regime. Our respondents freely acknowledged that the Soviet leaders gave the country guidance and firm direction, which in some ways advanced the long-range power and prestige of the nation. They granted that the regime well understood the principles of the welfare state, and cited as evidence its provision of free education and health services. The general necessity of planning was also allowed, indeed often affirmed, and the regime was praised for taking into its own hands the regulation of public morality and the conscious task of 'raising the cultural level' through support of the arts and the encouragement of folk culture.

Despite these virtues, however, the whole psychological style of ruling and of administration adopted by the Bolsheviks seems to have had the effect of profoundly estranging our respondents. A great gulf seemed to separate the rulers and the ruled, reflected in our respondents' persistent use of a fundamental 'we'-'they' dichotomy. 'They' were the ones in power who do bad things to us, and 'we' were the poor, ordinary, suffering people who, despite internal differences in status or income, share the misfortune of being oppressed by 'them'. Most did not know that Stalin had once asserted that the Bolsheviks could not be a 'true' ruling party if they limited themselves 'to a mere registration of the sufferings and thoughts of the proletarian masses' (Stalin 1933, v. 1:95–6). Yet our respondents sensed this dictum behind the style of Soviet rule. They reacted to it in charging the leaders with being uninterested in individual welfare and with extraordinary callousness about the amount of human suffering they engender in carrying out their plans. Our subjects saw the regime as harsh and arbitrary. The leaders were characterized as

Modal Personality and Adjustment to the Soviet System 333

cold, aloof, 'deaf' and unyielding to popular pleas, impersonal and distant from the people's problems and desires. The regime was seen not as firmly guiding but as coercive, not as paternally stern but as harshly demanding, not as nurturant and supportive but as autocratic and rapaciously demanding, not as chastening and then forgiving but as nagging and unyieldingly punitive.

The rejection of the regime was however by no means total, and the Bolshevik pattern of leadership was in many respects seen not as totally alien but rather as native yet unfortunately exaggerated. This 'acceptance' did not extend to the coldness, aloofness, formality, and maintenance of social distance, which were usually rejected. It did, however, apply to the pressure exerted by the regime, which were felt to be proper but excessive. Coercion by government was understandable, but that applied by the regime was not legitimate because it was so harsh. The scolding about backsliding was recognized as necessary, but resented for being naggingly persistent and caustic. And the surveillance was expected, but condemned for being so pervasive, extending as it did even into the privacy of one's friendship and home relations, so that a man could not even hope to live 'peacefully' and 'quietly'. The elements of acceptance within this broader pattern of rejection have important implications for the future of the post-Stalin leadership. They suggest that the regime may win more positive support by changing the mode of application of many of its authoritarian and totalitarian policies without necessarily abandoning these polices and institutions as such. Indeed in watching the public behavior of men like Khrushchev and Bulganin one cannot help but feel that their style of leadership behavior is much more congenial to Russians than was that of Stalin.

The preceding discussion strongly suggests that there was a high degree of incongruence between the central personality modes and dispositions of many Russians and some essential aspects of the structure of Soviet society, in particular the behavior of the regime. Most of the popular grievances were clearly based on real deprivations and frustrations, but the dissatisfactions appear to be even more intensified and given a more emotional tone because they were based also on the poor 'fit' between the personality patterns of many Soviet citizens and the 'personality' of the leaders as it expressed itself in the institutions they created, in their conduct of those institutions and the system at large, and in the resultant social climate in the U.S.S.R.

SOCIAL CLASS DIFFERENTIATION

Since personality traits found in the Russian sample are merely modal rather than common to the group at large, it follows that sub-groups can meaningfully be differentiated by the choice of appropriate cutting points on the relevant continua. As a way of placing the individuals in our sample on a common scale, three elements from the total range of characteristics previously described were selected. They were chosen on the grounds that they were most important in distinguishing the Russians as a group from the Americans, and also because they seemed meaningfully related to each other as elements in a personality syndrome. The three characteristics were: great strength of the drive for social relatedness, marked emotional aliveness, and general lack of well-developed, complex, and pervasive defenses. The two clinicians rated all cases for a combination of these traits on a three-point scale. Cases judged on the basis of a review of both interview and test material to have these characteristics *in a marked degree* were placed in a group designated as the 'primary set'. Individuals in whom these characteristics were clearly evident, but less strongly pronounced, were designated as belonging to a 'variant' set. The 'primary' and 'variant' sets together constitute a relative homogeneous group of cases who clearly revealed the characteristics that we have described as 'modal'. All the remaining cases were placed in a 'residual' category, characterized by markedly stronger development of defenses, and in most instances also by lesser emotional expressiveness and lesser social relatedness. This group was relatively the least homogeneous of the three because its members tended to make use of rather different combinations of defenses without any typical pattern for the set as a whole. Subjects placed in the 'residual' group appeared to differ more from those in the 'variant' set than the 'primary' and the 'variant' sets differed from each other. However, even the 'residual' pattern was not separated from the others by a very sharp break: emotional aliveness and relatedness to people were present also in some members of this group. Each of our 51 cases were assigned to one of four social-status categories on the basis of occupation and education. All those in group A were professionals and high administrative personnel most of whom had university training, and all those in the D group were either peasants, or unskilled or semi-skilled workers with no more than five years of education. Placement in the two intermediary categories was also determined by the balance of occupation and education, group B consisting largely of white-collar workers and semi-professional and middle supervisory personnel, and group C of more skilled workers with better education.

Table 1 gives the distribution of cases among the three personality types within each of the four status groups. It is evident that the primary pattern has its greatest strength in the lower classes, becomes relatively less dominant in the middle layers, and plays virtually no role at all in the top group. The 'residual' pattern predominates at the top level and is very rare among peasants and ordinary workers.[12]

TABLE 1. STATUS DISTRIBUTION OF PERSONALITY TYPES AMONG FORMER SOVIET CITIZENS

Status	Personality Type			Total
	Primary	Variant	Residual	
A	—	1	12	13
B	2	8	6	16
C	3	4	2	9
D	8	3	2	13
Total	13	16	22	51

[12] The method of assigning the cases to the three psychological groups was holistic and impressionistic. It is of interest to note, therefore, that when more exact and objective techniques were used on the Sentence Completion Test to rate a similar but larger sample of refugees on some differently defined personality variables, the relationship between occupation and education and the personality measures was quite marked in three out of five variables. See M. Fried (*op. cit.*).

Since the distinctive patterns of adjustment to the Soviet system by the various socio-economic groups will be the basis of extensive publications now in progress, we restrict ourselves here to a few general observations. First, we wish to stress that, as our interviews indicate, both the more favored and the rank-and-file share substantially the same range of complaints against the regime, find the same broad institutional features such as the political terror and the collective farm objectionable, and view the same welfare features such as the system of education and free medical care as desirable. In spite of these common attitudes our data suggest that personality may play a massive role with regard to some aspects of participation in and adjustment to the socio-political system. The educational-occupational level attained and/or maintained by an individual in an open-class society is one of the major dimensions of such participation. This is particularly the case in the Soviet Union, where professional and higher administrative personnel are inevitably more deeply implicated in the purposes and plans of the regime, are politically more active and involved, and are subjected to greater control and surveillance. It seems plausible that persons in whom the affiliative need was particularly strong, expressiveness marked and impulse control weak, and the defensive structures not well developed or well organized would be handicapped in competition for professional and administrative posts in any society; they certainly could not be expected to strive for or to hold on to positions of responsibility in the Soviet system.

The pattern of marked association between certain traits of personality and educational-occupational level clearly invites a question as to whether the personality really affected the level attained and held, or whether the appropriate personality traits were merely acquired along with the status. This question raises complex issues which we cannot enter into here. We do wish to point out, however, that the characteristics on which our psychological grouping was based belong to those that are usually formed at an early age and are relatively long enduring and resistant to change. At first glance this affirmation of the early origins of the patterns described seems to be inconsistent with their observed association with educational-occupational level. However, the contradiction exists only if one assumes that obtaining a higher education and a superior occupation in Soviet society is a matter either of pure chance or exclusively of ability, unrelated to family background and the person's own attitudes and strivings. The data on stratification and mobility in Soviet society show, however, that persons born into families of higher social and educational level have a much better chance than do others to obtain a higher education and professional training (Feldmesser 1953; see also Inkeles 1950). Consequently, many people of the professional and administrative class grew up in families of similar status, and in those families were apparently reared in a way different from that typical of the peasant and worker families.[13] Presumably this produced enduring effects on their personality formation, which were important prior to exposure to common educational experience.

In addition, mobility out of the lower classes may have been mainly by individuals whose personality was different, for whatever reason, from that of the majority of their class of origin. Such differences can easily express themselves in a stronger drive for education and for a position of status. We must also allow for the role played by the regime's deliberate selection of certain types as candidates for positions of responsibility. Finally, there is the less conscious 'natural selection' process based on the affinity between certain personality types and the opportunities offered by membership in the élite and near-élite categories. In this connection we are struck by the relative distinctness of the highest status level in our sample, since only one person with either of the two variants of the modal personality of the rank-and-file shows up among them. These results bear out the impression, reported by Dicks, of radical personality differences and resultant basic incompatibilities between the ruled population and the rulers. The latter, we assume, are still further removed from the 'modal pattern' than are our subjects in the élite group.

We have yet to deal with the question of how far our observations concerning a group of refugees can be generalized to the Soviet population and *its* adjustment to the Soviet system? The answer to this question depends in good part on whether personality was an important selective factor in determining propensity

---

[13] For a detailed discussion of *class differences* in the child-rearing values of pre-Soviet and Soviet parents see Alice Rossi (1954).

to defect among those in the larger group who had the opportunity to do so.[14] It is our impression that personality was not a prime determinant of the decision not to return to Soviet control after World War II. Rather, accidents of the individual's life history such as past experience with the regime's instruments of political repression, or fear of future repression because of acts which might be interpreted as collaboration with the Germans, seem to have been the prime selective factors. Furthermore, such experiences and fears, though they affected the loyalty of the Soviet citizen, were not prime determinants of his pattern of achievement or adjustment in the Soviet socio-political system.[15] The refugee population is not a collection of misfits or historical 'leftovers'. It includes representatives from all walks of life and actually seemed to have a disproportionately large number of the mobile and successful.

Though we are acutely aware of the smallness of our sample, we incline to assume that the personality modes found in it would be found within the Soviet Union in groups comparable in nationality and occupation. We are strengthened in this assumption by several considerations. First, the picture of Russian modal personality patterns which emerges from our study is highly congruent with the traditional or classic picture of the Russian character reported in history, literature, and current travellers' accounts.[16] Second, much of the criticism directed by the regime against the failings of the population strongly suggests that some of the traits we found modal to our sample and a source of strain

[14] It is impossible to estimate accurately how many former Soviet citizens had a real chance to choose not to remain under Soviet authority. The best available estimates suggest that at the close of hostilities in Europe in 1945 there were between two and a half and five million former Soviet citizens in territories outside Soviet control or occupation, and of these between 250,000 and 500,000 decided and managed to remain in the West. See G. Fischer (1952).

[15] Evidence in support of these contentions is currently being prepared for publication. A preliminary unpublished statement may be consulted at the Russian Research Center: A. Inkeles and R. Bauer (1954).

[16] After this article was completed we discovered a report based almost entirely on participant observation which yielded conclusions about modal personality patterns among Soviet Russians extraordinarily similar to those developed on the basis of our tests and interviews. See: Maria Pfister-Ammende (1949).

Modal Personality and Adjustment to the Soviet System 339

in its adjustment to the system are widespread in the population and pose an obstacle to the attainment of the regime's purposes *within* the U.S.S.R. Third, the differences in personality between occupational levels are consistent with what we know both of the general selective processes in industrial occupational systems and of the deliberate selective procedures adopted by the Soviet regime. Because of the methodological limitations of our study, the generalization of our findings to the Soviet population must be considered as purely conjectural. Unfortunately we will be obliged to remain on this level of conjecture as long as Soviet citizens within the U.S.S.R. are not accessible to study under conditions of relative freedom. We feel, however, that, with all their limitations, the findings we have reported can be of essential aid in furthering our understanding of the adjustment of a large segment of the Soviet citizens to their socio-political system and of the policies adopted by the regime in response to the disposition of the population.

17 CHILD REARING IN EASTERN EUROPEAN COUNTRIES[1]

Ruth Benedict

Systematic study of national character is an investigation into a special and paradoxical situation. It must identify and analyze continuities in attitudes and behaviors yet the personnel which exhibits these traits changes completely with each generation. A whole nation of babies have to be brought up to replace their elders. The situations two different generations have to meet—war or peace, prosperity or depression—may change drastically, but Americans, for instance, will handle them in one set of terms, Italians in another. Even when a nation carries through a revolution or reverses fundamental state policies, Frenchmen do not cease to be recognizable as Frenchmen or Russians as Russians.

The cultural study of certain European nations on which I am reporting[2] has taken as one of its basic problems the ways in which children are brought up to carry on in their turn their parents' manner of life. It accepts as its theoretical premise that identifications, securities, and frustrations are built up in the child

FROM Ruth Benedict, "Child Rearing in Certain European Countries," 1949, *American Journal of Orthopsychiatry*, 19:342–50. Copyright, The American Orthopsychiatric Association, Inc. Reproduced by permission.

[1] Presented at the 1948 Annual Meeting.

[2] Research in Contemporary Cultures, government-aided Columbia University Research Project sponsored by the Psychological Branch of the Medical Sciences Division of the Office of Naval Research. The Russian material was collected and organized under the leadership of Geoffrey Gorer and Margaret Mead, and I am especially indebted to Mr. Gorer's skill and insights; Prof. Conrad M. Arensberg directed the group gathering Jewish material, and Dr. Sula Benet organized the information on Poland. Thanks are due to these leaders and to all their co-workers.

Child Rearing in Eastern European Countries 341

by the way in which he is traditionally handled, the early discipline he receives, and the sanctions used by his parents. The study has been carried on in New York City by a staff of interviewers who have supplemented their work with historical, literary, journalistic and economic materials. The aims of the research have been to isolate exceedingly fundamental patterns and themes which can be tested and refined by study of local, class, and religious differences. It is believed that such preliminary hypotheses will make future field work in the home countries more rewarding, and such field work in the Old World is already being carried out under other auspices by students who have taken part in this research.

The Project has necessarily seen its work as a comparative study of cultures. It has blocked out large culture areas and their constituent subcultures. When a great area shares a generalized trait, the particular slants each subarea has given to these customs is diagnostic of its special values and the range of variation gives insight which could not be obtained from the study of one nation in isolation. This culture area approach commits the student, moreover, when he is working outside his own cultural area, to a detailed study of behaviors which, since they are not present in his own experience, have not been incorporated into his own theoretical apparatus. It is therefore a testing ground for theoretical assumptions and often involves a rephrasing of them.

The custom of swaddling the baby during its first months of life in Central and Eastern Europe illustrates well, in the field of child rearing, the methodological value of a culture area approach. It illustrates how the comparison of attitudes and practices in different areas can illuminate the characteristics of any one region that is being intensively studied, and the kind of inquiry which is fruitful. Specifically I shall try to show that any such student of comparative cultures must press his investigation to the point where he can describe *what is communicated* by the particular variety of the widespread technique he is studying. In the case of swaddling, the object of investigation is the kind of communication which in different regions is set up between adults and the child by the procedures and sanctions used.

Because of our Western emphasis on the importance of the

infant's bodily movement, students of child care who discuss swaddling in our literature often warn that it produces tics. Or with our stress on prohibition of infant genitality, it is subsumed under prevention of infant masturbation. Any assumption that swaddling produces adults with tics ignores the contradictory evidence in the great areal laboratory where swaddling occurs, and the assumption that it is simply a first technique to prevent a child from finding pleasure in its own body is an oversimplified projection of our Western concern with this taboo. Any systematic study of the dynamics of character development in the swaddling area is crippled by these assumptions. Infant swaddling has permitted a great range of communication.

Careful studies of mother-child relations in this country have abundantly shown the infant's sensitivity to the mother's tenseness or permissiveness, her pleasure or disgust, whether these are expressed in her elbows, her tone of voice or her facial expression. Communications of these sorts take place from birth on, and when a particular form of parental handling is standardized as "good" and "necessary" in any community, the infant has a greatly multiplied opportunity to learn to react to the traditional patterns. Local premises, too, about how to prepare a child for life will be expressed in modification of procedure in swaddling, and these detailed differences are means of communication to the child, no less than his mother's tone of voice. Any fruitful research in national character must base its work upon such premises and utilize them as basic principles in comparative study.

Swaddling is tightest and is kept up longest in Great Russia. The baby's arms are wrapped close to its sides and only the face emerges. After tight wrapping in the blanket, the bundle is taped with criss-cross lashings till it is, as Russians say, "like a log of wood for the fireplace." Babies are sometimes lashed so tight that they cannot breathe, and are saved from strangling only by loosening the bindings. The bundle is as rigid as if the babies were bound to a cradleboard, and this affects carrying habits and the way a baby is soothed in an adult's arms. It is not rocked in the arms in the fashion familiar to us, but is moving horizontally from right to left and left to right.

The swaddling in Russia is explicitly justified as necessary for the safety of an infant who is regarded as being in danger of destroying itself. In the words of informants, "It would tear its ears off. It would break its legs." It must be confined for its own sake and for its mother's. In the '30's the Soviet regime made a determined effort to adopt Western customs of child rearing and to do away with swaddling. Young women were trained to instruct mothers that a baby's limbs should be left free for better muscular development and exhibitions of pictures of unswaddled baby care were distributed widely. But swaddling persisted. Informants who have recently lived in Russia says constantly "You couldn't carry an unswaddled baby." "Mothers were so busy they had to make the child secure." Several hundreds of pictures of babies available at the Sovfoto Agency show the prevalence of swaddling; photographs taken in 1946 and 1947 still show the completely bunted baby with only the face exposed. This physical restriction of the baby is traditionally continued for nine months or longer. It is not accompanied by social isolation. Babies are kept where adults are congregated, and their little sisters and grandmothers act as nurses; they are talked to and their needs are attended to.

In many ways the infant apparently learns that only its physical movement is restricted, not its emotions.[3] The Russian emphasis upon the child's inherent violence appears to preclude any belief among adults that its emotions could be curbed. The baby's one means of grasping the outside world is through its eyes, and it is significant that in all Russian speech and literature the eyes are stressed as the "mirrors of the soul." Russians greatly value "looking one in the eyes," for through the eyes, not through gestures or through words, a person's inmost feelings are shown. A person who does not look one in the eyes has something to conceal. A "look" also is regarded as being able to convey disapproval more shattering than physical punishment. Throughout life the eyes remain an organ which maintains strong and immediate contact with the outside world.

The baby's physical isolation within its bindings appears to be related to the kind of personal inviolability Russians maintain in

[3] In this entire section I am indebted to Mr. Gorer's analysis.

adulthood. It is difficult for foreigners to appreciate the essential privacy accorded the individual in Russian folk life, for their pattern of "pouring out the soul" would be in most cultures a bid for intimacy, and their expressive proverb, "It is well even to die if there are plenty of people around," seems a vivid statement of dislike of isolation. These traits, however, coexist in Russia with a great allowance for a personal world which others do not, and need not, share. "Every man," they say, "has his own anger," and the greatest respect is given to one who has taken his own private vow—either in connection with a love affair or with a mission in life. Whatever an individual must do in order to carry out this personal vow, even if the acts would in other contexts be antisocial, is accepted. He must be true to himself; it is his *pravda*.

The Russian version of swaddling can also be profitably related to the tradition Russian attitude that strong feeling has positive value. Personal outbreaks, with or without intoxication, are traditionally ascribed to the merchant class and to peasants, but they were characteristic of all classes. Official pressure at present attempts to channel this strong feeling toward foreign enemies, but the uses of violence to the individual psyche seem to be stressed in traditional fashion in this modern propaganda.

Not only is violence in itself a means to attain order, but it is also relatively divorced from aggression against a particular enemy. In Czarist days "burning up the town," breaking all the mirrors, smashing the furniture on a psychic binge were not means of "getting even" or of avenging one's honor; they were "in general." Even the peasants characteristically fired the home of a landowner other than the one on whom they were dependent. This trait is prepared for in the first years of life by the relative impersonality of the swaddling. Even in the villages of Great Russia, moreover, there is constant use of wet nurses and *nyanyas,* older women who are engaged to care for the baby; there is consequently a much more diffuse relationship during the first year of life than in societies where the child's contact is more limited to that with its own mother. It is characteristic of Russia, also, that poems and folk songs with the theme of mother love are practically nonexistent. The Great Russian mother is not specifically a maternal figure; she is quite sure of her sex without having to produce children to prove that she is female—as the man also is sure of his sex.

The Polish version of swaddling is quite different from the Russian. The infant is regarded not as violent, but as exceedingly fragile. It will break in two without the support given by the bindings. Sometimes it is emphasized that it would be otherwise too fragile to be safely entrusted to its siblings as child nurses; sometimes that the swaddling straightens its bent and fragile legs. Swaddling is conceived as a first step in a long process of "hardening" a child. "Hardening" is valued in Poland, and since one is hardened by suffering, suffering is also valued. A man does not demean himself by retailing his hardships and the impositions put upon him. Whereas an Italian, for instance, will minimize his dissatisfactions and discouragements and respect himself the more for so doing, Poles characteristically tend to prove their own worth by their sufferings. A usual peasant greeting is a list of his most recent miseries, and Polish patriots have exalted Poland as "the crucified Christ of the Nations." From infancy the importance of "hardening" is stressed. In peasant villages it is good for a baby to cry without attention, for it strengthens the lungs; beating the child is good because it is hardening; and mothers will even deny that they punish children by depriving them of dessert and tidbits, because "food is for strengthening; it would be no punishment to deprive them of any food."

Another theme in Polish swaddling has reference to the great gulf fixed between clean and dirty parts of the body. The binding prevents the infant from putting its toes into its mouth—the feet are practically as shame-ridden as the genitals in Poland—or from touching its face with its fingers which may just before have touched its crotch or its toes. When the baby is unswaddled for changing or for bathing, the mother must prevent such shameless acts. Whereas the Russian baby is quite free during the occasional half-hour when it is unswaddled, the Polish baby must be only the more carefully watched and prevented. Polish decency is heavily associated with keeping apart the various zones of the body.

Although it was possible to sketch Russian infancy without describing details of nursing and toilet training, which are there warm and permissive, in Poland this is impossible. The high point of contrast is perhaps the weaning. In Russia supplementary food is given early; a very small swaddled baby has a rag filled with chewed bread tied around its neck; this is pushed down on its mouth as a "comforter" by anyone present. The baby is eating many foods long before it is weaned. In Poland, however, weaning is sudden. It is believed that a child will die if it is nursed beyond two St. John's Days of its life—or the day of some other saint—and therefore, when the child is on the average eighteen months old, the mother chooses a day for weaning. The child is not given an opportunity beforehand to accustom itself to eating solid food; the sudden transition is good because it is "hardening." It is further believed that a twice-weaned child will die and though many mothers relent because of the child's difficulties, it is necessarily with guilt.

Another contrast with Russia is a consequence of the strong feeling about the evil eye in Poland. Only the mother can touch the baby without running the danger of harming it; in the villages even the baby's aunts and cousins fall under this suspicion. Certainly no woman except the mother can feed the baby at the breast. During the spring and summer months the babies are left behind at home with three and four-year-olds since all older children go to help their parents in the fields. In house after house neglected children are crying and women incapacitated for the fields might advantageously care for them. But this is regarded as impossible.

The Polish child gets nothing from crying. He is hurried toward adulthood, and the steps which reach it are always ones which "harden" him; they are not pleasant in themselves. As a child he has tantrums, but the word for tantrums means literally "being stuck," "deadlocked." He does not cry or throw himself about as the Jewish child in Poland does; he sits for hours with rigid body, his hands and his mouth clenched. He gets beaten but he takes it without outcry or unbending. He knows his mother will not attempt to appease him. His defense of his honor in his later life is the great approved means of unburdening himself of resentments and turning them into personal glory. There are many Polish proverbs which say idiomatically and with great affect: Defend your honor though you die. The long process of childhood "hardening" lies back of their insult contest and their spirited struggles in lost causes.

The swaddling of the Jewish baby, whether in Poland or the Ukraine, has characteristics of its own. The baby is swaddled on a soft pillow and in most areas the bindings are wrapped relatively loosely around the baby and his little featherbed. The mother sings to the baby as she swaddles it. The specific stress is upon warmth and comfort, and the incidental confinement of the baby's limbs is regarded with pity and commiseration. People say in describing swaddling, "Poor baby, he looks just like a little mummy," or "He lies there nice and warm, but, poor baby, he can't move." Swaddling is also good, especially for boys, because it insures straight legs. There is no suggestion that it is the beginning of a process of "hardening" or that it is necessary because the baby is inherently violent. Rather, it is the baby's first experience of the warmth of life in his own home— a warmth which at three or four he will contrast with the lack of comfort, the hard benches, the long hours of immobility and the beatings at the *cheder,* the elementary Jewish school where he is taught Hebrew. In strongest contrast to the experience of the Gentile child, swaddling is part of the child's induction into the closest kind of physical intimacy; within the family the mother will expect to know every physical detail of her children's lives and treats any attempts at privacy as a lack of love and gratitude. The pillowed warmth of his swaddling period apparently becomes a prototype of what home represents, an image which he will have plenty of opportunity to contrast with the world outside, the world of the *goy.*

It is profitable also to relate Jewish swaddling to another pattern of Eastern European Jewish life: its particular version of complementary interpersonal relations. I am using "complementary" in a technical sense as a designation of those interpersonal relations where the response of a person or group to its vis-a-vis is in terms of an opposite or different behavior from that of the original actors. Such paired actions as dominance-submission, nurturance-dependence, and command-obedience are complementary responses. The Jewish complementary system might be called nurturance-deference. Nurturance is the good deed—*mitzvah*—of all parents, elders, wealthy, wise and learned men toward the children, the younger generation, the poor, and the still unschooled. In interpersonal relations these latter respond to the former with deference, "respect," but not with *mitzvah*. One never is rewarded in a coin of the same currency by one's vis-a-vis, either concurrently with the act or in the future. Parents provide for all their children's needs, but the obligation of the child to the parent does not include support of his aged parents when he is grown, and the saying is: "Better to beg one's bread from door to door than to be dependent on one's son." The aged parent feels this dependence to be humiliating, and this is in strongest contrast to the non-Jews of Poland, for instance, among whom parents can publicly humiliate their children by complaining of nonsupport. Among the Jews, a child's obligation to his parents is discharged by acting toward his own children, when he is grown, as his parents acted toward him. His aged parents are cared for, not by a son in his role as a son, but in his role as a wealthy man, contributing to the poor. Such impersonal benefactions are not humiliating to either party.

The swaddling situation is easily drawn into this Jewish system of complementary relations. The personnel involved in swaddling is necessarily complementary; it includes the binder and the bound. The bound will never reciprocate by binding the binder, and the Jewish binder conceives herself as performing a necessary act of nurturance out of which she expects the child to experience primarily warmth and comfort; she is rather sorry for the accompanying confinement but she regards random mobility as a sign of the baby's being uncomfortable. She is not, like the Polish mother, "hardening" the baby or preventing indecencies, or like the Russian mother, taking precautions against its destroying itself. She is starting the baby in a way of life where there is a lack of guilt and aggression in being the active partner in all complementary relationships and security in being the passive partner.

In swaddling situations the communication which is then established between mother and infant is continued in similar terms after swaddling is discontinued. Diapering of older babies is understood by Jewish mothers as contributing to the baby's comfort, and by Polish non-Jewish mothers as preventing indecencies by insuring that the baby's hands do not come in successive contact with "good" and "bad" parts of his body. In Rumania, where all informants from cities and towns stressed first, last and always that swaddling was necessary to prevent masturbation, the infant's hands, when he is too old to be swaddled, are tied to his crib, incased in clumsy mittens and immobilized by special clothing. His nurse or mother spies on him and punishes any slip.

The different kinds of swaddling communication which are localized in Central and Eastern Europe make it clear that the practice has been revamped to conform to the values of the several cultural groups. As in any culture area study, investigation discloses the patterning of behavior in each culture. The diversities do not confuse the picture; they enrich it. And the detailed study of this one widespread trait, like any other, throws light on the individuality of each cultural group, while at the same time it emphasizes the kinship among them.

DISCUSSION

MARGARET MEAD. I speak as a member of the research group on the basis of whose work Dr. Benedict has presented these results so that I find it most appropriate to comment on some of the theoretical implications of our experience.

We have attained considerable clarification, we think, of the problems of how to think about the way in which the child's experiences within a culture mould his character. Students of culture who have used child development as a way of describing the culture have recognized for a good many years that the Freudian model of pregenital development, especially in the systematic form relevant to cross-cultural comparisons elaborated by Erikson (1937, 1943, 1946), provided us with many clues, when we applied it to an exploration of which zones and which modes at which stages were frustrated, indulged or ignored in the course of child rearing. If a model of development like the Gesell-Ilg (Mead 1947) was used, it also provided us with important clues to understanding differences in character formation in different societies. We also found that it was not possible to make any simple cross-cultural statement, such as that permissive toilet training or long nursing or sudden weaning would have a single predictable effect in later character. Whenever any single practice was followed cross-culturally, a confusing number of contradictions were found, such as would have been the result if, to the material which Dr. Benedict presented today, we had applied a simple hypothesis that swaddling could be relied upon to produce a single set of effects. It has become increasingly clear over the last few years that it was necessary to include a variable, loosely described as "tone of voice" or the quality of the interpersonal relationship within which a given zone or stage of locomotion or mode of behavior was indulged and frustrated (Mead 1946; Fries 1947). I think that the research of the last six months makes it possible to proceed one step further and to advance the hypothesis that within the general framework of biological development the significant specific character-forming elements will be those through which the adults attempt to communicate with the child. This communication need not be an articulate type of "character education" but it is affect-laden and emphatic. Early toilet training followed out for some casual reason of household arrangement will have a very different, and possibly almost negligible effect, while toilet training at an age when it might be conceived to be less traumatic and more appropriate to the developmental stage may, because of the weight given it by the adult, have far stronger effects. By examining the system of communication between parent and child against a theoretical ground plan provided by the body itself, the pattern of family relationships in the society, and the tempo and rhythm of biological growth, we can distinguish those nuances of emphasis—as in the Russian communication to the baby that it is dangerously strong, the Polish that its body must be thought of as divided into good and bad parts, the Jewish that close warmth will defend it against a harsh outer world, and the Rumanian urban and town baby that touching its own body is a pleasure which his parents are concerned to deny him—all within the practice of swaddling during the early months of life.

There is also an aspect of our procedure in this research on contemporary cultures which has, I believe, important implications for psychiatry. In each of our areal groups members of the cultures being studied have worked as collaborators, and the research workers have been forced to take the trouble to phrase their results in ways which were not only scientifically satisfactory but were also culturally acceptable to those who were at one time both subjects and collaborators. This is a step which we felt no need to take as long as we described preliterate people who were unable to read our results. The psychiatrist has not yet faced the problem of how to phrase a diagnosis so that it is acceptable to the patient. Medical secrecy has made it possible to talk about the patient in ways which the patient would find intolerable. Furthermore, it has retarded any revision of a psychiatric vocabularly developed in the day when the early research workers, appalled by what they found in the unconscious, embodied their own repulsion in the vocabulary. The persistence of these practices can only serve to impede public acceptance of psychiatric concepts, and it should be possible to look forward to a time when psychiatric concepts will have such a degree of gentleness and inclusiveness that the patient could sit in at a staff conference where his own case was described.

18 IS THE OEDIPUS COMPLEX UNIVERSAL?

A SOUTH ITALIAN "NUCLEAR COMPLEX"[1]

Anne Parsons

INTRODUCTORY REMARKS

In the 1920's a famous debate took place between Ernest Jones and Bronislaw Malinowski which set forth some outlines of theoretical differences between psychoanalysis and anthropology which are still unresolved today.[2] On the basis of field work in the matrilineal Trobriand Islands, Malinowski drew the conclusion that the Oedipus complex as formulated by Freud is only one among a series of possible "nuclear complexes," each of which patterns primary family affects in a way characteristic of

FROM Anne Parsons, "Is the Oedipus Complex Universal? The Jones-Malinowski Debate Revisited and a South Italian 'Nuclear Complex.'" 1964, in Muensterberger and Axelrad, *The Psychoanalytic Study of Society*, Vol. III, pp. 278–301, and 310–26. By permission of the International Universities Press, Inc. Copyright International Universities Press, Inc.

[1] This paper is based on research carried out in Naples, Italy, in 1958–1960 on two grants from the National Institute of Mental Health, Bethesda, Md. (M-2105 and M-4301) and was written during the term of an interdisciplinary grant from the Foundation Fund for Research in Psychiatry. I am very much indebted to Merton J. Kahne, Donald S. Pitkin, David M. Schneider, Alfred H. Stanton, and to my father, Talcott Parsons, for many comments and discussions which have gone into the formulation of the ideas in ways which would be difficult to acknowledge specifically.

[2] Jones (1924) in a paper read before the British Psycho-Analytical Society first discussed three prior publications by Malinowski: "Baloma: The Spirits of the Dead in the Trobriand Islands" (1916) and two articles which were later published together as the first two sections of *Sex and Repression in Savage Society* (1927). The last two sections of this latter work were written in response to Jones's paper. For the most complete summary of the Trobriand field data, see Malinowski (1929).

Is the Oedipus Complex Universal?

the culture in which it occurs. In this perspective, Freud's formulation of the Oedipus complex as based on a triangular relationship between father, mother, and son appears as that particular nuclear complex which characterizes a patriarchal society in which the most significant family unit consists of mother, father, and child. The alternative nuclear complex which he postulated for the Trobriand Islands consisted of a triangular relationship between brother, sister, and sister's son, this in function of the nature of matrilineal social structure in which a boy becomes a member of his mother's kin group and is subject to the authority of his maternal uncle rather than the biological father. One of his most important observations was that in the Trobriand Islands ambivalent feelings very similar to those described by Freud with respect to father and son can be observed between mother's brother and sister's son. Relations between father and son, on the other hand, are much more close and affectionate; however, Malinowski felt that the father should not be considered as a figure in the kinship structure since the Trobrianders do not recognize the existence of biological paternity. The child is seen as conceived by a spirit which enters the mother's womb and later the father appears to him as the unrelated mother's husband.

In addition, Malinowski noted that the Trobrianders give a very special importance to the brother-sister relationship. While the brother has formal authority over the sister and is responsible for her support, their actual relationship is one of extreme avoidance, to the point that an object may be handed from one to the other by means of an intermediary. He characterized the brother-sister incest taboo as "the supreme taboo" from the Trobriand standpoint; while incest with other primary biological relatives and within the matrilineal kin group at greater biological distance is also forbidden, in no instance are the taboos as strict or surrounded by intense affects as in the brother-sister case. He also discerned, with his acute clinical eye, many evidences of the real temptations underlying the avoidance pattern, for example, in that while no Trobriander would admit to having such an incest dream, the questioning itself aroused a great deal of anxiety and often the assertion that "well, other people have such dreams, but certainly not me." He noted brother-sister incest to be a primary theme in Trobriand mythology, for example, in that love magic is seen as originating in a situation in which brother and sister actually committed incest and died as a result of it. He considered these variations from the European pattern of sufficient significance to uphold the view that the Oedipus complex is not universal.

Jones, in his 1924 paper, upheld with considerable vehemence the classical psychoanalytic point of view that it is. Thus while he felt that Malinowski's field data were in themselves interesting, he came to the conclusion that they did not point to the need for any important theoretical revisions in the pyschoanalytic framework. For the data on the Trobriand failure to recognize the biological relationship between father and son, he provided an alternative explanation, namely, that the nonrecognition was a form of denial covering affects originating in the Oedipus situation.[3] Much to Malinowski's dismay, this argument was carried to the point of the assertion that matrilineal social organization can itself be seen as a defense against the father-son ambivalence universally characteristic of the Oedipus situation. He also pointed out that Malinowski's observations of ambivalence between mother's brother and sister's son concerned adolescent and adult life, so that, theoretically, it is possible to see it as a secondary displacement in that there is an initial oedipal rivalry between father and son, but that in adult life the hostile feelings are displaced to the mother's brother. He also commented that similar patterns can be observed in Europe, for example, in that the hostile father figure may later be an occupational superior or rival, while the actual father remains a positive figure.

A re-examination of the debate in a contemporary perspective indicates that actually there are a number of intertwined issues. In the first place, it is characterized by a highly polemic character related to the newness and consequent defensiveness of both fields: for Jones "the" Oedipus complex appears as a kind of

---

[3] Not all anthropologists have accepted Malinowski's observations on this at face value; however, the data he presents indicate that the Trobrianders had formulated a reasonably coherent and intelligent picture of the facts of biology for a people lacking in any scientific framework.

Is the Oedipus Complex Universal? 355

point of honor upon whose invariance psychoanalysis would stand or fall, and exactly the same is true of some elements of Malinowski's argument, in particular those which touch on the resemblance between Jones's views and those of the older evolutionary anthropology which he himself did so much to overthrow. Thus, concerning the question of whether matrilineal social organization can be seen as a defense against oedipal affects, it seems difficult now to see how a complex social pattern could be based on the "denial" of an affect which occurs in the individual. But on the other hand, one can regret that Malinowski, in his rebuttal, went into a tirade against the evolutionary implications of this view rather than attempting to answer Jones's much more cogent point, namely, that Freud's concepts concern infantile life, and in this perspective it is quite possible that the hostility toward the mother's brother observed in adolescent and adult Trobrianders might be displaced from hostility initially experienced toward the father. What is perhaps most regrettable of all, given his status with regard to the psychoanalytic theory of symbolism, is that Jones never discussed in detail Malinowski's observations concerning the special importance of the Trobriand brother-sister relationship and the integrally related material concerning dreams and mythology.

When we look at the present state of theoretical knowledge, we might come to the conclusion that the question of whether or not the Oedipus complex is universal is one which should not be asked in such a way as to create the impression that there is a yes or no answer. In the first place, the theoretical assumption that there are infantile sexual wishes is one which has proved so useful, and has brought together such a variety of clinical facts, that it seems simply foolish to abandon the general Freudian scheme until such a point when we have an alternative that appears scientifically more valuable. In retrospect, one might say that the major point that Jones wished to maintain was simply the idea that there is an infantile sexual life. Secondly, the main point which Malinowski was supporting is now also so well established that we need not any longer be defensive about it—that human societies do structure family patterns in different ways according to laws of kinship, or particular phrasings of the incest taboo, that by no means can be derived directly from the biological facts of mating and reproduction. These latter simply cannot explain facts such as the extreme significance given to the brother-sister incest taboo by the Trobrianders in comparison to ourselves.

Taking these two points for granted, we might then proceed to ask again the same questions which were asked by Jones and Malinowski and to re-evaluate some of the major points made by each in the light of contemporary psychoanalytic and anthropological knowledge. It is this task which we have set ourselves in this paper. After some general theoretical considerations, we will discuss a particular case with respect to the possibility of formulating a third distinctive "nuclear family complex" differing both from Freud's patriarchal one and from the Trobriand matrilineal case.

Theoretical Points

Much of the Jones-Malinowski argument centered on the evidence presented by Malinowski to the effect that Trobriand Islanders are unaware of the facts of physiological paternity. The main importance of this material to Malinowski lay in its value for demonstrating the independence of social form biological kinship; certainly one of the major points which troubled him and has troubled many other anthropologists since about psychoanalytic theory is the implication that these two must overlap. However, while Jones's formulation leaves itself open to just this objection, one might now wonder whether in fact psychoanalytic theory does presuppose such an equivalence. One of the fundamental tenets of instinct theory is that an instinct is displacable according to source, aim, and object; but if we use the term "object" in a social sense, referring to either an external person who is the focus of a drive or to an internalized representation of a person, we might then say that the possibility of variant family structures is built into even Freud's earliest formulations. Moreover, Freud's theory, while it anchors affects and fantasies in biological concepts of instinct, might also better be seen as a psychological than a biological one; so that to the extent that it postulates universals, we should also see these psychologically rather than biologically.

Contemporary concepts of object relations and object representations[4] may make it possible to bring this point out more clearly than was done by Jones. Any clinician can cite from immediate experience a great many instances in which the object focus of oedipal affects has been a person other than the biological mother or father—an adopted parent, a more distant relative, or as in many cases today, a child therapist. Actually, Freud himself was very much concerned with the role played by domestics in the early sexual life of the Victorian upper status child. We might then say that the question of the Oedipus complex has two sides to it, the first related to instinct and fantasy, and the second to identification and object choice. But it is hard to believe that the latter processes are not in some way directly dependent on social structure and social norms, or the available possibilities for object choice and object representation.

In this perspective, the idea of the distinctive nuclear complex for each society becomes much more compatible with the psychoanalytic idea that there is an invariant series of developmental phases which is rooted in instinct; the social factor need only influence the object side. Using this assumption, we might interpret Jones's displacement hypothesis as saying that the passing of the Oedipus complex in the Trobriand Islands is equivalent to assimilating the polar distinction between two socially represented figures, the mother's brother and the mother's husband. Each of these then comes to have a differing or contrasting affective valence and one can even say that the boy identifies with both, but that each identification represents a different social function or aspect of personality. According to this view,[5] it is the social distinction which lies at the basis of the conscious representation, which could not even arise without the mediating effect of social exchange; if there were none, the biological drives would presumably arise nevertheless, but they would not give rise to a personality. Such a formulation seems much simpler

---

[4] See Jacobson (1954), T. Parsons (1958), and Stanton (1959).
[5] Which utilizes Durkheim's concept of collective representations (Durkheim 1915).

and less awkward than to say that first the Trobriand child goes through an Oedipus phase centered on the father, somehow acquiring a knowledge of biological paternity which adults in his society do not possess, then represses this knowledge and displaces the affects to the mother's brother. What we are saying is rather that conscious representation of objects by definition depends on collective representation, though their affective charge or valence may be rooted in unconscious or instinct-based constellations which are prior to culture.

This formulation would permit us to say that it does not make much difference whether the relevant figure is father or mother's brother; psychoanalytic theory requires only that the small boy have some available figure for masculine identification. However, a second aspect of the Oedipus theory raises a more difficult problem. This is that, according to Freud, the boy's hostility to the father arises from the fact that the latter has sexual relations with his mother; in other words, the Oedipus complex is rooted in sexual jealousy. However, in the Trobriand Islands, it is the biological father and not the mother's brother who has sexual relations with the mother. In fact, though it is not impossible that the mother have other sexual involvements as well, the one person who could not be a sexual object for her is precisely the maternal uncle, since he is, of course, her brother.

Here it seems that we have reached an insoluble impasse; either we must abandon the Malinowskian attempt to isolate distinctive nuclear complexes, saying that the initial oedipal object must always be the father since he is the actual sexual rival, or we must take the more empiricist "culturalist" viewpoint which abandons the idea of infantile sexuality altogether and says simply that various role patterns are learned in direct relation to social interaction. But since neither solution seems satisfactory (the second because it does not utilize instinct theory), we might do better to look further. Perhaps in reconsidering some of the various possible phrasings of psychoanalytic theory, we may find that some are more compatible with Malinowski's attempt than others.

It is well known that Freud's thinking contains many, not always compatible, interwoven strands. One of his earliest conceptionalizations was the trauma theory; this is the one which most directly influenced Malinowski and, moreover, most of the early workers in the field of culture and personality. According to the trauma theory, specific sexual events or observations take place in childhood which then have crucial consequence for adult personality and attitudes. In much of Freud's writing about infantile sexuality (before he reached his more general structural and dynamic formulations), he acts as if he were taking the trauma theory for granted, for example, when he portrays the Oedipus crisis as the point when the child observes or becomes aware of the "primal scene," asks questions about sexuality and comes to some conclusion about this matter and his own future sex role. This formulation presupposes a highly rationalistic child and a very direct relationship between environmental factors and psychosexual development. However, over the course of psychoanalytic history, the trauma theory has gradually slipped into the background; much of it today might well be given the status of myth. The main reason for this may well be that it simply has not worked; we certainly cannot try to predict today, nor does anyone, complex adult personality patterns from specific and limited kinds of infantile events. Applied in the anthropological field, however, the trauma theory very readily lent itself to the view that almost any kind of cultural difference could give rise to variations in the nature of the oedipal situation, and many of Malinowski's own convictions, like those of the later culture and personality theorists, were certainly derived from this kind of rough empirical evidence.

However, here we are concerned with the question of global structures rather than with specific items of socialization or other kinds of cultural behavior. With respect to family structure, trauma theory would lead us to believe that if it is in fact the father who has sexual relationships with the mother, then he should be the object of oedipal jealousy. However, in a somewhat different framework we could also reach the conclusion that this need not be so. It is often said that psychoanalysis began precisely at the moment when Freud abandoned the trauma theory, i.e., when he began to consider the verbal productions of his hysterical patients as fantasies. At this critical point he became much less concerned with the environmental question of whether or not his patients actually had been seduced in childhood and much more concerned with the questions which were formulated and reformulated throughout his later life: what are the instinctual roots of fantasy, and what are the inhabiting factors which can prevent instinct discharge on the biological plane and how do they operate? The work on hysteria, of course, led Freud right into the problem of the incest taboo, since his explanation of the genital inhibition associated with it was precisely that later objects may represent tabooed incestuous ones; moreover, he, at this point, began to interpret the relevant genetic sequences and drive constellations retroactively from fantasy and symbolic productions, rather than to postulate environmental events *ad hoc*. This shift went along with very close attention paid to the actual mental content of patients in all its details. In this perspective, we might come to the conclusion that if the brother-sister-sister's son triangle is most emphasized by the Trobrianders themselves in mythology and dreams, that this one indeed has a primary unconscious significance in Trobriand culture. Jones's main methodological mistake would then be that he did not pay sufficient attention to Malinowski's clinical detail and rather postulated a paternal trauma on the basis of theory alone. On this level, his formulation is logical, but it is as if he had tried to apply the genetic theory of hysteria to a schizophrenic patient without having tried to modify it to fit what the patient actually had to say.

But if we abandon trauma theory, it might be possible to postulate a distinctive genetic sequence that does not depend on the actual sexual relationships of which the child may be aware. Lacking the necessary material, we can only make a hypothesis, but to do this we might begin by summing up the three major facets of the brother-sister-sister's son triangle as it operates in adult life. First, it is very evident from the dream and myth material that even though there is a strict taboo, or just because there is one, brother and sister are to each other very highly cathected libidinal objects. Second, not only is the expression of any wishes for sexuality or intimacy forbidden, but also the relationship is one of respect, so that the expression of aggression is inhibited as well; the sister must show deference to her brother as an authority figure, and he, in turn, owes certain responsibilities to her. Third, the sister's son comes into this relationship in that he also owes respect to the mother's brother,

Is the Oedipus Complex Universal? 361

and for social continuity to be preserved, he must identify with him; for in time, of course, he will become a mother's brother with respect to his own sister's son.

Translating this into the genetic perspective, two difficulties arise. First, although this is not true in some other societies, the mother and father do share a habitation which is independent from that of the mother's brother. Second, as Jones points out, it may be difficult to conceive of the sister as a primary object (for example she may be younger and not present or an infant at the oedipal crisis), and later feelings about her may be displaced from the mother. In any event, one would expect the mother to form a part of the Oedipus triangle in almost any society since oedipal affects arise from the body closeness which is experienced in early infancy.

However, we can include the mother as a primary object and also make the mother's brother into the primary focus of masculine identification if we presuppose that much of the boy's early feelings about him derive from the special place which the uncle, as her brother, occupies in his mother's eye. Presumably, at a very early age the small boy becomes aware of the special importance which he has to her, both as an authority figure and as a primary object in her fantasy life. In this perspective the idea of sexual jealousy can be built into the triangular situation involving mother, brother, and son in that we might say that, by some process which is not yet fully understood, the boy becomes aware of the strong affective importance which the brother has for his mother; and when his jealousy and anger are awakened, he deals with them by identification. The mother's brother then becomes the primary rival. Moreover, assuming that the passing of the Oedipus complex is equivalent to an assimilation of social representations of objects into the child's mind, we could also assume that much of his perception of his mother is based on her role as sister, linked to the maternal uncle in the kin group to which he belongs. Having made this supposition, we could then suppose that the representations of the brother-sister relationship which are assimilated, in which the boy identifies with the brother role, then become transferred to the actual brother-sister relationship, within which the taboos are taught in the home very early in childhood. Such a formulation presupposes that identity and jealousy can both be transmitted through symbolic processes alone, without depending on particular observations or knowledge of parental sexual relations, but it would bring in the mother as a primary object, the distinctive aspect of the complex lying in the inclusion of her brother and the emphasis on her role as sister rather than father's wife.

Much of this is, of course, speculative since our knowledge of the possible range of perceptions of the oedipal child still has many gaps. However, such a formulation could reconcile the two assumptions with which we began, and moreover, could place the Oedipus complex in a more dynamic and wider social perspective, in that it would link up psychological knowledge with anthropological knowledge of kinship structure, given that we already know that this triangular relationship has a crucial status in the functioning of the matrilineal kinship system.

In a more general perspective, it should also be possible to say that each culture imposes restrictions on primary drives according to a particular pattern, and from the pattern of restrictions it should be possible to predict much of the cultural content from the assumption that symbols arise when a primary impulse is denied gratification. Such a possibility is found in the concept of repression, but perhaps comes out more clearly if we use the recent formulation of David Rapaport (1960), according to whom it is the fact of delay in drive expression which gives rise to the symbol, than in at least one facet of Jones's (1912) summary of the psychoanalytic theory of symbolism according to which there are biologically given types of primary symbolic content.

Returning to the Trobriand example, we could then say that the model for delay, or for the elaboration and maintenance of complex cultural productions, is provided by the brother-sister relationship. This latter would then be seen as the key relationship in a distinctive nuclear complex which can be used or interpreted on a number of levels: it is manifested directly in the myths of which brother-sister incest is the theme; it appears integral to matrilineal social structure; it presumably has genetic roots; and if we look to the actual experience of childhood and adolescence, we can see that quite concretely the brother-sister relationship is presented as the symbol of delay, for example, in

Is the Oedipus Complex Universal? 363

that while infantile sexual games are generally rather freely permitted, this is not the case between brother and sister, just as later in adolescence rather casual affairs are the rule, but between brother and sister the taboo is very strict. In other words, for the Trobriand Islands the brother-sister relationship has a special place on the borderline between instinct and culture; but it should also be possible to isolate such specially important relationships for other cultures as well.

SOME SOUTH ITALIAN CULTURAL COMPLEXES

At this point, I should like to attempt the description of a third nuclear complex, resembling neither the matrilineal one of the Trobriand Islands nor the patriarchal one described by Freud. The material concerns Southern Italy, but descriptions by other researchers indicate the existence of similar patterns throughout the Latin world and possibly even in pre-Reformation Europe. My own concrete observations were made primarily in the city of Naples where I carried out a study of working-class families; however, the basic pattern does not seem fundamentally different in other areas of Southern Italy or in other social class groups, though, of course, there are many variations in details. What I shall try to do is to bring together a number of facts from quite diverse areas—general cultural patterns, intrafamily behavior, and projective test material—in a way which depends on the framework sketched above.

The South Italian family system, similar in this respect not only to other Latin countries but also to much of the Mediterranean world, is in a certain sense intermediate between the kind of lineage system found in the Trobriand Islands and the discontinuous nuclear family characteristic of the industrial world. As we have seen in the Trobriand Islands, it is quite possible that units other than the biologically based mother-father-child one serve as the key axis of social structure; this is very often true of primitive societies where the latter unit usually is enclosed in some wider kinship unit which in turn defines patterns of social organization for the society as a whole. In industrial societies, on the other hand, it is often said that since there is such an elaboration of alternative nonkinship social structures (religious bodies, bureaucratic organizations, governments, etc.) the functions of the family have contracted to an irreducible minimum, i.e., the satisfaction of intimacy needs and the caring for small children. The family is discontinuous in the sense that it lasts only as long as particular individuals are alive; as children grow up they gradually move into a wider society and eventually form new families on their own rather than acquiring adult roles in a continuing social group. The world outside the family is seen in this perspective as a locus of positive achievement.

The South Italian family is an intermediate form in two senses. First, although there is no corporate lineage, since religious, economic, and political functions are handled by nonkinship organizations just as in any complex society, there is a rather loosely organized body of extended kin, the "parenti" which has some significance; one's "parenti," or relatives in a generic sense (usually meaning siblings of parents and their offspring), form the most immediate field of social relations and in theory at least are the persons on whom one can best count for aid in time of trouble. Second, while the family unit is the immediate biological one (with monogamous marriage, no legal divorce, and co-residence of husband, wife and minor children), this latter tends to be centripetal rather than centrifugal. In other words, parents, or in particular the mother, bring up children in such a way as to strengthen loyalties toward themselves rather than to move increasingly into a wider social context. This latter tendency is in turn associated with a definition of the world outside the family as hostile and threatening and very often as a source of temptations toward sexual or other forms of delinquency and dishonesty.

We can begin on the level of global culture patterns by examining a key complex of attitudes, namely, those surrounding the Madonna. The importance of the Madonna complex throughout the Latin world is evident to even the most casual observation; in the South Italian villages she stands in every church and along with the saints may be carried through the streets in procession, and in even the poorest quarters of the city of Naples she is likely to occupy some niche or other, decorated with the flowers or even gold chains brought by her children grateful for her favors. Moreover, every home has a private shrine, in which pictures or statues of the Madonna appear along with photographs of deceased relatives illuminated by a candle or lamp.

As a figure in Roman Catholic theology, the Madonna, of course, is only one element in a much wider religious complex. However, popular religion in Southern Italy does not always conform to theological doctrine, for example, in that it has a considerable admixture of magical beliefs and in that the Madonna and the saints are conceived of more as persons of whom one can ask a favor (Italian *grazia,* or a grace) than as ideal figures in a moralistic sense. The Madonna may also be seen in characteristic folk manner as a quite familiar figure who is very much part of daily life. One older woman has said, "The Madonna must have had a hard time when she was carrying the Savior, because people couldn't have known about the Holy Ghost and they always gossip about such things." Religion in general is seen in this concrete and living way, and religious vocabulary as exclamations, for example, *Madonna mia* and *Santa Maria,* are very much part of daily conversation.

The most important characteristic of the Madonna is that her love and tenderness are always available; no matter how unhappy or sinful the supplicant, she will respond if she is addressed in time of need. Acts of penitence may be carried out for her, for example, pilgrimages or even licking the steps of the church one by one and proceeding to the altar (today only in the most traditional rural areas). Even such acts of penitence, however, are apt to be conceived of as means of showing one's devotion in order to secure a favor, such as the recovery of a sick child. In this sense, the Madonna complex is based on an ethic of suffering rather than sin; the devotee seeks comfort for the wrongs imposed by fate rather than a guide for changing it.

The Madonna is quite obviously the ideal mother figure, and the relationship of the supplicant to her is conceived of as that of a child. The only family figures in the Christian pantheon are, of course, not lacking, that is, the father and the son. However, God the Father is usually conceived of as being so distant that he is unapproachable except through the intermediary of the Madonna or a saint; in Naples, the first cause theory of creation is very common, according to which God set the world in motion and then let it run according to its own devices. Christ, on the other hand, is perceived not as in many Protestant denominations as a representative of moral individuality, or even as an alternative comforting figure, but rather either as the good son who is truly and continually penitent or else in the context of suffering; as dramatized in Lenten rituals, the Madonna weeps when he dies martyrized by a hostile world. Of the three figures, it is the Madonna who has by far the greatest concreteness in the popular eye. Moreover, of all her characteristics one of the clearest is her asexuality: she conceived without sin and so became mother without being a wife.

Not only is the most apparent deity a feminine one, but also religion is defined as a primarily feminine sphere. Thus, while small boys may attend mass regularly in the company of women, as they approach puberty most of them are teased out of this by their male peers or relatives. The level of participation in religious functions (except for those touching on the secular such as fiestas) is in general very low for adult males; but at every Sunday mass one can observe crowds of young men waiting outside the door. The reason they themselves give for being there is that the girls are inside; thus, at the courtship phase religious participation becomes an opportunity for escaping surveillance, but with the difference that the girl's overt devotion increases and the reverse is true for the boy. Moreover, Southern Italy is noted for its anticlericalism, but, along with some socioeconomic aspects, a major feature of this anticlericalism is a joking pattern whose main consequence is to raise doubts concerning the ideals of purity which religion represents. This joking pattern is an important part of interaction in the male peer group which crystallizes around adolescence. It thus seems as if religion and adult male sexuality are conceived of as incompatible with each other.

The oppositional or skeptical trend which is represented by anticlerical joking is seen in a number of other cultural patterns as well; first, in swearing and obscenity which are extremely widespread. The particular expressions used can be divided into four groups: those wishing evil on someone else (e.g., "may you spit up blood," from the extreme anxiety evoked by the idea of tuberculosis); those reflecting on the dead ("curse the dead in your family"); those reversing religious values (the most com-

Is the Oedipus Complex Universal?

mon oath being "curse the Madonna"); and those reversing the values of feminine purity. The latter group includes graphic expressions for a variety of possible incestuous relationships with mother or sister, anal as well as genital, and can also be linked with the horn gesture (index and little finger extended) implying infidelity of the wife. Cursing may be engaged in by women as well as men, but it is far more characteristic of the latter, particularly the last two types.[6]

The context and seriousness of insult and obscenity is extremely variable; one may curse the Madonna on the occasion of stubbing one's toe, but raising the possibility of the "horns" or using the incestuous expressions with enough seriousness may also lead to murder. It is this subtle distinction of style and context which differentiates Neapolitan patterns from those found in association with lineage systems where there are more formalized distinctions between those kin relationships which permit joking or obscenity, and those which do not because they are based on respect.[7] But the essential point is that the frequency of obscenity as used by men is such that one might talk of any positive value as reversible into a potential negative one; the reversibility relation is in turn confirmed by the particular content choices.

A second index of the same oppositional or skeptical trend is found in the style of masculine behavior and in social interaction within the male peer group. From adolescence on, an important segment of male life takes place on the street corner, at the bar, or in the club setting which at least psychologically is quite separate from either the home or the church. But in this setting in contrast to the other two, it is masculine values which

---

[6] Women may in quarrelling with each other call each other prostitutes, but without reference to incest. They may also substitute euphemisms for actual curse words, such as *mannaggia alla marina,* literally "curse the seashore" for "curse the Madonna."

[7] See Radcliffe-Brown (1952:90–116). For the Trobriand Islands, obscene jokes are freely exchanged with the father's sisters but not with the mother's brother, and there are obscene expressions referring to mother, sister, and wife. Of these the most serious insult refers to sexual relations with the wife, a fact which is not quite congruent with the emphasis we have placed on the brother-sister taboo (see Malinowski 1927:104–108).

predominate over feminine ones. Not only are swearing and anticlerical joking characteristic, but most social interaction has a particular style which is partly humorous and partly cynical in quality; many features of both language and gesture point in the direction of skepticism. Moreover, attitudes toward all forms of higher authority, secular as well as religious, are far more negative than positive in emphasis. Much of this style has a ritualized quality to it, but again we have a further index of the reversibility in the masculine setting of values defined as positive in the feminine context. In addition, many male peer group patterns, in particular the emphasis on gambling and risk, are such that they provide a kind of counterpoint to the extreme emphasis on protection and security found in the Madonna complex.[8]

The second cultural complex which we will describe centers on courtship. Courtship is highly dramatized, and in the very important tradition of Neapolitan drama one can find over and over again the same plot: girl meets boy, this is kept secret from the family, or in particular from the father, father finds out (by catching them or by gossip from others), there is a big fight in which the girl or the fiancé stands up for the couple's rights against the father, father gives in at last, and here the play ends. Sometimes there are attempts on the part of the parents to marry a daughter to an old and ugly man for reasons of *interesse* or financial gain, but they are apt to be frustrated and never go without protest from the daughter. Says Rita in the early nineteenth-century play *Anella* when her father tries to marry her off to a rich but effeminate rag dealer:

> You can cut me up piece by piece, but that Master Cianno, I'll never take him. Poor me! Even if I had found him while Vesuvius was erupting, I wouldn't have gone near him. If I weren't your daughter but your worst enemy, even then I wouldn't think of marrying that sort of man. What sort of life would it be? (Davino 1957:125.)

The same play also serves to point up the very high degree with which courtship is romanticized and the particularly humble and

---

[8] See Vaillant (1958), Whyte (1943), and Zola (1963) for descriptions of relevant patterns.

Is the Oedipus Complex Universal?

supplicative position attributed to the young man. The following dialogue is addressed to Anella, standing in the balcony, by her suitor, Meniello:

> What sleep, what rest! What sleep, what rest can I have if I am in love, and the man in love is worse off than the man who is hanging on a rope and as soon as he gets a bit jealous, then the cord tightens. What sleep, the minute I close my eyes from exhaustion, jealousy makes me see my Anella up on her balcony surrounded by a crowd of lovers all looking up at her from below . . . what sort of sleep can you look for. And the worst of all is that I haven't even any hope of getting out of torment because I can't even ask her mother to give her to me as a wife because my dog's destiny made it happen that just to make a baker's dozen her mother is in love with me, too. You see what terrible things can happen in this world to torment a poor man in love!
>
> (Anella appears) Oh, Menie, is that you?
>
> (Meniello) Oh, beautiful one of my heart!
>
> (Anella) What on earth is wrong? I haven't even dressed yet, and you are up already. Why on earth are you so early? (op. cit.: 118–19).

The dialogue continues between Meniello's supplications and Anella's much more self-assured and often more mundane reassurances against his jealousy.

Courtship is not only a theme of popular drama; it is also one of the major topics of conversation and joking in everyday life. In one sense, the social norms surrounding it are very strict, in that there are patterns of chaperonage, parents have many active rights of control, and the whole area is surrounded with an aura of taboo. Above all, it is considered highly important that the young girl keep her virginity until she is able to stand in church in the white veil which symbolizes it. Thus, there is a very sharp polar distinction between the good woman and the bad woman, the virgin and the prostitute. The assumptions underlying courtship are linked up in turn with a metaphorical image from which one can derive many specific customs and sayings: in a similar bipolar fashion, the home is defined as safe, feminine, and asexual, while the street is defined as inherently dangerous, tempting, and freely accessible only to men. Thus, a woman of the streets is one who has violated the taboos and in a sense has taken over masculine prerogatives. Coming into the girl's home is a very crucial step in legitimate courtship (popular terminology distinguishes between the often quite casual "so-so engaged" or "engaged in secret," and the more formalized "engaged in the house," i.e., with parental knowledge and approval), and the doorway occupies a particular strategic intermediary position. Young girls usually become very excitable and giggly when they have the occasion for a promenade, and street phobias are a very common neurotic symptom in Italian women.

But a second aspect of the courtship complex is that in spite of the apparent strictness violations continually occur nevertheless, and the whole topic is treated with a particular kind of humorous ambiguity. Thus, while sexual matters are never referred to in serious or "objective" ways in everyday conversation, in a teasing or joking way they are an almost continuous focus of social exchange. The actual atmosphere or attitudes created by the strictness are far from puritan; it is rather as if the mothers and aunts and cousins who watch over the young girl with terrible threats about what will happen if she is "bad" are at the same time very much enjoying the possibility with her. One might by analogy to the many primitive societies in which there is a polar distinction between social relationships based on teasing or joking and those which are based on seriousness or formal respect, distinguish along the same lines between the Madonna complex and the courtship complex. For this reason, the distinction between the good woman and the bad woman is not as absolute as it might seem; often these may be alternative asexual and sexual images for the same woman, as when a father in anger calls his daughter a prostitute because she has come in late.

However, there is one point at which the sacred and the profane come together, and this is at the point of marriage, which almost without exception is symbolized by a church ceremony. Thus, while courtship is a secular process and while the idea of violation of chaperonage norms is often treated with humor, its more serious aim is nevertheless that it should end up in church with the young girl being able to stand "in front of the Madonna" in a white veil.[9] At the same time, marriage for the man symbolizes a kind of capitulation to the feminine religious complex, whose importance is denied in the male peer group setting by the pattern of sarcasm and secularization. In contrast to the girl, whatever prior sexual entanglements he has had lack significance. Thus, while at least in peasant areas even today the girl's "honor" may be verified by relatives after the wedding night, the whole question is seen as simply irrelevant on the sexual plane as far as men are concerned: said one informant, "How would anyone ever know if a man had it or not?"

There is, nevertheless, a sense in which the idea of honor is relevant to masculine identity as well as feminine. This is that the task of chaperonage is seen by the father (or brother) as a matter of maintaining his personal honor as well as the collective honor of the family. Thus, if a girl falls into disgrace, it will be said that the family honor has been lost, or that her father is also a *disgraziato* or lacking in grace. Moreover, whenever insults are cast at female kin, as in the oaths which reflect on the purity of mother, sister, daughter, or wife, the man is expected to consider this as a violation of his own personal integrity and to immediately come to their defense—in some instances with a knife. There are areas where the violation of the honor of a daughter or sister can lead to socially approved homicide, necessary to the defense of the family honor. This pattern is particularly characteristic of Sicily, where the brother's role is more important than in Naples. In eighteenth- and nineteenth-century Naples the task of protecting the honor of slum women was taken over by the Camorra, the most highly organized form reached by the Neapolitan underworld, which was not averse to using knives in order to force a reluctant man who had violated virginity into marriage.

We can now try to sum up some of the respective implications of the courtship complex and the Madonna complex as two contrasting sides of a global cultural pattern. One of these we have seen as a joking pattern and the other as a pattern of serious respect and desexualization, although the two meet and cross each other in the male peer group rebellion against the Madonna and in the culmination of legitmate courtship in the church

---

[9] Voluntary abstention from public church ceremony sometimes occurs when wearing the veil would be a shame in front of the Madonna.

wedding. The symbol that unites them is that of virginity, or an initial asexual image of femininity that can only be violated in the appropriate social circumstances. These contrasting but interdependent patterns in themselves give us some of the elements of a distinctive nuclear complex; the two most important elements are that of the sublimated respect of children for the ideal mother and that of the game in which erotic temptations continually come into clash with this image of feminine purity. In the latter context, the most important actors, as Neapolitan drama would suggest, are the girl, her father, and the prospective son-in-law. The key value is that of virginity or honor, and the father seeks to preserve it against all comers; it is here that we can look for a distinctive triangular situation.

Family Structure

At this point, we can turn to the more direct consideration of the family. We noted earlier that the primary unit is the nuclear family but that it is embedded in a larger kin group, and there is a high degree of continuity to the mother-child tie. The family is close in a certain sense, at least in that family ties and obligations outweigh all others, but family life is also characterized by a great deal of aggression and conflict. One way in which conflict is handled is by various patterns for the separation of roles, a result of which is the extrafamilial male peer group. After marriage, as well as before, many of the man's needs for comradeship and mutuality continue to be filled by the male peer group and much of the time he is out of the home. The woman, on the other hand, continues in close daily exchange with her natal family (perhaps less in the city than in the villages, and neighbors may also be important) so that many needs for mutual sympathy are fulfilled by mother and sisters or by other women. The division of the sexes is such that the marriage relationship is not often a focus of continuous intimate or reciprocal affective exchange. After the courtship phase and the honeymoon, it more often than not becomes very conflictual, principally because of the emotional ties which both partners retain to the natal family.

Is the Oedipus Complex Universal?

In actual fact, of course, there are a great many varied families as well as the noted regional variations; however, many of the observable norms and patterns can be interpreted from the above structural givens. For example, there is a variety of possible balances to the husband-wife versus primary family conflict. For Naples, the most common type of residence is in the vicinity of the wife's family, but the husband as an individual is likely to maintain important contacts with his own. Sometimes the couple together becomes assimilated into one family or another; women, for example, who have had particularly unfavorable relations with their own families, or who have lost a mother by death, are more likely to accept the mother-in-law as a mother surrogate, thus achieving a better relationship with her than is generally expected. The same may happen in the case of the man who marries into a fatherless family or one consisting of girls alone who may take over male roles in that family with relative success. This is unlikely if there are competing figures. Quarrels concerning where the couple should reside are very common, and they are accompanied by a great deal of mutual projection; thus, a man may complain that his wife is much too dependent on her mother and pays little attention to him, and then suggest as a solution to the problem that they move to the house next door to his mother. In extreme cases the two families may end up with quite violent feelings about each other; in studying schizophrenic patients, we found this to be common, and many marriages, while maintained in form, actually dissolved with each partner returning to his own home. The uncertainties of the conflict are intensified by the fact that in contrast to many simpler societies, there are no fixed rules of choice or subordination. A result of this uncertainty is that in situations of choice and conflict, it is more often the feminine point of view than the masculine one which prevails, since it is the woman who in daily life is most concerned with and most emotionally involved in matters pertaining to the family.

It is also the mother who is the primary personage in maintaining family unity, and many results of this can be observed; for example, ties with father or siblings are very likely to break up or become more distant on the death of the mother. Another consequence is seen in differential attitudes toward the remarriage of widows and in differing consequences of the death of parents. If a man is left without a wife, it is taken for granted that he will need a woman, and whether or not he has children, he is likely to find one, though often outside of legal sanction. Thus, many persons who have widower fathers simply state that they have drifted off somewhere, and the ties are no longer very real. On the other hand, a widow or a woman deserted by her husband may be condemned if she seeks alternative sexual attachments before her children marry; it is assumed that her primary loyalty is to them. Marriage, which in Naples is likely to take place either in the late teens or not until the late twenties or thirties, often in this latter instance follows very closely on the death of the parents. Remarriages when both partners have children are often conflictual on the grounds that each prefers his own offspring, and the stepmother is seen as in the Cinderella legend. She may do her best by the children, but even then the tie is never the same; the best possible solution to the loss of a mother is seen to be adoption by the mother's sister, who, because related by blood, will come much closer to fulfilling the maternal role. Marriage to the deceased wife's sister is not uncommon in the case of widowers, though practiced more in rural than in urban areas.

The importance of the mother-child tie as the axis of family structure is seen in some additional patterns characteristic of lower-class Naples. Where illegitimacy occurs, the child is legally recognized and brought up by the mother in about 50 per cent of the cases; such status is not formally approved but it does occur.[10] Fathers very rarely recognize illegitimate children, but there are, on the other hand, certain forms of semi-institutionalized polygamy, according to which a father may have two distinctive families, one of which is legal while the other is not. In contrast to the pattern of the affair where it is assumed that if the relationship is not socially sanctioned, precautions will be taken to avoid reproduction, it seems that aside from prostitu-

[10] Of the illegitimate children born in Naples in 1956, 51 per cent were legally recognized by the mother alone, as compared with 9 per cent by the father alone, 10 per cent by both parents, and 29 per cent remaining unrecognized. See Office of Statistics of the Commune of Naples (1959: 22).

Is the Oedipus Complex Universal?

tion it is usually assumed that children are the necessary and wanted consequence of any sexual relationship; thus, the rapid multiplication which often characterizes monogamous families also characterizes polygamous ones.

The major requirement for a husband is that he be able to feed and support his family. However, in the urban working class, it very often happens that he is not able to fulfill this task; thus, one common source of arguments is that the husband has not brought in any money. It is also the case in urban areas where the married woman often works in her own right; for example, women may be street vendors, artisans, domestics, etc. At the lower socioeconomic levels it is often the woman who has a better opportunity of earning money than the man. She is more motivated to work since she more willingly accepts a low-prestige or low-reward position because of concern for children, while for the man, peer group relationships or a kind of pseudo identification with the higher status groups offers a more immediately rewarding proof of masculinity. One of the primary symbols of peer group belongingness in Naples is the ability to offer food or drink to others, so that the man is faced with an inherent conflict in that what he spends to gain status in relation to other men is bread lost out of his children's mouths. Thus, a vicious circle may be set in motion in which the wife accuses the husband of irresponsibility, and the husband in turn goes off in anger and tries to recapture his self-esteem by taking risks at cards or by treating his friends to coffee. It is, moreover, the way of dealing with this situation which differentiates male relationships with wives and mothers; the mother, if she has anything at all, will give it to her son, but the wife expects the husband to hand everything over to her in the interests of the children. Thus, financial conflicts are one factor which can push a married man back to ask for support at home.

A second factor is the degree to which intrafamily behavior is characterized by rivalry between husband and children for the attention of the mother in her food-giving role. One symbolization of the difference between South Italian society and the more truly patriarchal Victorian one can be found in the nature of eating patterns and their relation to family social structure; in contrast to the regular ritualized mealtimes of the Victorian epoch, with father taking a commanding position at the head of the table, there is a highly irregular eating pattern (space often makes a regular dinner table impossible) in which each member of the family may eat according to his own preference at his own time, but in which the mother is almost continually involved in the process of feeding. In this structure the superior position of the father, and of sons as they grow up, is symbolized by the right to demand what they want and the right to complain if not pleased. When a man complains, the woman will try to do what she can, and as long as she has anything at all, she will give it; but the pattern also puts the husband on an equal subordinate basis with his children.

Thus, the ties to the primary family, the high significance of the maternal role, and the very great difficulties in making a living which characterize most of the working-class groups are such that in spite of appearances the husband and father does not actually enjoy much prestige or authority in the home. From this standpoint the male peer group can be seen as an escape; the man who gets totally "fed up" always has the possibility of leaving. Likewise, many of the male rage reactions, which give the impression that the Italian family is patriarchal, though much more stylized, have the quality of the child who throws his plate on the floor when he has had enough. Moreover, many of the status-gaining activities of the peer group can be seen as identifications with the feminine feeding role, for example, the high importance attributed to offering food or coffee. However, a second aspect of the masculine role in the home and its relations to sex segregation should not be neglected. This is that male rage may be seen as truly terrifying to women, so that kicking men out becomes necessary, and this goes with an image of masculinity as a kind of threatening force which is a disruptive factor in the feminine circle; images used in daily conversation clearly suggest the idea of phallic intrusion.

A few details on socialization can serve to round out the picture of family life. Children become a center of attention as soon as they are born and receive a great deal of physical handling which does not undergo systematic interruption; moreover, as they are weaned, substitute gratifications are provided so there is no significant discontinuity ending the oral phase of develop-

Is the Oedipus Complex Universal?

ment. However, it would be a mistake to conclude from this that they simply receive that much more of the "security" and maternal warmth which are currently so highly valued in the United States. In the first place, the mother may give little attention to any individual child, being busy and often having many; moreover, maternal behavior (in the sense of giving food and physical caresses) is so widespread that in actual social reality the maternal attachment is far from being exclusive. Rather, one might say that the circle of maternal objects progressively widens to include the family as a whole and in many respects strangers; along with this goes the learning of certain kinds of politeness and formality having to do with eating and giving.

In the second, handling of children is often very rough and unsubtle and includes a very high aggressive component.[11] As physical motility appears, it can be systematically frustrated by anxious adults who immediately bring back the wandering or assertive child to thrust a cookie into his mouth; one can see here the beginning of the forced feeding pattern which characterizes moments of tension in the family throughout life. An illustrative example concerns a three-year-old son of a gardener who picked up his father's tools and was immediately called back by mother with the tacit support of father. Children at this age may show considerable diffuse aggressivity and put on an unnatural amount of weight. Later, most of them learn to "talk back" with verbal rhetoric and gesture; these important components of South Italian culture might be seen as developed in counterreaction to muscular inhibition in that they become a major means for expressing individuality. A second relevant example concerns an eighteen-month-old girl who seemed hardly interested in learning to walk and was not yet able to talk; yet, held by her father she was able to perform fairly complex symbolic operations with her hands, such as snapping her fingers ten times when asked to count to ten.

For these early phases there seems to be little difference between the handling of the small girl and of the small boy, with

---

[11] It is roughest among the poorest and here also may be quite erotically stimulating as well. I am indebted to Vincenzo Petrullo for the suggestion that this latter may be the case because when children have to go hungry, erotic stimulation may be a means of maintaining their interest in life.

the single exception that the small boy is more likely to go unclothed from the waist down and to have his penis singled out for teasing admiration.[12] This open phallic admiration is characteristic of the behavior of mothers to sons, and in teasing intrafamily behavior the genital organs may be poked or referred to with provocative gestural indications. Children may also share beds with their parents or with each other even at advanced ages (crowding often makes this necessary)[13] though precautions are taken to prevent their observing parental intercourse. One young man was asked what he would do if he saw this; the answer was "I would kill them." Except for small children, modesty taboos are very strict, and while physical proximity within the family is very close with respect to anything except genital activity, this latter is surrounded with some secrecy.

There are, however, two crucial points at which sex difference is more prominent. The first is in the ritual of First Communion which ideally takes place at the age of six or seven. Around this age the growing attractiveness of the little girl is the focus of considerable teasing admiration from father or older brothers, uncles, etc., though these have not taken much interest in the very small child. One Neapolitan informant, for example, told me how his seven-year-old daughter had taken to getting into bed with him in such a seductive way that he finally had to slap her and kick her out. It did not surprise him in the least when I said that a famous Viennese doctor had made quite a bit out of this sort of thing. However, once the small girl's oedipal affects have been excited to this degree, it is also necessary that the culture find a resolution for them which it does in the ritual of First Communion; the small girl is dressed as a miniature bride, and at this point it must be impressed on her fantasy that she must delay fulfillment of her wishes until such a time as she can again appear in church in a white veil. Thus, a particularly elaborate cultural symbolization is provided for feminine oedipal wishes.

For the boy, on the other hand, there is much less in the way of such cultural elaboration of the Oedipus crisis, nor for that

---

[12] This pattern is even more characteristic of Puerto Rico (see Wolf 1952), where sex differences in modesty rules are also sharper.

[13] I know of examples of mothers sharing beds with adult sons, and also of a case of a mother who lost a child in infancy whereupon she asked a thirteen-year-old son to take the milk from her breast; he however, refused on the grounds that "she was my mother and I was ashamed."

Is the Oedipus Complex Universal?

matter is there any ritual symbolization of masculine status at adolescence, as there is in many other cultures where socialization at earlier stages is so exclusively in the hands of women. First Communion does take place, but masculine emphasis and degree of symbolization is simply less. Moreover, in many ways the boy's position at home is much more passive than that of the girl; the beautiful warm-eyed docility which one can observe in many boys in the Neapolitan slums might make for the envy of the American mother in the Hopalong Cassidy phase. The same degree of aggressive tension does not appear to be present, nor for that matter is there as much elaboration of the phallic "I want to be when I grow up" type of fantasy. What does differentiate the small boy from the girl is, first, the open admiration which may be shown for his purely sexual masculine attributes, and second, the fact that he has much less in the way of home responsibility and is in many ways favored by the mother; but since the father is so often out of the home, his socialization is placed in feminine hands almost as much as that of the girl.

In other words, while cultural ritual can be seen as providing a complex symbolic framework for feminine oedipal wishes, this is not true in the case of the boy, who may receive special privileges and an open acknowledgement of his physical masculinity, but no such elaborate social symbolization of it. Presumably, this should result in much stronger motivation for the delay of sexual wishes in girls than in boys. This kind of differential in turn becomes extremely important in adolescence, at which point the pattern of sex differentiation becomes a much sharper one, for it is then that chaperonage rules begin to apply to the girl, and the boy in turn acquires a special freedom to move out into the inherently dangerous and sexualized world of the street.[14] It is at this latter point that the prerogative of adult masculinity crystallizes, especially with respect to the quasi taboo on feminine inquisitions concerning masculine activities which take place outside the home.

---

[14] Boys are of course outside earlier too, the actual age and amount of time depending on the specific social milieu. The street gang in the slums may include girls and in some groups much of the family income may come from small boys. The important fact is the lack of any very formalized masculine authority over the boy.

Conclusions

We began, with reference to the Jones-Malinowski debate, by considering the possibility that each culture is characterized by a distinctive nuclear complex whose roots lie in its family structure. Our subsequent task has been to pull together various orders of data concerning Southern Italy in such a way as to portray such a nuclear complex which differs both from the brother-sister-sister's son triangle characteristic of the Trobriand Island and from the patriarchal complex isolated by Freud. In the South Italian data we have found that two cultural complexes, the sacred one centered on respect for the feminine Madonna figure and the secular joking pattern surrounding courtship and embodied in popular drama, also have their reflections in the actual patterning of family life and childhood experience and in the intrapsychic life of the individual as seen in projective tests. It is this continuity which has led us to the conclusion that it is possible to define a single global complex which can be perceived simultaneously either as intrapsychic or as collective, the representations which are passed on from generation to generation on the social level coming to be internalized in the individual in the form of representations of the self in relation to objects. The task which remains is the more precise summary of the outlines of the South Italian nuclear complex, comparing it with Freud's patriarchal one, and the drawing out of some more general implications with respect to research methodology and application.

Our principal supposition is that the two most significant among the biologically given family relationships are those between mother and son and between father and daughter. In the former instance the son occupies a subordinate position in the sense that authority stemming from the mother is fully internalized, and violations of it are subjectively sensed as inducing guilt, in comparison to the father-son relation where the son may openly express hostility or rebellion in such a way as to put the father in a negative light. In other words, respect for the mother is much stronger than respect for the father. We do not mean by this to

Is the Oedipus Complex Universal? 381

say that women dominate in any simple sense, since it is evident that many other taboos, such as the barring of feminine interference in areas of activity defined as masculine ones, act against this result, not to mention the open admiration and permissiveness which women usually show toward the masculinity of their sons. However, in many ways the mother-son relationship is qualitatively different from that of our own society or that of Freud, most notably in the continuation throughout life of what might be referred to as an oral dependent tie, i.e., a continual expectation of maternal solace and giving rather than a gradual or sudden emancipation from it.

It is this fact that might lead an American observer to speak of an "oral" culture, or one based on feeding as the dominant mode of libidinal interaction, in contrast to a hypothetical "anal" or "phallic" based one. However, this type of formulation we would consider quite inadequate both with respect to theory and the empirical facts. It is evident that types of interaction based on the exchange of gifts and food do have an extremely important role, though these result in very complex types of adult interaction which can by no means be derived directly from infantile roots. More important, however, is the theoretical postulate which would lead us to believe that the phallic phase of development nevertheless occurs. In other words, although he may not give up oral types of gratification, the boy nevertheless passes through a phase at which the wishes he experiences toward the mother are sexual and masculine in nature, and that, moreover, this phase will be associated with aggressive reactions against the subordinate feeding position. We can then trace some of the implications of these postulates rather than simply stopping with the "oral culture" formulation.

In this perspective we can better see some of the more general consequences of the fact that the masculine role is so little emphasized within the home and that cultural values center on the feminine image. From the genetic standpoint, we might say that while oral gratifications do not have to be renounced (although they do come to take more complex social forms), this is not true with respect to phallic and aggressive wishes toward the mother; these in fact must systematically undergo repression as they arise. In fact, to characterize the relation to the mother as one based on respect, in social language, is exactly the same thing as to say in psychodynamic language that sexual and aggressive wishes cannot be expressed directly. We then can ask what happens to these wishes, assuming that in some form they persist, and arrive at three kinds of formulation, each of which is relevant to the understanding of culture patterns. Through all of them the important contrast with Freud's formulation lies in the greater continuity of the relationship with the mother and the lesser continuity of that with the father.

First, referring back to the concept of the symbol as arising in precisely those areas where a culture both exploits (by actual affective closeness) and inhibits (by imposing of taboos) primary drives, we can say that the erotic wishes of the son toward the mother come to be sublimated, and it is precisely this fact which gives rise to the representation of the Madonna figure. Moreover, in her characteristics we can see both derivatives of the actual cultural reality, e.g., in that the dependent relationship of the penitent to the maternal figure is preserved, and some unrealizable aspects of fantasy, e.g., in that the Madonna became a mother without being a wife. This latter is, moreover, the characteristic which in itself represents oedipal repression, in that the Madonna is perceived as an asexual maternal figure. But in addition, and in contrast to the "oral culture" view which might say simply that mothers are more permissive, the Madonna is a "superego" figure; she could not be forgiving if she did not have a concept of sins which have to be forgiven. In this perspective we can say that oedipal wishes are repressed in such a way as to give rise to an internalized representation of the tabooed object, who then comes to play the role of conscience. However, the complication in this case is that the internalized object is in the case of men a feminine one; it is this which we mean by speaking of a matriarchal rather than a patriarchal "superego." What it leads to then is a masculine identification with a set of cultural values identifiable as feminine, or even as very concretely perceived according to a feminine body image. The most important of these is the respect for virginity, shared by men and women alike and manifested in the courtship taboos on entering the home of the girl who is sought before the relation is formalized. The identification of the girl

Is the Oedipus Complex Universal?

who is legitimately courted with the idealized mother is seen in the similar submissive relation adopted by the male; the infantile wishes underlying the image of the pure woman are also seen in a sometimes extreme degree of defensiveness concerning the issue of whether or not the purity is real and to be believed.

Second, however, impulses which are repressed can also be dealt with by displacement. It is in this respect that the significance of the masculine peer group and the definition of the sphere of life outside of the home, i.e., the sum total of masculinity as defined by the rebellion pattern which we have discussed, become apparent. Many of the patterns of the outside peer group are distinctively phallic in nature. Moreover, in many more concrete senses one can conceive of the outside world as the focus for aggressive and phallic wishes which must be displaced outside the home, e.g., the common situation of the male in anger who simply picks up and leaves, or the great importance of cursing. Thus, aggression which arises within the home may be dealt with by displacement outside it. One characteristic of the Madonna is that she is an ideal figure; ordinary mothers of course rarely approach her, in that they may not forgive, they may very often get angry or impatient, or they may in fact dominate in a very aggressively matriarchal way and in this event the recourse of the male is the privilege of exit. Women in turn support this form of expression of masculinity by respecting the taboo on interference and often by direct admiration and encouragement of even delinquent extrafamilial activities. In addition, anger which arises in a mother-son relationship conceived of as exclusive in fantasy may also be dealt with in a complex series of intrafamilial rivalries and jealousies within which the affective consequence of reality frustration vis-à-vis the mother may be expressed with respect to other family objects. Thus, displacement both within and outside the family is used to deal with aggressive impulses whose direct expression toward the mother is tabooed.

Third, erotic wishes may be displaced as well as aggressive ones, and it is here that we can find the source of the bipolar distinction between the good woman and the bad woman. The contrary image to the Madonna is, of course, that of the prostitute, and the close intertwining of the two images is seen at a great many points, e.g., in the obscenity patterns that reverse the values of feminine purity and in the family quarrels where even closely associated women may be accused of promiscuous impulses. The persistence of the early sublimations in later life is manifested in two crucial assumptions: first, that the sexualized woman may be appreciated in a naturalistic way but she is always perceived as on a lower spiritual plane than the pure one; and second, the idea of sexuality is almost inevitably associated with the possibility of betrayal and pluralization of the relationship, i.e., in that wives, sweethearts, and mistresses are continually suspected by men of wanting other partners than themselves as soon as the idea of sexuality comes into play.

It is facts such as these which lead us to postulate an underlying and persistent fantasy of an exclusive maternal object as a theoretical assumption. Because of repression, we cannot, of course, acquire direct information concerning the sexual aspect in most cases. One particularly important area of research, however, is found in schizophrenic cases where one may see gross breakdowns of cultural sublimations. One of two South Italian schizophrenic men whom I have seen intensively showed the sexual aspect of the mother-son relationship and the associated Madonna complex in a very transparent form: having many religious delusions; while praying to the Madonna he had open and bizarre erotic experiences and he was unable to distinguish consistently between maternal and erotic objects. The early history was probably one in which prolonged nursing merged into the awakening of genital feelings. However, the second case points up the need for care in separating local and individual variations from global patterns. Coming from a mountainous area where patriarchal patterns and a lack of sentimentality are more typical, the patient showed a much more autistic form of pathology of which the most conspicuous elements were warded-off homosexuality and an extremely submissive identification with the father. He rejected the breast of a wet nurse at an early age, and a crucial traumatic experience was a childhood seduction by an older brother.

One consequence of such a relationship, which fits many of the data we have concerning the South Italian family, is that it acts against social mobility in the broadest sense of the term by making for a very strong centripetal tendency. In other words, if a key axis of family structure is the relationship between mother and son, and if this relationship tends to maintain itself by the preservation of an infantile fantasy which is then dealt with by a complex series of social sublimations and displacements, rather than by attenuating its significance by dispersal or replacement by other objects, then we should have no theoretical basis for explaining the formation of new families. Rather we should expect each mother-son combination to simply continue until the death of the mother; the incest taboo alone does not seem sufficient for explaining the process of change, since nothing in South Italian norms prevents the adult son from obtaining immediate sexual gratification outside while continuing to occupy the emotionally more important position of son. It is at this point that we might turn to the examination of the father-daughter relationship, which can be seen as complementary to the mother-son one in defining a total structure.

The most important difference between these two lies in the dimension of continuity. The father is not continually and lovingly interested in his daughter as the mother is in her son, but rather his interest becomes particularly important at two points in the daughter's life history: the oedipal phase and the courtship phase. At both of these points the father is highly sensitive to the daughter's femininity, and the daughter is given considerable scope for exploiting this sensitivity in what is often a very active way. Moreover, while the taboo on incest between mother and son is as in all societies a very deep-lying one, it is very easy to come to the conclusion that the desexualization of the father-daughter relationship is not nearly as complete. Thus, in particular in instances where the mother has died, father-daughter incest is not an unheard of phenomenon and the possibility may be referred to even rather casually, as in the many stories about "that case in our village" that go around. In an American setting an openly incestuous perception might be taken as an indication of serious pathology, but we have no reason to believe this was the case for our informants. Their counterpart in the normal case where the taboo is preserved is found in the teasing behavior or embarrassed avoidance which characterizes the relation between the father and the sexually mature daughter or in the giggling embarrassment which women associate with the idea of being found out in their love relationships.

In other words, the incestuous impulses in the father-daughter relationship are quite close to the surface, in such a way that we might speak of a lesser degree of repression than is implied in Freud's concept of the Oedipus complex. There is of course a taboo but one might well speak of a persistence of the incestuous impulses on a preconscious level in such a way that they are openly expressed in cultural idiom, as in the frequent use of the word jealousy to describe the father's feelings about the daughter's suitors, and transformed into the joking pattern which is characteristic of the courtship complex.

The major significance of the triangle involving father, daughter, and prospective son-in-law, moreover, lies in the fact that it is to a much greater extent with respect to the daughter than to the wife or mother that the man plays an active role. When he himself is courting, he has to beg at the balcony for a well-protected woman whose virginity he has to respect, but in the case of his own daughter it is he who does the protecting and whose consent has to be sought by the prospective suitor. Thus, the most fully institutionalized masculine role in Southern Italy, one which is defined positively and not by rebellion, is that of the protection of the honor of the women who are tabooed. In turn, if the sexual affects felt toward these are quite close to the surface, considerable fantasy satisfaction must take place in a way which is active and masculine in contrast to the mother-son relationship, which in so many ways spreads into the marital one, where the male role is passive.

But in addition it is in the father-daughter relationship that we can find a mechanism of change which acts against the centrifugal family tendency. The courtship situation not only gives the father an active role but also has a particular affective style, namely, that of a sudden explosion in which erotic impulses break out with a dramatic intensity which suggests some underlying dynamic force. Moreover, in spite of the chaperonage norms, the behavior of young women at this point is not such as to suggest much innocence or ignorance of sexuality; they just as well as the young men seem propelled to rebel against the taboos, and they are very often teasers. We have also com-

Is the Oedipus Complex Universal?

mented at length on the ambivalent nature of the taboos themselves, in that while violations may be severely condemned explicitly, it often seems as if they were just as much encouraged. It almost seems as if the entire pattern of restriction and parental control were a kind of cultural fiction whose actual purpose is to cover something else; this is what we mean in characterizing it as a joking pattern.

In this perspective it is not at all difficult to postulate that much of the actual source of tension lies in the socially exploited incestuous tie between father and daughter. Thus, the South Italian girl does not appear as inhibited or naïve for precisely the reason that even though carefully kept away from outside men, she has in a great many indirect ways been treated as a sexual object by father (and brothers or other male relatives) both at puberty and during the oedipal crisis. Within the family the incestuous tension may be handled by joking (or avoidance[15]), but to the extent that the wishes generated seek a biological outlet, the daughter has to seek an object outside of the family—and the father has to rid himself of a woman whom he perceives as very desirable but cannot possess. We would then say that it is the strength of the incestuous wishes which accounts for the dramatic and explosive quality of the courtship situation; and the father-daughter relation, by accentuating incestuous tension and at the same time by imposing a taboo, acts as a kind of spring mechanism which running counter to the strong centripetal forces inherent in the mother-son tie has sufficient force as to cause the family unit to fly apart, resulting in the creation of a new one. In this context the insufficiency of the oral culture view again becomes apparent

One can then see the father's role in defending the honor of the daughter as the masculine counterpart of the Madonna identification; the father's incestuous impulses are sublimated in the active role which he plays toward the daughter in competition with her suitor. Since the sexual wishes cannot be fulfilled, the symbolic assertion of authority is much more important than the

---

[15] Casual joking and teasing between men and women within the family is characteristic of urban areas; in some country ones (where courtship taboos may be taken more seriously), there is more likely to be embarrassed avoidance, or *vergogna* (shame), between father and daughter.

actual outcome, a consideration which can explain the ritualized nature of the father's control over courtship and the gracefulness with which he eventually backs down. As the street vendor stated, his real wish is for his daughter's happiness, but in order to show that he is a man he has to be able to demonstrate the power he has over her, and over the still subordinate prospective son-in-law. The principal means he has at his disposal for doing this is by being obstinate in such a way as to increase the excitement of the drama—of which one could say the most important member of the audience for him is the daughter. Likewise, the complementary wishes of the daughter are sublimated in the pleasure which she experiences over the fact of being controlled, a pleasure which is evident in the courtship descriptions of women, however much they may verbally express resentment or rebellion. Moreover, just as the Madonna fantasy provides a feminine identity for men, so the courtship complex provides masculine modes of expression for women, in that in participating in an active teasing pattern the daughter may also identify with the father, as seen in the great importance which women attribute to their own capacity to make a stand in front of him which demonstrates that they really want a suitor.

In other words, while the mother-son tie acts primarily as a centrifugal one, in that it maintains itself in such a way as to make for an unbroken continuity of the primary family, the father-daughter tie acts in the inverse sense in that the incestuous tension, being much closer to the surface, has to seek an external outlet so that a kind of spring mechanism is generated. The two together make up a viable structure which can be differentiated from our own on two counts: first, it emphasizes the romantic cross-sex ties within the family far more than same-sex identifications, and second, it preserves incestuous fantasies in such a way that they may never be fully replaced by the actually sexual husband-wife relationship. Thus, though courtship is based on the idea of individual romantic love, this latter does not appear as a prelude to an intimate emotional interdependence between husband and wife, but rather as a temporary suspension of an equilibrium in which intergenerational ties are in the long run more significant. One might say that after the wedding the supplicant suitor returns in fantasy to his own

Is the Oedipus Complex Universal?

mother, and at the same time comes increasingly to resent the maternal aspects of his wife in such a way that he is again driven outside, much as in adolescence. The wife on the other hand may experience a parallel disillusion when she discovers that the husband is not the father of fantasy, and she comes increasingly to transfer her own affective needs to her son, and so the pattern repeats itself. The husband will of course have a reawakened interest in the family later, namely, when he has a daughter.[16] Thus, on both sides, it is having children, and in particular children of the opposite sex, which provides the principal affective source of commitment to the family.

We have up to this point given little systematic attention to the mother-daughter and father-son relationships, which we have conceived of as having a lesser cultural significance than the cross-sex pairs. This is, of course, not to say that they are inexistent or unimportant; but what we mean by a lesser cultural significance might come out more clearly if we draw a few brief contrasts with our own society and with the Oedipus complex as formulated by Freud.

The TAT responses for the mother-daughter card indicate a pattern that is quite classic in that the daughter appears to internalize maternal authority but she does so in an ambivalent way—contrasting with the romantic internalization found in the case of the son. Moreover, the actual mother-daughter relationship corresponds to that found in most societies; it is the mother who teaches the daughter the routine techniques of daily life. However, an additional feature of the TAT responses was that

---

[16] The importance of the father-daughter relationship becomes particularly apparent when we contrast South Italian patterns with those seen in other cultural groups where the rule is the matrifocal family, in which there is no stable husband-wife attachment and the only constant relation is between mother and child. The matrifocal family (found throughout the Caribbean and among working-class American Negroes) seems regularly to appear where masculine identity cannot be easily maintained on the basis of some real occupational achievement. The same conditions hold in Southern Italy and should be seen as underlying the matriarchal trends which we have described; however, with a few exceptions the monogamous family is nevertheless maintained. But the active role which the father has vis-à-vis the daughter must be one of the primary reasons for this, a view which should be considered by social agencies that often too readily seek to save daughters from fathers whom they see as acting solely from cruelty.

the informants themselves often stated that "these counsels are not very important," implicitly by comparison with those given during the courtship phase. But this comment gives us the possibility of tying together one global feature of South Italian values with the family nuclear complex: utilitarian accomplishments, notably in contrast to Protestant value systems, simply do not receive much emphasis. As our society sees the Oedipus complex, its outcome is that the child gives up the sexual fantasies centered on the parent of the opposite six and then identifies with the parent of the same sex, whom he or she takes over as an ego ideal. Thus, the small girl wants to grow up to be a woman like her mother, and fantasies that when she is, then she too will have a husband, this depending on how well she learns to carry out womanly tasks. But in small girls or young women in Southern Italy there is remarkably little in the way of the ego ideal, or the superior person one hopes to emulate. The necessary tasks are taken for granted, but the affectively more important matter is not becoming something one is not yet but rather guarding something one has already, namely, virginity. This in turn can be related back to the fact that the infantile wish is dealt with to a greater extent by symbolic replacement (the First Communion enactment of the role of the bride) of the cross-sex fantasy than by identification with the same-sex parent. In other ways the mother-daughter relationship acts as a centrifugal force in much the same way as that between mother and son, and the two go together in defining a somewhat static social tendency rather than an active accomplishing one.

The father-son relationship on the other hand seems to constitute an unresolved cultural problem, a fact which may have roots in economic conditions which make continuity of identity from father to son through occupational or social achievement very difficult to attain, though the nature of the family may in turn help to create such conditions. It is in examining the father-son relationship that the contrast between South Italian patterns and those described by Freud becomes clearest. The TAT responses do indicate that the father may be perceived by the son as a judging or condemning figure. However, when we have said that this does not give rise to an internalized paternal superego figure, what we meant was that on the whole our male informants did not present any social values going beyond their immediate relationship which the father represents, e.g., according to a pattern of "well he was tough but he did it to teach me to act like a man." Moreover, although they were adult men, they identified with the son figure far more than the father, and they saw the outcome as a simple mutual antagonism in which the father accuses the son of delinquency but the son justifies himself and his own rebellion, rather than channeling the rebellious forces into any kind of sublimated form.

In other words, father-son hostility simply leads to fights and antagonism rather than being restrained in the interest of higher social goals or symbols. The clearest case in this respect was that of the street vendor, who very explicitly relates the kind of decreasing social energy with respect to occupation—for which he is one of a great many representatives—to a failure to solve the problem of antagonism with the father in any creative way. But for Freud, of course, the exact opposite is true: in perceiving the great importance which hostile wishes against the father on the part of sons may have in psychodynamics, he also provides a cultural resolution in his view of repressed father-son rivalry, and its many derivatives in adult life, as a dynamic which can underlie superior creative achievements—including his own creation of psychoanalysis which resulted from his reactions to the death of his father and the contemporaneous intellectual competition with Wilhelm Fleiss.

In this perspective it is possible to look at Freud's formulation of the Oedipus complex in its wider cultural context in such a way as to bring out some of the contrasts with the South Italian complex. First we might sum up some of the essential characteristics of the latter in such a way as to make a comparison possible. We have seen the mother-son relationship as the primary axis of family continuity and emphasized the degree to which the son maintains a dependent position vis-à-vis the mother, dealing with sexual and aggressive feelings in a variety of ways among the most important of which is an identification with the feminine values of purity; we have also brought out the extent to which the father-daughter relationship provides a counterpoint pattern by a failure to repress deeply the incestuous element. We have also noted that cross-sex relationships are emphasized more than same-sex ones and have suggested that this may build both romantic and conservative elements into the social structure, in that the strength of intergenerational ties wins out over individually formed ones and in that the cross-sex emphasis acts against the creation of ego ideals which the individual seeks to achieve. Both the conservative and feminine emphasis are summed up in the importance given to virginity as a social symbol: virginity is something which is given and not acquired and it is given to women and not to men.[17]

But in discussing the Oedipus complex Freud is quite explicit about the fact that oedipal wishes are given up in such a way as to be replaced by identifications with the same-sex parent; where this does not take place the resulting phenomena are seen as pathological. Moreover, his formulations start from the assumption that the primary factor is rivalry between father and son; these two struggle with each other for the possession of a woman whose background position is taken for granted, just as is that of Sarah who waited until the age of ninety-nine for a son with only one outbreak of skeptical laughter and then did not complain when Abraham took Isaac off as a sacrifice to a patriarchal God. And finally he assumes a very high degree of capacity for delay or sublimation which takes the form of an ability, based on identifications, to turn instinctual impulses into future-oriented creative achievement. This in turn in his own thinking primarily takes the form of masculine imagery, e.g., penetrating reality in the interests of scientific conquest and overcoming resistance, whether in patients or in any other facet of reality.

What differentiates his view of the father-son relationship is then the very high degree of sublimation which he assumes to characterize the conflict: identification with the father, in his view and in his own life, even if ambivalent, does not result in the kind of open hostility and decreasing social energy which we saw in the case of the street vendor, but rather in a complex

---

[17] At least from the South Italian perspective, where the body referent is very clear: as a humorous response to the assertion that Freud defines femininity in terms of a lack of masculinity, we could again refer to the Neapolitan informant who, when questioned about the double standard, replied, "But how could you ever tell if a man had lost it or not?"

Is the Oedipus Complex Universal?

identification with a continuing tradition. As opposed to the South Italian view, it is the feminine sphere which is the lower and more naturalistic one, while father-son conflict gives rise to the most complex social sublimations, e.g., the many intellectual ties based on a patriarchal model which characterize Freud's life. This is not to say that he was insensitive to other human possibilities—the work on hysteria, and in particular the paper on transference-love, bear witness to a kind of paternalistic but subtly seductive appreciation of women, in many ways a more sophisticated variant of the South Italian father-daughter pattern; and of course his fantasy view of Rome as a romantic opposite to the active competition of his Viennese life is well known. But it is hard to doubt that Freud was a patriarch with a patriarchal view of man.

The sources of his patriarchal bias can be seen as twofold: the first in the Hebraic tradition which, as discussed in *Moses and Monotheism* (Freud 1939), was of considerable symbolic importance to him, and the second in elements common to Western society since the Reformation. From both perspectives one can see ways in which the Oedipus complex formulation ties in with broader cultural features. The historical importance of Moses lies in his having organized what was initially a series of patrilineal kin groups into a larger collectivity. The Old Testament makes many of the specific taboos and perceptions of the patrilineal kin group very clear: in the image of the thundering patriarchal God (which we can think of as arising when demands for respect taboo the expression of aggression against the father), in the emphasis on rivalry between brothers, in the tracing of lines of descent solely through men, and in the strong taboo against homosexuality (as seen in the story of Ham who was cursed for looking on his father's nakedness, and perhaps in the extreme anxiety which surrounds the idea of seeing God). From the second point of view, Freud does nothing more than reinforce and deepen our genetic understanding of values of active accomplishment and mastery of external reality, which in the degree of emphasis contrast post-Reformation Western society with many others and which can be thought of as masculine in style. In this perspective, moreover, the continuity between Freud's society and that of contemporary United States becomes apparent—the common elements being the emphasis on active mastery, the delay of gratification for future rewards by means of identification and ego ideals, and the emphasis on separation from early feminine attachments.

However, questioning of some of Freud's more narrowly patriarchal bias has been characteristic in this country and has had many reflections in psychoanalytic thinking, for example, in the much greater emphasis given to the mother-child relationship. This must certainly be related to the more egalitarian concept of the family, and one might say that psychoanalysis itself has been crucially involved in the elaboration of some new cultural values and images which are feminine in quality: the terms "warmth," "security," and "support," with all of their psychological and social ramifications, are evidence of this, and they in turn serve in the definition of norms for intimate relationships, for example, that the mother should send the child into the outside world, but not in such a sudden or traumatic way that he loses the sense of support of security.[18] In the same way, the ideal wife furthers her husband's extrafamilial activities by giving her support, in a way which may imply far more submissiveness than the Italian image of an intruding male presence which may on occasion be kicked out, and this goes with the positive rather than negative definition of the extrafamilial world. In addition, family patterns may in many ways make for a lack of differentiation between maternal and erotic aspects of love, in that the latter are not defined as "bad" or forbidden in themselves, but rather, in current American morality, tend to be legitimized precisely to the extent that they are assimilated to qualities such as "warmth" or "security." Thus, in contrast to many societies, we perceive no inherent conflict between family continuity and the sexual instinct. The details of this pattern and its cultural ramifications have yet to be described, but while it certainly involves major changes from nineteenth-century ideals of discipline and control or emphasis on masculine authority in the direction of a higher cultural valuation of the feminine role, it also seems likely that values such as warmth and security will

[18] Cf. the harsh separation characterizing early school life both in the Puritan and Orthodox Jewish traditions.

Is the Oedipus Complex Universal?

nevertheless remain subordinate to the primary social goal of mastery; we would not see these changes as working in the long run in the direction of matriarchy.[19]

In conclusion, we should like to say a few words on the subject of research methodology. Psychoanalysts who have continued to base their work on Freud's theory of instinct have often commented that work based on the concept of culture is likely to deal with motivation in a way which is behavioristic or even superficial. That many of the potentialities of Freud's theory were overlooked in much of the early work on culture and personality is, we believe, quite true. Among the reasons for this is a too-hasty attempt to take over the trauma theory in such a way as to postulate uncertain and often mechanical relationships between specific features of child training and adult personality or culture patterns, e.g., culture X is oral because it has a long nursing period, and culture Y is anal because toilet training is surrounded with anxiety. At the same time, in particular where it has not hesitated to deal with cultural patterns of meaning as expressed in symbolic form—for example, Mead and Bateson's [sic] (1942) attempt in *Balinese Character* to relate an entire ritual sequence to infantile experience—the field of culture and personality has also produced some quite new modes of thought. Similarly, beginning with Malinowski's work, the use of the psychoanalytic concept of affect and the emphasis on the more intimate dynamics of the family have added an entirely new dimension to the comparative study of kinship, the field which makes up the most solidly founded and scientifically based area of social anthropology. In contrast to the field of culture and personality, this latter is almost completely unknown in psychoanalytic circles, a fact which can lead one to believe that the assertion that the "culturalist" approach is a superficial one is as

[19] Grete Bibring (1953) has commented on some differences between European and American family patterns as reflected in comparative analytic case material. While noting important matriarchal trends in the latter setting, she comments that these are nevertheless not congruent with the total social context and may become pathogenic for this reason. One could add that matriarchalism in the sense of uncompensated female dominance in the family may be quite common as the result of various processes of social change, but that in the long run compensating social mechanisms should appear.

much based on attitudes concerning differences on theory and technique which have arisen within the psychoanalytic movement as it is on serious study of the actual work of anthropology.

Moreover, at the present time psychoanalysis is facing a crisis as the result of increasing pressures both from without and from within for more careful scientific demonstration and elaboration of its conceptual apparatus. One of the potential dangers of this situation is that psychoanalytic research will itself take an increasingly behavioristic direction, i.e., attempt to reduce concepts whose initial originality derived from their immediate perception of meaningful or symbolic phenomena to a form which is quantifiable or experimentally testable in a way which is independent of the interpretive sensitivity of the observer. But this latter, for the anthropologist just as much as for the clinically oriented psychoanalyst, is a factor which cannot or should not be left out of any attempt to create a truly human science of human behavior, however sophisticated we may become concerning the inevitable emotional or normative bias of individual observations. In this perspective the moment when Malinowski, alone in the Trobriand Islands, had to turn to the Trobrianders themselves for companionship—because in his isolation he had lost interest in the questions concerning evolution and the nature of primitive man which he had so heatedly debated with his colleagues in London—is to modern anthropology what Freud's discovery of transference is to psychoanalysis: both make the observer's sensitivity to what is happening around him a primary instrument of research, and both focus research on living human situations rather than artificially created ones.

But today one might say that the initial supposition of Malinowski and numerous other anthropologists that comparative work provides a particularly important means of testing and elaborating psychoanalytic concepts is no less relevant than it was a generation ago, both in that the variety of living cultures provides a natural laboratory setting and in that participant observation, or the attempt to at least hypothetically adapt the framework of a culture different from one's own, may provide an antidote for that part of observer bias that stems from the taking for granted of particular cultural suppositions, i.e., normative bias. In the latter respect, in fact, one might say that comparative

Is the Oedipus Complex Universal?

work is perhaps all the more necessary now that psychoanalysis, rather than being an isolated and badly misunderstood field of endeavor, has in itself become a source of social norms. One of the dangers of the latter situation is that personality attributes favoring psychoanalytic investigation may be postulated as components of an ideal "human nature" and in turn may be built into a theoretical apparatus. Many qualities common in Southern Italy, for example, may well appear as "ego weakness" from the standpoint of a therapist, but if we look at them in their own setting we may find ways in which they are adaptive and in turn use such observations to enlarge our concepts of the ego and adaptation (cf. A. Parsons 1961). A great variety of concepts and postulates also takes on new meaning or leads to new questions if they are applied in the comparative framework.

This paper in itself, moreover, raises many theoretical questions which we have not even tried to answer; for example, can one really say that some kinds of incest wishes are closer to consciousness in one society than in another, and if so, what does this imply for the concept of repression? Or, what are the theoretical consequences for concepts concerning psychopathology and delinquency of what we have called the lesser internalization of paternal authority in Southern Italy and its related social consequences such as the importance of negativism in the peer group setting? It is clear that failure to show a positive masculine identification in the occupational sphere cannot in itself be taken as an indication of psychopathic personality, if by the latter we mean the lack of any superego restraint, because it is by no means incompatible with a fully internalized respect for women and family norms: witness the affirmative role played by the Neapolitan underworld in the protection of virgins. But such facts should in turn lead us to seek a more careful definition of the superego, which, if it is indeed a universally found psychic apparatus laid down in early infancy, should be definable independently of variations in norms relevant to adults.

In other words, in a great many areas more careful and self-conscious comparative thinking might help us to tighten up some of our theoretical concepts and in particular to separate that which refers to early infantile life from that which defines normative expectations for the adult. Such attempts can in turn have immediate clinical implications for matters such as diagnosis and prognosis. Many social scientists have pointed out the ways in which normative bias may appear in diagnostic judgment when there are social differences between psychiatrist and patient; moreover, such biases follow some fairly consistent and predictable patterns. Thus, diagnoses such as "character disorder" and "psychopathic personality" are certainly overused for Italian male patients; when the neurotic acts out his difficulties outside the family, or even within it (as in the common example of the depressed and dependent man who beats his wife), he quite often gets into trouble with the law. Similarly for women, "oral" elements are commonly overemphasized (in the sense that significant areas of competence or of genital focus in intrapsychic conflict are overlooked) in the light of the greater restriction of life to the family setting. It would be our view that in this group one can individualize the major genetically rooted personality structures predictable from psychoanalytic theory (schizoid, depressive or cyclic, obsessional, and hysteric), but that the overt differences in phenomenology can be such that even the experienced diagnostician may have difficulty if he does not know the cultural expectations. Such difficulties in turn may have important implications for the evaluation of the depth of pathology or for treatment decisions.

In summary, we believe that comparative research has a potentially very important contribution to make in the light of the current need for further testing and elaboration of psychoanalytic concepts with respect to a variety of materials. Moreover, this is the case both for general social or cultural formulations and for more specific studies of psychopathology in ways which are relevant to the understanding of personality dynamics and which can have immediate applications for diagnosis and treatment. For the original question of whether the Oedipus complex is universal or not, we would sum up by saying that it is no longer very meaningful in that particular form. The more important contemporary questions would rather be: what is the possible range within which culture can utilize and elaborate the instinctually given human potentialities, and what are the psychologically given limits of this range? Or in slightly different terms:

what more can we learn about what Claude Lévi-Strauss (1949) has characterized as the "transition from nature to culture"? To answer fully questions such as these will require the equal and collaborative efforts of psychoanalysis and anthropology.

BIBLIOGRAPHY

Adorno, T. W. et al.
  1950, *The Authoritarian Personality*. New York, Harper and Bros.
Aitken, Barbara.
  1930, "Temperament in Native American Religion." *Journal of the Royal Anthropological Institute,* 60:363–87.
Allport, G. W.
  1943, "The Ego in Contemporary Psychology." *Psychological Review,* 50:451–478.
  1947, "Scientific Models and Human Morals." *Psychological Review,* 54:182-192.
Anastasi, Anne.
  1937, *Differential Psychology*. New York, Macmillan.
Bakke, E. Wight.
  1940a, *Citizens Without Work*. New Haven, Yale University Press.
  1940b, *The Unemployed Worker*. New Haven, Yale University Press.
Barnouw, Victor.
  1963, *Culture and Personality*. Homewood, Ill., The Dorsey Press.
Bateson, Gregory.
  1936, *Naven*. Stanford, Stanford University Press.
Bateson, Gregory, and Margaret Mead.
  1942, *Balinese Character: A Photographic Analysis*. New York, Special Publication of the New York Academy of Sciences.
Bauer, Raymond A.
  1952, *The New Man in Soviet Psychology*. Cambridge, Mass., Harvard University Press.
Bauer, Raymond A., Alex Inkeles, and Clyde Kluckhohn.
  1956, *How the Soviet System Works*. Cambridge, Mass., Harvard University Press.

Beaglehole, Ernest.
 1937, "Notes on Hopi Economic Life." New Haven, *Yale University Publications in Anthroplogy*, 15.
Beaglehole, Ernest, and Pearl Beaglehole.
 1936, "Hopi of the Second Mesa." Menasha, Wis., Memoirs of the American Anthropological Association, 44.
Beardsley, Richard K., Robert Ward, and John Hall.
 1959, *Village Japan*. Chicago, University of Chicago Press.
Beier, Helen.
 1954, "Responses to the Rorschach Test of the Former Soviet Citizens." Unpublished report of the Project. Russian Research Center. March.
Beier, Helen, and Eugenia Hanfmann.
 1956, "Emotional Attitudes of Former Soviet Citizens as Studied by the Technique of Projective Questions. *Journal of Abnormal and Social Psychology*, 53:143–53.
Bellah, Robert.
 1957, *Tokugawa Religion*. Glencoe, Ill., The Free Press.
Benedict, Ruth.
 1930, "Psychological Types in the Cultures of the Southwest." *Proceedings of the Twenty-Third International of Americanists*, September 1928:572–81.
 1934, *Patterns of Culture*. New York, The New American Library.
 1946, *The Chrysanthemum and the Sword*. Boston, Houghton Mifflin.
Bennett, John.
 1946, "The Interpretation of Pueblo Culture: A Question of Values." *Southwestern Journal of Anthropology*, 2:361–74.
Bibring, G. L.
 1953, "On the Passing of the Oedipus Complex in a Matriarchal Family Setting. In *Drives, Affects, Behavior*, R. M. Loewenstein, ed., pp. 278–84. New York, International Universities Press.
Billig, O., J. Gillin, and W. Davidson.
 1947–48, "Aspects of Personality and Culture in a Guatemalan Community: Ethnological and Rorschach Approaches." *Journal of Personality*, 16:153–87, 326–68.
Blackwood, Beatrice.
 1927, "A Study of Mental Testing in Relation to Anthropology." *Mental Measurement Monographs*, 4.
Boring, E. G.
 1946, "Mind and Mechanism." *American Journal of Psychology*, 59:173–192.

Bruner, Edward M.
  1956, "Cultural Transmission and Cultural Change." *Southwestern Journal of Anthropology*, 12:191–99.
Bruner, J. S.
  1951, "Personality Dynamics and the Process of Perceiving." In R. R. Blake and G. V. Ramsey, eds., *Perception and Approach to Personality*. New York, Ronald Press.
Buck, J. L.
  1937, *Land Utilization in China*. Chicago, University of Chicago Press.
Buck, Pearl.
  1931, *The Good Earth*. New York, The John Day Co.
Burrows, E. G.
  1952, "From Value to Ethos on Ifaluk Atoll." *Southwestern Journal of Anthropology*, 8:13–35.
Burrows, E. G., and M. E. Spiro.
  1953, *An Atoll Culture*. New Haven, Human Relations Area Files.
Bushnell, J.
  1958, "La Virgin of Guadalupe as Surrogate Mother in San Juan Atzingo." *American Anthropologist*, 60:261–65.
Cancian, F.
  1961, "The Southern Italian Peasant: World View and Political Behavior." *Anthropological Quarterly*, 34, 1:1–17.
Carstairs, G. Morris.
  1957, *The Twice Born*. London, Hogarth Press.
Cassirer, E.
  1944, *An Essay on Man*. New Haven, Yale University Press.
Caudill, William.
  1949, "Psychological Characteristics of Acculturated Wisconsin Ojibwa Children." *American Anthropologist*, 51:409–27.
  1958, *The Psychiatric Hospital as a Small Society*. Cambridge, Mass., Harvard University Press.
Cohen, Yehudi.
  1961, *Social Structure and Personality: A Casebook*. New York, Holt, Rinehart & Winston.
Curtis, Edward S.
  1922, *The North American Indian*, Vol. XII. Norwood, Mass., The Plimpton Press.
Cushing, Frank H., Jesse W. Fewkes, and Elsie Clews Parsons.
  1922, "Contributions to Hopi History." *American Anthropologist*, 24:253–98.

Davino, Gennaro.
   1957, "Anella: Tavernara A Portacapuana." In Trevisani, G., ed., *Teatro Napoletano dalle origini,* 2 vols. Bologna.
de Castro, Josui.
   1952, *The Geography of Hunger.* Boston, Little, Brown.
De Jorio, A.
   1832, *La Mimica degli Antichi Investigata nel Gestire Napolitana.* Naples, dalla stamperia e carteria del fibreno.
Dennis, Wayne.
   1940, *The Hopi Child.* University of Virginia Institute for Research in the Social Sciences, Monograph 26. New York, Appleton-Century.
   1941, "The Socialization of the Hopi Child." In L. Spier, A. I. Hallowell, and S. S. Newman, *Language, Culture and Personality,* pp. 259-71. Menasha, Wis., Sapir Memorial Publication Fund.
Devereux, George.
   1957, Dream Learning and Individual Ritual Differences. *American Anthropologist,* 59:1036-45.
DeVore, Irven.
   1965, *Primate Behavior: Field Studies of Monkeys and Apes.* New York, Holt, Rinehart & Winston.
De Vos, George, and Hiroshi Wagatsuma.
   1959, "Psycho-cultural Significance of Concern Over Death and Illness Among Rural Japanese." *International Journal of Social Psychiatry,* 5:6-19.
   1961, "Value Attitudes Toward Role Behavior of Women in Two Japanese Villages." *American Anthropologist,* 63:1204-30.
Dicks, Henry V.
   1952, "Observations on Contemporary Russian Behavior." *Human Relations,* 5:111-74.
Dollard, J., and N. E. Miller.
   1950, *Personality and Psychotherapy.* New York, McGraw-Hill.
DuBois, Cora.
   1944, *The People of Alor.* Minneapolis, University of Minnesota Press.
Duijker, H.C.F., and N. H. Frijda.
   1961, *National Character and National Stereotypes: a trend report prepared for the International Union of Scientific Psychology.* New York, The Humanities Press.
Durkheim, Émile.
   1897, *Suicide,* Glencoe, Ill., The Free Press, 1951.

1915, *The Elementary Forms of the Religious Life.* Glencoe, Ill., The Free Press, 1958.

Eggan, Dorothy.
1943, "The General Problems of Hopi Adjustment." *American Anthropologist,* 45:357–73.
1949, "The Significance of Dreams for Anthropological Research." *American Anthropologist,* 51:177–98.
1955, "The Personal Use of Myth in Dreams" in Scheok (ed.), *Myth, A Symposium. Journal of American Folklore,* 68:67–75.

Eggan, Fred.
1950, *Social Organization of the Western Pueblos.* Chicago, University of Chicago Press.

Elkin, Henry.
1940, "The Northern Arapaho of Wyoming." In Ralph Linton, ed., *Acculturation in Seven American Indian Tribes.* New York, Appleton-Century.

Emerson, Ralph Waldo.
1841, Self-reliance. In N. Foerster, ed., *American Poetry and Prose.* 1934. Boston, Houghton Mifflin.

Erikson, E. H.
1937, "Configurations in Play-Clinical Notes." *Psychoanalytic Quarterly,* 6.
1943, *Observations on the Yurok: Childhood and World Image.* University of California Publications in American Archaeology and Ethnology, 46, No. 10. Berkeley.
1946, "Figure 1, A Chart of Modes and Zones." In Leonard Carmichael, ed., *Manual of Child Psychology.* New York, Wiley and Sons.
1950, *Childhood and Society.* New York, W. W. Norton.
1956, "The Problem of Ego Identity." *Journal of the American Psychoanalytic Association,* 1:56–121.

Evans-Pritchard, E. E.
1940, *The Nuer.* London, Oxford University Press.
1953, *Kinship and Marriage Among the Nuer.* London, Oxford University Press.
1956, *Nuer Religion.* London, Oxford University Press.

Fainsod, Merle.
1953, *How Russia Is Ruled.* Cambridge, Mass., Harvard University Press.

Feldmesser, R.
1953, "The Persistence of Status Advantages in Soviet Russia." *American Journal of Sociology,* 59:19–27.

Fenichel, Otto.
　1945, *The Psychoanalytic Theory of Neuroses.* New York, W. W. Norton.
Fewkes, Jesse Walter.
　1903, *Hopi Katcinas.* Bureau of American Ethnology, 21st Annual Report (for 1899–1900), pp. 3–126, plates II–LXVIII.
Field, Margaret J.
　1960, *Search for Security: an Ethnopsychiatric Study of Rural Ghana.* London, Faber and Faber.
Fischer, G.
　1952, *Soviet Opposition to Stalin.* Cambridge, Mass., Harvard University Press.
Forde, C. Daryll.
　1931, "Hopi Agriculture and Land Ownership." *Journal of the Royal Anthropological Institute,* 61:357–405.
Fortes, Meyer, and E. E. Evans-Pritchard, eds.
　1940, *African Political Systems.* London, Oxford University Press.
Fortune, R. F.
　1927, "On Imitative Magic." A thesis presented for the diploma in anthropology, University of Cambridge. Unpublished.
Fosbrooke, H. A.
　1948, "An Administrative Survey of the Masai Social System." *Tanganyika Notes and Records,* 26:1–50.
French, Thomas M.
　n.d., "Guilt, Shame and other Reactive Motives." Unpublished Mss.
Frenkel-Brunswik, Else.
　1955, "Differential Patterns of Social Outlook and Personality in Family and Children." In M. Mead and M. Wolfenstein, eds., *Childhood in Contemporary Cultures.* Chicago, University of Chicago Press.
Freud, Anna.
　1946, *The Ego and the Mechanisms of Defense.* New York, International Universities Press.
Freud, Sigmund.
　1900, *The Interpretation of Dreams.* New York, Basic Books, 1955.
　1905, *Three Essays on Sexuality.* In Standard Edition, Vol. VII. London, Hogarth Press.
　1908, "Civilized Sexual Morality and Modern Nervousness." In Collected Papers, Vol. II. London, Hogarth Press, 1924.
　1910a, *Leonardo Da Vinci: A Study in Psychosexuality.* New York, Random House, 1947.
　1910b, "Psychogenic Visual Disturbance According to Psycho-an-

alytical Conceptions." In *Collected Papers*, Vol. II, pp. 105–12.

1926, *Inhibitions, Symptoms, and Anxiety*. London, Hogarth Press, London, Hogarth Press, 1924.

1917, *Beyond the Pleasure Principle*. In Standard Edition, Vol. XVIII. London, Hogarth Press, 1955.

1936.

1930, *Civilization and Its Discontents*. London, Hogarth Press.

1936, *The Problem of Anxiety*. New York, W. W. Norton.

1939, *Moses and Monotheism*. New York, Vintage Books, 1958.

Fried, Marc.

1954, "Some Systematic Patterns of Relationship Between Personality and Attitudes Among Soviet Displaced Persons." Unpublished Report of the Project. Russian Research Center. October.

Fried, Marc, and Doris Held.

1953, "Relationships between Personality and Attitudes among Soviet Displaced Persons: A Technical Memorandum on the Derivation of Personality Variables from a Sentence Completion Test." Unpublished Report of the Project. Russian Research Center. August.

Fries, Margaret.

1947, "Diagnosing the Child's Adjustment Through Age Level Tests." *Psychoanalytic Review*, 34:1.

Fromm, Erich.

1939, "Selfishness and Self-Love." *Psychiatry*, 2:507–24.

1941, *Escape From Freedom*. New York, Farrar & Rinehart.

1943, "Sex and Character." *Psychiatry*, 6:21–31.

Garth, T. R.

1931, *Race Psychology: A Study of Racial Mental Differences*. New York, McGraw-Hill.

Geertz, Clifford.

1957, "Ritual and Social Change: A Javanese Example." *American Anthropologist*, 59:32–54.

Gladwin, Thomas.

1961, Oceania. In F. L. K. Hsu, ed., *Psychological Anthropology*, pp. 135–71. Homewood, Ill., The Dorsey Press.

Goldfrank, Esther S.

1945, "Socialization, Personality, and the Structure of Pueblo Society (with Particular Reference to Hopi and Zuni)." *American Anthropologist*, 47:516–39.

Goldstein, K.

1940, *Human Nature in the Light of Psychopathology*. Cambridge, Mass., Harvard University Press.

Gorer, Geoffrey.
   1943, *Themes in Japanese Culture*. Transactions of the New York Academy of Sciences, ser. 2, 5:106–24.
Hack, John T.
   1942, *The Changing Physical Environment of the Hopi Indians of Arizona*. Papers of the Peabody Museum of American Archaeology and Ethnology, Harvard University, Vol. XXXV, No. 1. Cambridge, Mass.
Hall, C. S.
   1954, *A Primer of Freudian Psychology*. Cleveland, World Publishing Co.
Hall, C. S., and G. Lindzey,
   1957, *Theories of Personality*. New York, John Wiley and Sons.
Hallowell, A. I.
   1942, "Acculturation Processes and Personality Changes as Indicated by the Rorschach Technique." *Rorschach Research Exchange*, VI:42–50.
   1950, "Personality Structure and the Evolution of Man." *American Anthropologist,* 52:159–73.
   1951a, "Cultural Factors in the Structuralization of Perception." In J. H. Rohrer and M. Sherif, eds., *Social Psychology at the Crossroads*. New York, Harper and Bros.
   1951b, "The Use of Projective Techniques in the Study of the Sociopsychological Aspects of Acculturation." *Journal of Projective Techniques,* 15:27–44.
   1955, *Culture and Experience*. Philadelphia, University of Pennsylvania Press.
   1960, "Self, Society, and Culture in Phylogenetic Perspective." In S. Tax, ed., *The Evolution of Man*. Chicago, University of Chicago Press.
Hanfmann, Eugenia
   1957, "Social Perception in Russian Displaced Persons and an American Comparison Group." *Psychiatry,* 20:131–49.
Hanfmann, Eugenia, and Helen Beier.
   1954, "Psychological Patterns of Soviet Citizens." Unpublished Report of the Project. Russian Research Center. August.
Hanfmann, Eugenia, and J. G. Getzels.
   1955, "Interpersonal Attitudes of Former Soviet Citizens as Studied by a Semi-projective Method." *Psychological Monographs,* Vol. 69, No. 4, whole number 389.
Haring, D. G., ed.
   1956, *Personal Character and Cultural Milieu*. Third edition, revised. Syracuse, Syracuse University Press.

Hartmann, H., E. Kris, and R. M. Loewenstein.
  1951, "Some Psychoanalytic Comments on 'Culture and Personality.'" In G. B. Wilbur and W. Muensterberger, eds., *Psychoanalysis and Culture*, pp. 3–31. New York, International Universities Press.
Hearn, Lafcadio.
  1905, *Japan: An Attempt at Interpretation*. New York, Macmillan.
Henry, William E.
  1947, "The Thematic Apperception Technique in the Study of Culture-Personality Relations." *Genetic Psychology Monographs*, Vol. 15.
Hilgard, E. R.
  1948, *Theories of Learning*. New York, Appleton-Century.
Hockett, Charles F., and Robert Ascher.
  1964, "The Human Revolution." *Current Anthropology*, 5:138–68.
Hollingshead, A. B., and F. C. Redlich.
  1958, *Social Class and Mental Illness*. New York, John Wiley and Sons.
Honigmann, John J.
  1954, *Culture and Personality*. New York, Harper and Bros.
Honigmann, John.
  1961, "North America." In *Psychological Anthropology*, F. L. K. Hsu, ed., pp. 93–134. Homewood, Ill., The Dorsey Press.
Howell, P. P.
  1954, *A Manual of Nuer Law*. London, Oxford University Press.
Hsu, Francis L. K., ed.
  1953, *Americans and Chinese*. New York, Schuman.
  1954, *Aspects of Culture and Personality*. New York, Abelard-Schuman.
  1961, *Psychological Anthropology*. Homewood, Ill., The Dorsey Press.
Hughes, Charles C., et. al.
  1960, *Peoples of Cove and Woodlot: Communities from the Viewpoint of Social Psychiatry*. New York, Basic Books.
Hull, C. L.
  1943, *Principles of Behavior*. New York, Appleton-Century.
Hunt, Robert.
  1965, "A History of the British and American Anthropological Study of National Character." Unpublished PhD. dissertation, Northwestern University.
Inkeles, Alex.
  1950, "Stratification and Social Mobility in the Soviet Union: 1940–1950." *American Sociological Review*, 15:465–79.

Inkeles, Alex, and Raymond Bauer.
 1954, *Patterns of Life Experiences and Attitudes under the Soviet System.* Russian Research Center. October.
Inkeles, Alex, and Daniel J. Levinson.
 1954, "National Character: the Study of Modal Personality and Sociocultural Systems." In G. Lindzey, ed., *Handbook of Social Psychology*, Vol. II. pp. 970–1020. Cambridge, Mass., Addison-Wesley.
Irving, J. A.
 1949, The comparative method and the nature of human nature. Phil. Phenom. Res., 9:545–56.
Isaacs, Susan.
 1931, "The Experimental Construction of an Environment Optimal for Mental Growth." In C. Murchison, ed., *Handbook of Child Psychology*. Clark University Press; Oxford University Press.
Jacobson, E.
 1954, "The Self and the Object World: Vicissitudes of their Infantile Cathexes and their Influence on Ideational and Affective Development." In R. S. Eissler et. al., eds., *The Psychoanalytic Study of the Child,* 9:75–127. New York, International Universities Press.
Jamieson, E., and P. Sandiford.
 1929, "The Mental Capacity of the Southern Ontario Indians." *Journal of Educational Psychology,* 19:536–51.
Joffe, Natalie F.
 1940, The Fox of Iowa. In *Acculturation in Seven American Indian Tribes,* Ralph Linton, ed. New York, Appleton-Century.
Jones, E.
 1912, "The Theory of Symbolism." *Papers on Psychoanalysis.* Boston, Beacon Press, 1961.
 1924, "Mother-Right and Sexual Ignorance of Savages." In *Essays in Applied Psychoanalysis,* 2:145–73. New York, International Universities Press, 1964.
Kaplan, B., ed.
 1961, *Studying Personality Cross-culturally.* Evanston, Ill., Row, Peterson.
Kardiner, A.
 1939, *The Individual and His Society.* New York, Columbia University Press.
Kardiner, Abram, with the collaboration of R. Linton, Cora DuBois, and J. West.
 1945, *The Psychological Frontiers of Society.* New York, Columbia University Press.

Kennard, E. A.
- 1937, "Hopi Reactions to Death." *American Anthropologist,* 39: 491–96.

Kinietz, W. Vernon.
- 1940, *The Indians of the Western Great Lakes, 1615–1760.* Occasional Contributions from the Museum of Anthropology of the University of Michigan, No. 10.

Klineberg, Otto.
- 1935, *Race Differences.* New York.

Klopfer, Bruno.
- 1944, "Form Level Rating." *Rorschach Research Exchange,* VIII: 164–77.

Klopfer, Bruno, Mary D. Ainsworth, Walter G. Klopfer, and Robert R. Holt.
- 1954, *Developments in the Rorschach Technique,* Vol. I: *Technique and Theory.* New York, World Book Co.

Kluckhohn, Clyde.
- 1941, "Patterning as Exemplified in Navaho Culture." In L. Spier, A. I. Hallowell, and S. S. Newman, eds., *Language, Culture and Personality,* pp. 109–30. Menasha, Wis., Sapir Memorial Publication Fund.

Kluckhohn, Clyde, and Henry A. Murray.
- 1953, "Personality Formation: The Determinants." In Kluckhohn, Murray and Schneider, *Personality in Nature, Society and Culture,* pp. 53–67. New York, Alfred A. Knopf.

Kluckhohn, Clyde, H. Murray, and D. Schneider.
- 1953, *Personality in Nature, Society and Culture.* 2nd edition, revised. New York, Alfred A. Knopf.

Krige, E. S., and J. D.
- 1943, *The Realm of a Rain-Queen.* New York, Oxford University Press.

Kroeber, A. L.
- 1948, Anthropology. New York, Harcourt Brace.

Kroeber, A. L. and Clyde Kluckhohn.
- 1952, "Culture: A Critical Review of Concepts and Definition." Papers of the Peabody Museum of American Archaeology and Ethnology, Vol. XLVII, No. 1.

Lanham, Betty.
- 1956, "Aspects of Child Card in Japan: Preliminary Report." In Haring, ed., *Personal Character and Cultural Milieu,* pp. 565–83. Syracuse, Syracuse University Press.

Leach, E. R.
  1954, *Political Systems of Highland Burma*. London, G. Bell and Sons.
Le Clercq, Chretien.
  1910, *New Relation of Gaspesia*. Translated and edited by W. F. Ganong. Toronto.
Leighton, Alexander, et. al.
  1963, *Psychiatric Disorder Among the Yourba*. Ithaca, Cornell University Press.
Lévi-Strauss, C.
  1949a, "L'Analyse Structurale en Linguistique et en Anthropologie." *Word*, 1:35–53.
  1949b, *Les Structures Elémentaires de la Parenté*. Paris, Presses Universitaires de France.
Levy, D. M.
  1943, "Hate as a Disease." *Journal of Educational Sociology*, 16: 354–58.
Lévy-Bruhl, Lucien.
  1926, *How Natives Think*. London, Allen and Unwin.
  1928, *The Soul of the Primitive*. London, Allen and Unwin.
Lewin, K.
  1935, *A Dynamic Theory of Personality*. New York, McGraw-Hill.
  1942, "Field Theory of Learning." In 41st *Yearbook*, National Society for the Study of Education. Bloomington, Ill., Public School Publishing Co.
Lindzey, Gardner, ed.
  1954, *Handbook of Social Psychology*. 2 vols. Reading, Mass., Addison-Wesley Publishing Co.
  1961, *Projective Techniques and Cross-cultural Research*. New York, Appleton-Century.
Linton, Ralph.
  1936, *The Study of Man*. New York, Appleton-Century.
Lynd, Robert S., and Helen M. Lynd.
  1937, *Middletown in Transition*. New York, Harcourt, Brace.
Malinowski, B.
  1916, "Baloma: The Spirits of the Dead in the Trobriand Islands." *Journal of Royal Anthropological Institute*, 46:353–430.
  1925, "Magic, science and religion." In Needham, ed., *Science, Religion and Reality*. London, Macmillan Co.
  1927, *Sex and Repression in Savage Society*. London, Routledge and Kegan Paul, 1953.
  1929, *The Sexual Life of Savages*. London, Routledge and Kegan Paul, 1953.

Mandelbaum, David, ed.
 1951, *Selected Writings of Edward Sapir*. Berkeley and Los Angeles, University of California Press.
Mann, Cecil.
 1940, "Mental Measurements in Primitive Communities." *Psychological Bulletin*, 37:366–95.
Masson, R. L.
 1890, *Les Bourgeois de la Compagnie de Nord Ouest*. 2 vols. Quebec.
Mastriani, F.
 1871, *I Vermi: Studi Storici Sulle Classe Pericolose in Napoli*. 4 vols. Naples.
Mead, Margaret.
 1928, *Coming of Age in Samoa*. New York, W. W. Morrow.
 1930a, "American Educational Problems in the Light of South Sea Experiments." *Proceedings of the 18th Annual Schoolmen's Week*. Philadelphia.
 1930b, *Growing Up in New Guinea*. New York, W. W. Morrow.
 1931, "The Primitive Child." *Handbook of Child Psychology*.
 1932, *The Changing Culture of an Indian Tribe*. New York, Columbia University Press.
 1935, *Sex and Temperament*. New York, W. W. Morrow.
 1939, "Researches in Bali, 1936–39; on the Concept of Plot in Culture." *Transactions, New York Academy of Sciences*, Ser. 2, 2:24–31.
 1942, *And Keep Your Powder Dry*. New York, W. W. Morrow.
 1946, "Research on Primitive Children." In L. Carmichael, ed., *Manual of Child Psychology*. New York, John Wiley and Sons.
 1947, "On the Implications for Anthropology of the Gesell-Ilg Approach to Maturation." *American Anthropologist*, 49:69–77.
 1959, *An Anthropologist at Work: Writings of Ruth Benedict*. Boston, Houghton Mifflin.
 1965, *Anthropology, a Human Science*. New York, Van Nostrand.
Merton, Robert K., and Patricia K. Kendall.
 1946, "The Focused Interview." *American Journal of Sociology*, 51:541–57.
Middleton, J., and David Tait, eds.
 1958, *Tribes Without Rulers: Studies in African Segmentary Systems*. London, Routledge and Kegan Paul.
Miller, N., and J. Dollard.
 1941, *Social Learning and Imitation*. New Haven, Yale University Press.

Miller, Walter B.
1955, "Two Concepts of Authority." *American Anthropologist,* 57: 271-89.
Mintern, Leigh and W. W. Lambert.
1964, *Mothers in Six Cultures.* New York. John Wiley and Sons.
Moller, H.
1951, "The Meaning of Courtly Love." *Journal of American Folklore,* 73, 287:39-52.
1959, "The Social Causation of the Courtly Love Complex." *Comparative Studies in Society and History,* 1, 2:137-63.
Montgomery, Ross G., Watson Smith, and John Otis Brew.
1949, *Franciscan Awatovi: The Excavation and Conjectural Reconstruction of a 17th-century Spanish Mission Establishment at a Hopi Indian Town* . . . Papers of the Peabody Museum of American Archaeology and Ethnology, Harvard University, Vol. XXXVI. Cambridge, Mass.
Moss, L. W., and W. H. Thomson.
1958, "The South Italian Family: Literature and Observation." *Human Organization,* 18, 1:35-41.
Moulton, Harold.
1952, Editorial, Chicago *Sun Times,* Jan. 21, 1952.
Mowrer, O. H.
1939, "A Stimulus-Response Analysis of Anxiety and its Role as a Reinforcing Agent." *Psychological Review,* 46:553-65.
Murray, H.
1938, *Explorations in Personality.* New York, Oxford University Press.
Nelson, John Louw.
1937, *Rhythm for Rain.* Boston, Houghton Mifflin.
Nequatewa, Edmund.
1933, "Hopi Courtship and Marriage: Second Mesa." Edited by Mary-Russell F. Colton. Museum of Northern Arizona, *Museum Notes,* 1933, 5:41-14.
1936, "Truth of a Hopi and Other Clan Stories of Shung-opovi." Ed. by Mary-Russell F. Colton. Museum of Northern Arizona, *Bulletin* 8.
1944, "A Mexican Raid on the Hopi Pueblo of Oraibi." *Plateau,* 16:45-52.
Norbeck, Edward and Margaret.
1956, "Child Training in a Japanese Fishing Community." In Haring, ed., *Personal Character and Cultural Milieu.* Syracuse, Syracuse University Press.

Office of Statistics of the Commune of Naples.
   1959, *Annuario Statistico del Commune di Napoli: Anno 1956*, 21. Naples, Stabilimento Tipografico Francesco Giannini & Figli.
Opler, Marvin K. (ed.)
   1959, *Culture and Mental Health—Cross-cultural Studies.* New York, Macmillan.
Page, Gordon B.
   1940, "Hopi Land Patterns." *Plateau,* 13:29–36.
Parsons, Anne.
   1960, "Family Dynamics in South Italian Schizophrenics." *Arch. Gen. Psychiat.,* 3:507–18.
   1961, "A Schizophrenic Episode in a Neapolitan Slum." *Psychiatry,* 24:109–21.
Parsons, Elsie Clews.
   1927, "Witchcraft Among the Pueblos: Indian or Spanish?" *Man,* 27:106–12, 125–28.
   1933, "Hopi and Zuni Ceremonialism." *Memoirs of the American Anthropological Association,* No. 39. Menasha, Wis.
   1936, *Hopi Journal, by Alexander M. Stephen.* 2 vols. New York, Columbia University Press.
   1939, *Pueblo Indian Religion.* 2 vols. Chicago, University of Chicago Press.
Parsons, Talcott.
   1949, *Essays in Sociological Theory, Pure and Applied.* Glencoe, Ill., The Free Press.
   1951, *The Social System.* Glencoe, Ill., The Free Press.
   1958, "Social Structure and the Development of Personality: Freud's Contribution to the Integration of Psychology and Sociology." *Psychiatry,* 21, 4:321–40.
Parsons, Talcott, and Robert F. Bales, with James Olds, Morris Zelditch, Jr., and Philip E. Slater.
   1955, *Family, Socialization and Interaction Process.* Glencoe, Ill., The Free Press.
Petrullo, V.
   1937, "A Note on Sicilian Cross-Cousin Marriage." *Primitive Man,* 10, 2:8–9.
Pfister-Ammende, Maria.
   1949, "Psychologische Erfahrungen mit sowetrussischen Flüchtlingen in der Schweiz." In M. Pfister-Ammende, ed., *Die Psychohygiene: Grundlagen und Ziele.* Bern, Hans Huber.
Phillips, Arthur.
   1944, *Report on Native Tribunals.* Nairobi, Government Printing Office, Colony and Protectorate of Kenya.

Piaget, J.
  1926, *The Language and Thought of the Child*. New York, Harcourt, Brace.
  1928, *Judgment and Reasoning in the Child*. New York, Harcourt, Brace.
  1929, *The Child's Conception of the World*. New York, Harcourt, Brace.
  1930, *The Child's Conception of Physical Causality*. New York, Harcourt, Brace.
Piers, Gerhart, and Milton Singer.
  1953, *Shame and Guilt: A Psychoanalytic and a Cultural Study*. Springfield, Ill., Charles, C. Thomas.
Pitkin, D.
  1959, "Land Tenure and Family Organization in an Italian Village." *Human Organization,* 18, 4:169–73.
Postman, L.
  1951, "Toward a General Theory of Cognition." In J. H. Rohrer and M. Sherif, eds., *Social Psychology at the Crossroads*. New York, Harper and Bros.
Pratt, D.
  1960, "The Don Juan Myth." *American Imago,* 17:321–35.
Price-Williams, Douglas.
  1961a, "Analysis of an Intelligence Test Used in Rural Areas of Central Nigeria." *Oversea Education,* 33:124–33.
  1961b, "A Study Concerning Concepts of Conservation of Quantities among Primitive Children." *Acta Psychologica,* 18:297–305.
  1962a, "Abstract and Concrete Modes of Classification in a Primitive Society." *British Journal of Educational Psychology,* 32:50–61.
  1962b, "A Case Study of Ideas Concerning Disease among the Tiv." *Africa,* 32:123–31.
Radcliffe-Brown, A. R.
  1952, *Structure and Function in Primitive Society*. Glencoe, Ill., The Free Press.
Ramirez, S. and R. Parres.
  1957, "Some Dynamic Patterns in the Organization of the Mexican Family." *International Journal of Social Psychiatry,* 3:18–21.
Rapaport, D.
  1960, "The Structure of Psychoanalytic Theory." *Psycholigical Issues,* Monograph 6. New York, International Universities Press.
Rasmussen, Vilhelm.
  1920, *Child Psychology*. London, Gyldendal.

Riesman, David.
  1950, *The Lonely Crowd*. New Haven, Yale University Press.
Roseborough, H. E., and H. P. Phillips.
  1953, "A Comparative Analysis of the Responses to a Sentence Completion Test of a Matched Sample of Americans and Former Russian Subjects." Unpublished Report of the Project. Russian Research Center. April.
Rosenblatt, Daniel, Mortimer Slaiman, and Eugenia Hanfmann.
  1953, "Responses of Former Soviet Citizens to the Thematic Apperception Test (TAT): An Analysis Based upon Comparison with an American Control Group." Unpublished Report of the Project. Russian Research Center. August.
Rossi, Alice.
  1954, "Generational Differences Among Former Soviet Citizens." Unpublished Ph.D. Thesis in sociology, Columbia University.
Rubel, Arthur.
  1965, "The Mexican-American Palomilla." *Anthropological Linguistics*, 7:92–97.
Sargent, S. S., and M. W. Smith.
  1949, *Culture and Personality*. New York, The Viking Fund.
Schilder, Paul.
  1942, *Goals and Desires of Man*. New York, Columbia University Press.
Schneider, D., and K. Gough, eds.
  1961, *Matrilineal Kinship*. Berkeley and Los Angeles, University of California Press.
Schrier, A. M., H. Harlow, and F. Stollnitz.
  1965, *Behavior of Non-Human Primates*. New York, Academic Press.
Sears, Robert R., Eleanor Maccoby and Harry Levin.
  1957, *Patterns of Child Rearing*. Evanston, Ill., Row, Peterson.
Segall, Marshall, D. T. Campbell, and M. J. Herskovits.
  1963, "Cultural Differences in the Perception of Geometric Illusions." *Science*, 139:769–71.
Seward, Georgene, ed.
  1958, *Clinical Studies in Culture Conflict*. New York, Ronald Press.
Siegal, Bernard, ed.
  1959, *Biennial Review of Anthropology*. Stanford, Stanford University Press.
  1961, *Biennial Review of Anthropology*. Stanford, Stanford Univerity Press.
  1963, *Biennial Review of Anthropology*. Stanford, Stanford University Press.

Bibliography

1965, *Biennial Review of Anthropology*. Stanford, Stanford University Press.

Simmons, Leo W., ed.
1942, *Sun Chief: The Autobiography of a Hopi Indian*. New Haven, Yale University Press.
1945, *The Role of the Aged in Primitive Society*. New Haven, Yale University Press.

Singer, Milton.
1961, "A Survey of Culture and Personality Theory and Research." In *Studying Personality Cross-Culturally*, B. Kaplan (ed.), pp. 9–90. Evanston, Row, Peterson.

Smelser, Neil J. and Wm. T. Smelser. (eds.)
1963, *Personality and Social Systems*. New York, John Wiley and Sons.

Southall, Aidan W.
1956, *Alur Society: A Study in Processes and Types of Domination*. Cambridge, England, Heffer and Sons.

Spence, K. W.
1947, "The Role of Secondary Reinforcement in Delayed Reward Learning." *Psychological Review*, 54:1–8.
1950, "Cognitive Versus Stimulus Response Theories of Learning." *Psychological Review*, 57:159–72.

Spindler, George D.
1955, "Sociocultural and Psychological Processes in Menomini Acculturation." *University of California Publications in Culture and Society*, 5. Berkeley and Los Angeles, University of California Press.

Spindler, Louise.
1956, "Women and Culture Change: A Case Study of Menomini Indians." Unpublished Ph.D. dissertation, Stanford University.

Spiro, M. E.
1950, "The Problem of Aggression in a South Sea Culture." Unpublished Ph.D. dissertation, Northwestern University.
1951, "Personality and Culture: The Natural History of a False Dichotomy," *Psychiatry*, 14:19–46.
1952, "Ghosts, Ifaluk, and Teleological Functionalism." *American Anthropologist*, 54:497–503.
1961a, "An Overview and a Suggested Reorientation." In Hsu, F. L. K., ed., *Psychological Anthropology*. Homewood, Ill., The Dorsey Press.
1961b, "Social Systems, Personality and Functional Analysis." In Kaplan, ed., *Studying Personality Cross-Culturally*. Evanston, Ill., Row, Peterson.

Srole, Leo et. al.
  1962, *Mental Health in the Metropolis: The Mid-Town Manhattan Study,* Vol. 1. New York, McGraw-Hill.
Stalin, Joseph.
  1933, *Leninism.* New York, Modern Books, Vol. I.
Stanton, A. H.
  1959, "Propositions Concerning Object Choices." In *Conceptual and Methodological Problems in Psychoanalysis,* L. Bellak, ed., pp. 1010-37. New York, Annals of the New York Academy of Sciences.
Stanton, A. H., and M. Schwartz.
  1954, *The Mental Hospital.* New York, Basic Books.
Stephen, Alexander M.
  1936, *Hopi Journal.* 2 vols. Ed. by E. C. Parsons. New York, Columbia University Press.
Steward, Julian H.
  1931, "Notes on Hopi Ceremonies in Their Initiatory Form in 1927-1928." *American Anthropologist,* 33:56-79.
Sully, J.
  1926, *Studies of Childhood.* New York, D. Appleton.
Thomas, W. I., and Dorothy Swaine Thomas.
  1928, *The Child in America.* New York, Alfred A. Knopf.
Thompson, Laura.
  1945, "Logico-aesthetic Integration in Hopi Culture." *American Anthropologist,* 47:540-53.
  1947, "Review of 'Hopi Horizons: A Film Study of an Indian Tribe.'" *American Anthropologist,* 49:464-65.
Thompson, Laura, and Alice Joseph.
  1944, *The Hopi Way.* Lawrence, Kansas, U. S. Indian Service.
  1947, "White Pressures on Indian Personality and Culture." *American Journal of Sociology,* 53:17-22.
Thorpe, W. A.
  1950, "The Concepts of Learning and Their Relation to Those of Instincts." In *Physiological Mechanisms in Animal Behavior: Symposia of the Society for Experimental Biology,* No. 4. New York, Academic Press.
Thwaites, Reuben Gold, ed.
  1896-1901
  The Jesuit Relations and Allied Documents. 73 vols. Cleveland.
Titiev, Mischa.
  1938, "The Problem of Cross-Cousin Marriage Among the Hopi." *American Anthropologist,* 40:105-11.

1943, "Notes on Hopi Witchcraft." Michigan Academy of Science, Arts and Letters, *Papers,* 28:549–57.

1944, *Old Oraibi: A Study of the Hopi Indians of the Third Mesa.* Papers of the Peabody Museum of American Archaeology and Ethnology, Harvard University, XXII, No. 1. Cambridge, Mass.

1946, "Review of 'The Hopi Way.'" *American Anthropologist,* 48:430–32.

Tolman, E. C.

1934, "Theories of Learning." In F. A. Moss, ed., *Comparative Psychology.* New York, Prentice Hall.

1938, "The Determiners of Behavior at a Choice Point." *Psychological Review,* 45:1–45.

1949, "The Psychology of Social Learning." *Journal of Social Issues,* supplementary series, No. 5, Vol. 15.

Tooth, Geoffrey.

1950, *Studies in Mental Illness on the Gold Coast.* H. M. Stationary Office, Colonial Research Publications, No. 6.

Trevisani, G., ed.

1957, *Teatro Napoletano dalle origini.* 2 vols. Bologna, Tip. Mareggiani.

Vaillant, R.

1958, *The Law.* New York, Alfred A. Knopf.

Verga, G.

1953, *Little Novels of Sicily.* New York, Grove Press.

Vogt, Evon.

1951, *Navaho Veterans, a Study of Changing Values.* Papers of the Peabody Museum of American Archaeology and Ethnology, XLI. Reports of the Rimrock Project Values Series, No. 1. Cambridge, Mass., Harvard University Press.

Voth, H. R.

1901, *The Oraibi Powamu Ceremony.* Field Columbian Museum Publication 61, Anthropological Series, Vol. III. Chicago.

1905, *The Traditions of the Hopi.* Field Columbian Museum Publication 96, Anthropological Series, Vol. VIII. Chicago.

Wallace, Anthony F. C.

1952, *The Modal Personality Structure of the Tuscarora Indians.* Smithsonian Institution, Bureau of American Ethnology. Bulletin 150. Washington, Government Printing Office.

1961, *Culture and Personality. Studies in Anthropology.* New York, Random House.

Wallis, Wilson D., and Mischa Titiev.

1945, "Hopi Notes from Chimopovy." Michigan Academy of Science, Arts and Letters, *Papers,* 30:523–55.

White, Leslie A.
 1949, *The Science of Culture.* New York, Farrar, Straus.
Whiting, Alfred F.
 1939, "Ethnobotany of the Hopi." Museum of Northern Arizona, *Bulletin* 15, Flagstaff, Arizona.
Whiting, J. W. M.
 1941, *Becoming a Kwoma.* New Haven, Yale University Press.
 1961, Socialization Process and Personality." In Hsu, ed., *Psychological Anthropology,* Homewood, Ill., The Dorsey Press.
Whiting, J. W. M., and I. Child.
 1953, *Child Training and Personality.* New Haven, Yale University Press.
Whiting, J. W. M. et. al.
 Field Manual for the Cross-Cultural Study of Child Rearing, Social Science Research Council (mimeographed).
 "Inculcation of the Mechanisms of Social Control." In *Field Guide for a Study of Socialization in Five Societies,* by Whiting, I. Child, W. W. Lambert, et. al. Laboratory of Human Development, Harvard University (mimeographed).
Whorf, B. L.
 1941, "The Relations of Habitual Thought and Behavior to Language." In Spier, Hallowell, and S. S. Newman eds., *Language, Culture, and Personality.* Menasha, Wis., Sapir Memorial Publication Fund.
Whyte, W. F.
 1943, *Street Corner Society: Social Structure of an Italian Slum.* Chicago, University of Chicago Press.
Wolf, K. R.
 1952, "Growing Up and Its Price in Three Puerto Rican Sub-Cultures." *Psychiatry,* 15, 4:401–33.
Zola, I. K.
 1963, "Observations of Gambling in a Lower Class Setting." *Social Problems,* 10, 4:353–61.

INDEX

Aberle, David F., 79–139
Abortions, 173, 174, 176
Acculturation, male-female comparison, 56–78
Achievement (*See also* Drives; Prestige systems; Striving): Americans and, 263, 264–65, 268, 278, 318, 321–22, 327; guilt feelings among Japanese and, 261–88; Iatmul *Naven* ceremony and, 204–12; repression and, 391, 392; Russian, 338
Admiralty Islands, 213, 215
Adolescence (*See also* Children): Hopi, 107; Indian-Ladino, 145–46, 148–49; Italian, 366, 367, 379; Kaska, 46–48; Oedipus complex and, 355, 363–64; psychoanalytic theory and, 25, 29; Samoan, xvi
Adorno, T. W., 195
Advertising, 300, 308
Affiliation, need for, 317–18, 327, 328–30, 336
Africa, 185–203
Age groups, 193, 194, 216
Aggression-nonaggression, xv, xvii, 293, 344 (*See also* Hostility; Violence); Chinese, 295, 302–3; guilt feelings and, 264n, 287; Gusii-Nuer, 186–201 *passim;* Hopi, 80, 83, 96, 99, 105, 108, 120, 126–36 *passim;* Ifaluk, 239, 249; Indian-Ladino, 140–47 *passim;* Italian (Oedipus complex), 372, 377, 379, 381ff, 391, 393; Kaska, 40, 41; Russian, 319, 344; training in, 197–99 (*see also* specific people)
Agriculture: Chinese, 301–4, 305–6, 308; Gusii, 193n; Hopi, 82–84, 88, 93–95, 96, 97, 108, 128, 129, 134, 137; Soviet, 314, 329, 336
Aitken, Barbara, 137n
Alcohol. *See* Drunkenness
Allport, G. W., 243n, 244n
Alorese, the, xiv
Altruism, 29
Alus, 240–50
Ambivalence, 29, 47, 147, 266, 272, 321, 353, 354, 370, 386, 389. *See also* Polarities; Roles
American Indians, 33–48, 49–55, 56–78, 79–139 (*See also* specific people); Mesoamerican, 140–82
Americans (U.S.), 376, 393 (*See also* American Indians; Mesoamericans); Chinese values and, 293, 294–95, 300–11 *passim;* Italian personality and, 376, 389; Japanese achievement and, 263, 264–65, 268, 278; Japanese beliefs and, 251–60; Russian personality and, 316, 318, 319–27, 334
Anal stage of development, 11, 25, 26, 29
Anastasi, Anne, 51–52
Ancestors, 257, 292
Anella (Davino), 368–69
Anger, 124–25, 127, 383. *See also* Aggression; Conflicts; Hostility
Animal learning, 243–44
Animism, children's, 213–37
Anthropology, psychological, ix–xix
Anticathexes, 14, 16, 17, 20, 22–23, 25
Anticlericalism, 366, 367
Anxiety, 8, 17–24, 26 (*See also* Aggression; Hostility; Tension; Trauma); castration, 27–29; culture change and, 57, 61, 62, 67, 72, 75–76; Hopi, 80, 83, 125, 126, 127, 138; Ifaluk ghosts and, 248, 249; Indian-Ladino, 140–50; Japanese, 265, 276ff, 286; Kaska, 34, 47; mental disorders and, 163, 165
Approval, need for, 318–19
Arapaho Indians, 57
Arensberg, Conrad M., 340n
Argentine, 167
Arranged marriage, 261, 267–68, 274ff
Ascher, Robert, xvii
Ascribed status, 100, 131
Aspirations (*See also* Achievement; Drives; Values): Japanese, 260, 273
Assaults, Gusii and, 189
Assertiveness, Kaska, 36–39
Authoritarianism (*See also* Authority): Gusii, 190–91, 192, 193, 194; Japanese, 260, 263n; parent-child relations and, 195–201; Russian personality and, 315, 323, 326–27, 333
Authority (*See also* Authoritarianism): Americans and, 320, 322, 326; Chinese and, 300; Hopi, 84–86, 100; Kaska concept of, 38, 40–43; Oedipus complex (Italian) and, 360, 361, 368, 376, 380, 387–88, 389, 394; political values and,

185–203 *passim;* Russians and, 318, 319, 320, 322–24, 326–27, 330ff
Autonomy, 318–19, 321, 327, 328. *See also* Self-reliance
Awatovi, 81

Babcock, Charlotte G., 264n
Bakabi, 81
Bakke, E. Wight, 138
Bales, Robert F., 74n
Balinese Character, 39, 395
Bateson, Gregory, xii, xvi, 34, 39, 204–12, 395
Bathing, Ifaluk ghosts and, 245, 246, 248, 249
Bauer, R., 313n, 328, 330, 338n
Beaglehole, E. and P., 91n, 92n, 94, 103, 122n
Beating. *See* Whipping
Bed-wetting (enuresis), 102n
Begging, 169, 170, 173, 181
Beier, Helen, x, 312–39
Beliefs (*See also* Religious beliefs; Supernaturalism; Values; Worldviews): Hopi, 86, 88, 95–102, 120–37 *passim;* Ifaluk ghosts and, 238–50 *passim;* Italian, 365–98 *passim;* Japanese achievement and, 262ff; Japanese morale and, 251–60; learning and, 240ff, 248–50; nature of, 252–54
Bellah, Robert, 265n
Benedict, Ruth, x, xvii, 179–82, 268, 284, 340–51
Benet, Sula, 340n
Bennett, John, 80n
Berens River Saulteaux, 54
Beyond the Pleasure Principle (Freud), 12
Biard, Father, 50, 52
Bibring, Grete, 394–95n
Billig, O., 143n
Birth trauma, 18
Bisexuality, 28–29
Blackfoot Indians, 57
Blood feuds. *See* Feuds
Bogonko, 191
Bolsheviks, 332, 333
Boring, E. G., 243
Breast(s), 40; feeding (*see* Nursing; Weaning)
Bressani, on Indians, 49–50
British, 186–87, 189, 199, 200, 201
Brother-sister relationship, 353–54, 356, 360–63, 367n, 371. *See also* Siblings
Bruner, Edward M., 201
Bruner, J. S., 245
Buck, J. L., 302
Buddhism, 257, 286
Buffooning. *See* Joking
Bulganin, N. A., 333
Burial, 102, 286n
Burrows, E. G., 239, 246

Cadillac, on Indian intelligence, 51
Cameron, Duncan, 51n
Camorra, 371
Canoe-making ceremony, 204–12
Caroline Islands, 239
Cassirer, E., 243
Caste system (*See also* Prestige systems; Status): Indian-Ladino, 142, 145, 146, 147
Castration complex, 27–29
Castro, Josui de, 303
Cathexis, 13–29 *passim,* 360
Catholicism, 59, 71, 73, 364
Caudill, William, 57, 264n, 268
Ceremonialism: Hopi, 85, 86–88, 94–95, 104–8, 114, 125, 126; Iatmul *Naven,* 204–12; Ifaluk ghosts and, 240, 242; Indian-Ladino, 143, 144; Japanese, 257, 286n; Manus, 236
Change, impetus to, 292, 293
Chaperonage, 369, 370, 371, 379, 386
Charms (*ramus*), 221, 231–32
Chiang Kai-shek, 306
Chiefs: Gusii-Nuer, 187–89, 190–91, 193; Hopi, 85–86, 87, 94, 96, 98, 123, 133n; Ifaluk, 239; "sacred," 256
Children (child-training) (*See also* Family; Nursing; Parents; Punishment; Socialization): achievement ceremony, 204–12; American, 311; authoritarianism and, 195–203 (*see also* Authoritarianism; Authority); Chinese, 291–311 *passim;* Hopi, 79–120 *passim;* Ifaluk ghosts and, 242, 245–50; Indian-Ladino, 143–49 *passim;* Italian, 353–98 *passim;* Japanese values and, 254–88 *passim;* Kaska, 34–48; Nuer-Gussi, 194–201; Oedipus complex in (*see* Oedipus complex); personality development in, xi, 3–29;

Index   423

Pilaga, 167–82; thought (animism) in, 213–37
China, family and economy in, 291–311
Christianity, 43, 119, 120, 143, 257, 284, 285, 286, 365. *See also* specific sects
Clan(s) (*See also* Family; Kinship; Lineage): Chinese, 291, 292; Hopi, 85–86, 88–93, 94–95, 106, 123; Ifaluk, 239
Class differentiation, 334–38. *See also* Prestige systems; Status
Cognition, xii, 241, 242, 248, 250, 324–25, 326. *See also* Perception
Collective representations, 357n, 358
Colton, on Hopi suicide, 101
Commerce and industry (business; manufacturing; trade): Chinese and American, 294–311 *passim*
Communication, parent-child, 341, 342, 350
Communists: Chinese, 307; Japanese, 252; Soviet personality and, 312–39, 342–46, 350
Competitiveness, 301, 308. *See also* Achievement; Cooperativeness; Drives; Striving
Complementary relations, 347–48
Compulsiveness, 9, 23–24, 42, 43n; Indian-Ladino, 144, 145
Conative functioning, 325–26, 331
Conflicts, 19, 168, 239, 320, 321, 372ff, 391–92. *See also* Aggression; Ambivalence; Anxiety; Dispute settlement; specific people
Conformity-nonconformity (*See also* Authority; Submission): American, 308; Chinese, 292, 293; Hopi, 129, 136, 137n; Indian-Ladino, 141; Japanese, 263, 265
Conscience, 6, 15, 18, 23, 263, 382
Conscious, the, 22
Conservatism, 9, 57, 69, 70, 71
Constancy principle, 11–12
Cooperativeness (*See also* Drives; Striving): Gusii, 193; Hopi, 96, 136, 137, 138; Iatmul, 208, 211; Ifaluk, 130; Indian-Ladino, 143; Pilaga, 169, 181
Coues, on Indian intelligence, 49
Courts, Gusii-Nuer, 187–89, 193, 200
Courtship: Hopi, 91, 107; Italian, 366, 368–72, 380, 382, 385–89; Pilaga, 171

Crafts, Chinese, 295–300 *passim*
Criticism, freedom in, 324, 326, 331
Crying, 35, 245, 246, 283, 345, 346
Cults, culture change and, 59, 60, 61, 71
Culture(s): cross-cultural research, ix–xviii; determinism and, 238–50 *passim;* intelligence and, 51–52; personality and, xiii–xviii *passim* (*see also* Personality); self-regulating processes and, 151–66; systems of belief, 253–54, 255–57 (*see also* Beliefs; specific people); variables of, x–xvii, 52
Curer societies, 132
Curtis, Edward S., 132n
Cushing, Frank H., 95n

Daughters (*See also* Children; Family; Parents): Hopi, 88–93; Italian, 368–72ff, 385ff; Kaska, 44–47
Davidson, W., 143n
Davino, G., 368–69
Death (*See also* Burial; Disease: Mourning): among Hopi, 96–102, 108, 120–26, 129, 130, 134; Ifaluk ghosts and, 240, 242, 248; Italian family and, 373; Japanese values and, 254, 255, 257, 258, 269–73, 277, 278, 283–85, 286n
Death instincts, 11–12
Decision-making (*See also* Authority): Chinese, 292; Gusii-Nuer, 186, 187–89, 191, 195, 200, 202, 203
Defectors, 313, 314ff, 337–38
Defense mechanisms, 14, 18, 22–24, 25, 320, 327, 334, 336
Deference, 347; Gusii-Nuer, 190, 191; Kaska, 41, 45
Dennis, Wayne, 80n, 102, 103, 104, 105n, 107, 119
Dependency-independency, 24, 26, 347, 348 (*See also* Cooperativeness; Helplessness; Security); Chinese and American, 291–311 *passim;* Italian, 381, 382, 391; Kaska, 35, 37, 38, 40, 41, 42–43, 46; Russian and American, 318, 319, 327, 330, 331
Depressive reactions, 264–65n, 324
Determinism, cultural, 238–50 *passim*
Deviance: culture change and, 58, 61, 70, 71, 72, 73; mental disorder and, 151, 166

DeVore, Irven, xvii
De Vos, George, 261–88
Diapering, 348
Dicks, Henry V., 318, 320, 321, 323, 337
Dilemmas, 320–21, 327. *See also* Ambivalence
Discipline (*See also* Authority; Punishment; Whipping): authoritarianism and, 196; East European, 341ff; Gusii-Nuer, 196, 197; Hopi, 89, 104–8, 113, 116n, 119; Ifaluk, 246; Indian-Ladino, 143, 148, 149; Kaska, 41, 42; Russian, 331; Western traditional, 285
Disease (sickness; illness) (*See also* Mental illness; Shananism): guilt and, 265n; Hopi and, 86, 88, 96–102, 108, 120–37 *passim*; Ifaluk ghosts and, 240, 242, 248; Indian-Ladino, 142, 143; Japanese achievement and, 269, 273, 278, 281, 283–84; Manus, 228
Displacements, 10, 19, 20–22, 23, 25, 29; Oedipus complex and, 354, 356, 357, 358, 383
Dispute settlement, Gusii-Nuer, 187, 188–89, 193, 195, 198, 199, 200
Divorce, Hopi, 91, 92–93
Dollard, U., 241–42, 249
Dreams, 4, 355, 360. *See also* Hallucinations
Drives, 362 (*See also* Aspirations; Impulses; Instincts; Motivation(s); Striving); achievement and, 263ff; learning and, 242, 249; Oedipus complex and, 362, 382, 383; success and, 301, 302, 304, 308–11
Drunkenness, 145, 147, 153, 170n, 281
"Dry father," 301
DuBois, Cora, xiv
Du Peron, on Huron intelligence, 50
Durkheim, Émile, xi, 357n

East Africa, 203
East Indies, ix
Eating, 12, 25–26, 375, 377. *See also* Food; Hunger
Economy, personality and, xi–xii, xviii, 138; American, 293, 294–95, 300, 302, 304, 305, 308–11; Chinese, 291–311; Gusii-Nuer, 191–92; Hopi, 82–84, 108, 137, 138; Ifaluk, 239; Italian, 374–75, 390; Pilaga, 169, 170, 173, 175, 176, 179; Russian, 314, 329, 330–39
Education (learning; teaching) (*See also* Children; Socialization): adjustment to Soviet system and, 313–14, 315, 316, 335, 336–37; animism and, 214, 215, 219, 233, 234, 235–36, 237; Ifaluk ghosts and, 238–50; Indian-Ladino, 148–49; intelligence and, 50, 51; parent-child communication, 341, 342, 350
Egalitarianism, 190, 191, 192, 193, 194, 200–3; parent-child relations and, 196–201, 394
Eggan, Dorothy, 80n, 89, 92n, 102, 103, 106, 119, 125n
Ego, 3–7, 13–18 *passim*, 21–26 *passim*, 244n, 249 (*See also* Ego-ideal; Superego); Japanese, 287; Kaska, 33–48; Russian, 325, 327
Egocentricity, Kaska, 35, 38, 41, 42, 43, 44, 46
Ego ideal, 6, 15; Japanese achievement and, 263, 265, 266–67, 287; Oedipus complex and, 390, 391, 393
Eidos, defined, xii
Elites: culture change and, 59–60, 61, 70–74; Russian personality and, 328, 335, 337, 338
Elkin, Henry, 57
Elopement, 156
Emerson, Ralph W., 292
Emotions (*See also* Ambivalence; Ethos; Personality; Repression; Security; specific aspects, emotions, people): belief systems and, 253, 254, 257, 259, 262ff (*see also* specific people); illness and, 184 (*see also* Mental illness; Neuroses)
Emperor system, morale and, 251–60
Empiricism, Kaska, 42
Employers-employees, Chinese, 296–301
Endocrine glands, 29
Energy, psychoanalytic theory and, 3–4, 8, 10, 11, 12–29 *passim*
Engagement. *See* Courtship
Entrepreneurs, 299–311 *passim*
Envidia, 142, 146
"Episodes Test," 316
Erikson, E. H., 287–88, 320, 349
Erogenous zones, 11, 25

Index

Escape from Freedom (Fromm), xi–xii
Espanto (magical fright), 146, 148
Ethic(s), 365 (*See also* Morality; Values); Chinese, 291ff; Hopi, 95–102, 108, 125; Japanese, 262–88 *passim;* Western traditional, 284–86, 287
Ethos: defined, xii, xvi, Iatmul, 204–12; Indian-Ladino compared, 140; Kaska, development of, 34–48
Europeans (whites) (*See also* specific countries, people): child rearing in, 340–51 (*see also* specific countries); Chinese migration and, 304, 305; Indian culture change and, 74, 75; Indian intelligence and, 49–55 *passim; Naven* transvesticism and, 209
Evans-Pritchard, E. E., 185, 186, 190, 192, 193, 194, 196, 198
Evil eye, 346
Evolution, psychological anthropology and, xvii, xviii
Expiation, achievement as, 269, 272
Expressive roles, 74n, 75, 76
Eyes: "evil," 346; feelings and, 343

"Face," 263, 286
Failure, 33, 34, 264. *See also* Achievement; Striving; Success
Fainsod, Merle, 328
Family (*See also* Fathers; Kinship; Marriage; Mothers; Parents): Chinese economy and, 291–311; Gusii-Nuer, 191–92, 195–201, 203; Ifaluk, 239, 245–48; Italian (Oedipus complex), 352–63ff, 372–98; Japanese achievement and, 256–57, 258, 262–88; Jewish, 347–48; Kaska, 44–48; personality and experiences in, xiff, 3–29; Pilaga, 169; Russian adjustment and, 314, 318, 328, 333, 337
Fantasy, 26, 27, 40 (*See also* Dreams; Hallucinations; Myths); culture change and, 61; intelligence and, 54; Oedipus complex and, 357, 359–60, 378–90 *passim;* verbalization and, 150
Farberow, Norman L., 264n
Farms and farming. *See* Agriculture
Fathers (*See also* Children; Family; Marriage; Oedipus complex; Parents; specific people): development of child's personality and, 23, 27–29
Fear (*See also* Aggression; Anxiety; Hostility; Tension; specific people): learning process and, 242, 263
Fechner, constancy principle of, 12
Feldmesser, R., 337
Fenichel, Otto, 39
Feuds, 186, 187, 188, 189, 199
Fewkes, J. W., 113n
Filial piety, 257, 285, 291, 306
First Communion, 378, 390
Fischer, G., 338n
Fixations, 22, 24, 25
Fleiss, Wilhelm, 391
Flexibility, 41, 43, 62, 75
Food (*See also* Eating; Hunger): child-rearing and, 345–46 (*see also* Nursing); Iatmul *Naven* ceremony and, 206, 207; Italian male status and, 375, 376, 381; leeching, Kaska, 38; Pilaga hostility and, 167–82; Russian personality and, 318, 345–46
Forde, C. D., 94n
Foreordination, belief in, 95
Form level rating, 53
Fortes, Meyer, 193, 194
Fortune, R. F., 216, 217, 224n, 234
Fosbrooke, H. A., 193
Fox Indians, 57, 193
Frames of reference, 244–45, 246
France, 50
Free enterprise, 308
French, Thomas M., 263
Frenkel-Brunswik, Else, 195, 196
Freud, Anna, 22
Freud, Sigmund, xi, xviii, 3–29, 249, 263, 270; Oedipus complex concept of, 27–29, 352–53, 355, 356, 357, 358–59, 380, 381, 385, 389, 391, 392–95
Fried, Marc, 316n, 335n
Friendship, 318, 322, 328, 333
Fries, Margaret, 350
Fromm, Erich, xi–xii, 41, 46, 48
Frustration, 19, 21, 341; Ifaluk, 246; Indian-Ladino, 143, 147, 148, 149

Geertz, Clifford, x
General Motors Corp., 309
Generosity, 38. *See also* Presents
Genitalia (*See also* Sexuality): personality development and, 25, 26–

29, 360, 377, 378, 381; shame and, 345
Germany, 314, 338
Getutu tribe, 191, 194
Getzels, J. G., 316n
Ghosts, 224, 226–29, 236, 238–50. *See also* Spirits; Supernaturalism
Gifts. *See* Presents
Gillin, John, 140–50
God(s), 293, 393 (*See also* Religious beliefs); Chinese and American view of, 293, 295, 308, 311; Ifaluk, 240; Indian-Ladino view of, 141, 143; Italian view of, 365; Japanese, 254, 255, 257, 285, 286; Kaska view of, 43
Goldfrank, Esther S., 80n, 102
Goldstein, K., 243
Gorer, Geoffrey, xix, 264, 340n, 343n
Gossip, 135, 136, 137, 142
Grant, Peter, 52
Group membership: American, 318, 319, 320; Chinese economy and, 292–312 *passim;* cultural change and, 58, 59–78 *passim;* Indian-Ladino, 141, 142, 143, 146; Pilaga, 172; Russian, 318, 319, 328
Group personality, xiv. *See also* National character
Growing Up in New Guinea (Mead), 216
Guardian spirits, 98, 122, 125, 127, 226–28
Guatemala, 149, 151
Guilds, Chinese, 296, 299, 300
Guilt feelings, 6, 34, 321–22, 323, 327, 380 (*See also* Anxiety; Shame; specific people); achievement and, 261–88 *passim;* mental disorders and, 164
Gusii, the, 185–203

Hack, John T., 82n
Hall, Calvin S., xiii, 3, 21, 243
Hallowell, A. I., xv, 49–55, 57, 60, 244
Hallucinations, 4, 14, 159, 162, 164
Hanfmann, Eugenia, x, 312–39
Hanks, L. M., 57
"Hardening," child rearing and, 345, 346, 347, 348
Hate (*See also* Hostility): as cultural variable, xvii; psychoanalytic theory of personality and, 12, 23

Hearn, Lafcadio, 263
Held, Doris, 316n
Helplessness (*See also* Dependency; Security): Hopi, 99, 136; Ifaluk, 246; Kaska, 33–34; Russian, 323
Henry, Jules, 103n, 166–82
Herding: Hopi, 82, 83, 93; Pilaga livestock, 171
Herodotus, xiv
Hilgard, E. R., 243
Hirano, Kei, 275n, 282
Hockett, Charles F., xvii
Homesteads, Gusii, 192
Homosexuality, 29, 47, 92
Honigmann, John, 33–48
Honor, 371, 372, 386, 387
Hopei province, 299
Hopi Indians, 79–139
Hostiles (Hopi faction), 81, 82
Hostility, 22, 23, 27, 391 (*See also* Aggression; Conflicts; Hate); achievement and, 264–65n, 267; Hopi, 80, 126, 127, 128, 134–36; Ifaluk, 249; Kaska, 41; Oedipus complex and, 354, 355, 358, 380; Pilaga cultural determinants of, 167–82; Russian and American, 324, 331
Hotevilla, 81, 105
Households (*See also* Family; Kinship; Lineage): Hopi, 88–93, 94; Japanese, 273; mental disorder and, 165; Pilaga, 167, 168–70, 177
Howell, P. P., 185, 187, 188, 190
Hsu, Francis L. K., xvi, 291–311
Hull, C. L., 240, 241, 242, 244
Humility, 99, 124n
Hunger, 4, 8, 9, 11, 15, 167ff, 180. *See also* Eating; Food
Hunt, Robert, xii
Huron Indians, 49, 50
Hypotheses, belief systems and, 245, 246, 247, 249

Iatmul tribe, 204–12
Id, the, 3ff, 6–7, 8, 13–17
Identification, process of, 13–15, 16, 19–20, 27, 29, 266, 341; Oedipus complex and, 357, 358, 361, 362, 382, 388, 390ff
Ifaluk, the, 238–50
Illegitimacy, 374
Illness. *See* Disease
Imitation, 19. *See also* Identification

Index

Impulse control, 319–20, 323, 326, 327, 331, 336. *See also* Drives; Instincts
Incest, 27, 28, 397; Oedipus complex (Italian) and, 353–67 *passim*, 385–88, 397
Independence (independency). *See* Dependency-independency
Indians. *See* American Indians; specific people
Individual-centered orientation, 292–93
Infancy (*See also* Children; Nursing; Weaning; specific countries, people): national character and, 341–51; psychoanalytic theory of personality and, 18–29 *passim;* sexuality (Oedipus complex) and, 355, 358, 359, 363 (*see also* Oedipus complex; Sexuality)
Infanticide, female, 170–71, 175
Infantilisms, 24
Infidelity, 122, 123, 124n, 125, 126, 276, 367. *See also* Promiscuity
Ingratiation, Kaska, 44–45
Inheritance, Chinese, 304, 305
Initiation: Gusii, 197; Hopi, 80, 86, 97, 106–8, 113–20, 133
Ink blots, 218, 220, 229–30. *See also* Rorschach test
Inkeles, Alex, x, 312–39
Instincts, 3, 5–17 *passim*, 26, 356–63, 392. *See also* Drives; Impulse control; specific instincts
Instrumental roles, 74–76
Intelligence, Northeastern Indians', 49 55
Internalization process, 239, 266–67, 287, 380, 382, 397. *See also* Education; Political values; Socialization
Interpersonal relations (*See also* Children; Family; Parents; Relationships): East European, 347–48, 350; Gusii-Nuer, 200; Hopi, 128, 134; Ifaluk, 245; Indian-Ladino, 142; Japanese, 262ff; Jewish, 347–48; Kaska, 33, 39, 45–48; mental disorder and, 162–66; Pilaga, 167, 168, 170, 180, 181; Russian and American, 317–19, 322, 325, 326
Intimacy-isolation. *See* Isolation
Introjection, 6
Introspection, culture change and, 72
Iroquois Indians, 51

Irving, J. A., 243
Isaacs, Susan, 235
Isolation-intimacy, 320, 321, 327, 343
Italians, 345, 363–98

Jacobson, E., 357n
Japanese, 251–60, 261–88, 303, 304, 307
Jealousy, sexual, 358, 359, 361, 362, 386
Jesuits (*Jesuit Relations*), 49, 50, 51, 52
Jesus Christ, 43, 365. *See also* Christianity
Jewish child rearing, 346–48, 350, 394n
Joffe, Natalie F., 57
Joking (teasing): Hopi, 89, 133; Iatmul *Naven* ceremony, 205; Indian-Ladino, 144; Italian, 266, 267, 269, 370, 371, 378, 380, 385, 386, 387
Jones, Ernest, 352, 353–56, 357, 360, 361, 362
Joseph, Alice, 80n, 82n, 83, 90n, 91n, 95n, 102, 103n, 114n

Kaplan, Bert, 58n
Kardiner, A., xiv, xv, 35, 39, 99, 100, 262
Kaska Indians, 33–48
Katcina society, 86, 90, 95, 101, 104, 106–7, 111–20
Kennard, E. A., 80n, 95, 96, 100n, 101
Kenya, 185, 189, 193n
Khrushchev, N. S., 333
Kinietz, W. V., 51
Kinship systems, 395 (*See also* Family; Lineage; Relationships); Chinese, 291ff; Gusii-Nuer, 196, 198; Hopi, 84–86, 88–90, 120, 126, 127, 129, 132, 134, 137; Indian-Ladino, 141; mental disorder and, 159, 164–66; Oedipus complex and, 353–54, 355, 356, 362, 363ff, 372; Pilaga, 172
Kivas, 85, 95
Klineberg, Otto, 51
Klopfer, Bruno, 53, 64, 68n
Kluckhohn, Clyde, xiv, 134n, 313n
Krige, E. S., 43n
Krige, J. D., 43n
Kroeber, A. L., xiii, xvii, 244n
Kung, H. H., 309

Lactation, 174, 175
Ladinos, 140–50, 153, 157
Lalemant, Jerome, 50
Land and landholding, 93–94, 133, 142, 300, 301–5, 306. *See also* Property
Language: animism and, 216, 234–35, 237; behavior and, 243
Lanham, Betty, 264n
Latency period, 24–25
Leach, E. R., 194n
Leadership (*See also* Authority; Chiefs): Gusii-Nuer, 186, 187, 194, 199; Russian personality and, 322–24, 329–39 *passim*
Learning. *See* Children; Education; Socialization
Le Clerq, on Micmac intelligence, 50
Leighton, Alexander, x, 251–60
Le Jeune, Father, 50
Lenin, N., 330
Leonardo da Vinci, 21
Levin, Harry, 197
LeVine, Robert A., 185–203
Levinson, Daniel J., 312n, 316n
Lévi-Strauss, Claude, 398
Levy, David M., 41, 179
Lévy-Bruhl, Lucien, xvii, 213–14
Lewin, K., 241, 244n
Libido, 11, 360, 381
Life-history, Hopi, 79–139
Life instincts, 11, 12
Lindzey, Gardner, xv, xviii, 3
Lineage (See also Family; Kinship systems): Gusii-Nuer, 185, 186, 189, 191, 193, 194, 195, 196, 199, 202; Hopi, 85; Ifaluk, 239, 248; Italian, 364, 367; Japanese, 273
Linton, Ralph, 86n
Litigation, Gusii, 189, 199, 200
Livestock, 171. *See also* Herding
Lobvedu, the, 43n
Logic, 252–53, 255, 257–58
Loss, identification and, 20
Love, 37, 38, 42, 394 (*See also* Dependency; Emotions; Family; Sexuality); as cultural variable, xvii; psychoanalytic theory of personality and, 12, 23, 29
Love marriages, Japanese, 267, 274, 276ff
Lynd, R. S., 138

Maccoby, Eleanor, 197
Mackinac, 51

Madonna complex, 364–68, 370, 371, 382, 384, 387
Madonnas, Freud on Da Vinci's, 21
Magic. *See* Beliefs; Supernaturalism; Witchcraft; specific beliefs, people
Malenkov, G., 329
Males (*See also* Fathers; Marriage; Parents; specific people): compared to females in culture change (Menomini Indians), 56–78; Oedipus complex (Italian) and, 358, 366, 368, 369–72ff
Malinowski, B., xii, xvi–xvii, 352–56, 358, 359, 360, 367n, 395, 396
Manus tribe, 213–37
Maria (case history), 152–66
Marriage (*See also* Family; Parents): American, 311; Gusii-Nuer, 196–97; Hopi, 85, 88, 90–93, 99, 107, 108, 120–28, 129, 134; Indian-Ladino, 143; Italian, 364, 370–71, 372ff; Japanese, 261–88 *passim;* mental disorder and, 156, 162; Pilaga, 171–76
Masai, the, 193
Masau'u, 108, 118, 121
Masson, R. L., 51n, 53
Mastery: American emphasis on, 393; Kaska striving for, 36, 37, 42
Masturbation, 26, 27, 103, 348–49
Matriarchilism, 389, 394, 395n
Matrifocal families, 389n
Matrilineal societies, 85–86, 239, 352, 353, 354, 355, 356, 362
Mead, Margaret, xvi, xvii, 34, 39, 213–37, 340n, 349–51, 395
Medicine men. *See* Shamanism
Melanesia, 215, 216
Memory, 49
Menomini Indians, culture change and, 56–78
Mental illness, xiii (*See also* Neuroses; Schizophrenia); self-regulating processes and, 151–66
Mesoamericans, 140–82
Methodology, in culture research, 56, 57, 58ff, 395–98
Mexico, 81, 101
Micmac Indians, 50
Micronesia, 239
Middle class, culture change and, 71, 74
Migration, Chinese, 304–5
Miller, N., 241–42, 249
Miller, Walter B., 193
Missionaries, 285. *See also* Jesuits

Index 429

Mistrust. *See* Trust-mistrust
Mobility. *See* Social mobility
Modal personality technique: adjustment to Soviet system and, 312–39; culture change (Menomini) and, 63ff
Modesty, 378
Moenkopi, 81
Moral anxiety, 17–18, 23
Morale, belief systems and, 251–60
Morality (*See also* Ethic(s); Values; specific aspects, people): superego and, 6, 15–16, 17–18
"Moral masochism," 270, 272, 284
Moses and Monotheism (Freud), 393
Mothers (*See also* Children; Family; Marriage; Parents; Women): aggressive behavior and permissiveness by, 198; Chinese, 291; culture change and, 77; development of child's personality and, 25–29 *passim* (*see also* specific people); East European, 342ff; Hopi, 88–90, 91, 102–9; Ifaluk, 246–48; Italian (Oedipus complex), 353ff, 372ff; Japanese, 264, 268ff; Kaska, 35–48 *passim;* Pilaga, 175–79; *waus* as, 204–9 *passim*
Motivation(s), 395 (*See also* Achievement; Dependency; Drives; Striving); Indian-Ladino, 144, 146; Japanese, 254, 263ff, 267ff; Kaska, 34–48; Russian, 321, 327
Moulton, Harold, 310–11
Mourning, 212, 286n
Mowrer, O. H., 249
Muramatsu, Tsuneo, 261
Murray, Henry A., xiii–xiv, 317
Myths (myth-making) (*See also* Fantasy): animism and, 214, 236–37; Oedipus complex and, 354, 355, 360

Naples, Italy, 363–98
Narcissism, 29
Nathaniel (in Hopi life-history), 126–27
National character, xiv, 312–39, 340–51. *See also* specific countries
Nationalists, Chinese, 306–7, 309
Native-orientation, culture change and, 58–78 *passim*
Navaho Indians, 57, 83, 85, 134n
Naven behavior, 204–12

Need, instinct and, 8, 9
Needs, Russian personality and, 317–19, 328–30
Nequatewa, Edmund, 91n, 95, 101
Nervousness, 21. *See also* Anxiety; Tension
Neuroses: Indian-Ladino, 146; Italian, 370, 378; systems of belief and, 253
Neurotic anxiety, 17–18, 23
New Guinea, 204, 213, 241n
New York City, 341
Niiike (Japan), 261, 262n, 267, 268, 275ff
Nisei (Japanese-Americans), 264–65n, 268
Norbeck, Edward, 264n
Norbeck, Margaret, 264n
Northeastern Indians, 49–55
Nuclear family complex, 352, 356–63ff, 372ff
Nuer, the, 185–203
Nursing (breast-feeding) (*See also* Weaning): East European, 344, 345–46; Hopi, 102, 103; Ifaluk, 246; Indian-Ladino, 145; Italian, 376, 384; Japanese, 264; Kaska, 35; Pilaga, 175, 176, 178
Nurturance (*See also* Dependency; Security): Rusisan personality and, 322, 326, 333, 347, 348

Obedience. *See* Authority; Conformity; Submission
Object, instincts and, 9, 10, 13–20ff, 356, 357–63, 380, 383ff
Object-choice, 13–15, 21, 22, 29, 357–63
Occupation: adjustment to Soviet system and, 314, 316, 335, 336–39; identification and, 389n, 390, 391
Oedipus complex, xvii, 27–29, 266, 352–98; Italian and universality of, 352–98; Japanese, 282; Kaska, 41, 43
Ojibwa Indians, 57, 60
On obligations, 273, 274
Opler, Marvin K., 264n
Opler, Morris, x, 251–60
Optimism-pessimism, 320–21, 327, 330
Oraibi, 80ff
Oral needs, Russian, 318, 319, 327, 329

Oral stage of development, 11, 25–26, 29; Italian, 376, 381, 382, 388, 398; Kaska, 38

Other-directed orientation, 263. *See also* Conformity; Situation-centered orientation

"Others," Russian awareness of, 325

Ottawa Indian intelligence, 51

Overpopulation, 302–3

Overprotection, Kaska, 42

Pain principle, 4–5, 17 (*See also* Pleasure principle); Ifaluk ghosts and, 246, 247, 248

Parents (parent-child relations) (*See also* Children; Family; Fathers; Mothers): American, 311; authoritarianism and, 195–201; Chinese, 291–311 *passim;* East European, 340–51; Gusii-Nuer, 195–99; Hopi, 102–9ff, 119ff; Ifaluk, 245–48; Italian (Oedipus complex), 353ff, 372ff; Japanese, 256–57, 261–88; Jewish, 347–48; Kaska, 38–48 *passim;* Pilaga, 179, 180; psychoanalytic theory of personality and, 6, 15, 18–29 *passim*

Parsons, Anne, 352–98

Parsons, E. C., 85–86n, 92, 95n, 100n, 101, 114n, 132n

Parsons, Talcott, 74n, 75, 100, 284n, 357n

Passivity: Indian adaptation, 140, 143; Kaska adaptation and, 35–36, 37, 38, 39, 43; Russian, 321, 326, 327

Patriarchal societies, 353, 356, 375, 376, 380, 382, 384, 392–95

Patrilineal groups, 196

Paul, Benjamin D., 151–66

Peacefulness, Hopi, 79, 96. *See also* Conflicts; Cooperativeness

Peasants, 50–51, 55, 335, 337, 344; swaddling and, 344, 345

Penis envy, 28

Perception, xii, xvii, 238–50, 324–25, 362. *See also* Cognition; Learning; specific people

Peri, 216, 229

Permissiveness: aggressive behavior and, 198–99; Indian-Ladino, 145, 148; Italian, 380, 382; Japanese, 264; Kaska, 41, 42

Personality (behavior; character): as central to study of human behavior, x, xiii; cultures and, xiii–xvii (*see also* specific people); definitions of, xiii, xv; ethos and, xii, xvi (*see also* Ethos); modal technique, 63ff, 312–39; psychoanalytic theory and development of, xi, xviii, xix, 3–29, 395–98; national (*see* National character; specific people); psychological anthropology and study of, ix–xix *passim*

Personalization, 223–25, 235

Petrullo, Vincenzo, 377n

Peyote cult, 59, 60, 61, 71, 73, 76

Pfister-Ammende, Maria, 338n

Phallic stage of development, 25, 26–29. *See also* Genitalia; specific people

Phillips, Arthur, 189n

Phillips, H. P., 316n

Phratries, Hopi, 85

Piaget, M., 214

Piers, Gerhart, 263

Pilaga Indians, 167–82

Pleasure principle, 4, 5, 6, 13, 17, 25, 29; Ifaluk ghosts and, 246, 247, 248

Poland, 345–48, 350

Polarities, 320–21, 327, 370. *See also* Ambivalence

Political systems, Russian adaptation to, 312–39

Political values, internalization of, 185–203; Gusii-Nuer, 185–203; Japanese, 251–60

Polygamy, 374

Polygyny, 175, 186, 203

Postman, L., 245, 247

Powamu society, 86, 106–7, 113, 116n, 119

Preconscious, the, 23

Pregenital stages of development, 25–29

Pregnancy, Pilaga, 173, 174, 175, 176

Presents (gifts): Hopi, 104, 107, 112, 113n, 115; Iatmul *Naven*, 205, 206, 207; Italian, 381

Prestige systems (*See also* Caste system; Status): Hopi, 80, 87, 108, 129, 131–33; Indian-Ladino, 141, 142, 143; Japanese emperor and, 256; Pilaga, 171, 181

Pride (*See also* Prestige systems; Self-esteem; Status): Iatmul, 208, 209, 211

Primary process, 4, 13, 14

Index

Primary relationships (*See also* Interpersonal relations; Relationships): Chinese economy and, 292, 293, 305, 308, 310
Profit systems, Chinese and American, 300
Projection, xvii, 22, 23, 39–40, 99–100, 249, 260
Projective tests, 262n, 315–17, 320, 321, 380. *See also* Tests
Promiscuity (philandering), 47–48, 108, 122–26 *passim*, 383. *See also* Infidelity; Prostitution; Sexuality
Propaganda, 258, 259
Property (*See also* Land; Wealth): American, 310; Chinese, 304; Gusii-Nuer, 192; Hopi, 93–95; Pilaga, 167, 171, 181
Prostitution, 367n, 369, 370, 374, 383. *See also* Promiscuity
Protestantism, 285, 365, 390
Psychoanalytic theory of personality, xi, xviii–xix, 3–29, 395–98
Psychocultural center of gravity, 65–78
Psychological adaptations, culture change study in, 56–78
Psychological anthropology, ix–xix
Psychological (psychic) variables, x–xvii
Psychological warfare, 351–60
Pueblo Indians, 81, 83, 85, 132n
Puerto Rico, 377
Punishment, 6, 15, 23, 345 (*See also* Discipline; Permissiveness; Sanctions; Whipping); Gusii-Nuer, 187–89, 196, 197, 200; Hopi, 89, 104–8, 113–20; Ifaluk ghosts and, 240, 242; Indian-Ladino, 145; Japanese, 264, 266, 269, 270, 286n; Manus, 235; mental disorder as, 164–65; Russian, 323

Radcliffe-Brown, A. R., xviii, 367n
Rapaport, David, 362
Rasmussen, V., 214
Reaction formation, 22, 23, 320
Reality anxiety, 17–18, 23
Reality principle, 5, 22, 29
Reality testing, 5
Reflections in water beliefs, 229
Reflex actions, 4, 13
Refugees, 314ff, 337–38
Regression, 22, 24, 36, 37, 38, 179, 180

Regressive character of instincts, 9, 12
Relationships (relatedness) (*See also* Family; Interpersonal relations; Kinship systems; Lineage): American, 308–11; Chinese, 291–312 *passim*; Gusii-Nuer, 191–93, 194, 196–201; Hopi, 88–93, 120–29; Iatmul *Naven* and, 204–12; Indian-Ladino, 142; Italian (Oedipus complex), 353–63ff, 372ff; Pilaga, 167, 168, 170, 180
Religious beliefs, xii (*See also* Ceremonialism; Supernaturalism; Witchcraft; World-views; specific religions); American, 293, 295, 308, 311; Chinese, 294; culture change and, 59–60, 71, 73; Hopi, 86, 88, 95–102, 104–8, 117, 120–28, 131, 137; Ifaluk, 238, 240, 241; Indian-Ladino, 143; Italian, 364ff, 380; Japanese, 254, 255, 256, 257–60, 287; Kaska, 41, 43; Manus, 234, 236
Repetition compulsion, 9
Repression, xvii, 20, 22–23, 25, 27–28; Oedipus complex and, 286, 362, 382, 383–84, 391, 397
Reservation life, Indian culture change and, 73, 74
Residence, 372–73; matrilocal, 171, 174, 175, 239; patrilocal, 196
Responsibility, sense of: Hopi, 96, 100, 104, 129, 138; Indian-Ladino, 146; Japanese, 265, 268; Kaska, 41, 42; Russian, 328, 330
Restitution, 179, 180
Restlessness, Freud on, 21
Retentive character, development of, 26
Rewards, 6, 15, 107, 133, 242. *See also* Punishment; specific people
Riesman, David, 195, 263
Roheim, G., 39
Roles: Japanese achievement and, 266, 268, 271, 274, 276, 286, 287; mental disorder and, 163; *Naven* ceremony and, 208–12; Oedipus complex and, 358, 359, 361, 362ff (*see also* Identification; Oedipus complex); Russian political, 327ff
Rorschach test, xiv, xv, 315 (*See also* Ink blots); Indian-Ladino anxiety, 143–44, 145–46; Menomini culture change and, 57–73; Northeastern Indians' intelligence, 53–55

Roseborough, H. E., 316n
Rosenblatt, Daniel, 316n
Rossi, Alice, 337n
Rumania, 348–49, 350
Russians, adjustment to Soviet system by, 312–39

Samoa, xvi, 256
San Carlos, 140–50
Sanctions, 21, 87, 91, 262ff, 286, 321, 323, 341. *See also* Punishment; specific people
Saulteaux Indians, 51n, 52, 53–55, 57
Scapegoats, 127
Schilder, Paul, 41
Schizophrenia, 360, 373, 384
Schrier, A. M., xviii
Scolding, 104, 272, 323, 333
Sears, Robert R., 197
Secondary process, 5, 14
Security-insecurity, 341, 394 (*See also* Dependency-independency); Chinese and American, 292–312 *passim;* Ifaluk ghosts and, 247, 248; Indian-Ladino, 140–50; Italian, 368; Japanese, 253–56, 259–60, 262ff; Kaska, 33–48 *passim;* Pilaga, 172, 173, 176, 177; Russian, 318
Segmentary lineage systems, 185, 186, 189, 191, 193, 194, 195, 199, 202
Self-control, Russian and American, 318, 319, 320, 326
Self-esteem, Russian and American, 321–22, 327
Self-reliance (self-confidence), 33–39 *passim,* 42, 292–312 *passim*. *See also* Dependency-independency; specific people
Self-sacrifice, Japanese achievement and, 268, 269–73, 276
Self-view, Kaska, 33–48
Selling and buying, Chinese and American, 297–99, 303
Seward, G. H., 264n
Sexuality (attitudes, instincts), 6, 10, 11, 12, 15, 25, 26–29 (*See also* Homosexuality; Incest; Love; Marriage; Promiscuity); Hopi, 89, 91–92, 93, 103–4, 122; Iatmul, 204–12; Indian-Ladino, 143; Italian, 364, 366ff; Japanese, 276–88; Kaska, 40, 47–48; Oedipus complex and, 355–63ff (*see also* Oedi-

pus complex); Pilaga, 171, 173–76; Western Christian, 280, 284–85
Shamanism (medicine men), 97, 98, 100, 143, 153, 157–58, 159, 161
Shame (*See also* Guilt feelings): Japanese achievement and, 262–63, 264–65, 266–67; Russian and American, 321–22, 327, 330–31; sexuality and, 345, 387n
Shintoism, 257, 286
Schneidman, Edward S., 264n
Siblings (*See also* Brother-sister relationship; Children; Family): Hopi, 103, 104; Ifaluk, 246–47, 248; Italian, 373; Kaska, 45–46; Pilaga, 169n, 176, 178, 179, 180
Sicily, 371
Sickness. *See* Disease
Simmons, Leo W., 79, 101, 110, 112, 113n, 122, 125n
Sin (evil), 285–86, 293; Ifaluk ghosts and, 240, 242, 249; Italian Oedipus complex and, 365, 366, 382
Singer, Milton, 262
Sisters. *See* Brother-sister relationship; Children; Daughters; Family; Siblings
Situation-centered orientation, 291–93
Skepticism, 366, 367
Social forms, personality and, 167
Socialization, 29, 241n (*See also* Children; Education; Family; Parents); culture change and, 77; Gusii-Nuer, 195; Hopi, 105–8, 109, 129, 136; Italian, 376ff; Kaska, 35–48
Social mobility, 337, 338, 384; culture change and, 73–74
Social theory, validity of, xviii
Societies, religious, 86–88, 90, 95, 97, 98, 100, 104, 106–7, 111–20, 131, 132
Socio-cultural variables, x–xvii; culture change and, 73–74
Socio-political systems, adjustment to, 312–39
Sons (*See also* Children; Family; Fathers; Mothers; Parents; specific people): Oedipus complex universality and, 353–98 *passim* (*see also* Oedipus complex)
Soong, T. V., 309

Index

Sorcery, 96–100, 121, 168, 169. *See also* Supernaturalism; Witchcraft
Southall, A. W., 193, 194
Soviet Union: adjustment to sociopolitical system, 312–39; child rearing in, 342–46, 350
Soyoko, 104–5, 116, 118, 119
Spanish America, 81, 82n
Spence, K. W., 241
Sphincter control. *See* Toilet training
Spindler, George, 56–78
Spindler, Louise, 56–78
Spirits, 353 (*See also* Ghosts; Supernaturalism); Manus, 225–29; mental disorder and, 153, 158–61, 164
Spiro, Melford E., xvi, 238–50
Spontaneous animism, 214, 215, 218, 221, 223–26, 230, 233, 236
Stalin, Joseph, 328, 332, 333
Standards, multiple, 292
Stanton, A. H., 357n
Stateless societies, political values and, 185–203
Status (*See also* Prestige systems; Roles; specific people): adjustment to political systems and, 395; ascribed, 100, 131; authoritarianism and, 190–91, 193; caste system, 142, 145, 146, 147; culture change and, 58–78 *passim,* 141; feeding role and, 375, 378
Stealing, 38
Steward, Julian H., 106, 113n
Striving (competitiveness), 36, 43n, 142, 263ff, 301, 308, 325–26, 331. *See also* Achievement; Drives; Motivation; Self-reliance
Sublimation, xvii, 21, 25, 29, 371, 382, 392
Submission (*See also* Authority; Conformity; Self-sacrifice): Gusii, 190, 200; Iatmul, 208; Indian-Ladino, 143; Italian, 382, 394; Kaska, 41, 42; Russian, 318, 322, 330
Success drives (*See also* Achievement; Drives; Failure; Motivation; Striving): Chinese and American, 301, 302, 304, 308–11
Sucking, 9, 11, 21, 97, 247. *See also* Nursing
Sudan, 185
Suffering, 332, 345, 365, 366. *See also* Self-sacrifice

Suicide, 101, 265n, 271, 273, 284
Sully, J., 214
Sumi, Taeko, 271n
Sun clan, Hopi, 123, 124, 129
Superego, 3–7 *passim,* 13–17 *passim,* 20, 21, 28 (*See also* Ego); in guilt and achievement, 263, 266–67, 287; Oedipus complex and, 382, 390, 397
Supernaturalism (*See also* Religious beliefs; Witchcraft; World-views): animism (Manus) and, 218, 221, 224, 225–29; Chinese, 294; Hopi, 104–8, 112–20; Ifaluk, 238–50; Indian-Ladino, 141, 143; Japanese, 253–54, 255, 256, 257; mental disorder and, 153, 158–61, 164
Superstitions, 238, 346. *See also* Religious beliefs
Suspicion. *See* Trust-mistrust
Swaddling, 341–51
Swearing (cursing; obscenity), 366–67, 371, 383
"Sworn brother," 301
Symbolism, 23; Oedipus complex (Italian) and, 360, 362–63, 369, 370, 375, 378, 379, 382, 390–96 *passim*

Talayesva, Don C., 79, 97, 98, 109–33
TAT, 261, 268, 269ff, 315, 389, 390
Tchinals, 225, 228–29, 230, 236
Teasing. *See* Joking
Tension, 3–4, 5, 9, 15–29 *passim,* 170, 377 (*See also* Aggression; Anxiety; Conflicts; Hostility); culture change and, 62, 72, 77, 239
Tests (testing), 51–55, 229–30, 315–17, 320–21, 396. *See also* specific studies, tests
Thematic Apperception Test. *See* TAT
Theories of Personality, xiii
Thirst, 11
Thomas, W. I., 129
Thompson, Laura, 80n, 82n, 83, 90n, 91n, 95, 97, 100, 102, 103n, 114n
Thorpe, W. A., 243
Thought processes (*See also* Cognition; Perception): animism in children, 213–37
Threat(s), 19, 72 (*See also* Aggression; Anxiety; Hostility); Ifaluk ghosts and, 245, 246, 247; Japanese achievement and, 271; Rus-

sian personality and, 324, 327; security and, 140–50 (*see also* Security)
Tics, 342
Timidity, 99 See also Aggression
Titiev, M., 80n, 82n, 83n, 84n, 85, 88n, 89, 90n, 91n, 92n, 93, 94, 98, 99, 102, 105n, 111, 114n, 116n, 121n, 122, 124n, 132
Toilet training, 26; East European, 345, 350; Hopi, 102, 103; Ifaluk, 246; Indian-Ladino, 145; Kaska, 40, 41, 43; Japanese, 264
Tolman, E. C., 241, 243n
Tonga, 256
Tradition, beliefs and, 248–49
Transitional syndrome, culture change and, 59, 60, 61, 71, 72, 73
Transvesticism, 207, 209–12
Trauma(s), 18, 24, 28, 36–39, 41, 42; Oedipus complex and, 358–59, 360, 395
Trobriand Islands, xvii, 352, 353, 354, 355, 356, 357–58, 360, 362–63, 396
Trust-mistrust: Hopi, 80, 110–20, 125, 126, 129, 133, 137; Russian, 320, 327, 330
Tumin, Melvin, 140
Tuscarora Indians, xvi, 63
Two-heartedness, 97, 99, 123, 124, 125

United States. *See* American Indians; Americans (U.S.)

Vaillant, R., 368n
Values, 244, 253ff, 393 (*See also* Beliefs; Motivation(s); specific people); culture change and, 58–78 *passim;* political, internationalization of, 185–203, 251–60
Variables: intelligence testing and, 52; learning theories and, 244; political behavior and, 200–3; psychological and socio-cultural, x–xvii, 73–74
Verbosity (verbalization; volubility), 142, 149–50, 318, 377
Violence, 278–80 (*See also* Aggression; Hostility); infant swaddling and, 343, 344, 345, 347
Virginity, 369, 371, 382, 386, 390, 392
Visions, 4. *See also* Hallucinations

Vogt, Evon, 57
Voth, H. R., 95, 101, 107

Wagatsuma, Hiroshi, 261, 262n, 286n
Wallace, Anthony F. C., xiv, xv, 63, 64
Wallis, Wilson D., 99, 121
Warrior societies, 132
Waus, 204–12
Wealth, 95, 171, 191, 193, 299, 301, 306, 307–11. *See also* Land; Property
Weaning, 35, 103, 145, 148, 264, 345–46, 376. *See also* Nursing
Weber, Max, 265n
Welfare state, 314, 330, 332, 335
Whipping (beating), 104, 106–8, 113–20, 159, 172, 173, 192, 196, 206, 345
White, Leslie A., 238
Whiting, Alfred E., 82n, 97n, 98n, 113n
Whiting, J. W. M., xviii, 195, 241n
Whyte, W. F., 368n
Wish, instinct and, 8, 9
Wish-fulfillment, 4, 13, 14
Witchcraft, 80, 96–100, 108, 111, 116–35 *passim,* 143, 146–47, 148. *See also* Supernaturalism
Withdrawal, 72, 143, 165, 176, 177
Wives. *See* Marriage; Women
Wolf, K. R., 377n
Women (*See also* Daughters; Marriage; Mothers; Sexuality; specific people): compared to men in culture change, 56–78; Ifaluk ghosts as, 248; mental disorder and, 163, 165; *Naven* ceremony and, 204–12; Oedipus complex and, 366–98 *passim* (*see also* Oedipus complex)
Work patterns, 141, 142, 146, 265, 266, 269, 271, 272, 283, 318, 331–32. *See also* Achievement; specific people
World-views, 33–48, 95–102, 140–41, 245, 248, 253–57, 291ff, 364ff. *See also* Beliefs; specific people
World War II, x, 251–60, 270–71, 313, 338n
Wowochim society, 107–8

Yokioma, 99, 133

Zola, I. K., 368n